KU-258-575

WORLD TEXTILES

THE
PAUL HAMLYN
LIBRARY

WITHDRAWN

TRANSFERRED FROM

THE
CENTRAL LIBRARY
OF THE
BRITISH MUSEUM

2010

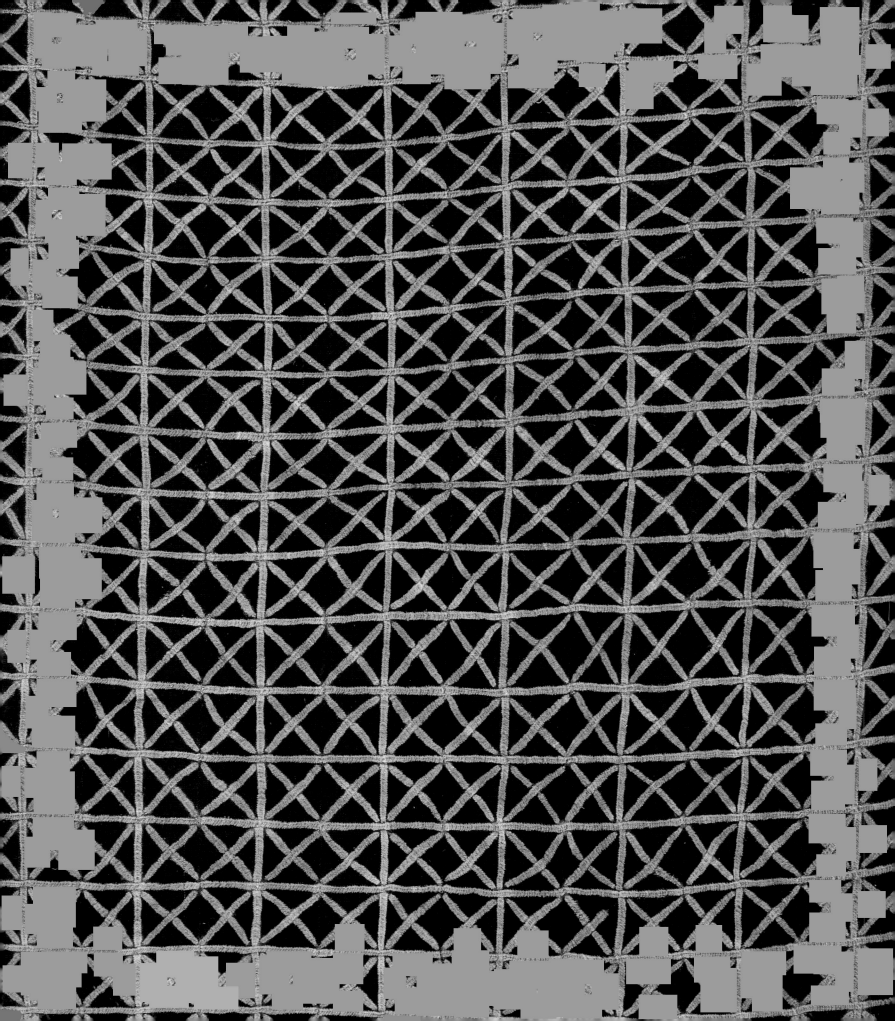

WORLD TEXTILES

A VISUAL GUIDE TO TRADITIONAL TECHNIQUES

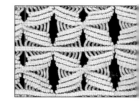

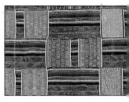

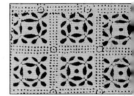

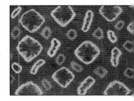

JOHN GILLOW AND BRYAN SENTANCE

WITH 778 ILLUSTRATIONS, 551 IN COLOUR

Thames & Hudson

FOR YVONNE GILLOW AND FOR POLLY

Had I the heavens' embroidered cloths
Enwrought with golden and silver light,
The blue and the dim and the dark cloths
Of night and light and the half light
I would spread the cloths under your feet:
But I, being poor, have only my dreams;
I have spread my dreams under your feet;
Tread softly because you tread on my dreams.

He Wishes for the Cloths of Heaven
John Keats

page 1, Embroidered shawl, from the Indonesian island of Sumba, worked in chain stitch; page 2, Indigo-dyed cloth made by the Mossi people of Burkina Faso with a pattern created by the stitched-resist technique; page 3, Raphia apron made by the Kuba of the Congo (formerly Zaire), employing patchwork, embroidery and stitched dye resist; page 5, Nineteenth-century tapestry-woven Kashmir shawl; page 6, left, Maranau woman's marriage 'malong', from Mindanao in the Philippines, with tapestry-woven silk bands; page 6, top, Black Miao girl's embroidered jacket; page 6, centre, Kano stripweave cotton blanket, Nigeria; page 6, below, Blanket, from Nagaland, India, with a central band painted with images of animals and trophy heads; page 7, above, left, Woman's tie and dye silk shawl from Tajikistan; page 7, above, right, Chauhan *rumal*, from Sind, Pakistan, sewn together from strips of cloth edged with sawtooth appliqué; page 7, below, right, Meghwal *choli*, from Sind, Pakistan, decorated with embroidery and mirrors.

Any copy of this book issued by the publisher as a paperback is sold subject to the condition that it shall not by way of trade or otherwise be lent, resold, hired out or otherwise circulated without the publisher's prior consent in any form of binding or cover other than that in which it is published and without a similar condition including these words being imposed on a subsequent purchaser.

First published in the United Kingdom in 1999 by Thames & Hudson Ltd,
181A High Holborn, London WC1V 7QX

Design by David Fordham

© 1999 Thames & Hudson Ltd, London

All Rights Reserved. No part of this publication may be reproduced or transmitted in any form or by any means, electronic or mechanical, including photocopy, recording or any other information storage and retrieval system, without prior permission in writing from the publisher.

British Library Cataloguing-in-Publication Data
A catalogue record for this book is available from the British Library

ISBN 0-500-01950-9

Printed and bound in Singapore by C.S. Graphics

5956

CENTRAL LIBRARY
THE BRITISH MUSEUM
WITHDRAWN

BM7 (GL)

Man is the shuttle, to whose winding quest
And passage through these looms
God order'd motion, but ordain'd no rest.

Henry Vaughan (1622–95), *Silex Scintillans, Man*

CONTENTS

INTRODUCTION   8

1 MATERIALS   16

Skin and hide 20 • Wool and hair 22 •
Felt 24 • Woollen yarn 26 • Cotton 28 •
Silk 30 • Bark 32 • Linen 34 • Other bast
fibres 36 • Raphia and leaf fibres 38

2 NON-LOOM TEXTILES   40

Netting, linking and looping 44 • Crochet 46 •
Knitting 48 • Textured knitting 50 • Multi-
coloured knitting 52 • Braids 54 • Sprang 56 •
Macramé 58 • Ply-splitting 60 • Lace 62 •
Twining and wrapping 64

3 LOOM-WOVEN TEXTILES   66

Tabby weave 70 • Twill 72 • Satin weave 74 •
Tapestry weave 76 • Warp-faced weave 78 •
Weft-faced weave 80 • Damask 82 •
Supplementary warp 84 • Supplementary
weft (continuous) 86 • Supplementary
weft (discontinuous) 88 • Brocade 90 •
Stripweave 92 • Double weave 94 •
Velvet 96 • Tablet weaving 98

4 PAINTED AND PRINTED TEXTILES   100

Daubed textiles 104 • Painted textiles 106 •
Pen work 108 • Woodblock printing 110 •
Polychrome woodblock printing 112 •
Stencilling 114

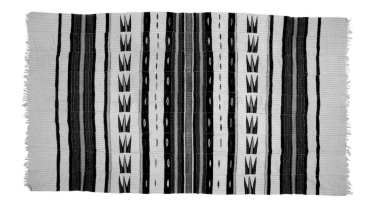

7 EMBROIDERY 168

Running stitch 172 • Satin stitch 174 • Surface satin stitch 176 • Chain stitch 178 • Cross stitch 180 • Herringbone stitch 182 • Couching 184 • Bokhara couching 186 • Blanket, buttonhole and eyelet stitch 188 • French and Pekin knots 190 • Drawn-thread and pulled-thread work 192 • Needleweaving 194 • Whitework 196 • Needlepoint 198 • Smocking 200 • Tambour work 202

5 DYES 116

Indigo 120 • Tie and dye 122 • Stitched resist 124 • Leheria and mothara 126 • Starch-resist by hand 128 • Stencilled starch-resist 130 • Wax-resist: Chinese knife 132 • Wax-resist: canting 134 • Wax-resist: printed 136 • Mordant techniques 138 • Warp ikat 140 • Weft ikat 142 • Compound and double ikat 144

8 EMBELLISHMENT 204

Metal thread 208 • Mirrors 210 • Coins and sequins 212 • Shells 214 • Bead embroidery 216 • Bead weaving 218 • Feathers 220 • Porcupine quills 222 • Ephemera 224 • Fringes 226 • Tassels 228

6 SEWING 146

Appliqué 150 • Reverse appliqué 152 • Molas 154 • Leather and felt appliqué 156 • Braid and ribbon work 158 • Patchwork 160 • Quilting 162 • Patchwork quilts 164 • Padded and stuffed work 166

Glossary 230

Further reading 232

Collections 235

Sources of illustrations 238

Acknowledgments 238

Index 239

INTRODUCTION

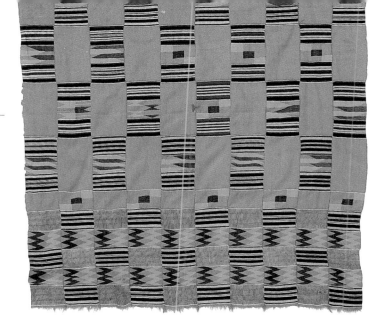

THE history of the world can be read in textiles; the rise of civilizations and the fall of empires are woven into their warp and weft along with the great adventures of conquest, religion and trade. The greatest highway ever made, the Silk Road, was not for the transportation of gold or armies, but for the trading of the most luxurious and desirable commodity of all, silk textiles.

Study of the traditional textiles of the world reveals at times an amazing diversity of techniques and styles, while at others we can only wonder at the way in which cultures separated by vast distances have developed such similar solutions to problems of design and construction. Sometimes only a limited number of solutions may be possible, but the frequency of similarities in techniques and the choice of motifs and symbols makes one wonder if this is evidence of ancient unrecorded trade routes or if it is substantiation of Jung's theory that we have a collective unconscious.

THE PURPOSE OF THIS BOOK

THERE are many valuable volumes that concentrate either on an intensive study of one specific aspect of textile construction or decoration, such as weaving, dyeing or embroidery, or are devoted to the textiles produced in one geographic region. In this book, by displaying the fabrics of many places side by side, we hope to provide a basis for comparison and thereby a greater understanding of the techniques involved and a greater awareness of the diversity of stylistic interpretation. Our main priority in the selection of illustrations has been to choose not only the most beautiful textiles from the widest possible geographical range, but also those that show the techniques most clearly.

Our rather ambitious aim has been to include as many techniques as possible, often, in the interests of space, in a generalized rather than a specific form, and to provide illustrations from as much of the world as we possibly can. Many of the textiles illustrated were collected on our own travels over the last twenty-five years, and

Opposite: This patchwork quilt from Banni Kutch in North-West India can be read like a textile compendium. Its construction involved a diverse range of techniques and it shows examples of printing, dyeing, embroidery, patchwork and appliqué.

Above: A kente cloth woven by the Ashanti of Ghana. Long strips, which have been woven by men on narrow looms, are sewn together to form a voluminous toga-like garment with a distinctive chequerboard effect.

Below: This selection of metal, plastic and wooden knitting needles demonstrates the variety of materials that have been exploited to manufacture textiles. The four needles on the left are for 'circular' knitting without a seam and the small one on the right is for knitting cables.

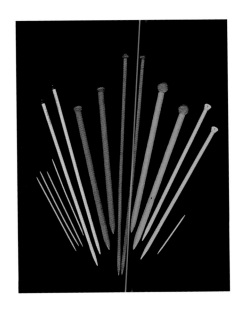

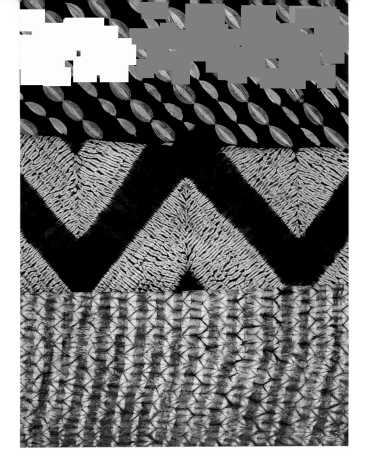

Above, left: *Indigo-dyed textiles from the Gambia. Indigo is a unique, colourfast dye that has been in use for more than 4,000 years. The patterns have been produced by tightly sewing the cloth before dyeing which prevents the dye penetrating into the areas designated for the white patterns.*

Above, right: *'Casae ex arundine textae' (huts built of reeds). Zulus weaving a hut out of flexible branches.*

others were generously lent by travellers, collectors and enthusiasts to whom we are much indebted.

WHAT IS A TEXTILE?

THE word 'textile' comes from the Latin verb *texere*, a word which was used by the Romans to mean 'to weave', 'to braid' or 'to construct'. It is a fairly versatile word, open to interpretation, which was even used by Livy in the context of building when he wrote of '*casae ex arundine textae*' (huts built of reeds). In fact, whether it is a basket, a blanket or a wattle and daub hut, the techniques employed have much in common. Therefore, rather than confining our choice of fabrics and structures according to arbitrary, academic parameters, we have made a personal selection of what to include in this book based on our own interpretation of what is appropriate and what will bring a greater understanding of the subject as a whole.

THE HISTORY OF TEXTILES

TEXTILES are made of perishable materials and only survive the millennia when preserved under exceptional circumstances such as the felts discovered buried in the permafrost of Noin Ula in Mongolia which date from around the 4th century BC, or the weavings found in the pre-Columbian tombs preserved by the dry air of the Peruvian coast. However, much has been learned from written sources and even from ancient carvings and artefacts. Egyptian tombs contain paintings of spinning and the weaving of linen while, in the *Odyssey*, the Greek poet Homer describes how Penelope, the hero's wife, evaded the attentions of her unwelcome suitors by weaving a large and delicate shroud for her father-in-law, Laertes, a scene illustrated on a 5th-century BC vase. The story of the development of textiles is therefore largely a yarn spun from deduction and conjecture rather than hard evidence. Archeological finds, though, point to a high level of skill and sophistication at an astoundingly early date.

RIGHT: PENELOPE AT HER LOOM, FROM A GREEK VASE, 5TH CENTURY BC.

BELOW: AN ANCIENT EGYPTIAN TOMB PAINTING OF WOMEN WEAVING ON A SINGLE HEDDLE LOOM.

10

THE FIRST FABRICS

ONE of the most basic needs of mankind is protection from the elements. Early hunters utilized the skins of animals they had killed for food. The excavation of Neolithic sites has yielded evidence that tools were used to scrape the hides clean and that needles made from bone slivers were used to sew them together. The first prestigious garments were probably the skins of rare or dangerous animals worn by daring hunters. In many northern regions, such as amongst the Inuit of the Northern Territories of Canada, skins are still the preferred mode of dress since a satisfactory substitute for the insulation they provide against the cold and damp has never been found.

In some tropical regions, such as Fiji, Samoa and Central Africa, an alternative to leather was acquired by stripping the inner bark off certain trees and beating it until it became soft and flexible. A similar material – felt – was developed by pastoral communities who were inspired by the matted coats of sheep and goats.

As the craft of basket-making became more and more refined, it became feasible, with twining and interlacing, to employ an enormous variety of animal or plant fibres in the construction of flexible fabrics. Experimentation by succeeding generations also saw the development of techniques to make more flexible fibres and the invention of spinning which was used in different parts of the world to make yarn from wool, linen, cotton or silk.

Above: *Unyoro men, from Uganda, dressed in cloth made from the bark of* ficus natalensis.

Below, left: *Woven textiles decorated using the warp-ikat technique. Before weaving the cloth, the pattern is established by carefully tying and dyeing the warp yarn in preselected places. These examples were made in, from left to right, Bokhara, Uzbekistan; Oaxaca, Mexico; Flores, Indonesia; Aleppo, Syria; Sarawak, Malaysia.*

Below: *A Samoyed family of herdsmen from Siberia. In cold, wet weather they wear their reindeer-skin garments with the fur on the inside.*

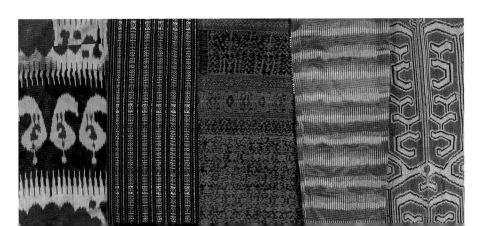

LEARNING TO WEAVE
IN 16TH-CENTURY
MEXICO, FROM THE
CODEX MENDOZA.

The development of better-quality yarns and further experiments with their manipulation resulted in fixed structures on which warp threads could be stretched out to maintain tension, while a weft thread was painstakingly woven in and out with the fingers. The true loom was developed from this structure with the invention of the heddle, a device that made the process quicker and simpler by raising alternate warps all at once, opening a shed through which the weft could be passed.

Above, right: *An old woman in traditional Welsh costume. She is using four needles to knit seamless woollen socks.*

Right: *A group of Aborigine men, from Australia, decorated with paint and flowers. They are about to participate in a magical ceremony to make edible snakes abundant.*

Below: *A shawl, from Ahmedabad, in North-West India, with a pattern printed using carved wooden blocks. The finished item has been glazed with egg-white to impart a sheen. For centuries, textiles have been produced in India specifically for export. Shawls like this are intended for the Yemeni market.*

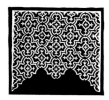

ABOVE: CLAMPED-
RESIST DYED TEXTILE
FROM AHMEDABAD,
GUJARAT, NORTH-
WEST INDIA.

THE DECORATION OF TEXTILES

THE evolution of the decoration of textiles followed several unrelated routes. One developed from the textures produced by the actual process of construction and the effect of colour variations such as stripes, bars and checks. From these humble beginnings weaving specialists ultimately explored the complexities of tapestry, brocades and supplementary warp or weft patterning.

Another route, that of decoration applied to the surface of a piece of finished cloth, was probably developed from body painting and tattooing, initially employing the same pigments and dyes, and eventually achieved the sophistication of batik, ikat and multi-coloured printing.

From the experience of tailoring cloth, patching and mending it, and the need to use every available scrap of material, the sewing skills required for the making of appliqué, quilting and patchwork were developed, while the decorative possibilities of the stitches themselves led to the refined art of embroidery.

Above: *A Pueblo Indian wearing a Navaho tapestry-woven blanket. The tribes of the south-west were the only North American peoples to develop the use of the true loom. With the introduction of sheep's wool towards the end of the 16th century, blanket weaving became an art form. The most famous exponents are the Navaho.*

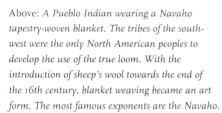

Above, right: *An exquisite 19th-century ivory fan from Belgium. A painted central panel floats on an intricate ground depicting landscapes and flowers worked in Brussels needlepoint lace. Both needlepoint and bobbin lace were made in Brussels, often with parts of the process performed by different women under the aegis of a master.*

SPINNING A YARN

THROUGH the history of textiles run tales of magic, romance and industrial espionage. The very act of telling a story is known as 'spinning a yarn'.

The gods themselves are the greatest exponents of the textile arts. Athene, goddess of wisdom, was challenged to a weaving competition by the conceited Arachne. The latter, of course, lost and for her presumption was turned into a spider to spin and weave forever. In Scandinavia parents told their children that the stars we now know as Orion's belt represented the distaff with which Frigga, the wife of Odin, spun the clouds.

Penelope is not the only heroine whose fate was ravelled up in her textile skills. Vassilisa the Beautiful, a Russian peasant girl, eventually married the Tsar who was impressed by her needlework, and many a princess or lazy girl has needed the assistance of a goblin or spirit such as Tom Tit Tot or Rumplestiltskin to weave prodigious quantities of yarn or even straw into gold.

As for industrial espionage, the secret of silk, so one story tells, was smuggled out of China by a princess who hid silkworms in her elaborate coiffure, while the arcane knowledge of Flemish weavers was stolen in the 14th century by an English cat burglar who climbed on the roof of a weaving shed in Bruges.

TRADITIONAL TEXTILES

THE availability of a particular material has led to localized specialization in specific techniques. When this is combined with the dictates of social values and the influence of climate and lifestyle, a community's textiles develop distinctive traditional characteristics. A cut-pile raphia cloth from the Congo (formerly Zaire) bears little resemblance to a silk brocade sari from Benares, India, but each epitomises the culture that has produced it. Tradition is not static. It is a living thing that evolves gradually with all the influences on a community – contact with outsiders, prosperity or hardship,

WOMAN SPINNING, CHINESE STONE CARVING FROM THE HAN DYNASTY.

Left: *A bolster cover from Swat-Kohistan, Pakistan. Dense patterns are typically embroidered in satin stitch or darning stitch using red silk floss thread on a background of black cotton. Pre-Islamic motifs such as the Tree of Life and solar discs are still in use.*

Below, left: *A Spanish woman wearing a heavily fringed* manton de Manila *embroidered with flowers.*

Right: *Magigabow, a Seminole Indian from Florida. He is wearing a blanket decorated with distinctive appliqué built up in superimposed layers like the molas of the Kuna of Panama. By 1910, this technique had been supplanted by machined patchwork.*

climatic change. Within a community, rural or urban, a sense of identity and belonging is marked by the clothes that people wear and the textiles they make. Tradition does not exert a stranglehold, but provides a foundation on which a fertile imagination may build. Within this framework the opportunity to display one's wealth or status through the use of expensive materials such as silk and metal thread, or the construction of outfits requiring time-consuming weaving or embroidery such as the 'eight knives' robes commissioned by Yoruba men in Nigeria exists. As does the chance to show one's marital status, which is the case in the Andes where unmarried men advertise their availability to potential wives through the patterns knitted into their caps. All over the world a major part of a girl's youth has traditionally been spent sewing a trousseau or dowry for her bottom drawer in preparation for the day she begins a new life in her own home as a married woman.

In many places, whatever the religious inclination, garments are embellished with magical designs to protect the wearer from evil spirits and accidents or to attract good luck and the protection of supernatural powers.

Much time and expense is lavished on textiles for no better reason than vanity and the love of beauty. The most sublime outlet for innovation must surely be the clothing lovingly embroidered by devoted mothers for their children such as the sparkling mirrorwork jackets embroidered by women in Gujarat, India, and Sind, Pakistan.

It could be argued that the manufacture of traditional objects by hand gives a very real sense of identity and belonging, something so often lacking in the depersonalized world of mass-production. Communities grow and change. Tradition and textiles evolve. It is only when a way of life ceases to be viable and a community dies that tradition dies out. There have been many instances in the past of attempts to subjugate cultural groups by banning their traditional dress. Such was the case after the defeat of the Jacobite army at Culloden, Scotland, in 1746 when an Act of Parliament was passed banning the wearing of tartan on pain of transportation for seven years. At the beginning of the 20th century Kemal Atatürk, the first President of modern Turkey, banned the wearing of the fez as part of his plan to drag Turkey into the modern world. During the Cultural Revolution (1966–68) the Chinese government banned the wearing of traditional costume by ethnic minorities such as the Tibetans. However, even today, many communities around the world retain their traditional costume as a living symbol of their cultural identity.

CONCLUSION

THESEUS, escaping from the Labyrinth, followed the route he had marked with a ball of yarn. In the interest of clarity, on this journey through the textile maze, we have chosen to follow a sequence which we hope will give a comprehensive outline of each technique described and will generally lead on to a greater understanding of the technique that follows.

We have tried to select textiles that represent living cultures and that are still individually made using methods that have been employed for generations. Traditional textiles are a statement of identity that say, 'This is where I am from. This is what I do. This is who I am!'

A 19TH-CENTURY CARTER IN A TRADITIONAL SMOCK, FROM DORSET IN SOUTHERN ENGLAND.

Above: *A Caucasian peasant woman wearing a traditional costume of a skirt, blouse and apron enhanced with embroidery and pulled-thread work.*

Below: *A toran, door hanging, from Gujarat in India. The opulent encrustation of sequins and couched gold-thread embroidery is typical of the Indian love of glitter and glamour.*

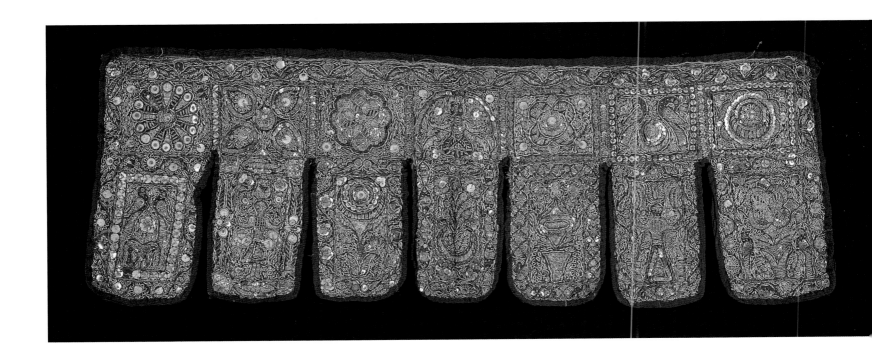

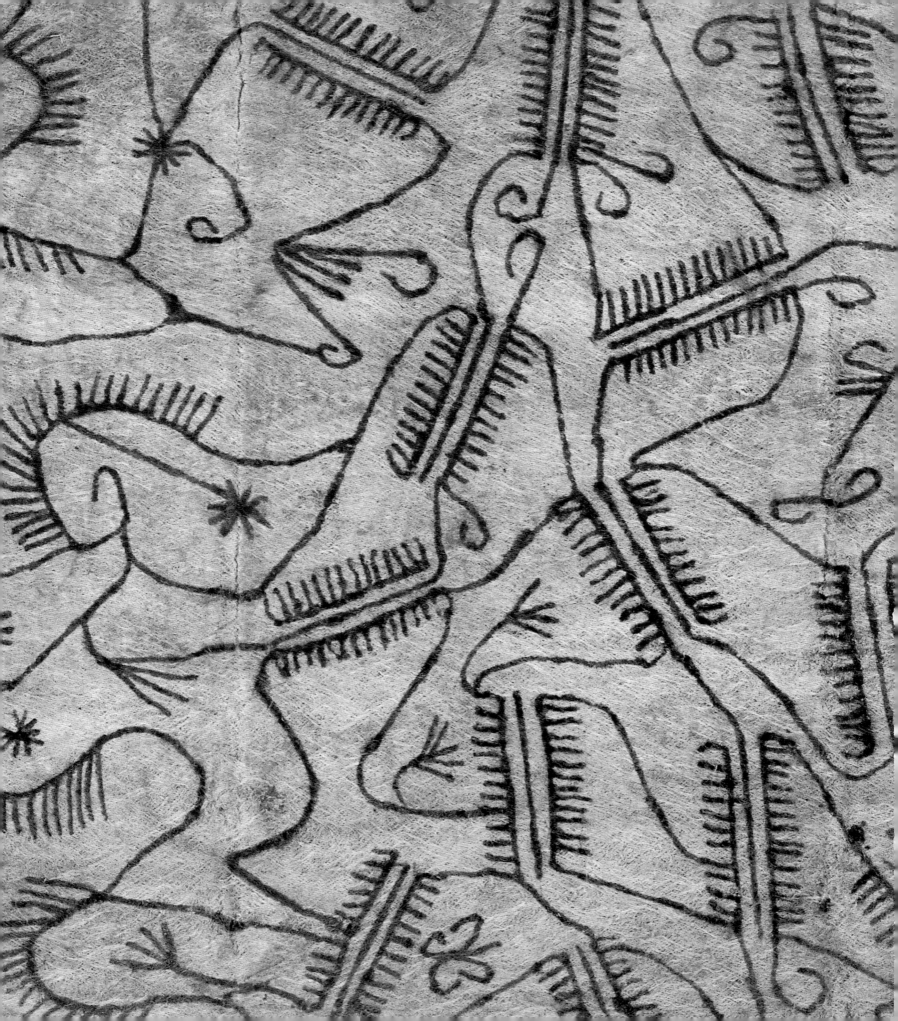

MATERIALS

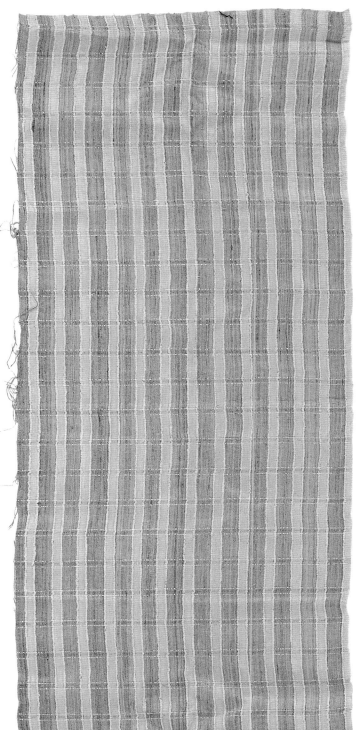

FAR LEFT: PYGMY
BARK CLOTH FROM
THE CONGO
(FORMERLY ZAIRE).

NEAR LEFT: TUSSAR,
WILD SILK, YARDAGE
FROM MADHYA
PRADESH, INDIA.

BELOW: KUBA RAPHIA
CLOTH FROM THE
CONGO (FORMERLY
ZAIRE).

MATERIALS

THE Earth has so many diverse regions, such climatic, topographic and biological variety that many different materials have been exploited and methods have evolved to process them. Different regions are home to different flora and fauna, sheep require grazing, silk worms need warmth, raphia palms only thrive in the tropics. For millennia the only materials that could be utilized were those that were locally available and specialized expertise was developed in the exploitation of specific resources. Over the centuries the evolution of the global market and the establishment of trade routes have made the same materials available at a price to everyone who inhabits this planet.

LUXURY

MATERIALS that are not easily obtained, because they are difficult to grow or must be acquired through trade, become desirable as a sign of wealth and status. Specialized, often city based, 'luxury' crafts have evolved to process these materials, frequently to a high level of sophistication.

Above: *Two Basque women, from the French Pyrenees, winding wool into a ball in preparation for knitting. Leaning against the woman on the left is a distaff used in spinning.*

Left: *An Iban woman, from Sarawak, Malaysia, using a cotton gin. The fluffy bolls of the cotton plant are crushed between the rollers of the gin, as though being squeezed in a mangle. As the cotton fibres are pulled out, seeds, burrs and impurities are extracted.*

Left: *Indian cotton workers. The large bows are held above a pile of cotton and struck with a mallet. The vibrations cause the cotton fibres to separate and fluff up.*

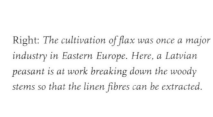

Right: *The cultivation of flax was once a major industry in Eastern Europe. Here, a Latvian peasant is at work breaking down the woody stems so that the linen fibres can be extracted.*

Right: *A Samoan woman preparing* tapa *cloth. Once the bark of the paper mulberry tree has been beaten out into a sheet resembling a tough, papery felt it is decorated with the juices of tropical plants.*

RELIGION

RELIGION has been another powerful influence on the use of certain materials. In Hindu and Buddhist cultures the orthodox shun the use of leather and other by-products of the slaughter of animals, while Muslim men are traditionally forbidden to wear silk next to their skin. Paradoxically, this led to the invention of *mashru*, a silk textile woven in satin weave with a cotton weft, that lies next to the skin. *Mashru* means 'permitted' in Arabic.

The other side of the coin is that religious ceremony, particularly in the Christian church, has always been enhanced with fine embroidery and expensive materials. For all the major creeds, workshops, specializing in many of the textile crafts, have grown up to supply the market.

MODERN MATERIALS

INDUSTRIALIZATION and new technology have led to the development of many cheap synthetic materials which have often supplemented or replaced natural fibres. Although 'synthetic' and 'traditional' are not harmonious terms, in many places man-made fibres have been adopted enthusiastically into folk textiles. In West Africa the Yoruba of Nigeria have created dazzling effects by weaving lurex into their cloth and in Pakistan it is possible to find embroidered blouses of which the main feature is couched cellophane.

Left: *Peasants, from the Czech Republic, extracting bast fibres from hemp stalks after the First World War.*

Above: *Weaving on a vertical loom in Cameroon, using fibres extracted from the fronds of the raphia palm.*

SKIN AND HIDE

Since prehistoric times the skins of small animals and the hides of large ones have provided a tough, but flexible, material suitable for making clothes and a wide range of useful equipment.

Rawhide

A fresh skin begins to rot very quickly and must be cured by drying or salting, all the flesh having first been scraped away. This produces a strong, but inflexible, material called rawhide. When wet, rawhide can be bent and moulded and then it becomes stiff and hard when left to dry. The Plains Indians of North America, who pursued a nomadic lifestyle largely dependant on the herds of buffalo, used rawhide to make large envelopes or parfleches for transporting food and belongings, and as shields for battle and frames for saddles.

Left: An elite Aztec warrior dressed in jaguar skins, from the Codex Mendoza.

Above: *A dyed and painted leather bag or bolster cover with patterns and colouring typical of Moroccan leatherwork.*

Far left: *This large sheet of leather was used to cover a camel's load, from Sind in Pakistan. It is decorated with leather appliqué and embroidery in thick thread.*

Below: *A pair of brain-tanned leather gauntlets embroidered with cut-glass beads, made around 1900 by Native Americans of the Plateau region.*

Leather

To produce the flexible and versatile material we call leather, a longer process called tanning is necessary. After the flesh and hair have been scraped away and the curing completed, the skin or hide is either smoked, rubbed with animal or fish oils, or immersed in a solution of vegetable matter or chemicals. In much of the world this is traditionally carried out in pits. Some solutions, such as that of oak bark, require immersion for as long as a year. Finally, the leather is rinsed, dried and oiled to make it waterproof.

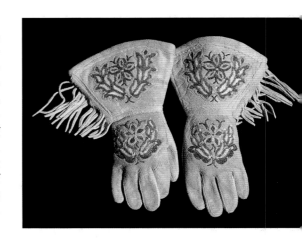

Above: *A Ruthenian woman, from the Western Ukraine, wearing traditional costume. The large sheepskin waistcoat is embellished with embroidery and leather appliqué.*

Right: *A Hungarian sheepskin coat with punched leather appliqué. Sheepskin garments can still be seen in many rural areas of Eastern Europe where they have been a feature of costume since time immemorial.*

Above: *A sheepskin waistcoat with floral embroidery, from the Carpathian Mountains of the Ukraine. Similar waistcoats are also worn in the mountainous regions of Afghanistan.*

Uses

Leather may be dyed, tooled, cut, moulded or stitched to provide a wide range of strong, hard-wearing items including shoes, belts, bags and protective clothing. For centuries, the leather work of Morocco, using hide transported across the Sahara from Sokoto in Nigeria, has been particularly admired for its quality, suppleness and craftsmanship.

Right: *Nahraminyeri, a Ngarrindjeri woman, from South Australia, wearing a possum-skin cloak with a pouch for her child, 1880.*

Left: *Lamo, a cheerful, but ragged, boy, from Leh in Ladakh, Northern India, wearing a woollen goncha. This is typical of the traditional costume worn by inhabitants of the Himalayas who are of Tibetan stock.*

Above: *A wool kilim, from Uzbekistan, made using mainly natural-coloured wool. The patterns have been created with a combination of soumak weaving and embroidery, also in wool. The distinctive hooked-wave motifs are often referred to as 'running dog'.*

WOOL AND HAIR

Tʜᴇ hairy coats of many wild animals provided our ancestors with fibres that could be manipulated in a number of ways to create textiles. Clothes made of wool were worn in Sumeria at least 4,000 years ago. In most parts of the world one species, or sometimes more, has been domesticated and bred selectively to produce high-quality wool or hair – for instance, sheep and goats in Europe, Africa and Asia, camels in Central Asia, and alpaca and vicuña in South America. The Salish people of the American North-West coast even kept packs of small, white-haired dogs, probably Pomeranians, for their wool. The most widely reared animal is the sheep and the finest wool is cashmere, which is actually made from the soft chest hairs of Himalayan goats.

Above: *A sleeveless pullover knitted by a man from Hazarajat, Afghanistan.*

The properties of wool and hair

Aɴɪᴍᴀʟs have hair or fleece to create an insulating layer to conserve their body heat and to repel rain. Woollen textiles retain these properties and are therefore greatly valued in cold regions. Wool also keeps heat out and is widely used by desert peoples for tents and clothing. Each individual hair is covered in tiny scales which not only repel moisture, but also cause the fibres to mat together, giving greater strength and density. These scales impart a lustrous appearance. Natural oils, such as lanolin, are secreted from glands near the hair follicles. Clothing made up without losing this greasiness remains to some extent waterproof and is very practical for sailors and fishermen. The pullovers of the Aran Islands, off the West coast of Ireland, and Guernsey, one of the Channel Islands, retain a distinctive oily smell.

Finally, wool has a wavy quality called crimp which causes the fibres to wrap around each other during spinning, thus making a stronger yarn. The springiness of the crimp also means that woollen clothes keep their shape well.

Above: *Natural-coloured wool products from Bolivia. On a sheep and vicuña wool poncho lie two double-weave sheep's wool belts, an alpaca hat and a sheep and alpaca wool money pouch.*

Left: *A shepherd's woollen coat, from the mountainous Chitral valley of North Pakistan, embroidered with multi-coloured wool. In the cold hills and mountains of the world, wool is not only the material most readily available, but it also provides the best protection against the elements.*

Aʙᴏᴠᴇ: Sᴜᴍᴇʀɪᴀɴ ʀᴜʟᴇʀ ᴡᴇᴀʀɪɴɢ ᴀ sᴋɪʀᴛ ᴏғ ᴛᴜғᴛᴇᴅ ᴡᴏᴏʟ, 2600 BC.

FELT

Although the oldest known felt textiles, those discovered at the Scythian burial site of Pazyryk in Siberia, can only be dated to about 500 BC, it seems likely that felt was the first wool fabric used by mankind. Wool felts unaided – the scaly surface of the fibres ensures that damp wool quickly becomes matted and irreversibly tangled even while still on an animal's back. In spring, wild sheep moult and shed lumps of matted fleece. For our ancestors to have observed this and then to have tried to induce the effect artificially would have been but a small innovative step.

Opposite, above: A woman's apron, from Guizhou in China, made of felted silk filaments.

Below: A felt rug or numdah from Kirghizia. The pattern was laid out with dyed wool fibres before the rolling process.

Opposite, inset: Felt cloaks on the plains of Anatolia have been made in the same way for the last 3,000 years.

Traditional felt making

IN Central Asia, where felt making has an ancient history, felt has been made in the same way for many generations. The sheep are washed in a river and shorn and the resulting fleece is then beaten with sticks to remove grit and burrs – spiny seed heads or any unwanted particles of vegetable matter. To separate the fibres further, the wool may then be combed or carded and if coloured felt is required, the wool may be dyed at this point. Next, the wool is spread evenly on a reed mat that has been sprinkled with soapy water and then the wool is sprinkled with hot water, rolled up inside the reed mat and tied up into a bundle. This is rolled backwards and forwards for several hours, usually under the forearms of a group of kneeling

A felt bag, folded like an envelope, with wool tassels and patterns of cloth appliqué, from North Afghanistan.

women. The result, when the bundle has been unwrapped and dried, is a densely intermeshed fabric that can be cut, stitched or moulded.

Uses

FELT, in a variety of thicknesses, is used in Europe, Asia, North Africa and South America in the construction of warm boots, hats, coats, bags, rugs and coverings for the tents, yurts or gers in which they live.

Below: A donkey-cart cover, from Kashgaria in Chinese Turkestan, where such items are regarded as cheap and disposable. The dynamic, geometric pattern has been achieved using two different colours of natural, undyed wool.

WOOLLEN YARN

To convert wool fibres into a form that can be manipulated more easily they must be spun into yarn. First the wool needs to be carded or combed to remove impurities, disentangle the fibres and align them in one direction.

Carding

THE Romans are credited with the invention of carding. By mounting the prickly heads of teasels on a wooden cross called a *carduus* (Latin for thistle) they were able to brush or tease the fibres into alignment. This eventually evolved into a pair of wooden blocks with rows of bent wire teeth set into a leather pad on each surface. A small amount of wool is carefully stroked between them until all the fibres are parallel. It is then removed and gathered into a loose bundle, called a rolag, ready for spinning.

Combing

BY combing wool from a longer-haired sheep with long-tined combs, longer, better-separated fibres are produced that are used to weave smooth-surfaced worsted cloth.

ABOVE: ENGLISH WOMAN AT HER SPINNING WHEEL, MID-17TH CENTURY.

Left: *A herdsman's blanket woven in Rajasthan, India, from locally produced yarn. The main ground is of undyed yarn with a pattern of supplementary weft weaving. Because Rajasthan is mostly desert, it can become extremely cold at night and a blanket is essential.*

Right: *Woollen hand-loom woven cloth, from Lhasa, Tibet, used for edging men's garments. After weaving, the cloth is decorated with rows of crosses, traditionally achieved by pressing the bunched up cloth through a wide-gauge wooden sieve into dye vats or alternatively by block printing.*

Opposite, near left: *A hand-knitted Fair Isle hat, from the Scottish Shetland Islands, with the popular 'snowflake' motif, worked in typically pale-coloured wool.*

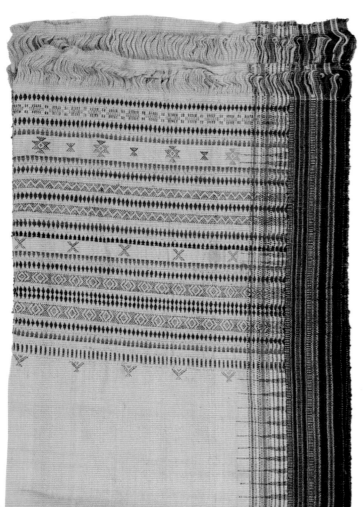

Spinning

THE simplest way to twist wool into strands is to roll it between the fingers, but a spindle is employed to achieve greater uniformity and length. The spindle is basically a stick with a weight, or whorl, at the bottom. Fibres are drawn out from the rolag, which is sometimes attached to a distaff, and fastened to the top of the spindle which is then set spinning either freely suspended in the air or with its tip on the ground. The spinning twists the fibres together into yarn. As the spun yarn gets longer it is wound around the spindle and more fibres are drawn out from the rolag. A spindle spun clockwise will produce a Z twist and spun anti-clockwise it will produce an S twist. The spinning wheel is merely a more mechanized method of achieving a consistent yarn.

Uses

AS yarn, wool can easily be knotted, twined or interlaced into a diverse range of warm, flexible textiles suitable for everyday wear in cooler climates such as Northern Europe and the high altitudes of the Andes or the Atlas Mountains of North Africa.

Above: *A Romanian man at Sighetu market, with a woollen cape draped over his shoulder.*

Near right: *A chullo,* from Puno in Peru, *knitted in a pleasing combination of dyed and naturally coloured wools.*

Far right: *A Bolivian* chullo *with intricately patterned bands depicting animals and birds. Many Bolivian knitters are illiterate and mistakes often occur in the lettering.*

COTTON

COTTON is obtained from the hairy fibres surrounding the seed-head of a semi-tropical plant of the genus *Gossypium*. It can be spun into a strong, fine thread or yarn that is ideal for even weaving and so has become one of the most popular and widely used of all textile materials, although garments made from it are most suitable for warmer climates. The oldest known cotton yarn was produced in Mohenjo-Daro in Pakistan 3,000 years ago.

Processing cotton

WHEN the fluffy cotton seed-heads or bolls open they are plucked and ginned. Ginning is the removal of the seeds by rolling the bolls under an iron or wooden rod or by squeezing them through a special mangle called a cotton gin. Then the fibres are untangled and fluffed up into a loose mass by beating them with sticks or by plucking the string of a bow against them. Finally, the mass is gathered into a rolag and spun, with spindle or wheel, into yarn or thread.

Uses

BECAUSE of its strength, smoothness and fineness, cotton is excellent for making densely woven, hard-wearing rugs and cloth. Calico, for example, is a sturdy, unbleached cotton fabric named after Calicut, a town on the Indian Malabar coast, where it was originally woven. On the other hand, this strength and fineness facilitate the weaving of delicate, loosely woven fabrics such as muslin which originally came from Mosul in Iraq.

Above: *A cotton flag from Ghana. The banners of the Fante men's societies are decorated with appliqué pictures that convey allegorical messages.*

Below: *A huilpil,* woman's poncho, *from Chiapas in Mexico, woven from undyed, naturally coloured cotton yarn with patterns of birds and flowers.*

Opposite: *A Yoruba indigo-dyed cotton cloth. Machine stitching has been used to resist the dye and make the pattern.*

Opposite, inset: *Two small Buddhist monks, from Myanmar (Burma), dressed in cotton robes dyed with saffron or turmeric.*

RIGHT: WEAVING COTTON IN PERU, FROM A POT OF THE MOCHE PERIOD (AD 300–500).

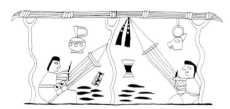

Below: *A 'hunting cloth', from Herat in Western Afghanistan, embroidered on a cotton ground with cotton thread.*

ONE

SILK

FOR generations, the secrets of silk manufacture, shrouded in myth and mystery, were known only to the Chinese. The desire for this most fabulous of fabrics led to the establishment of the greatest trade route the world has ever known – the Silk Road – which stretched from Lanzhou in China to Rome in Italy, where silk togas cost their weight in gold. Legends tell how in the 6th century AD two monks smuggled the cocoons of a few silk worms to Byzantium in hollowed-out walking sticks and so brought the knowledge of sericulture, the rearing of silk worms, to the West.

Sericulture

THE finest silk is made by the caterpillar of the silk moth, *Bombyx mori*, which only feeds on the leaves of the white mulberry tree, *Morus alba*. As it is a delicate creature, sensitive to noise and draughts, it is impossible to rear on a large scale and so a cottage industry grew up which carefully nurtures the greedy grubs until they reach three to four inches long and spin themselves a cocoon. The cocoon is dried in the sun to kill the pupa inside before it can become a moth and damage the filament by eating its way out.

Reeling silk thread

REELING silk is a specialist's job. The cocoons are thrown into a cauldron of boiling water to soften the gum that binds the filaments together. With great care several filaments at a time are reeled onto a bobbin to make one long, smooth thread. The more filaments that are wound together, the thicker the thread will be and therefore the heavier the cloth woven from it. The finest shawls are woven from thread made by reeling together the filaments of only four cocoons.

Floss silk and embroidery threads are spun using damaged and inferior filaments. Wild silk is collected in China, Eastern India and Africa from the cocoons of uncultivated *Antheraea* moths, but it yields a coarser thread. The Ashanti people of Ghana, among others, acquire their silk threads by unravelling silk textiles imported from Europe.

Uses

SILK is highly prized as the raw material of luxury fabrics since it is soft and has a beautiful sheen. It is easy to dye, has surprisingly good insulating properties and is strong enough to have been used in the manufacture of parachutes.

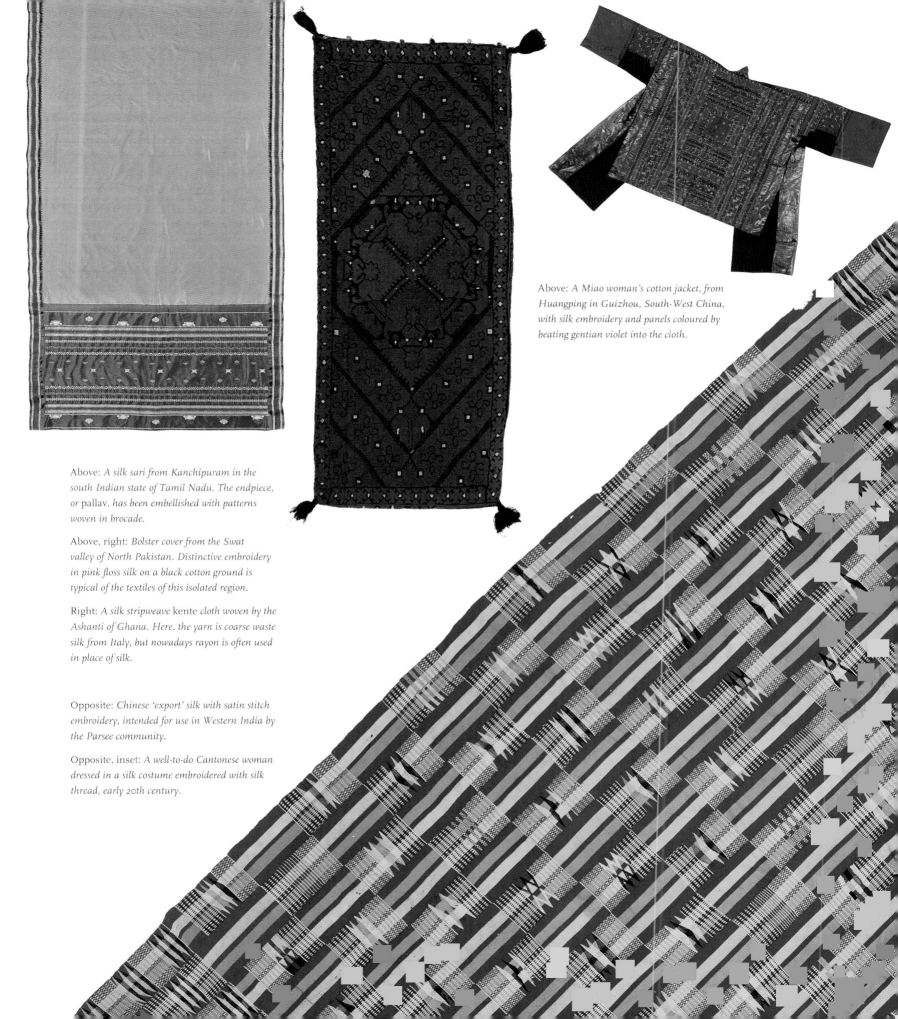

Above: *A silk sari from Kanchipuram in the south Indian state of Tamil Nadu. The endpiece, or pallav, has been embellished with patterns woven in brocade.*

Above, right: *Bolster cover from the Swat valley of North Pakistan. Distinctive embroidery in pink floss silk on a black cotton ground is typical of the textiles of this isolated region.*

Right: *A silk stripweave* kente *cloth woven by the Ashanti of Ghana. Here, the yarn is coarse waste silk from Italy, but nowadays rayon is often used in place of silk.*

Opposite: *Chinese 'export' silk with satin stitch embroidery, intended for use in Western India by the Parsee community.*

Opposite, inset: *A well-to-do Cantonese woman dressed in a silk costume embroidered with silk thread, early 20th century.*

Above: *A Miao woman's cotton jacket, from Huangping in Guizhou, South-West China, with silk embroidery and panels coloured by beating gentian violet into the cloth.*

BARK

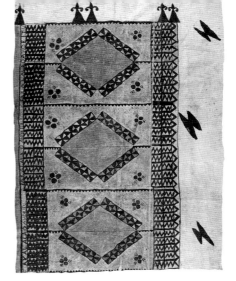

O<small>NE</small> of the oldest methods of obtaining clothing without weaving cloth on a loom was to make it from the inner bark of certain trees. This method was fairly widespread, and is still found in well-wooded areas in Africa, South-East Asia and Polynesia.

Bark cloth

I<small>N</small> Indonesia and Polynesia the inner bark of the paper mulberry tree, *Broussonetia papyrifera*, is used to make cloth, while in Central Africa the preferred source is a species of fig tree, *Ficus natalensis*. In Central Africa a sheet of bark is removed from the tree, steamed to soften it and then placed over a log and beaten with grooved wooden mallets until the fibres become felted together. The fibres lie longitudinally and beating causes the fabric to stretch widthways, resulting in a large sheet of cloth.

In Tonga *tapa* cloth is made by stripping a whole sapling of its outer bark, soaking it in sea-water for about two weeks and then stripping off the inner bark. This is cut into thin strips which are then beaten against a flattened log with a hardwood beater. This process felts the bark, giving it strength and flexibility, and more than doubles its width. The strips are then pasted together with arrowroot to form a very large cloth and painted or stencilled with the sap of certain trees, which stains them black or brown.

The bark of the fig tree oxidizes to the rich reddish brown typical of African bark cloth, while the *tapa* cloth made from the paper mulberry remains off white.

Opposite: A large tapa *cloth from Fiji. The geometric stencilling has been applied so densely that the pattern appears to be in cream on brown rather than vice versa.*

Opposite, insets, from top to bottom: Basu Fondong, King of Cameroon in the 1920s, wearing bark cloth strikingly decorated with hand-painted flowers; a Samoan girl wearing tapa *cloth with a typical bold, monochrome pattern; an Ainu couple, from North Japan, dressed in garments made of woven elm-bark fibre.*

Bark fibre

O<small>N</small> the American North-West coast the Tlingit and Kwakiutl wove blankets from the shredded bark of the red cedar. The Ainu of Hokkaido, Japan, traditionally wear garments woven from the thin bark of the atsui tree or of elm-bark fibre.

Uses

B<small>ARK</small> cloth was once common day-to-day wear, but its use has largely been superseded by cotton except for ritual and ceremonial use. In Fiji the creamy ground of *tapa* cloth is stencilled with bold floral and geometric shapes in brown and black.

Above, right: A large tapa *cloth, from Tonga, more than three metres long. As mulberry bark does not stretch much, large sheets are made by joining strips together with arrowroot paste.*

Right: Painted bark cloth from Astrolabe Bay, Papua New Guinea.

Below: The Kuba people of the Congo (formerly Zaire) use raphia textiles for everyday use, but prefer bark cloth for ceremonial use. This wrap-around apron is made of bark cloth with an embroidered raphia edging.

LINEN

BAST fibres are obtained from the stalks of certain dicotyledonous plants. The supreme example of a bast fibre is linen, which is made from the stems of the flax plant, *Linum usitatissimum*. A shirt-like garment (*c.* 2800 BC) from the Egyptian Early Dynastic period is the oldest surviving specimen of linen cloth.

ABOVE: *LINUM*
USITATISSIMUM,
THE FLAX PLANT.

Left: *Embroidered linen dress panel from Ramallah, Palestine.*

Below: *Turkish linen towel with silk embroidery.*

Processing flax

FIRST the seeds are removed by rippling or pulling the stems through a coarse comb. The stems are soaked in water so that the bast fibres can be separated easily from the woody parts. This is called retting. Then the stems are broken by beating or crushing them in a hinged wooden device called a brake. Finally, the stems are tapped and stroked to free the bast fibres from the unwanted woody portions and combed through a hackle with iron teeth. The end product is a fine fibre that can be spun into tough thread or yarn.

Uses

SINCE Ancient Egyptian times linen cloth has been used for making fine-quality clothing worn by the wealthy or by the general populace on special occasions. It is a popular base for needlework and to this day, although cotton has replaced it for daily use, beautifully embroidered linen shirts and blouses are the preferred costume for weddings in Eastern Europe. The terms 'bed linen' and 'table linen' are still in common usage, although most sheets and tablecloths are now made from cheaper materials.

Above: *Greek linen coverlet with cross-stitch embroidery around the border. The warps and wefts of linen cloth are easy to count which makes it an ideal base for counted-thread embroidery.*

Right: *A long linen chemise, from the Balkans, with counted-thread embroidery in wool yarn on the sleeves and hems. Red, the colour of life, is the most widely used colour in Eastern European embroidery.*

Below: *A Norwegian girl, from Hardanger, wearing a skaut, the traditional linen headgear of a married woman.*

Right: *The sleeve of a Bulgarian linen blouse embroidered with cotton and silk thread.*

Left: *A group of Atayal women from the hills of Taiwan (then Formosa). Their traditional square cloaks, embroidered with complex, geometric designs in red, black and blue wool, are woven from 'China grass' or ramie fibre.*

Above: *A Miao man's smock from Guizhou in South-West China. It has been made from tough ramie or hemp fibre and the cotton yoke has been decorated with abstract geometric patterns embroidered in silk.*

OTHER BAST FIBRES

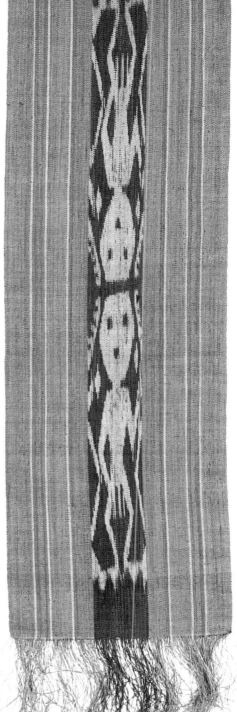

MANY other plants are prepared in much the same way as linen, although the bast fibres they yield are generally much coarser and more suitable for finger weaving than loom weaving.

In West Africa a large number of plants of the genus *Hibiscus* are used, notably *Urena lobata* and *Sida rhombifolia*. In Borneo the lemba plant, *Curculigo latifolia*, which grows wild, is harvested for its fibres. The Indian province of West Bengal has an economy largely based on the processing of jute, *Corchorus capsularis* and *C. olitorius*. Various members of the nettle family, genus *Urticaceae*, have been exploited in Asia and North America including ramie, *Boehmeria nivea*, a native of China and the East Indies.

The milkweed, genus *Asclepia*, was widely used by the indigenous peoples of North America. The plant most extensively cultivated for its bast fibres must be hemp, *Cannabis indica*, which has been grown in Asia, Europe, Africa and North America.

Similar fibres

IN the Philippines the abaca palm, *Musa textilis*, a small banana-like plant, provides tough, silky fibres used in the weaving of warp ikat.

Uses

MOST bast fibres are used in the manufacture of matting, netting, rope and string. Strong bags, belts and burden straps constructed from bast twine are also widespread. Canvas woven from hemp and linen is a tough material that can be made up into bags, tarpaulins, tents, sailcloth and work clothes. Hemp-woven skirts are much valued in South-East Asia as they keep their pleats much longer than skirts made of cotton.

Above, left: *A Mandaya mantle, from Mindanao in the Philippines, made from abaca fibre dyed and woven using the warp-ikat technique.*

Above, centre: *A warp-ikat selendang, from Kalimantan, Indonesia, woven from wild-orchid fibres.*

Above, right: *A galla covers the back of the neck of Banjara women in India. It is embroidered with bast fibres.*

RAPHIA AND LEAF FIBRES

Raphia, or raffia, is a grassy fibre extracted from the leaves of a palm tree, *Raphia ruffia* or *R. taedigera*, that grows extensively round the fringes of the tropical forests of Central and West Africa and on the island of Madagascar. The mature leaves can grow as long as fifty feet (15.25 metres), but only the young leaflets are used.

Preparing raphia

The leaflets are cut from the palm before they reach six feet (1.8 metres) in length. The soft tissues of the underside of the leaf are stripped away with the edge of a knife or peeled off by hand to leave behind the upper epidermis. These translucent fibres are tied in hanks and dried in the sun. Finally, each fibre is split lengthways with the fingers, a comb or a snail shell to produce a silky strand three to four feet (90 cm–120 cm) long.

Uses of raphia

Raphia is most familiar in Europe and North America as a grassy string used by gardeners, but in fact it is used to make some silky, even luxurious, textiles. Most raphia textiles, like those of the Congo (formerly Zaire) and the Côte d'Ivoire, are smaller than four feet by three feet (120 cm x 90 cm) as their size is limited by the length of a raphia strand, although dance skirts are made by sewing several woven pieces into a long strip. The Kuba of the Kasai River area of the Congo (formerly Zaire) make distinctive velvety textiles using embroidery and cut pile. In Madagascar raphia fibres are twisted together to make a yarn long enough to weave on a loom, while in Nigeria lengths are sometimes simply knotted together.

Other leaf fibres

On the Tanimbar Islands, warp-ikat cloths are woven from fibres obtained from the lontar palm, *Borassus fiabelliformis*, and in other parts of Indonesia threads are obtained from *Sago* and *Pandanus* palms. In the south-west region of North America the fibres of the yucca, *Yucca aloifolia*, were once used in the making of sandals and baskets, while another New World plant, *Agave sisalana*, was introduced to the Canary Islands by the Spanish for the manufacture of sisal and its use has since spread to many other tropical parts of the world.

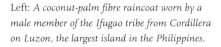

Left: *A coconut-palm fibre raincoat worn by a male member of the Ifugao tribe from Cordillera on Luzon, the largest island in the Philippines.*

Right: *A patchwork and appliqué raphia-fibre dance skirt made by the Kuba of the Congo (formerly Zaire). The most common motif in Kuba craftwork is comma-shaped, known as* shina mboa, *the tail of a dog.*

Opposite: *Kuba raphia textiles. The base cloth is woven by men and the embroidery, also in raphia, is executed by women.*

Opposite, inset above: *A Portuguese farmer protected from the rain by a raincoat made of grass.*

Opposite, inset below: *Chinese coolies wearing rice-straw raincoats.*

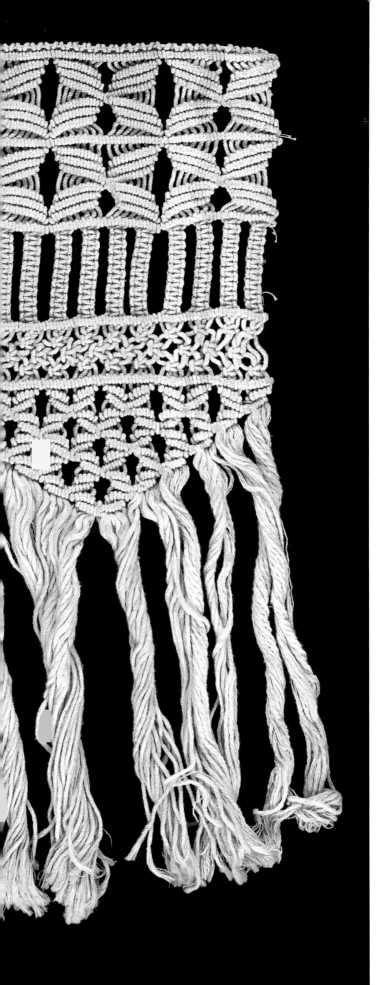

NON-LOOM TEXTILES

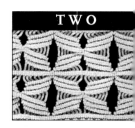

LEFT: ENGLISH 19TH-
CENTURY COTTON
MACRAMÉ.

BELOW: HAMMOCK OF
INTERLINKED COTTON
WARPS FROM MERIDA
IN MEXICO (DETAIL).

NON-LOOM TEXTILES

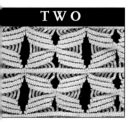
THE first textiles fabricated by mankind were made by manipulating fibres with the fingers. It has been suggested that the craft of basketry was invented by primitive man and that the techniques developed were then applied to constructing other fabrics. A number of techniques were developed that involved looping, knotting, interlacing or twining strands together. The major difference between early baskets and textiles was not so much in the techniques, but in the choice of materials. The more resilient and flexible a fibre used, the more supple the fabric constructed from it. Some of the methods that evolved are so effective that in parts of the world, such as central and eastern North America, the loom was never devised and even with the introduction of the true loom by colonists the techniques of working only with the fingers were not replaced.

PORTABILITY

WITH non-loom textiles the very fact that a bulky loom is not required and that equipment is minimal means that work in progress is often portable and easy to pick up at any convenient moment. This is, of course, of prime importance to those who do not have a sedentary lifestyle or who are unable to devote prolonged periods to a single task. The supreme example of a portable technique is knitting, a craft that is practised by men and women all over the world and is today one of the most common of all domestic textile crafts. On the Scottish islands of the Outer Hebrides there are still experts who are able to knit with one hand, while attending to their domestic

Above: *A young Breton knitter, from Finistère, France, wearing a lace cap.*

Above: *An English fisherman, from East Anglia, wearing a knitted pullover while mending his nets.*

Right: *Making bobbin lace in the streets of Burano near Venice in Italy.*

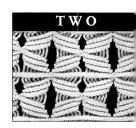

Right: *Amazonian Indians weaving baskets. Many techniques are common to both basketry and textile construction.*

Below: *French shepherd. Knitting can be carried out anywhere.*

chores, nursing the baby or stirring the supper, with the other. In the days of whaling and global exploration, sailors, away from home for months or even years at a stretch, spent a considerable amount of time knitting themselves articles of clothing or knotting lengths of twine into useful articles.

FRAMES

To maintain their structure and regular shape many textiles, such as crochet, only need to be held firmly by the fingers, but others need to be attached to a fixed point or stretched on some form of frame, as is necessary in sprang. These simple devices are rudimentary relatives of the loom.

WARP AND WEFT

Most techniques that do not need a loom require only one set of elements – they are either weft-based like netting, knitting and crochet, or warp-based like sprang, macramé and braiding.

Right: *A Tongan woman making an apron from crocheted twine.*

Far right: *Ishwar Singh from Jaisalmer in Rajasthan, Western India – a great exponent of ply-split work – making a camel girth out of goat hair.*

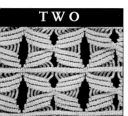

TWO

A NET is a structure built up horizontally by connecting each row of weft to the previous one. The connection may be linked, knotted or looped, but has the appearance of being structured on the diagonal. All textiles made like this have a fair degree of elasticity.

Technique

THE foundation of most netted fabrics is a horizontal thread or cord attached at either end to some sort of frame. A manageable length of yarn is then wound onto a shuttle or bobbin and loosely attached to the foundation cord in a series of loops. On reaching the edge, the yarn is worked back in the opposite direction, looping through the previous row and creating a new set of loops on to which the following row is attached. For a flexible structure the yarn is simply passed through the loops, but if a stronger fabric, such as that required for fishing, is being manufactured then the yarn may be attached to the previous row with a suitable knot like a sheet bend.

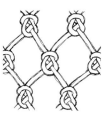

LINKED BAG FROM MEXICO.

FISHING NET.

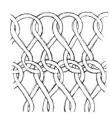

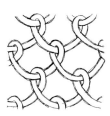

LOOPED BAG FROM ECUADOR.

BILLUM FROM NEW GUINEA.

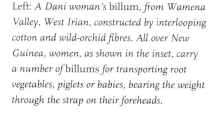

Left: *A Dani woman's* billum, *from Wamena Valley, West Irian, constructed by interlooping cotton and wild-orchid fibres. All over New Guinea, women, as shown in the inset, carry a number of billums for transporting root vegetables, piglets or babies, bearing the weight through the strap on their foreheads.*

There are many variations on this basic principle. The density and strength of a looped or netted structure may be greatly reinforced by linking several rows together at the same time, introducing extra horizontal elements, crossing the yarn in a figure of eight or simply pulling the work tighter.

Above, left and centre: *Two bags, or shigra, from Ecuador, made by tightly looping yarn spun from fibres obtained from the cabuya plant.*

Above, right: *A general purpose bag, used by the Hani tribe of Yunnan in China, made from hemp fibres with a structure of interconnected looping.*

Uses

THE most obvious application of this technique is the manufacture of nets for fishing and storage or for use as hammocks. When the fibres or threads are worked tightly, strong, yet flexible, bags can be constructed. Such bags can be found all over the world, often incorporating fibres of several colours to build up decoration. Among the most interesting examples are the *billums* of New Guinea which are constructed in hourglass or figure-of-eight looping using a needle threaded with *Pandanus* fibre.

Right: *The embroidered border at the end of a Russian towel, embellished with a simple netted fringe and enhanced with beads threaded onto the yarn.*

Right: *Details of woollen socks, from North Afghanistan, with interlooped tops. They are intended to be worn inside riding boots at bozkashi contests, a form of free-for-all polo where a headless calf is used instead of a ball.*

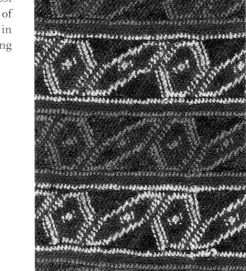

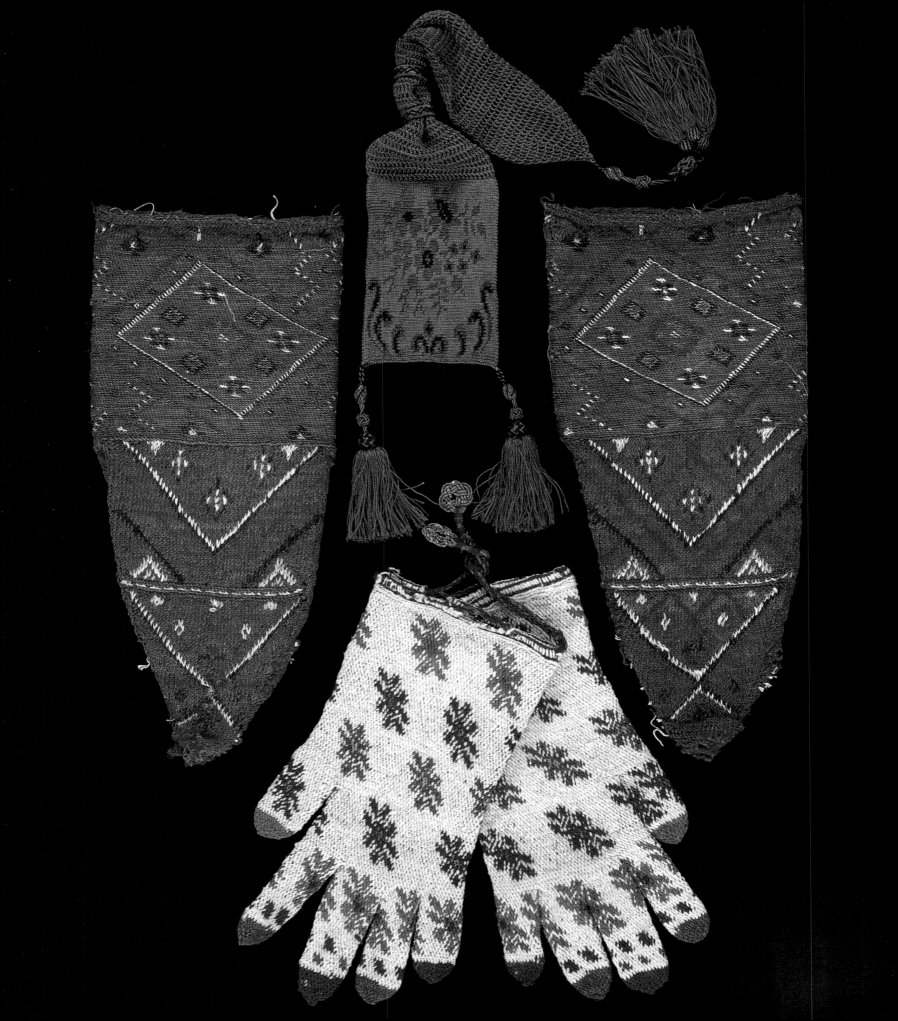

CROCHET

CROCHET, which derives its name from the French for 'hook', is a doubly interlooped structure worked with a hook made of wood, metal, bone or plastic. As it is a simple technique requiring only a hook and yarn, crochet work can easily be carried around and worked on at any convenient moment.

Technique

THE foundation of every piece of crochet is a chain. First a slip loop is tied and then a loop is pulled through this with the hook. A succession of loops are then worked through each other, one at a time, until the chain has reached the required length. To build a crocheted fabric subsequent rows are added by working a new sequence of loops, each one of which is hooked through the previous loop and also through the previous row.

Variations on the basic stitch involve increasing the number of loops carried on the hook or linked together at the same time.

Below: *Tablecloths with crocheted borders made in England before the First World War.*

Uses

CROCHET, usually worked in wool, cotton or silk, lends itself easily to the making of open work, and such is the variety of stitches and their possible applications that the number of different articles that can be crocheted is almost limitless. As crochet is such a simple, but versatile, technique and work in progress is so easily transported, it has been adopted by the inhabitants of many lands and adapted to local materials and requirements.

Opposite: *A selection of crocheted items, including a pair of socks, from Dubrovnik in the Former Yugoslavia; an English 'miser's purse' dating from the late 19th or early 20th century; and a pair of gloves from the Hunza Valley in Pakistan.*

Above: *A Spanish señorita wrapped in a crocheted woollen shawl.*

Below: *A tough bag with a narrow neck manufactured from crocheted cotton yarn in Kutch, North-West India.*

KNITTING

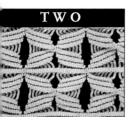

KNITTING is a technique where an interlooped textile is created by horizontally manipulating a weft yarn with two or more needles. Traditionally wool is used, although sometimes cotton. The Egyptian Copts, a Christian sect who became famous for their skill, are credited with inventing the first true knitting. As Christianity spread, knitting spread with it, travelling as far as Peru with the Conquistadores in the 16th century. Although it originated in a hot climate, knitting is now most often practised in temperate or cold countries and requires only an adequate supply of yarn. In Europe and Central Asia sheep or goat wool is used, but in the High Andes of Bolivia and Peru alpaca, llama or vicuña hair is more readily available and is knitted into beautifully soft garments. Plain, functional sweaters knitted with naturally oily wools are the choice of seafaring and fishing folk such as the inhabitants of Guernsey and the other Channel Islands.

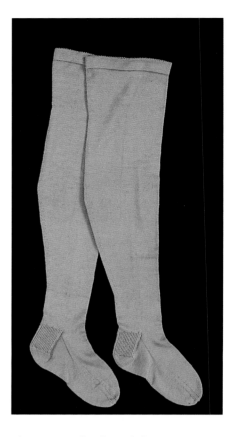

Above: *A pair of woollen socks knitted in France. Seams can be avoided by circular knitting on three or four needles.*

Opposite: *A multi-coloured blanket knitted using recycled wool.*

Opposite, inset: *Scottish fisherman in a knitted hat.*

Above: *A knitted cotton altar cloth from Mexico.*

Technique

A FIRST row of stitches is cast on by looping the yarn onto one needle, pulling a second loop through the first with the other needle and picking the new loop up beside the first. A third loop is pulled through the second and so on until there are sufficient stitches for the required width. A second row is then knitted by pulling a new series of loops through the first, one stitch at a time. This is repeated until sufficient rows have been knitted to make one panel. When all the separate panels have been knitted they are stitched together to make the final garment. It is possible to knit tubular items like socks and hats in one go, without a seam, by using three or four needles.

The texture of the knit can be made more interesting by varying the stitch. For plain, or knit, stitch the loop of yarn is pulled through to the front, while for purl stitch it is pulled through to the back.

The most widely knitted fabric uses stocking stitch which makes a smooth fabric comprised of alternate rows of plain and purl. When it is reversed, with the purl side as the face, it is called reverse stocking stitch.

Far left: *Eastern European knitted and beaded hat.*

Near left: *English 19th-century knitted purse.*

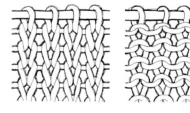

PLAIN OR KNIT STITCH.   PURL STITCH.

Popularity

THE fact that knitting is simple to learn, needs no special equipment, other than a pair of needles, and is portable has ensured the survival of knitting as a domestic, as well as a commercial, textile craft. In any moment of leisure or when the hands are not required for other work, whether while watching sheep or watching television, knitting can be done.

TEXTURED KNITTING

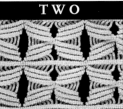

THE most famous textured knitting of all is Aran. Developed on the Irish Aran Islands to protect fishermen from the hostile elements, Aran sweaters are knitted in natural white wool which does not detract from the bold, raised patterns of cables and bobbles. It is possible to buy imitations as far away as Kathmandu in Nepal.

Technique

CABLES imitate plaited or twisted rope. To achieve this effect one set of elements is slipped onto an extra needle and pulled over or under another set of elements to change the order in which the stitches are knitted. To emphasize the texture, the cable is worked in stocking stitch on a background of reverse stocking stitch. Using a cable needle, a number of different patterns can be created. Although textured patterns can be built up without the use of cable needles, by comparison they are dull and two dimensional.

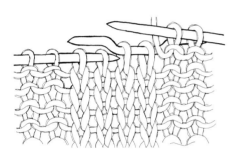

Opposite: *A child's woollen pullover from the Aran Islands off the Atlantic coast of Ireland. The panels are knitted in two-rib diamond cable. Warm woollens are considered indispensable for withstanding the harsh weather to which these islands are exposed.*

Opposite, inset above: *An English fisherman wearing a knitted pullover that identifies his home port as Lowestoft.*

Opposite, inset below: *An Aran Islander, from Inishmaan, wearing a textured pullover under his jacket.*

Above, right: *English knitted woollen socks, or stockings, with a ribbed texture. In some parts of England and Scotland women still make their families hand-knitted socks.*

Right: *A woollen pullover, from Kathmandu in Nepal, knitted in imitation of the Aran style. The central pattern is a horseshoe cable.*

Uses

FISHERMEN all around the coasts of Britain have relied for generations on warm, weatherproof pullovers, knitted for them by their womenfolk. Navy blue is the most typical colour, but textured patterns on selected parts of the garment – neck, chest, sleeves or shoulders – were once a sure way of knowing whether a fisherman was from Whitby, Lowestoft or Guernsey. Sadly, these garments are now seldom made at home and plain, machine-knitted jumpers have become the usual mode of dress.

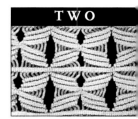

MULTI-COLOURED KNITTING

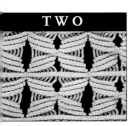

Just as the introduction of dyed yarn increased the range of effects that could be achieved in weaving, so did many cultures build up a treasury of motifs and patterns in knitting. To this day men in the Andes record their marital and social status in the hats and belts they knit and the repertoire of designs used in the Scottish Shetland Islands includes motifs (such as the Armada cross) supposedly derived from the wrecks of ships from the dispersed Spanish Armada of 1588.

In recent years knitting skills have been given a new lease of life amongst refugees, such as those from Afghanistan, who knit to their own designs using wool unravelled from garments given to them by aid organizations.

Above: *Guatemalan bag. By using different yarns and by varying the tension of the stitches, it is possible to produce delicate, gauzy fabrics or tough, hard-wearing objects like this bag knitted with a typically Guatemalan colour scheme.*

Technique

The process of knitting in colour is very much like weaving with a supplementary weft, in that an extra colour can float across the back of the knitting, surfacing when required to take over the pattern. It is possible to use several colours in a single row, but the more strands of yarn used, the harder they become to manipulate and the bulkier the fabric will be.

Because knitting is a horizontal process it is easiest to build up patterns in bands or rows of repeated motifs. This can be observed all over the world from Fair Isle in Scotland to Afghanistan and from Norway to Bolivia.

Opposite: *A knitted hat, or chullo, from Bolivia. Hats knitted from vicuña, alpaca or sheep's wool are worn by both sexes all over the Andes.*

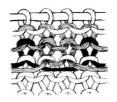

Left: Multi-coloured knitting seen from the back.

Opposite, inset: *Villagers in Western Macedonia wearing hand-knitted socks.*

Above: *Bulgarian woollen socks. Patterned socks are knitted in many parts of the world, often by men while watching over their sheep. In Afghanistan, many socks are now knitted for export using recycled wool.*

Right: *Bag, puttees and socks knitted from woollen yarn by Sarakat nomads in Northern Greece.*

BRAIDS

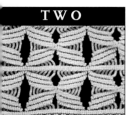

Although the word braid is often used to describe any narrow textile, irrespective of the method of construction, technically, a braid is a band manufactured by interworking a group of warp strands together diagonally across the width of the fabric. When carried out with a large number of strands, the interlacing bears a strong resemblance to a woven textile using both warp and weft. A technically more precise term is oblique interlacing.

The three-strand plait has been universally used, particularly by women, for keeping hair tidy, sometimes in quite complex styles as can be observed in West Africa. One of the most elaborate plaited coiffures is that used by Khampa women in Tibet who braid their hair into 108 plaits, a religiously significant number for Buddhists.

RIGHT: SCOTTISH DIRK
WITH BRAIDED GRIP.

Opposite, above: *Khampa girl, from Eastern Tibet, with her hair plaited into 108 braids.*

Opposite, inset: *John Henry, the factor of the Hudson's Bay Company at Lower Fort Garry, Manitoba, Canada, wearing an Ojibway sash constructed by oblique interlacing.*

Below: *A Hazara woven storage bag, or juval, from central Afghanistan, embellished with tassels and a fringe of interlaced braids.*

Technique

A NUMBER of strands are suspended side by side from a foundation thread and each strand is interlaced diagonally to one edge, passing alternately over and under every other strand on the way. The strands originating on the left all travel to the right and all the strands on the right travel to the left. As each strand reaches the selvedge it changes direction and travels back across to the opposite side. In North America this is called double-band plaiting. In multiple-band plaiting a larger number of strands are used. These are divided into groups and from each group half the strands travel to the right and half to the left.

The introduction of coloured strands allows the creation of a variety of patterns which may be made more intricate by changing the direction in which selected strands are interlaced. Braids can be flat, tubular, solid and even three-dimensional.

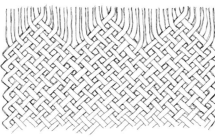

ABOVE: MULTIPLE-BAND PLAITING.

Uses

A s the technique of plaiting or braiding lends itself best to the manufacture of narrow fabrics a few inches wide, it is most often used for making straps, belts and bags. Quite often plaits may be used to make fringes to secure the ends of larger textiles. The finest examples of textiles made with this technique are the Assumption sashes made by the Native Americans of the Great Lakes area. These are made of finely spun worsted wool with colourful repeated zigzag patterns.

Above, left: *Wool sash, from Cherokee, North Carolina, North America, with linked elements to allow more complexity.*

Above, right: *A double-weave belt, or chumpi, from Bolivia, with a braided end.*

Below, left: *Tablet-woven band, from Turkey, finished with oblique interlacing and tassels.*

Below, centre: *Simple braided camel anklets acquired at Yalikavak market in Turkey.*

Below, right: *The braided end of a tablet-woven baggage strap, from Cappadocia in Turkey.*

SPRANG

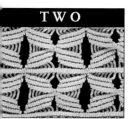

SPRANG is an ancient method of making a stretch fabric. Although similar in appearance to netting, it is constructed using only warp without any added weft elements. Much used before the invention of knitting, the earliest archaeological evidence of sprang is a hair-net made in around 1400 BC found in a Danish bog.

Opposite: Three sprang pyjama cords from Sind in Pakistan. The fine band on the right is made with a circular warp and has a distinctive pattern of holes near each end.

Technique

A SET of warp threads are always stretched between two beams or in a rectangular frame. A fabric can then be created by manipulating the warp threads, row by row, interlinking, interlacing or intertwining them. Small sticks may be set in to prevent the work in progress unravelling. Because the threads are fixed at top and bottom, any textile structure created at the top will also be created in mirror image at the bottom. If, after they have been worked, each row and the complementary row created at the bottom are beaten with a flat stick, forcing them to opposite ends of the warp, a compacted fabric will grow, one half growing from the top downwards, the other from the bottom upwards.

Eventually the two halves will grow until they almost meet in the middle. The unworked threads between them must be secured in place to prevent the whole structure unravelling. It is also possible to create two identical textiles by cutting the threads at this point.

Uses

ONCE used to make clothing, hats and gloves in many parts of the world, sprang is still in traditional use in Guatemala and Colombia for the making of bags and hammocks and in Pakistan for the construction of elaborately patterned silk draw-strings for trousers. Now almost universally superseded by knitting, it has experienced something of a vogue in the art-textile world as a medium for decorative hangings.

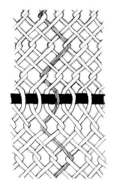

ABOVE: INTERLACED SPRANG WITH RETAINING BATTEN.

Right: A small Colombian bag, a mechita, constructed from agave fibres in interlaced sprang. The warps are stretched on a portable frame with a central rod that is tucked under the left arm while work is in progress. Unravelling is prevented by inserting a roll of fibres into the final sheds and tucking it up inside the finished bag. The mechita is still manufactured and in everyday use, although examples constructed with synthetic materials are now appearing.

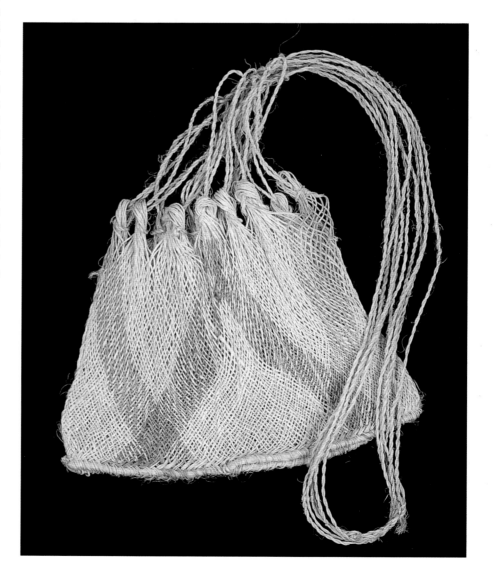

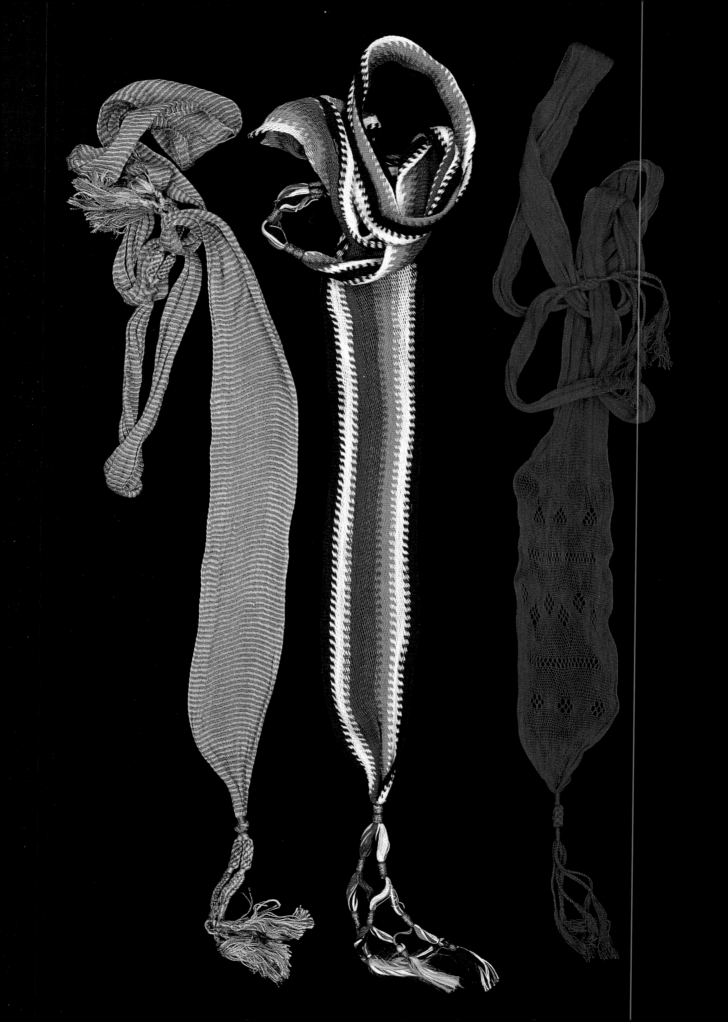

MACRAME

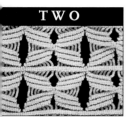
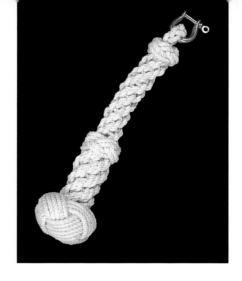

MACRAME is a knotting technique used to make fringes, decorative braids and other articles. It is of ancient Near Eastern origin and reached Spain through the Moorish invasions (8th century onwards) and Italy through the Crusades (11th to 13th centuries). From Europe it was disseminated to other parts of the world largely by sailors. It came into popular vogue in the 19th century and has been in and out of fashion ever since.

Above: *A ship's bell rope, acquired in Scotland, featuring three-dimensional knotting and Turk's heads.*

Below: *Cotton macramé fringes such as this were in widespread use in the 19th century as domestic decorations in Victorian England.*

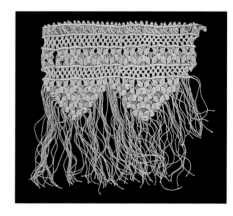

Technique

MACRAME can be worked on a knotting board of cork or similar soft, but rigid, material on which the cords can be held in position. Every piece of macramé is started from a holding cord *(see diagram opposite)*. The working threads are doubled and attached to the cord using double half hitches, or larks heads, and packed closely together across its width. As a guide to planning the work, the doubled threads need to be four times

Left: *An embroidered apron, from Bulgaria, with a fringe dominated by rows of diagonal knotting.*

as long as the finished work. However, some knots or sinnets (several knots worked in succession to form a bar) are likely to take up even more thread so allowance must be made for this. On the other hand, an open knotted pattern will take up less thread.

The work proceeds downwards, joining sets of cords at intervals using a few basic knots and many variations, the main ones being the square knot, half hitch, double half hitch and the Josephine knot. Common variants include the picot, square knot sinnet, corkscrew sinnet and alternating square knots.

To finish off, loose ends can be knotted into tassels or worked into horizontal cording.

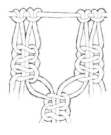

LEFT: INTERLOCKED BRAIDS OF FLAT OR SQUARE KNOT SINNIT.

Above: *A Victorian English mantlepiece fringe worked in unbleached cotton yarn, 19th century.*

Above, right: *Turkish blue glass 'eye' bead, or bonjuk, a good luck talisman, suspended from a macramé strap.*

Below: *Cotton macramé fringe from Spain.*

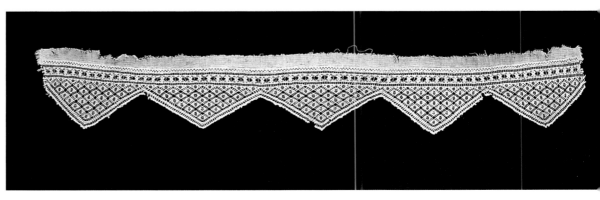

PLY-SPLITTING

PLY-SPLITTING work is one of the simplest forms of textile structure, a technique almost exclusively used in the manufacture of animal trappings. Cotton cord or sisal is sometimes employed, but the chosen material is most often goat hair.

Technique

IN Rajasthan in India a villager will spin out yarn from a bundle of either black or white goat hair. This yarn is doubled and then folded in four and twisted to make a four-ply cord. The looped ends of the four-ply cords are then slipped onto a wooden stick or spindle. An expert girth maker can use as many as sixty separate strands.

The basic structure of ply-splitting work is similar to plaiting in that the warp elements travel diagonally down the fabric from selvedge to selvedge. However, instead of passing over and under each other, one four-ply cord is untwisted sufficiently to allow another to be threaded through it. By varying the initial sequence in which the strands are attached and by choosing whether to thread one strand through another or have the other pass through it, it is possible to build up a range of patterns.

There are several basic pattern structures that can be formed using variations on this technique. The resulting girths can be monochrome (usually in black), have a black-and-white diagonally chequered pattern or alternately black-and-white horizontal waves. The most visually interesting structures, obtained with four-ply yarn that is half white, half black, are geometric or figurative with the pattern appearing in negative on the reverse.

Uses

THE villagers of Western Rajasthan in India are particularly adept at making camel girths using this technique. Ply-split darning is a similar technique in which one strand is used as a weft and threaded through a set of warp elements. Ply-split textiles can be found in Egypt, Turkey, Greece, Nepal, India and Japan.

Above, left: *A ply-split bottle bag from Rajasthan, North-West India. The intersections are concealed by mirrors.*

Above, right: *Two hollow, tubular straps, from Rajasthan, North-West India, constructed by ply-split darning with a needle.*

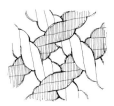

LEFT: INTERLACED DIAGONAL ELEMENTS.

Opposite: *Ply-split camel girths from Rajasthan in North-West India. Most camel girths are made using a combination of natural-coloured light and dark goat hair to create a two-colour pattern. The girth on the right has a polychrome pattern created by the diagonal interlacing of dyed cotton cords.*

Right: *Ply-split darning as used by the Sarakat nomads of Northern Greece for constructing borders for clothes.*

LACE

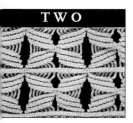

LACE is a European invention, made by the poorest of women to adorn the clothing of the rich. Probably the most recent traditional textile-making technique to come into existence, it seems to have originated in Italy or Dalmatia (the coastal region of the Former Yugoslavia) in the 15th century, but the technique and the fashion for its use spread rapidly to countries as far apart as England and Russia. It was later introduced to other parts of the world by Christian missionaries whose vestments were ornamented with lace cuffs and collars. Generally speaking, peasants are and were the lacemakers in Eastern Europe, but in Western Europe lacemaking was a profession. Hand-made lace was always expensive, and the death-knell of the lace-making industry in Western Europe was sounded in 1818 when the first bobbin net was machine-made in France. But in the conservative societies of Eastern Europe, peasant women continued to create bobbin lace to decorate their festival clothing. Tape lace was a speciality in Eastern Europe, especially in Russia.

Bobbin lace

BOBBIN (or pillow) lace is worked over a firm pillow on to which a paper pattern has been fixed. Needles are inserted into the pattern to support the work and a number of threads, weighted by bobbins of wood or bone, are twisted and interlaced around them to create an open-work mesh. There are many regional styles, from that of the cottage industries of rural England to the sophistication of Brussels and the Mediterranean styles of the islands of Malta and Cyprus.

Needle lace

MORE time consuming than bobbin lace, needle (or needlepoint) lace has always been more expensive. Using a needle, long chains of buttonhole stitches are worked which are looped and linked up as the work progresses to form net-like patterns. Once known as the Queen of Lace, complicated figurative patterns can be created with as many as one hundred stitches to the inch.

Tatting

TATTING is a form of lace-making worked with a small shuttle. Knots and loops or picots are worked on a ground thread which is drawn into rings or semi-circles and built up into delicate patterns.

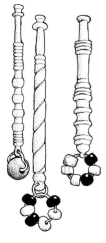

LACE BOBBINS.

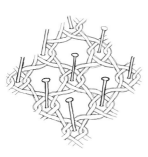

BOBBIN LACE.

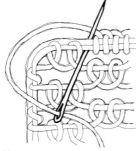

NEEDLEPOINT LACE.

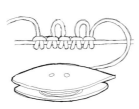

TATTING SHUTTLE AND PICOTS.

Left, above: *Two Greek linen bobbin lace or copanelli valances in torchon technique. The top one is unbleached.*

Far left: *Branscombe tape lace from England.*

Near left: *A pair of Italian Reticella needle-lace collars.*

Opposite: *A tatted doily from Western Europe.*

Opposite, inset above: *Maltese girls learning the craft of lacemaking.*

Opposite, inset centre: *A 'bourgogne', a traditional lace headdress from Normandy, France.*

Opposite, inset bottom: *Russian peasants wearing tape-lace decorated skirts.*

TWINING AND WRAPPING

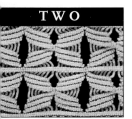

Twining and wrapping need some sort of frame for their construction, use a warp and a weft and greatly resemble loom-woven textiles. The warps and wefts are, however, manipulated by hand and, therefore, need no system of heddles to open a shed. The similarities to basket-making methods suggest that these techniques may have been in use over a much larger area of the world before the invention of the true loom. In places, twining and wrapping techniques are used in combination with loom-weaving techniques.

Weft twining

For the manufacture of a weft-twined textile a set of warps are suspended from a fixed rod. To maintain tension, weights are often attached to the bottom. The weft strands are then worked in pairs. One strand passes over a warp, the other under. The strands are then twisted around each other so that the first strand will pass under the next warp and the other over it. In this way, the weft twists and twines across the fabric from one selvedge to the other. The most amazing textiles woven using this method are the Chilkat blankets made of cedar-bark fibre by the indigenous people of the North-West coast of Canada and Alaska, and the phormium fibre cloaks worn by the Maoris of New Zealand.

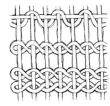

WEFT TWINING.

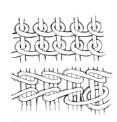

WEFT WRAPPING AND SOUMAK.

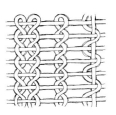

WARP TWINING.

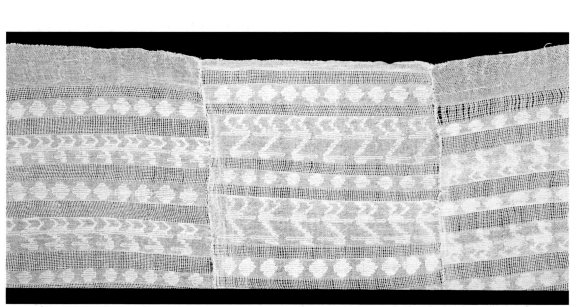

Warp twining

Much as in weft twining, it is possible to bind in the weft by twisting and twining the warp. This is an ideal technique for the construction of long narrow bands. Warp-twined textiles can also be woven with tablets.

Weft wrapping

In this technique the weft threads do not merely pass over and under the warps,

Left: A loosely woven cotton textile from Mexico with raised patterns of supplementary wefts and openwork sections of gauze weave. The combination of different techniques has created interesting textures and patterns even though only one colour has been used.

they are actually wrapped right around them. In the case of *soumak*, a technique popular in Balouchistan, Anatolia and the Caucasus, the weft wraps around several warps at a time. Fine, hard-wearing bags and rugs are woven in *soumak*, sometimes with the addition of a ground weft.

Gauze weaves

Gauze weaves, woven for centuries in China and South America, are very similar to warp-twined textiles except that the warps cross and are anchored by a pick of the weft and then uncross before the next pick. They do not twine around each other. Like *soumak*, gauze is often incorporated into a loom-woven ground weave.

Above: *A bag for transporting goods by camel, from Malatya in Eastern Turkey. The patterned areas are woven in* soumak.

Above, right, inset: *Pataragurai, a Maori chief, wearing a cloak of weft-twined phormium fibres.*

Right: *A narrow-necked bag, shaped like a tobacco pouch, made in Gujarat in North-West India from densely twined goat hair.*

Far right: *Ceremonial sling, or honda, made from wool and camelid hair by men in Bolivia. The cradle for the stone is wrapped and the cords are braided.*

GAUZE WEAVE WITHOUT FIXED WARP ENDS.

GAUZE WEAVE WITH DOUP AND FIXED ENDS.

FAR LEFT: EWE
STRIPWEAVE CLOTH
FROM AGOBZUMBE
IN GHANA.

LEFT: TWELFTH-
CENTURY TAPESTRY-
WOVEN BURIAL TEXTILE
FROM THE NAZCA
DESERT OF PERU.

BELOW: SILK BROCADE
WEAVING FROM THE
INDONESIAN ISLAND
OF LOMBOK.

THREE

LOOM-WOVEN TEXTILES

LOOM-WOVEN TEXTILES

WEAVING is quite simply the art of interlacing one element in and out of another. Interesting fabrics can be woven using the fingers alone, but the most complex and sophisticated results are achieved using a loom.

THE LOOM

THE most basic loom is a wooden frame which the warp threads are suspended from or stretched across. The weft threads are then woven in and out of the warp from side to side. To keep the warps tensioned evenly, thus ensuring a consistent piece of cloth, different solutions have been found. A suspension loom, as used by the Tlingit Indians of Alaska or the Lapps of Northern Scandinavia, is vertical with weights attached to the warp. The horizontal drag loom, used by the Yoruba of Nigeria, for instance, has the warps attached to a heavy weight on a sledge, while body-tensioned looms, such as those used in parts of Indonesia, rely on the weight of the weaver's body to keep the warp taut. Large cloth is usually woven on looms with the warp attached to a beam fixed to each end of the frame.

Above: *A Javanese woman weaving tabby-weave cloth on a semi-automized loom. A shed is open ready for the passage of the shuttle.*

Below: *An Ashanti weaver at Bonwire in Ghana using a double-heddle loom to weave narrow strips which are then sewn together to make* kente *cloth.*

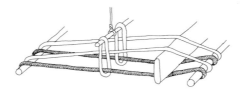

ABOVE: OPENING A SHED WITH A SHED STICK ON A SINGLE-HEDDLE LOOM.

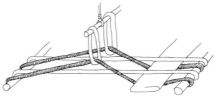

ABOVE: OPENING THE COUNTERSHED BY LIFTING THE HEDDLE ROD.

Right: *By an old Inca wall in Cusco, a Peruvian woman sits making double-weave belts, or* chumpi, *on a body-tensioned loom. She is using a heddle and three shed sticks.*

Left: *A Navaho woman, outside her hogan in Arizona, North America, making a tapestry-weave blanket on an upright loom. Although the Navaho use a very simple form of loom, they are famous for weaving blankets and rugs of great beauty and complexity.*

Above: *Weaving long narrow strips in Ghana on a drag loom. The warps are tensioned with a heavy stone on a sledge.*

Below: *An Ewe weaver at a double-heddle loom in Ghana. He uses his hands to manipulate the shuttle and his feet to operate the heddles for opening the sheds.*

OPENING THE SHED

To facilitate the interlacing of the weft, a shed stick is threaded over and under alternate warp threads to open a space, or shed, through which the weft can be passed more easily. A countershed then has to be opened and the sequence in which the weft passes over and under the warp altered. To do this, the threads pressed down by the shed stick are attached through loops or heddles to a rod that will pull them above the other threads when it is raised. This is called a heddle rod. By having two or more heddle rods, it is possible to raise a variety of combinations of warp threads and so weave increasingly complicated textiles.

BINDING SYSTEMS

There are three basic methods of interlacing the warp and weft together – tabby, twill and satin weave. They are called binding systems and differ in the number of warps the weft crosses before passing to the other face of the fabric.

TABBY WEAVE

THREE

Technique

Tabby or plain weave is the simplest form of woven cloth. Each pick, or passage of the weft from side to side, passes over one warp, under one, over one and so on. On its return passage the sequence is reversed. If the warp and weft are composed of yarn of equal weight they will be equally visible in the finished weave which will therefore have a balanced, criss-cross texture. By varying the colour of the warps, longitudinal stripes are produced and by varying the colour of the weft, horizontal stripes are produced. By varying the colours of both warp and weft a pattern of checks is achieved.

LEFT: WARP AND WEFT ARE BALANCED.

Uses

As tabby is the easiest cloth to weave it is also the most widespread and is universally employed for everyday wear and use. A balanced tabby weave provides an ideal surface for printing, painting or embroidery and is also easy to cut and sew.

Distribution

Tabby or plain-weave cloth is produced wherever people use a loom, but certain fabrics are produced with distinctive qualities. Examples of these are the light-weight, cotton muslin originally developed in Mosul in Iraq, tough calico from Calicut in India and heavy-duty canvas woven from hemp or flax and used for sails or as a base for fine embroidery.

Above: *English embroidery sampler, 1818. Balanced tabby weave is the ideal ground for counted-thread embroidery.*

Opposite: *A balanced tabby-weave silk shawl from Turkmenistan. The vertical stripes are created by the colours of the warp threads and the horizontal bands by the colours of the wefts. Where they cross, checks are formed.*

Opposite, inset left: *A Myanmarese (Burmese) youth wrapped in a comfortable, checked tabby-weave lungi.*

Opposite, inset right: *Tabby weave is cheap and easy to produce, but here it is worn by Foumba, a former king of the Kilema district of Uganda.*

Above: *A bandhani tie and dye shawl from Jamnagar in Gujarat, India. The material is a loosely woven, tabby-weave silk.*

Right: *Checked tabby-weave yardage, from Guatemala, with compound-ikat patterning created by resist-dyeing the yarn before weaving.*

Left: *Twill-woven Scottish tartans, from left to right, Royal Stewart, Dress Gordon and Lindsay. The colours normally used for tartans are sombre and harmonious because they were originally based on the available natural dyes.*

Top: *Tweed cloth woven in a herringbone pattern on the Isle of Harris in the Outer Hebrides.*

Above: *Woollen cloth, from Gilgit in Northern Pakistan, woven in herringbone twill.*

TWILL

Technique

IN twill each passage of the weft through the warps goes over two, under one, over two, under one. In the next passage the same sequence is repeated, but staggered, to produce a textured effect with raised diagonals. The degree of staggering will affect the angle of the diagonal. A number of variations are possible and by careful sequencing different patterns such as chevrons, lozenges and herringbone can be made.

Above: *Tapestry-weave cloth with a twill binding system from Kirman in Iran. A similar technique is often used in the manufacture of Kashmir shawls.*

Below, left: *A Scottish piper in full costume.*

THREE

 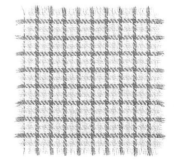

Above: *Four samples of tweed cloth, from the Isle of Mull, Scotland, showing some of the patterns that can be created with a twill binding system.*

LEFT: TWILL WEAVE.

Uses

TWILL weaving produces a thick, firm fabric ideal for outdoor and working clothes such as the tough, woollen Harris tweed made on Harris Island in the Outer Hebrides, the tartan plaid used by Scottish highlanders for kilts, shawls and blankets or cotton denim first used to make overalls in the California gold rush of 1849.

Tartan

THE simple technique of weaving checked woollen cloth allows for an enormous number of combinations with the limited range of colours available from natural dyes. During the 17th century distinctive arrangements began to be associated with specific families, and districts in Scotland. By the 18th century wearing tartan had become a sign of clan allegiance and national identity to such an extent that after the defeat of Bonnie Prince Charlie at Culloden in 1746 an Act of Parliament was passed banning the wearing of Highland dress.

Today, the sale of tartan cloth to tourists ensures the survival of this textile. Although not often worn as daily attire anymore, many Scotsmen still choose to wear a kilt on special occasions.

SATIN WEAVE

Technique

SATIN has a much more loosely bound weave than tabby or twill. The weft thread passes over one warp thread, under four or more, over one and so on. This produces a weave in which the face shows virtually only the warp and the reverse is nearly all weft, so the texture is particularly smooth, especially if the warps are silk or viscose. The weft threads are often of cotton, both for strength and economy.

ABOVE: WARPS LIE
OVER SEVERAL WEFTS.

Uses

SATIN textiles are widely used in Europe and Asia for blouses, skirts and pyjamas because of their glossy sheen and texture. *Mashru* fabric woven in Turkey, Syria and India is a luxury fabric with a silken warp and a cotton weft. The literal meaning of *mashru* is permitted. According to Islamic custom, silk should not be worn against the skin; with the satin

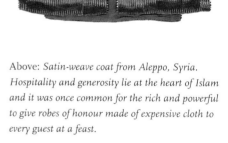

Above: *Satin-weave coat from Aleppo, Syria. Hospitality and generosity lie at the heart of Islam and it was once common for the rich and powerful to give robes of honour made of expensive cloth to every guest at a feast.*

Left: *Indian* mashru *was once exported to the Middle East in large quantities. This contemporary example, from Aleppo, shows a style with plain and patterned bands popular in the 19th century. The fuzzy effect is created by dyeing the warps with the ikat-resist technique, so that they vary in colour along their length.*

Left, inset: *Armenian teachers and pupils in the 1920s. Until the early 20th century,* mashru *was the everyday costume worn by many inhabitants of Asia Minor, whether scholar, chief or Kurdish mountaineer.*

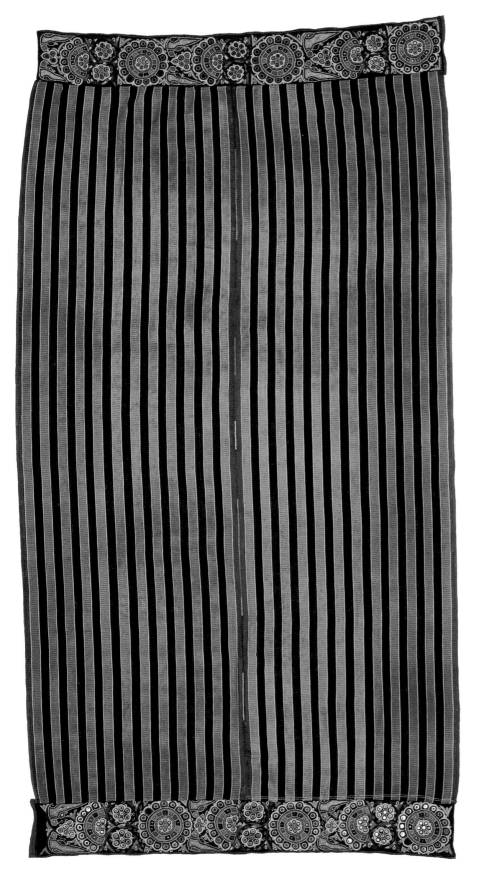

weave of *mashru*, silk is only shown on the face of the fabric and it is cotton that brushes against the skin. In this way the proprieties of custom are preserved.

In Central Asia, as well as in the Middle East, *abr* (satin-weave ikat-dyed) robes of honour are traditionally given at feasts or worn by the wealthy. The Tajik and Uzbek women of Central Asia still wear *abr* trousers and tunics on a daily basis.

Left: *A festive* mashru *shawl, or odhni, from Kutch in North-West India. The margins are decorated with sparkling mirrorwork and embroidered with patterns of flowers and parrots.*

Below: *Silk coat from Damascus in Syria. The leaves of two mulberry trees are required to feed enough silk worms to spin sufficient silk to make one coat. Several coats may be worn when the weather is cold.*

TAPESTRY WEAVE

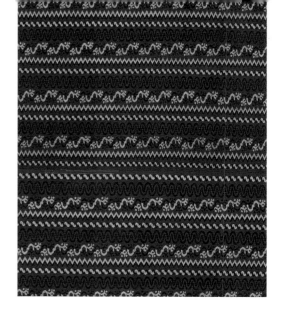

Above: *A silk sarong, from Amarapura, Myanmar (Burma), woven in a variation of tapestry weave known as* Lun taya *or thousand bobbin.*

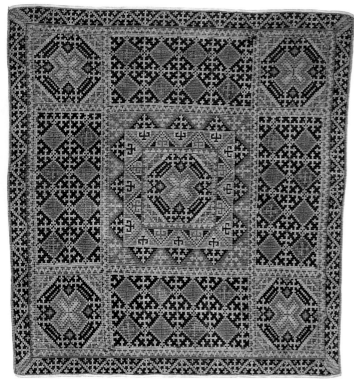

Above: *A subtly coloured, tapestry-woven cotton kerchief, or pis, from the Sulu Islands in the Philippines.*

Below: *A brightly coloured, tapestry-woven woollen serape, or shawl, from Mexico.*

Technique

WHEN weaving a weft-faced textile it is not necessary for a weft thread to pass all the way from one edge to the other (selvedge to selvedge). At any chosen point a new weft thread of a different colour may be substituted and woven in. In this way, any number of colours may be introduced and blocks of pattern built up. This technique may also be described as using a discontinuous weft.

Uses

BECAUSE this technique has so few practical restrictions it has been used to create decorative and pictorial clothing, carpets, rugs and tapestries, often on a large scale. The word tapestry, now used to mean a woven wall hanging, actually comes from the French *tapis* meaning a carpet. When speaking of carpets, the term *kilim* is often used to denote a rug executed in tapestry weave.

Distribution

TAPESTRY weave is practised in many parts of the world. Some of the oldest and most beautiful decorative textiles were woven in Ptolemaic Egypt using the tapestry method. Many examples survive from the early Christian era and are popularly known as Coptic weavings. This tradition is kept alive in contemporary Egypt with the fine tapestries woven in the workshops of Wissa Wassef at Harrania near the pyramids at Giza. Also of surpassing beauty were the famous twill-tapestry shawls of Kashmir, Northern India. Of very complex design, in the 19th century work on a single shawl was split between two or more looms. These shawls, known as *jamawars*, are still woven at Basohli near the North-West Indian town of Jammu. Particularly fine prestige textiles are woven in tapestry in Iran, South-East Asia and South America.

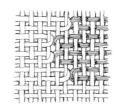

LEFT: TAPESTRY WEAVE.

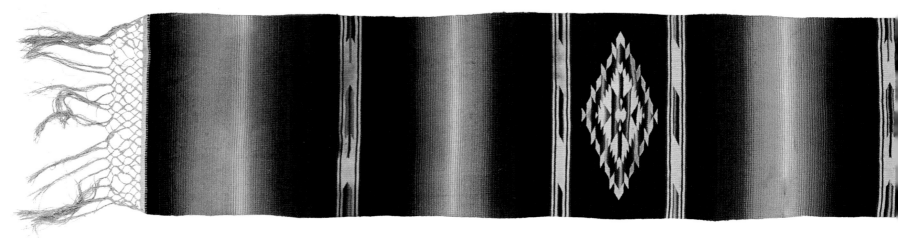

THREE

Above: *Chinese 19th-century insignia.*

Below: *Early 19th century Kashmiri* jamawar.

Bottom: *Woollen shawl with tapestry-woven borders from Kulu in India's Himalayan foothills.*

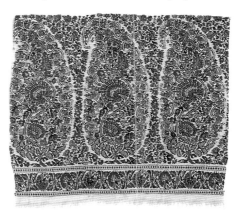

Above: *A modern Egyptian tapestry-weave panel from the workshop founded by Dr Ramses Wissa Wassef at Harrania.*

Right: *A fragment of tapestry-woven cloth made by Christian Copts in 6th-century Egypt.*

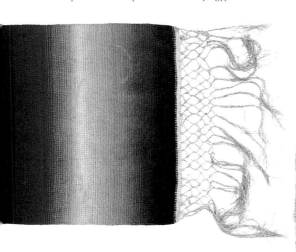

WARP-FACED WEAVE

THREE

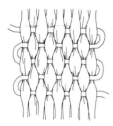

A WARP-FACED weave is one in which the weft has been obscured by the warp threads and any pattern, most commonly longitudinal stripes, is therefore carried by the warp.

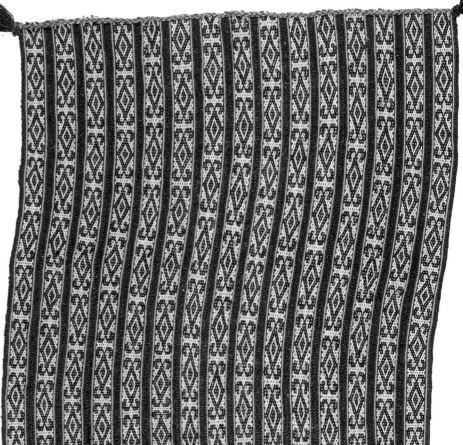

Above: *Bolivian coca bag with complementary warp patterns.*

Below: *An Uzbek* ghudjeri, *from Afghanistan, made from narrow woven strips sewn selvedge to selvedge.*

Opposite: *Warp-striped cotton blanket from Guatemala.*

Opposite, inset: *A Mende chief, from Sierra Leone, wearing warp-striped cloth.*

Technique

THE pattern of a warp-faced fabric is laid down in the initial setting up of the warps – the colour of the yarn is changed at intervals to ordain the width and frequency of the stripes. To ensure its dominance, the warp must be more densely packed than the weft or made of a thicker yarn. More complicated patterns can be woven if selected warp strands are periodically made to float across the weft or behind it, as in satin weave.

LEFT: WARPS OBSCURE WEFTS.

Distribution

WARP-FACED, longitudinally striped textiles are found in all parts of the world where any kind of loom exists. The popularity of striped textiles is ensured not only by the ease of their construction, but also by their dynamic effect. Serviceable, hard-wearing items such as blankets and cloaks intended for day-to-day use are frequently decorated with warp-faced stripes. In both rich and poor countries, the variations possible in the colour and width of stripes has often been used as a means of differentiating affiliation, whether tribal or collegiate.

Belts, bands and sashes for securing loads or fastening clothes are frequently woven with warp-faced patterns and often elaborated with floats and complementary warps.

Complementary warps

IF more than one set of warps is used, floating short distances on opposite faces of the fabric, these can be made to change places periodically to create a pattern, one face the reverse of the other.

Below: *Yoruba indigo-dyed, warp-striped cloth from Nigeria.*

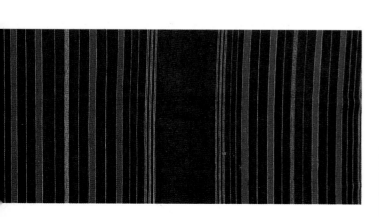

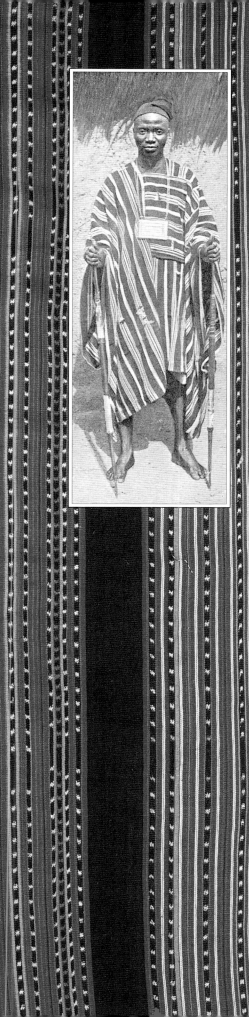

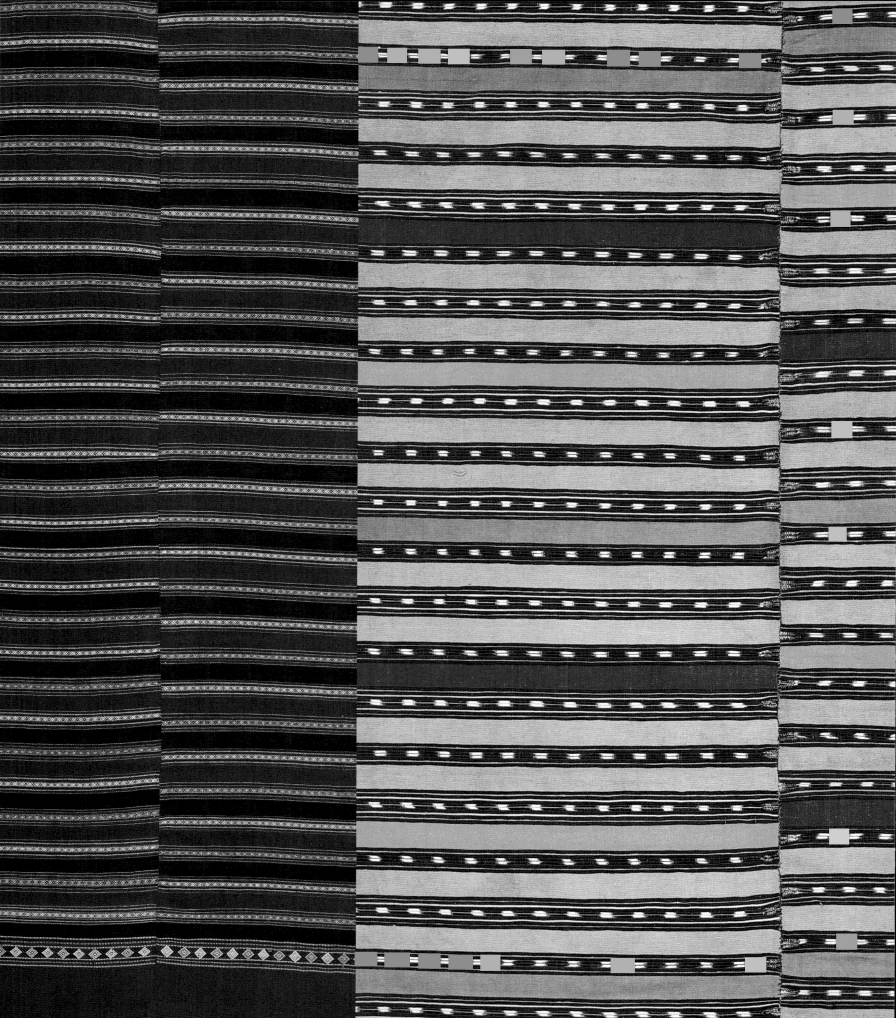

WEFT-FACED WEAVE

THREE

A WEFT-FACED weave is the reverse of a warp-faced weave. The wefts are more densely packed than the warp or are of heavier weight and so the warp threads are obscured and dominated by the wefts, which therefore carry the pattern. A weft-faced pattern will run across a textile in horizontal bands.

Technique

FOR a textile to be weft-faced, the weft threads must be appreciably thicker than the warps or more densely packed. A common example of the former is the combination of a woollen weft and a cotton warp. To achieve the latter, although warps and wefts may be of equal thickness, the wefts are beaten down hard with a comb or beater, so that in any given surface area they predominate.

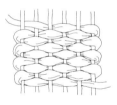

LEFT: WEFTS OBSCURE WARPS.

Complementary wefts

JUST as a pattern can be created with complementary warps, if more than one set of wefts is used, floating short distances on opposite faces of the fabric, these too can be made to change places periodically to create a pattern, one face the reverse of the other.

Opposite, left: *A woman's shawl, from North-East Thailand, woven in two pieces. The pattern of horizontal bands is enhanced with supplementary weft details.*

Opposite, right: *A Mexican blanket woven in two pieces. The weft-faced pattern has been emphasized with weft ikat that shows as white dashes.*

Right: *A Kano stripweave from Nigeria. The textile is made up of strips that run vertically, but the weft-faced pattern appears to run horizontally.*

Uses

SHAWLS and ponchos are most commonly woven in weft-faced weaves. Weft-faced weaves keep their shape better than warp-faced ones and are most often used for complex patterning.

Above, right: *Aprons with weft-faced stripes can be found all over the world, from Wales to Tibet. These two matrons are from Hardanger in Norway.*

Right: *A Tibetan woman's weft-striped woollen apron sewn together from three pieces. The stripes are seldom perfectly aligned.*

Below, right: *A Kano stripweave cotton cloth from Nigeria. The details are worked in supplementary weft.*

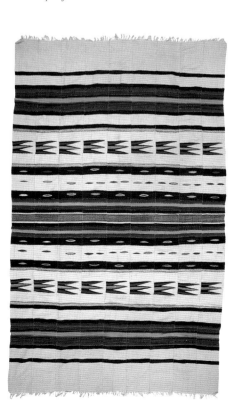

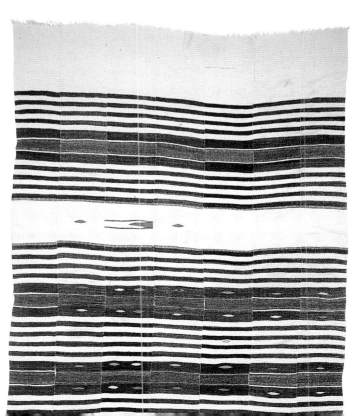

DAMASK

THE Chinese had been weaving figured silk fabrics for hundreds of years before they were introduced to Europe via the Middle East. They became known as 'damask' after the Syrian city of Damascus, which may have been where these textiles were first encountered by the Crusaders.

The play of light

DAMASKS are self-patterned textiles woven, most often, in silk or linen in one colour. The pattern motifs are thrown into relief by the way light falls on the fabric and is reflected differently by the lustrous fibres of areas of pattern and ground. The effect is subtle, shimmering and glamorous.

ABOVE: THE DOMINANCE OF EITHER THE WARP OR WEFT CHANGES TO CREATE THE PATTERN.

Left: *Korean damask pojagi used to wrap gifts given to a bride by the groom's parents.*

Above: *A silk damask duffle bag, from Korea, used for carrying a bottle of spirits. In Korea, special cloths are used to carry or protect many things. They may be made of silk, cotton or ramie and are decorated according to the means of the owner.*

Technique

DAMASKS are essentially satin-weave textiles, although on occasion a twill binding system may be employed. While the pattern motifs are being woven, the silky warps float over a number of wefts before being bound in. When an area of background is reached the warps are made to float across the wefts on the reverse face. This results in the motifs being shown in warps (which lie vertically) and the background being shown in wefts (which lie horizontally). Light falling on vertical and horizontal threads is reflected differently and so as the fabric moves and light strikes it at different angles it seems to shimmer.

The Chinese pioneered the use of a drawloom equipped with a large number of heddles. This enabled the weaver to lift warps individually, with the help of several assistants, and so weave very complicated patterns. At the beginning of the 19th century Joseph Marie Jacquard of Lyons in France invented an automated apparatus 'programmed' with a system of punched cards that selected and lifted the warps in a desired sequence. The process of weaving damask and other fancy weaves subsequently became quicker, easier and cheaper.

Uses

WOVEN in silk, damask makes a glamorous dress fabric. In Europe linen damask continues to be the classic choice for tablecloths and napkins. Damask woven with warp and weft composed of different fibres has often been used for curtains and upholstery.

Above: *Silk damask dress fabric woven in Europe in about 1800. European damasks have often featured bold patterns of flowers and birds.*

Above, right: *A Chinese woman wearing a wide-sleeved damask jacket decorated with auspicious symbols.*

Right: *English tablecloth from the 1920s with damask-figuring thrown into relief, in places, by contrasting colours in the warp and weft.*

Below: *A detail of a Chinese robe made of silk brocade fabric. Motifs of flowers and auspicious symbols are common features of Chinese brocades.*

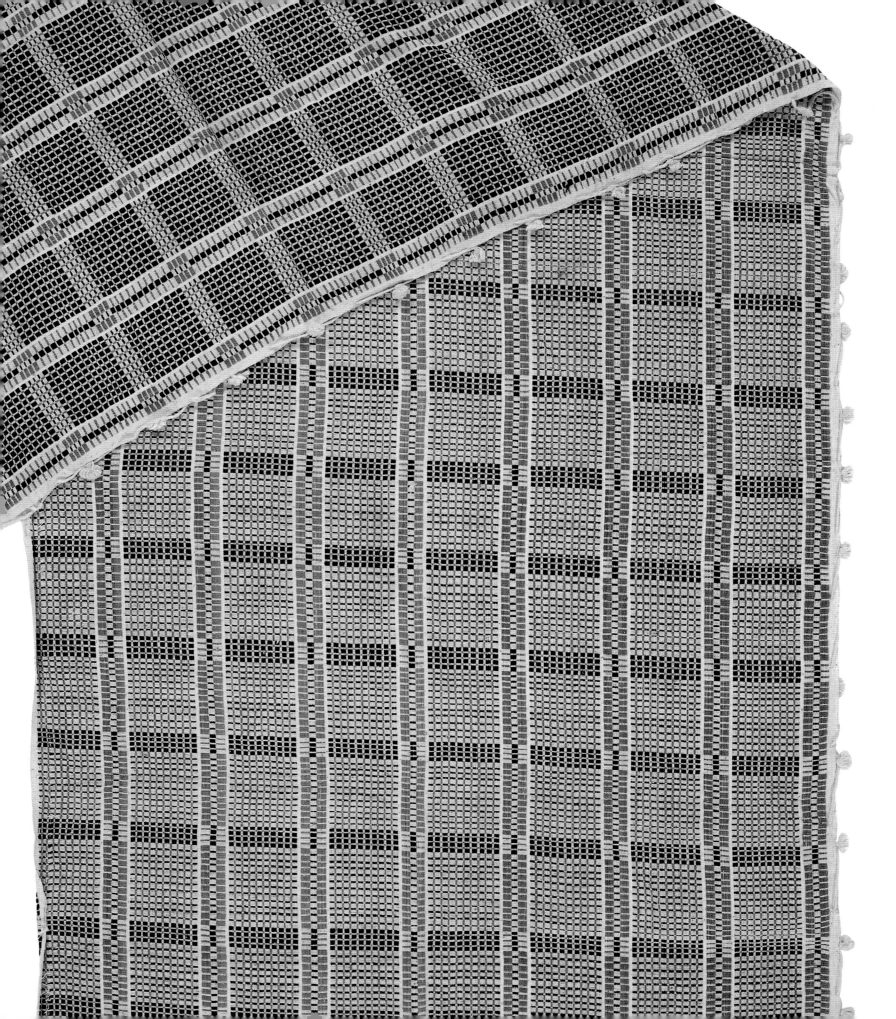

SUPPLEMENTARY WARP

DECORATION can be incorporated into a ground weave with the use of extra, or supplementary, warps which play no part in the basic structure.

Technique

IN Indonesia the ground warp threads are laid out on a two-heddle, continuously warped body-tension loom and the supplementary warp threads which are thicker and lighter in colour are laid over them. The weaver then places a bamboo stick between the ground and extra-warps, near the warp beam, to ensure that the two sets of warp do not get entangled. A small model of the pattern made of string and sticks is used as a guide to setting out the extra-warp pattern. Many small wooden splints are then set into place, picking up the appropriate supplementary warp threads to form a pattern as the weft is introduced. As weaving progresses, the splints are lifted in sequence to form a supplementary pattern in twill weave. Where the splints are lifted, the extra-warp threads will appear on the surface to form the pattern, otherwise they appear on the underside as a continuous float. Weaving with extra warps causes problems with tensioning, so constant adjustments have to be made with both the ground and supplementary warps.

Distribution

SUPPLEMENTARY-warp textiles are woven in very few parts of the world – they are most prevalent in Eastern Indonesia, particularly on the islands of Bali, Timor and the Moluccas, and most notably in Sumba. In East Sumba, noblewomen weave a sarong known as *Lau pahudu*. Its lower border has mythological motifs worked in a supplementary warp of heavy, light-coloured yarn against a dark background weave. Long sashes are also woven in the same technique. The tourist demand for these pieces is now so high that, breaking with tradition, young men as well as young women weave them on back-strap looms with very long warps.

Above: *The border of a woman's* tapis, *from Sumba, decorated with men at prayer worked in supplementary warps.*

THREE

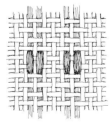

LEFT: THE PATTERN HERE IS CREATED BY SUPPLEMENTARY WARPS FLOATING ABOVE THE WEFTS.

Opposite: *Syrian bath towel. The supplementary warp pattern appears in negative on the reverse.*

Right: *Antoni weaving, from Timor, an Indonesian island, with the borders and lizards created by supplementary-warp floats.*

Far right: *Supplementary-warp* selendangs *from Sumba, an eastern Indonesian island. Human figures appear on many Sumban weavings.*

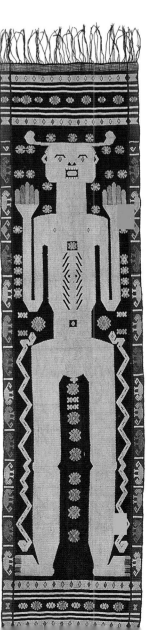

SUPPLEMENTARY WEFT (CONTINUOUS)

THREE

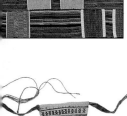

Extra or supplementary wefts can be introduced into a weave to add decoration to an otherwise plain cloth. As with supplementary warps, these are decorative and are not an essential part of the structure. The supplementary weft is usually of a different colour and thicker than the yarn used for the ground weft. A continuous supplementary weft is one that passes right across the weave from selvedge to selvedge.

Technique

To build up a pattern an extra-weft thread must be made to appear or disappear by floating it across several warp strands at strategic points. This type of weave is called a weft float. The supplementary weft, when it does not appear on the face of the cloth, floats on the reverse and is periodically bound in to the ground weave to maintain the integrity of the structure.

With elaborate continuous supplementary weft designs the decorative motifs characteristically appear as a dark pattern against a lighter ground, whereas on the reverse the design will appear in negative, a light pattern against a dark background. A supplementary weft may be woven in with the ground weft or by the opening of a separate shed.

WEFT INLAY.   WEFT FLOATS.

Distribution

Elaborate and beautiful continuous supplementary weft cloths are woven in many parts of the world. Weavers in Europe, Asia, North Africa and Latin America are the producers of almost all of these fabrics. Probably the most beautiful are those woven in the remote hills of Sam Neua in Northern Laos for use as sashes, stoles and curtains.

Far left: *A cotton belt, from Timor, with decorative elements worked in silk supplementary wefts.*

Above: *Moi tribesman from Annam, Vietnam. The man's shirt is decorated with supplementary wefts.*

Right: *Laotian silk and cotton shawl, from Sam Neua, with continuous and discontinuous supplementary weft patterns.*

Opposite, above, left: *Detail of a Mexican shawl with bird pattern.*

Opposite, above, right: *An Itneg mantle from Luzon in the Philippines.*

Opposite, below, left: *Cotton curtain, from central Laos, decorated with supplementary weft threads.*

Opposite, below, right: *A woven cotton square, from Lombok, Indonesia, with a simple pattern of supplementary wefts.*

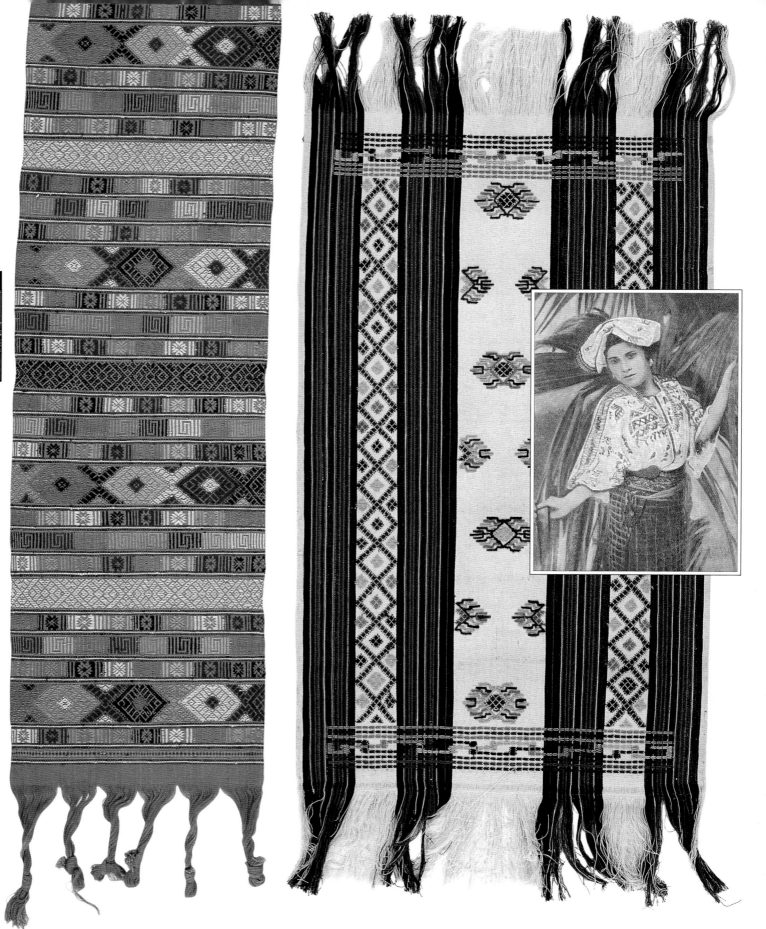

88

SUPPLEMENTARY WEFT (DISCONTINUOUS)

Just like a continuous supplementary weft thread, a discontinuous weft thread is decorative and not an essential part of the textile's structure, but is woven into selected places only, as in tapestry weave, and not into the full width of the cloth from selvedge to selvedge.

Technique

The most effective way of employing discontinuous supplementary wefts is with the use of floats, introducing them either into the same shed as the ground weft or into one of their own. They are not entered at the selvedge, but at the point at which the pattern is to be begun, unlike continuous supplementary wefts which must traverse the full width of the fabric.

For a different effect a weft inlay may be employed. This consists of a supplementary weft that is laid in with the ground weave. As it does not float the effect is more subtle, although stronger as it is less likely to snag.

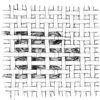

DISCONTINUOUS WEFT INLAY.

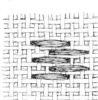

DISCONTINUOUS WEFT FLOATS.

Distribution

Textiles with a pattern woven with a discontinuous supplementary weft are found all over the world, often in combination with continuous supplementary wefts. Weft inlay is used with particular vigour for working the motifs of animals and domestic objects in the stripweaves of the Ashanti and Ewe peoples of Ghana.

Opposite: *Bhutanese textiles. Discontinuous supplementary weft patterns frequently appear as isolated motifs rather than in bands as is typical of continuous supplementary weft weavings. The sash on the left has been woven using both techniques.*

Opposite, inset: *A girl, from Mixan, in the 1920s. Her cotton blouse, with discontinuous supplementary weft patterns, is of a type that can still be seen in Guatemala today.*

Right: *A Kach'in woman's apron, from Myanmar (Burma), worn with the wefts, and therefore the bands of patterns, running vertically.*

Left: *Coverlet, from Laos, in which the use of discontinuous supplementary wefts has created an effect resembling tapestry weaving.*

Above: *Discontinuous supplementary weft weaving from Laos.*

Above, right: *A Guatemalan head wrapping made by surface weft packing, a cross between tapestry and supplementary weft weaving.*

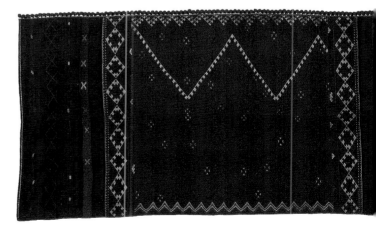

BROCADE

BROCADES are finely woven luxury fabrics worn in many parts of the world on ceremonial occasions or as an indication of status. Although the term 'brocade' refers to a textile woven with a supplementary weft of a material different to that of the ground weft, it is generally used to signify a silk textile with rich figuring worked with gold or silver supplementary weft threads.

Metal thread

IT is possible to draw gold and silver out into very fine wire. This wire is wound tightly around a silk or cotton core to produce a thread sufficiently flexible and durable for weaving or embroidery. When metal threads are utilized as supplementary weft threads they catch the light with a subtle shimmer suffused with mystery and enchantment.

Distribution

FINE brocades are woven in Europe, all over the Muslim world, and in India and South-East Asia. The vast majority of these are worked with metal thread. China and parts of South-East Asia have a tradition of silk brocades. The opulent and beautiful *kinkhab* of Benares, India, and the *songket* of the Indonesian islands of Sumatra and Bali are so complex that a specialist is employed to set up the intricate system of heddles required.

Opposite: *The sumptuous silk brocade* pallav *of a Baluchar sari woven at Murshidabad in Bengal, Eastern India. It features a pair of* butti *cones and a border of galloping horsemen.*

Opposite, inset: *A Palestinian elder wearing a brocade turban.*

Left: *Supplementary-weft Bulgarian apron woven on a narrow loom in two strips. To qualify as brocade the supplementary wefts must be of a different material from the ground weft.*

Right: *A 19th-century Chinese sleeveless coat made from floral silk brocade with auspicious calligraphy on the shoulders.*

Above: *Silk* songket *brocade from Singaraja, Bali. Balinese* songket *is most often woven in gold and mulberry.*

Left: *Minangkabau* songket *brocade, from Sumatra, woven in typical gold and red.*

STRIPWEAVE

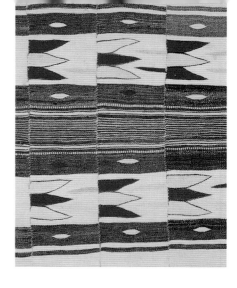

IT is a widespread practice to sew two separately woven pieces together to make one textile which is too large to be woven in one piece on any available loom. This is the method of construction, for example, of rugs made by the Balouch in Afghanistan or of *hinggi* mantles woven on Sumba in Indonesia. In a very few places textiles are made by sewing together a large number of very narrow strips. Apart from the *ghudjeris*, or horse blankets, of Uzbekistan virtually all stripweaves are to be found in West Africa. The best known is the *kente* cloth of Ghana.

Above: *Detail of a Kano stripweave, from Nigeria, with both continuous and discontinuous supplementary-weft patterning.*

Opposite, above: *Fulani woollen blanket from Mali.*

Opposite, below, left: *An Ashanti woman's rayon* kente *cloth woven in Bonwire village, Ghana.*

Opposite, below, right: *An Ashanti* kente *cloth.*

Opposite, inset: *Prempeh, last of the Ashanti kings, wearing a cotton stripweave.*

Technique

CLOTH is woven on double-heddle looms in extremely long strips from 4–10 inches (10.2 x 25.4 cm) wide which are cut into shorter strips and sewn together, selvedge to selvedge. Woollen blankets are woven in Mali, but usually cotton, silk or rayon is used to weave a voluminous toga-like garment for men and a smaller cloth for women.

The stripweave *kente* cloths woven in Ghana by the Ashanti and Ewe tribes have a distinctive checkered appearance. This is achieved by alternately weaving a section warp-faced, and therefore showing the longitudinal stripes of the variously coloured warp threads, and then a section weft-faced, which shows as a horizontal band. An extra pair of heddles is used with the warp threads grouped in sixes so different sheds can be opened for weaving the weft-faced sections. Supplementary weft floats are used to introduce motifs depicting animals, drums, combs, hands and so on into the warp-faced sections.

ABOVE: ALTERNATING WARP-FACED AND WEFT-FACED WEAVES.

Left: *Ewe stripweave cloth from Ghana. Ewe weaving can be identified by its restrained use of subtle colours. A wide variety of motifs, representing objects such as chickens, drums and combs, are woven with supplementary-weft inlay.*

Right: *A Fulani sheep's wool* khasa, *or blanket, from Mali, constructed from strips about 20 cm (7⅞ in) wide. Second-hand Fulani blankets are traded all over West Africa.*

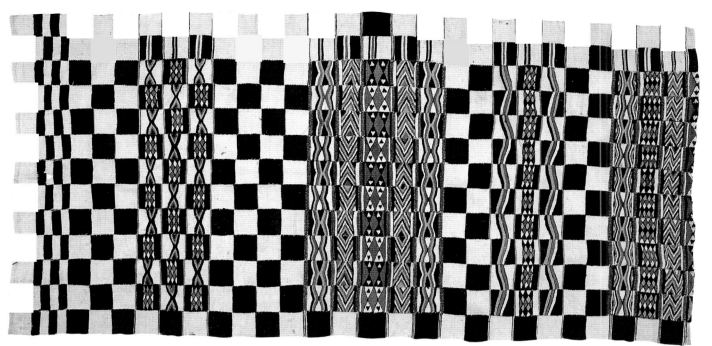

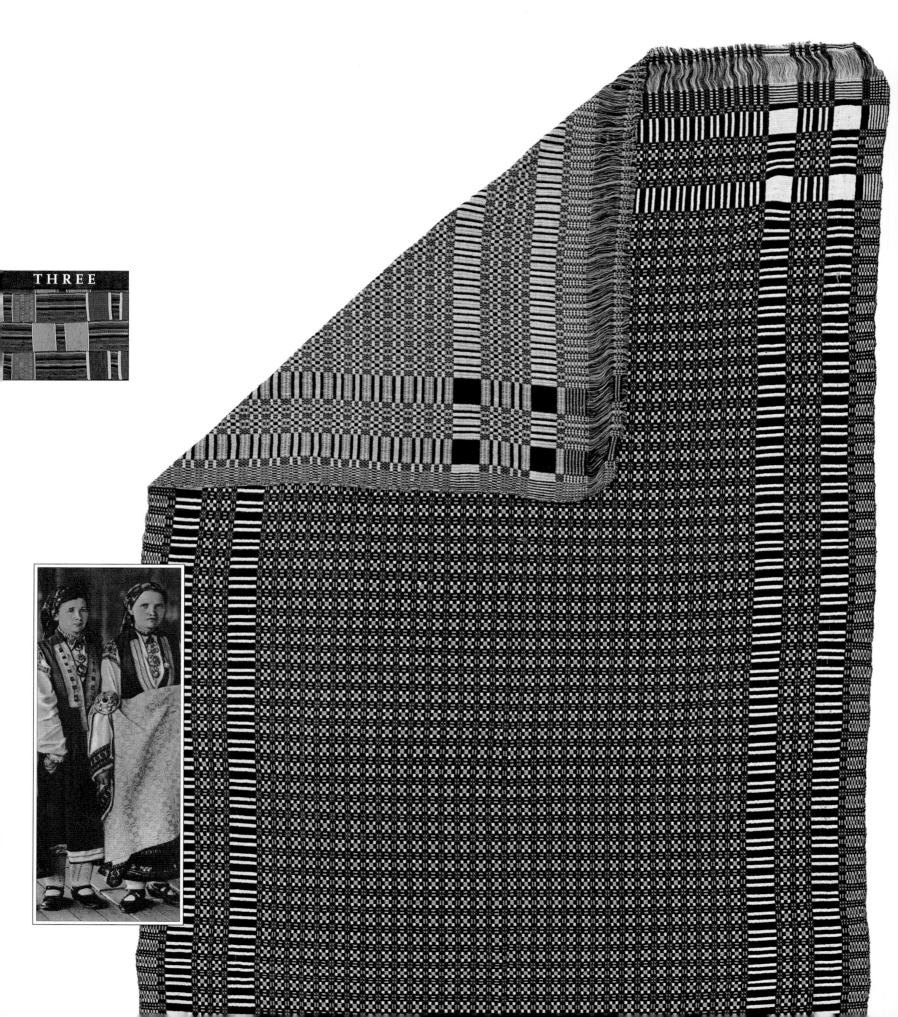

THREE

DOUBLE WEAVE

MANY textiles are woven in such a way that the front and back are quite different in appearance. Double weave or double cloth, however, is an unusual technique in which the 'front' and 'back' are actually woven as independent layers, one above the other, occasionally swapping places to interlink and create a pattern.

Technique

TWO sets of warps are set up one above the other and either separate wefts are woven in or one weft is used for both layers which links them at one selvedge (double-width weave) or at both (tubular weave). With the aid of four or more heddles, the warps are periodically lifted from one level to the other, causing the two layers to change place. As the two layers are composed of different colours or materials, a pattern is created with one face of the fabric the negative of the other.

LEFT: A PATTERN IS CREATED WHERE THE LAYERS INTERSECT.

manufacture of traditional blankets continues to be a thriving industry in central Wales.

Emigrants took the knowledge of how to make double-weave cloth to the New World where it continued to be manufactured by colonists, such as those in Virginia in the USA and Ontario in Canada.

Archaeological excavations in central Peru have shown that double weaves were produced by the Chancay people who thrived between AD 1000 and 1476. The Quecha and Aymara of Ecuador, Bolivia and Peru continue to produce intricately woven double-weave belts and hat-bands to this day.

In the Punjab and the Pakistan province of Sind, cotton double-weave textiles, known as *khes*, are woven in sections and sewn together and used as bedding.

Uses

TEXTILES woven in double weave, particularly when made of wool, are thick and warm. They have, therefore, been widely used in cooler climates for shawls, blankets and coverlets.

Distribution

DOUBLE weave is a technique in widespread use in Europe and examples can be found from Scotland, Spain, Germany, Poland and Italy. The

Above: *A double-weave throw, from the Blue Ridge Mountains in North America, incorporating wool dyed in the distinctive Williamsburg blue. The technique was probably introduced to the region by settlers from the British Isles.*

Below: *Double-weave woollen belts, or* chumpi, *from La Paz in Bolivia. Andean textiles include motifs derived from indigenous wildlife and fabulous creatures taken from myth and heraldry.*

BELOW: HOWLING SPIRITS FROM A PERUVIAN DOUBLE-WEAVE FRAGMENT WOVEN SOME TIME BEFORE AD 1450.

Opposite: *A simple, but boldly patterned, double-weave blanket, or* khes, *from Panipat in India. The pattern can be seen in negative on the reverse.*

Opposite, inset: *Latvian women, one with a double-weave blanket. Double-weave cloth is most often woven in symmetrical, geometric patterns.*

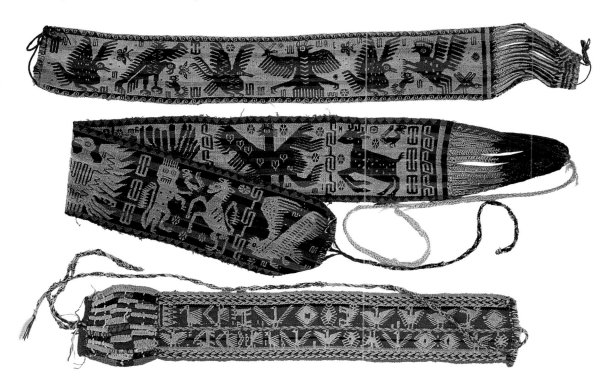

VELVET

VELVET is a luxury fabric with a short, densely piled surface traditionally woven from silk. The pile may uniformly cover the face of a textile (solid velvet) or it may produce a pattern by only appearing in selected places (voided velvet). The pile can be very long (plush) or of two or more lengths (pile on pile). Velvet textiles are often of several colours, may have a pattern stamped onto them and may even be printed.

THREE

Technique

THE distinctive pile of velvet is produced by means of supplementary warps which are raised over grooved metal rods inserted into an open shed just like the weft. When weaving has proceeded far enough for the raised warps to be secure they are cut along the groove in the rod with a sharp knife to form dense tufts and the rods are then removed. Sometimes the loops are left uncut for a coarser effect or patterns may be made up from a combination of cut and uncut areas ('cisele' velvet).

Right: *English machine-made upholstery velvet of about 1880, printed with a pattern in the Jacobean style.*

Other piled textiles

FABRICS similar to velvet can be woven with a supplementary weft – for instance, velveteen, which has a solid pile, and corduroy, which has a ribbed pile. Particularly interesting pile cloths are the embroidered raphia textiles made by the

LEFT: PILE OF CUT AND UNCUT LOOPS.

Above: *English Jaspé velvet made in 1640. The patterns are created by areas of cut and uncut pile and void ground.*

Right: *Spanish table carpet, from Alpujarra, woven in about 1750 with wool pile and linen ground weave.*

Above: *Russian roller-printed velvet. Mass-produced fabric, like this, was printed with contemporary versions of traditional motifs, such as the medallion, or gul, to be sold to the Central Asian market.*

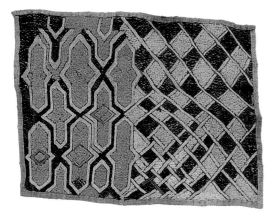

Above: *Kasai velvet, Kuba cut-pile raphia cloth from the Congo (formerly Zaire).*

Kuba of the Congo (formerly Zaire), sometimes referred to as Kasai velvet. The pile is created by sewing a fine raphia strand under the warp thread of a ready-woven base cloth, so that both ends are above the surface, and then they are cut off short with a knife.

The pile of many fine rugs and carpets is created by knotting or wrapping yarn around the warps of a ground weave. The denser the knots, the higher the quality of the carpet.

Left: *A skilfully woven child's hat, from Uzbekistan, with an ikat pattern with a velvet pile.*

Above: *Opulent Hazara velvet gown, from central Afghanistan, embellished with gold-thread embroidery.*

Right: *A Moroccan woman in a velvet gown with a luxurious texture reminiscent of fur.*

TABLET WEAVING

THREE

Tablet weaving is an ingenious method of making narrow bands, belts and straps. The earliest known textiles that were irrefutably woven with tablets were found in a grave at El Cigarellejo in Spain and have been dated to around 375 BC. Although requiring only a small work station, weaving in progress is not readily transportable as it is essential that tension is maintained to prevent twisting. The most sophisticated exponents of this technique are therefore sedentary rather than nomadic.

Turkish tablet woven bands, from top to bottom:
Goat hair animal strap from Western Turkey.

Camel bag tie, from Cappadocia, Turkey, with a wavy pattern produced by turning all the tablets in the same direction.

A long, finely woven band from Eastern Turkey.

Technique

Warps are stretched on a long narrow loom or between the weaver and a fixed point and not threaded through a system of heddles, but through the corners of tablets made of card, wood or bone, which lie flat against each other like a pack of cards. The tablets are most often square, although many shapes including triangles, hexagons and octagons have been used. According to the intricacy of the pattern anything between seven and three hundred may be used to weave a single band. Each tablet separates the warps threaded through it, lifting some and forcing others down, thus effectively opening a shed through which to pass the weft. By twisting the tablets, individually or in groups, different warps are raised and lowered and different sheds can be opened.

Each time a tablet is rotated, the warp threads twist around each other and so most tablet weaving can be identified by this distinctive warp-twined appearance.

LEFT:
THREADED
TABLET.

ABOVE: TWINING
WARPS.

Camel bag tie, from Sivas in East Turkey, mounted on a plain wool band for reinforcement.

Double-faced cotton belt from Bhutan.

Double-faced Greek cotton band depicting two of the Evangelists.

Above: *A dagger belt, from the Yemen, woven on a tablet loom. The brocade pattern has been created with the addition of heddles to open sheds for a supplementary weft of gold thread.*

Uses and distribution

THE high ratio of tablets to warp threads (far higher than is practicable with heddles on a loom) means that a diverse range of complex and intricate warp-faced patterns can be woven, such as the magical cotton belts of Sulawesi in Indonesia worked with Arabic lettering. It is even possible to open two sheds at the same time and produce double weave.

Tablet weaving is employed all over the world from Norway to Morocco and from China to Spain for the construction of narrow bands to be used as belts, sashes, straps and animal trappings.

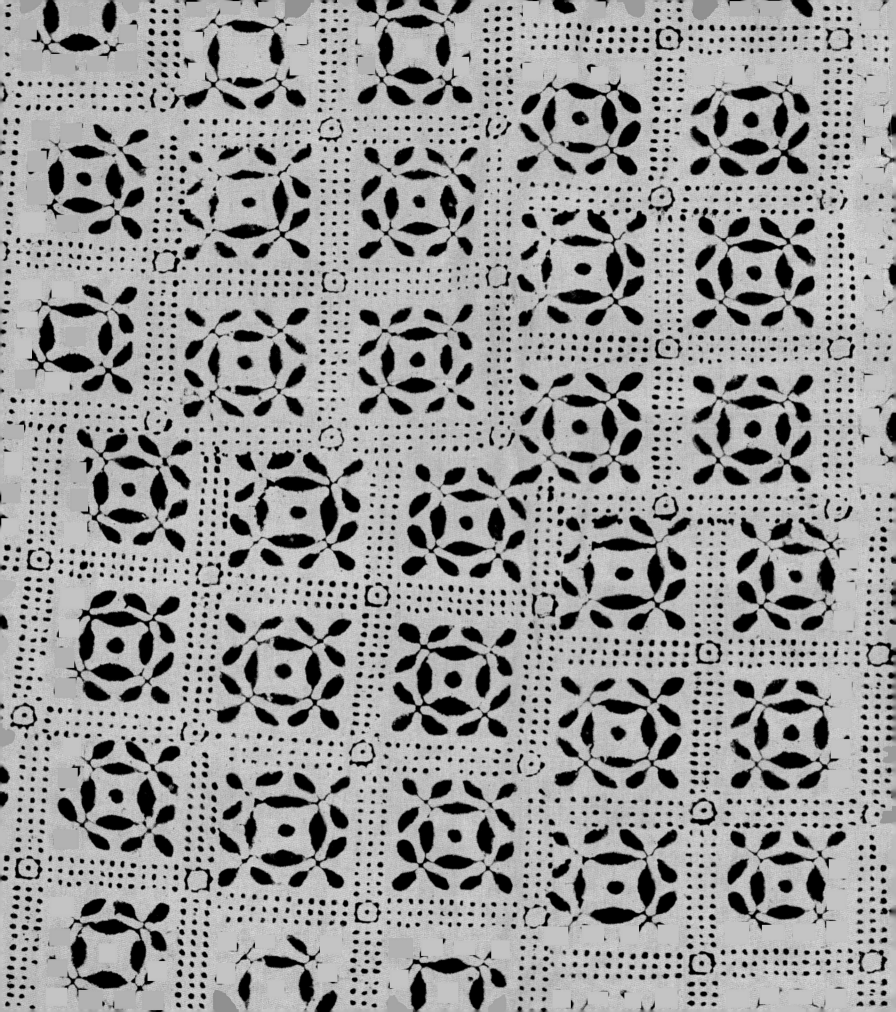

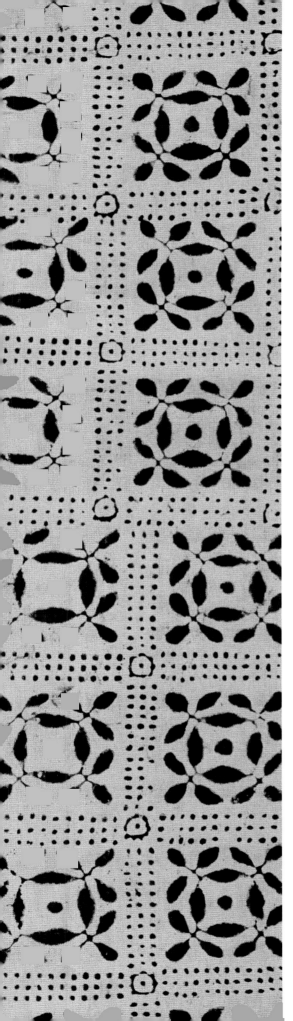

FAR LEFT: SYRIAN
COTTON CLOTH
PRINTED WITH A
WOODEN ROLLER.

LEFT: DETAIL OF
PAINTED BARK CLOTH
FROM ASTROLABE
BAY, PAPUA NEW
GUINEA.

BELOW: NEPALESE
PRINTED MUSLIN
FROM KATHMANDU.

FOUR

PAINTED AND PRINTED TEXTILES

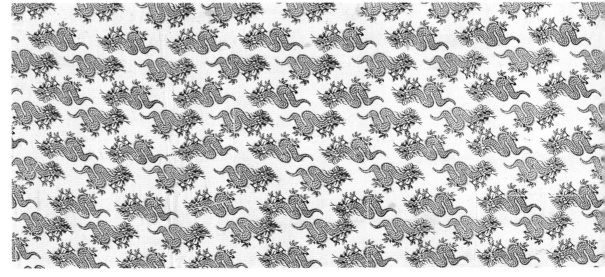

PAINTED AND PRINTED TEXTILES

PAINTINGS from prehistoric times survive on the walls of caves in many parts of the world. A large number of the images depicted served a magical purpose, attracting good luck through the medium of sympathetic magic, the process whereby imitating an action can cause it to happen in reality.

Left: *Tonga islanders playing spillikins in a hut decorated with a large bark cloth painted with geometric patterns with the sap of local trees.*

Above: *Until the disruption of their lifestyle by white colonists, the indigenous inhabitants of Australia disdained the use of clothing. On ritual occasions they decorated their bodies with paint and flowers.*

The first personal decoration was the painting of the body with earth pigments to provide magical protection, denote status or to enhance personal beauty. Tattooing is an extension of this process. Similar designs could be applied to hide or cloth with fingers, sticks or knives. To this day, textiles that serve a particularly esoteric purpose, like the hunting cloths of Herat in Afghanistan or the ceremonial initiation shirts of the Poro men's society of the Côte d'Ivoire, are painted by hand by choice because the high concentration required focuses the life force or thaumaturgic energy and endows the textile with a power of its own.

Left: *Using a* kalam *to draw the ink outlines on a* kalamkari *cloth in Kalahasti, Andhra Pradesh, India.*

Right: *Bakoumba Coulibaly, a Bambara artist, painting the patterns on a bogolanfini mud cloth at Fanimbongou in Mali.*

Left: *An Indian textile artist, outside the G.P.O. in Ahmedabad, Gujarat, India, drawing the outlines of a* mata-ni-pachedi *using lampblack. A finished example of his work hangs on the wall behind him.*

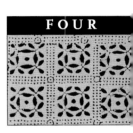

EARTH PIGMENTS

THE colouring agent most readily available to primitive peoples was mud. By selecting mud from different sources and mixing it with a variety of substances, a subtle range of shades of black, red, yellow, brown and white could be made. One of the strongest earth pigments is ochre, prized to this day by the Masai of Kenya for the rich red it yields which they use to colour their garments, hair and bodies. Earth pigments, such as umber, sienna and ochre, are also still used in the manufacture of paint for artists and decorators.

TECHNIQUE

THE first application of pigment to cloth was most probably by hand, and then in progressive order with a stick, a chewed stick and animal hairs attached to a stick to form a brush. All these implements could be used to create a flowing linear pattern. Alternatively, a design could be created by printing onto the cloth with an object such as a shell, stick or hand dipped into pigment. From these primitive origins it did not take man long to make a stamp from clay, wood or metal, shaped to any particular design that took his fancy.

Above: *A Ghanaian craftsman carving stamps from calabash, a large gourd, for printing* adinkra *motifs onto cloth. Every stamp has a symbolic meaning.*

Right: *Printing metallic patterns onto cloth at Indore, Madhya Pradesh, India. Brightly coloured cloth like this is used for shawls and saris by Indian women from all walks of life.*

Far right: *A Muslim woman, from Jodhpur, in the Indian state of Rajasthan, printing patterns on cotton cloth with a wooden block.*

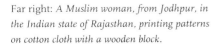

DAUBED TEXTILES

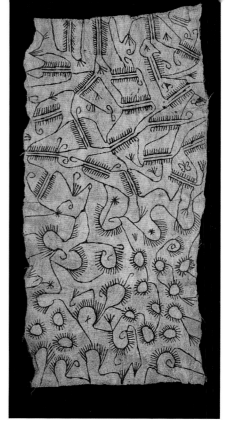

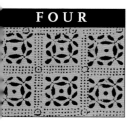

FOUR

J̲ᴜsᴛ as prehistoric peoples painted their magical images on the rock walls and caves of every continent, they painted the skins and hides that they wore.

Native American hide paintings

Oɴ the prairies of North America, until late in the 19th century, the Plains Indians continued to record and commemorate the great events and adventures of their lives, as well as their magical visions, on the buffalo-hide robes they wore and on the covers of the tipis in which they lived. The humble medium they used was pigment derived mainly from earth and rocks applied with a stylus of bone or wood. The final painting was often protected with size made from boiled horn, hide scrapings or cactus juice.

Painted magic

Aʟᴛʜᴏᴜɢʜ the Native Americans of the Plains were adept at decorating clothing and equipment with beads or quillwork, like the artists of many other cultures, when decoration took on a magical significance they preferred to

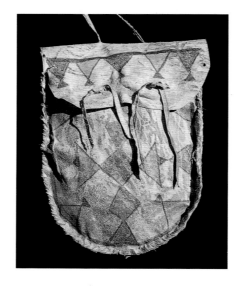

Above: *A painted rawhide pouch acquired at the Sioux reservation at Pine Ridge in South Dakota, North America.*

paint the motifs directly by hand. The Ghost Dance shirts worn in the 1880s and 1890s, hand painted with motifs of birds, animals and stars, were believed to render the wearer bulletproof.

Bogolanfini mud cloths

Oɴᴇ of the most striking of all daubed textiles are the bogolanfini 'mud cloths' of Mali. These are decorated with geometric patterns in white on a black background – the result of painting previously dyed cloth with river mud, applied with a bamboo splint or metal spatula, and bleaching colour from the exposed, unpainted areas with a solution of caustic soda, peanuts and millet. 'Mud cloth' is traditionally worn as ceremonial costume at rites of passage.

Top: *Loincloth of bark cloth made by a pygmy tribe in the Congo (formerly Zaire). The mysterious, flowing, linear pattern appears to have been applied with a stick.*

Left: *A tapa bark cloth from Tonga. A brush, made by sharpening the dried key of a pandanus fruit, is sometimes used to paint patterns with pigment made from the bark of the koka tree, Bischovia javanica.*

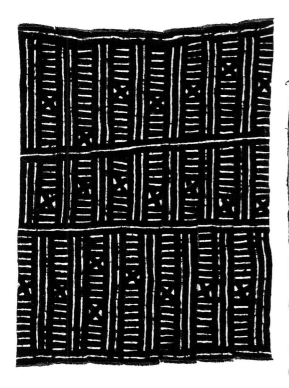

Above and below: *Bogolanfini mud cloths made by the Bamana of Mali. The ground is made by sewing together narrow strips of cotton cloth.*

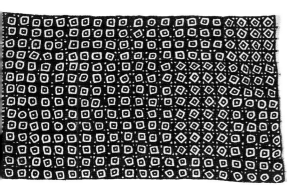

Other daubed textiles

MEMBERS of the Senufo's Poro men's society of the Côte d'Ivoire wear daubed cloths for ceremonial dress which are decorated with crocodiles, turtles, snakes and masked figures. The designs are drawn out with a green paint made from leaves and with mud applied with the edge of a knife. Some of the bark *tapa* cloths of Tonga are also decorated by daubing on the patterns freehand.

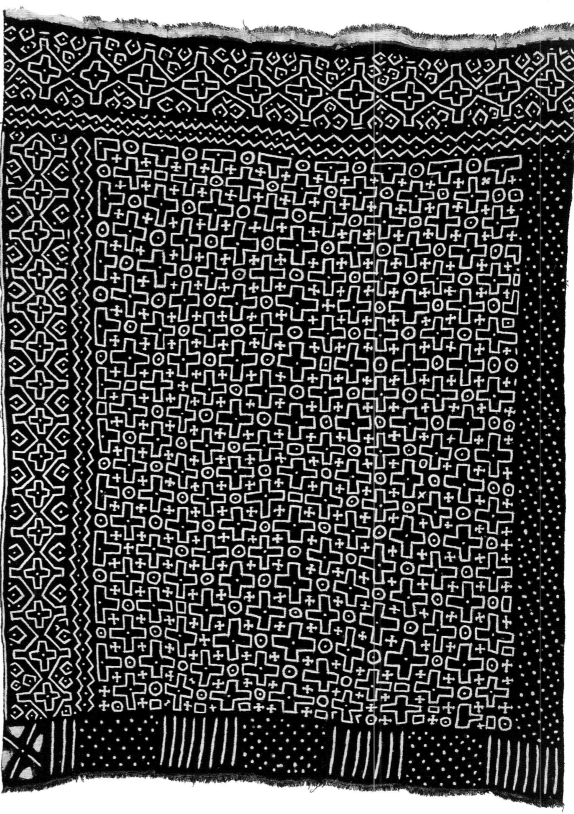

Above: *The dense application of mud on this Bamana mud cloth from Mali results in an intricate negative pattern of exposed, bleached areas.*

PAINTED TEXTILES

The introduction of a brush or absorbent applicator that will hold a reserve of pigment and can be manipulated with fluidity allows a much greater degree of sophistication than a finger, knife or stick.

Paints

PIGMENTS are the raw materials of colour. They may be derived from earth, minerals, animals, insects or plants, but all need to be mixed with other substances, usually oils or fats, to achieve a sufficiently fluid consistency for controlled painting. Gum arabic, exuded by certain acacia trees, is a particularly good medium.

Technique

TEXTILE painting for religious and educational purposes is frequently carried out according to very strict rules about composition and colour. The sequence of painting is also often scrupulously adhered to – so that the colours will not run, the cloth is first coated with starch or size, a sort of glue. Outlines are drawn in and then painting proceeds, one colour at a time over the whole fabric, beginning with the lightest colour and ending with the darkest. The outlines are then repainted over in black. Finally, the eyes of the focal figure are painted and the picture brought to life.

Uses

PAINTS remain on the surface of fabrics and are therefore vulnerable to wear and tear. For this reason painted textiles are seldom used for clothing – more often being employed for religious, educational or decorative purposes. In many places large, painted cloths are used as illustrations and backdrops by professional storytellers for the recitation of epic tales such as that of the Pabuji in Rajasthan, India, or of the Paladins in Sicily. Great care is also taken over the painting of spiritual works such as the thankas of Tibetan Buddhism.

Roghan

ROGHAN work was once practised in many places in the Indian subcontinent, but is now restricted to the village of Nirona in Kutch. Roghan is a thick, bright paste which is used to decorate inexpensive textiles with geometric patterns. Safflower, castor or linseed oil is boiled up until it forms a thick residue which is then mixed with chalk and coloured pigment. This is applied to the cloth with a stick or metal rod. It may also be printed on with a metal block.

Above: A section of a painted par, *from Bhilwara in Rajasthan, India, used in the telling of the story of the folk hero Pabuji, who appears in the centre.*

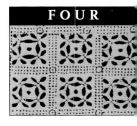

FOUR

Below: A mata-ni-pachedi shrine cloth, from Ahmedabad in Gujarat, India, depicting the mother goddess in her fearsome form of Durga. These painted cloths are used to decorate shrines visited by low-caste Hindus to ask for help from the goddess during times of misfortune. On this cloth she is shown armed with the weapons of the other gods to fight the buffalo demon, Mahisha. The outlines and details may be printed or drawn on, while the large areas are painted in with a brush made from a chewed stick.

Opposite, above, left: *Painted bark cloth from Colombia.*

Opposite, far left: *Delicately patterned, painted cotton textile from Ecuador.*

Opposite, right: *Roghan work* odhni, *or shawl, made in Kutch, North-West India, to be sold in Sind, Pakistan.*

PEN WORK

Kalamkari

THE Persian word 'kalamkari' can be literally translated as 'pen work'. The use of a Persian name for these Indian fabrics proves their popular demand as trade items. They have been exported from the south-east coast of India since the 16th century to Persia, South-East Asia and Europe.

Technique

COTTON cloth that has been specially prepared is spread out on the ground or on a low bench and outlines are sketched out freehand with charcoal. The lines are then carefully drawn over with a *kalam*. The *kalam* is a sharpened length of bamboo with a felt or wool pad tied to the point. The flow of ink is controlled by finger-tip pressure on the ink-soaked pad. Larger areas are then filled in with another *kalam* with a flattened and softened tip. The colours are achieved partly with paint and partly with the application of dyestuffs and mordants.

Uses

LIKE all painted cloths, *kalamkaris* are vulnerable to wear and so they are primarily reserved for use as religious hangings. They are often decorated with scenes from the Hindu epics, the *Mahabharata* and the *Ramayana*. The craftsmen of Masulipatnam in Andhra Pradesh in India, however, concentrated on the production of floral and geometric patterns demanded by Muslim customers and later by Europeans. These fabrics, that we think of as chintzes (from the Hindi word for 'painted'), were often glazed to make them more durable.

FOUR

A large Persian kalamkari, *from Isfahan, used by storytellers to illustrate the adventures of the kings and heroes of the great Persian epic, the* Shahnama.

Three kalamkari *paintings from Kalahasti in the eastern Indian state of Andhra Pradesh.*

Above: *In an episode from the* Ramayana, *Ravana, the demon king, creates a magical deer to lure Rama and his brother, Lakshman, into the forest, leaving Sita, Rama's wife, unguarded.*

Right: *Before the battle of Kurukshetra, Krishna recites the* Bhagavad Gita *to teach his hesitant cousin, Arjuna, his duty.*

Below: *The avatars, or incarnations, of Vishnu, top row, from left to right, Matsya, Kurma, Varaha, Narasimha and Vamana; bottom row, Parashurama, Rama, Balarama, Krishna and Kalki, who is yet to come.*

WOODBLOCK PRINTING

THE idea of using an object or utensil to impress repeated and identical designs into pottery can be traced to prehistoric times. The Chinese developed the use of wooden blocks for letterpress printing about two thousand years ago and soon after cloth was being printed in both China and India. Today, printed fabrics are produced all over the world.

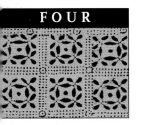

FOUR

Woodblocks

To ensure crisp carving and sharp detail, woodblocks are made by cutting into the end grain of densely grained hardwoods such as ash, box, sycamore or pearwood. To avoid excessive weight, the pattern may be divided up and different sections of it carved on different blocks.

Technique

FIRST a sheet of cloth, most often cotton, is laid out on a level surface. Then, a tub or bowl is filled with pigment and a cloth pad placed over the surface to soak it up. The printing block is pressed on this pad with sufficient pressure to pick up just the right amount of colour. The block is then placed carefully on the cloth to be printed and struck with the heel of the hand or with a mallet. This process is repeated, carefully aligning the block each time, until the entire cloth has been patterned.

Uses

BECAUSE block-printing can be employed to produce patterned cloth so quickly and efficiently, it is both cheap and popular. As the colours can be created through the application of resilient inks and dyes, hard-wearing textiles can be made suitable for everyday use as clothing, bedspreads or decoration.

Adinkra

THE Ashanti of Ghana use stamps cut from calabash gourds to print *adinkra* cloth. There are many different motifs, each having magical or allegorical meaning, and these are printed in groups on a large cloth that has been marked out in squares. The ink, derived from bark and iron slag, is always black or dark brown and the background is usually either white or bark dyed blue-black. *Adinkra* cloths are not used on a daily basis, but on ritual and special occasions such as funerals.

Above: *A Shiah Muslim shrine cloth with medallions of Arabic calligraphy printed in Ahmedabad, Gujarat, India.*

Below: *Detail of Indian block-printed yardage from Madhya Pradesh.*

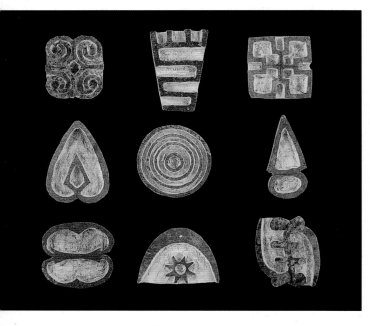

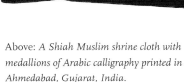

Far left: *Stamps carved from calabash shells for printing* adinkra *cloth.*

Left: *Block-printed prayer flags, from Bhutan, featuring* lung ta *wind horses.*

Opposite: Adinkra *cloth from Ghana. The cloth has been divided into squares, each of which has been filled with prints of one allegorical motif.*

Opposite, inset: *A Ghanaian schoolmaster. The double ram's horn motif means, 'It is the heart and not the horns that leads the ram to bully.'*

POLYCHROME WOODBLOCK PRINTING

By using a number of printing blocks, each cut to print a different part of the pattern, it is possible to produce sophisticated, multi-coloured designs. It is not uncommon for nine or ten colours to be used on a single textile. Of course, the more colours used, the greater the time and labour required for cutting the blocks and printing and, therefore, the more expensive the product.

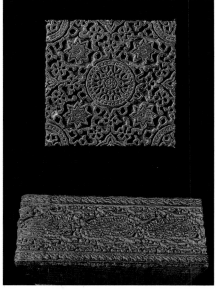

Above: *Wooden printing blocks from Gujarat, India. The Gujaratis are expert carvers and crisp, floral carvings can be found ornamenting the façades of the family palaces of merchants and princes.*

Technique

The process for printing with several blocks is the same as for printing with one. One colour is applied at a time using the appropriate block or blocks. To ensure that each subsequent colour registers properly whole blocks are often cut to shape or have registration notches cut in their sides. The most efficient method is to set brass pitch pins into the corners for accurate alignment.

Mass production

The invention of multiple block-printing opened the doors for manual mass production. The economy of India

Left: *Printed cotton, Masulipatnam, Andhra Pradesh, India. Patterns like this may use ten or more differently carved blocks.*

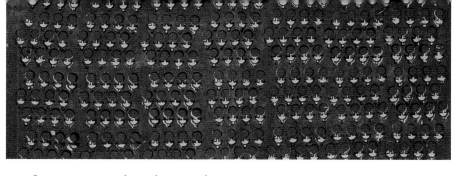

was for many years dependent on the export of printed cloth until overwhelmed by competition from English and Scottish factories in the 18th and 19th centuries.

Distribution

INDIA, with its mastery of dyeing techniques and the use of mordants, has always produced the world's most sophisticated polychromatic block-prints. Fifteenth-century block-prints from Gujarat have been excavated at Fostat near Cairo. Gujarat and particularly the city of Ahmedabad are still the most important centres in India for both the domestic and export markets. Iran, Central Asia and Europe have also been important centres of the block-printing industry.

Right: Simple, but striking, patterns are often composed of borders of concentric bands. In the 20th century, Indian printed cloth has satisfied a global demand for cheap patterned fabrics.

Above: *Detail of hand-printed cotton yardage from Jodhpur in Rajasthan, India. Before the fabric was dyed green, the pattern was printed with a resist paste. After dyeing, the red pigment was printed onto the light, undyed areas.*

Above: *Printed cotton from Iran. The* butti *or* boteh *cone motif associated with Paisley dominates this design. It can be found on many textiles, including Persian rugs and Kashmir shawls.*

FOUR

STENCILLING

Above: A 19th-century Japanese stencilled kimono. More frequently, the Japanese stencil on a resist paste and then dye the cloth. This would have produced a light pattern on a dark background.

STENCILLING is a widespread technique used either to implant a design directly, or to apply starch in the dye-resist process. The stencil is in essence a mask with a carefully cut hole in it so that pigment can be applied to selected areas only. This mask might be made of metal, oiled paper or even banana leaves. The most sophisticated stencils of all are made in Japan.

FOUR

Technique

THE Japanese learned how to use stencils in the 8th century. The weakness of stencils was the ties that had to be left once the pattern had been cut out. These were fragile and broke easily, so stencils were previously bold and clumsy. The Japanese came up with an ingenious solution that transformed stencilling into the art form now known as *katazome*. Sets of identical stencils are cut with a long, thin knife from sheets of paper made from waterproofed mulberry fibre. One sheet is brushed with adhesive and silk threads or strands of hair are glued on in several directions like a net. A second sheet is then glued on top. The hairs reinforce the stencil and make it possible to cut very intricate shapes that will not fall apart. Ink (or starch when resist dyeing) is then pounced through the stencil with a soft brush. Great subtlety can be achieved by varying the amount of colour on the brush or the pressure applied.

LEFT: INUIT STENCIL FROM BAFFINLAND, 1961. 'TWO MEN DISCUSSING THE HUNT.'

Below: Nineteenth-century tent decoration from Rajasthan, India. The details and outlines are printed and the large red areas filled in with a stencil.

Opposite: Detail of bark cloth from Fiji. Pigment is rubbed through a banana-leaf stencil with a wad of tapa.

Screen printing

SCREEN printing is a development of the Japanese stencil. Silk or organdie is stretched across a wooden frame and parts of it are masked off with paper or acetate which subsequently sticks to the silk because of the printing ink. Ink is then poured into the frame and forced through the silk with a rubber squeegee onto a sheet of fabric. Where the silk has been masked, the ink is unable to penetrate and cannot reach the fabric beneath. The wooden frame, or screen, is then lifted clear and the design can be repeated on a further section of cloth. Several screens may be used to build up as many colours as are required.

Left: A painted 'hunting cloth', from Herat, Afghanistan, intended to appease the spirits of hunted animals. The flowers and details of the pattern have been applied with a stencil.

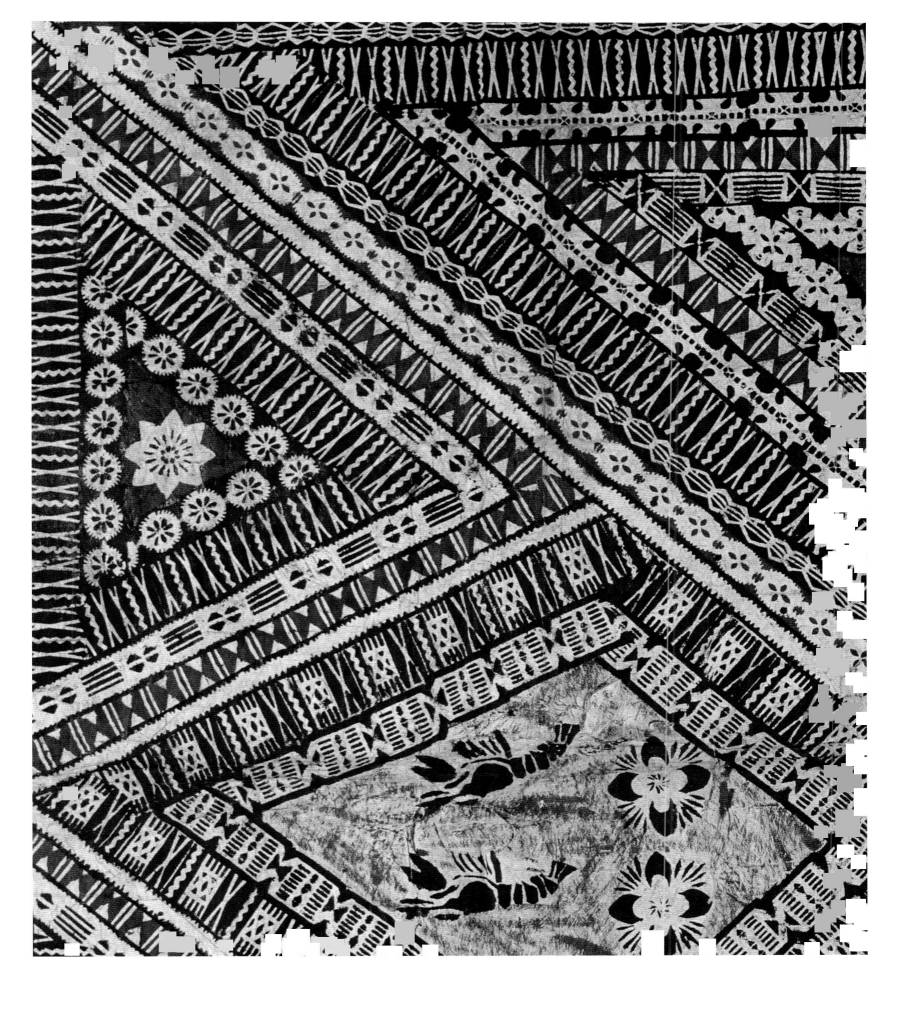

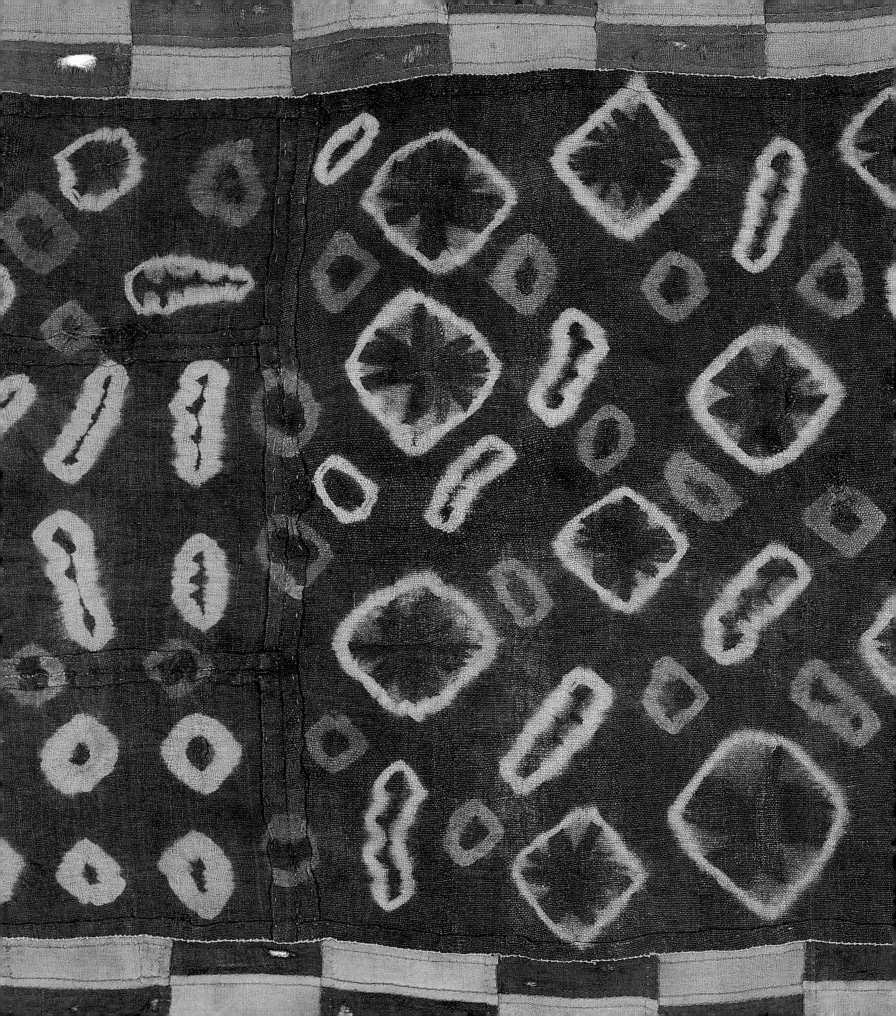

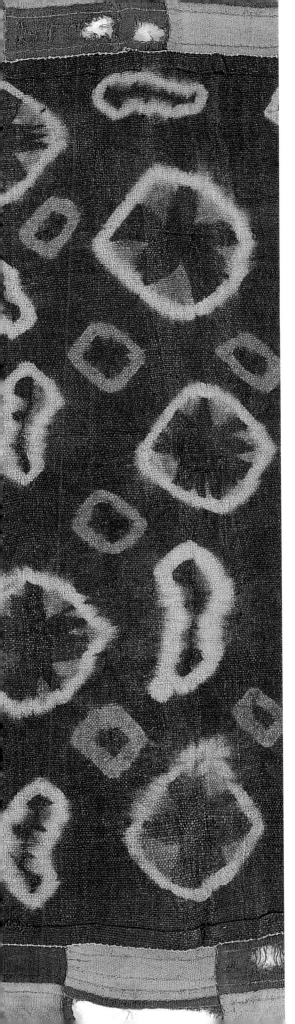

LEFT: KUBA RAPHIA SKIRT WITH STITCHED-RESIST DECORATION, THE CONGO (FORMERLY ZAIRE).

BELOW: BAGOBO MAN'S TIE AND DYE KERCHIEF FROM MINDANAO, PHILIPPINES.

BOTTOM: ERSARI *JALLAR* DYED WITH MADDER AND COCHINEAL, TURKMENISTAN.

RIGHT: DYED TURBAN LENGTHS, RAJASTHAN, INDIA.

DYES

DYES

YES are absorbed into the very fibres of textiles, ensuring a much longer lifetime than paints and pigments which are applied to the surface of a textile and are therefore vulnerable to wear and tear. At its most basic, dyeing is a process in which yarn or fabric is immersed in a solution produced by boiling up selected raw materials or dyestuffs. In origin these may be animal (*murex* shell for purple), vegetable (onion skins for yellow) or mineral (iron oxide for red).

Above: *A dyer at Barmer in Rajasthan, India, mixing together the ingredients for a yellow dye. He is in the process of adding myrobalan flowers to the mix. Many dye recipes are closely guarded secrets.*

FIVE

Above, right: *Black walnut, a source of black and brown dye.*

Right: *Dyed woollen yarn for sale at the Kashgar yarn market in Xinjiang, China.*

Below: *A woman, from the village of Biashia, Guizhou, China, drawing out wax-resist patterns on cotton cloth with a Chinese knife.*

SUBSTANTIVE DYES

ANY substances are capable of yielding colours or stains, but few are resilient enough to withstand repeated washing or exposure to sunlight. Those dyes that give a fast, lasting colour without the need for extra chemical processes are known as substantive dyes. Amongst these highly prized dyestuffs are walnut (for black), orchil lichens (for mauves), and, the king of dyes, indigo.

ADJECTIVE DYES

OST natural dyes such as cochineal or madder are not fast unless the yarn or fabric to be dyed is first treated with a mordant which makes it more absorbent and helps the dye to bite. Different dyes require different mordants, but most mordants used today are of mineral origin such as alum, tin, chrome or iron, although the oldest and most widespread is urine.

ANILINE DYES

IN the 1850s, as the result of a search for a use for coal tar (the waste product of coal gas) and analysis of the chemical structure of indigo, the first reliable alternative to natural dyes was developed in Britain. These aniline dyes (from *anil*, the Arabic word for indigo) became available in an astounding range of colours which, combined with their fastness, consistency and ease of use, made them so popular worldwide that in many places the craft of dyeing with natural dyes was virtually forgotten.

Above: *Woman drawing batik with a canting, Java.*

FIVE

Above: *Man printing batik patterns with a cap in Jogjakarta, Java. The pattern is known as* parang *and was once reserved for use only by members of the court.*

Above, right: *Using a wooden block to print the red onto* ajrakh *cloth at Dhamadhka, Kutch, North-West India.*

THE SURVIVAL OF NATURAL DYES

ALTHOUGH the use of aniline or chemical dyes is now the norm, in a number of places, such as the Highlands and Islands of Scotland, the subtlety of natural dyes is still appreciated and there has been a resurgence in their use. In other places where particular dyes are used for reasons of beauty, prestige, custom and symbolism their use has never been threatened.

Left: *Untying wefts for weft-ikat cloth at Sukarara, Lombok, Indonesia. The pattern was resist dyed into the wefts before they were woven. This may involve tying, untying and retying the yarn several times to dye different parts of the pattern in different colours.*

Right: *Weaving double ikat, where both the weft and warp have been resist dyed, Tenganan, Bali.*

INDIGO

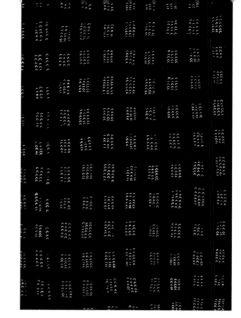

INDIGO is the oldest dyestuff known to man, having been in use since 2500 BC, if not before, during the Old Kingdom of Ancient Egypt. Requiring expertise and patience to produce, indigo-dyed textiles have been valued the world over for their fast, deep blue colour and until the advent of aniline dyes indigo was the most widely used dye of all. Various plants growing in tropical regions are used to make indigo, including members of the genus *Indigofera* in India, China, the Americas and the East Indies, *Baptisia tinctoria* also in the East Indies, *Lonchocarpus cyanescens* in West Africa and *Polygonum tinctoria* in Japan. Woad, *Isatis tinctoria*, with which Ancient Britons so famously painted themselves, is a form of indigo.

Technique

THE preparation of indigo for dyeing is an arcane and complicated process. The indigo dyestuff is almost always extracted from plants by boiling, but in West Africa the leaves are sometimes simply rolled into a ball and dried. Although indigo is a substantive dye and needs no mordant, it must be fermented and deoxidized in an alkaline solution to make it soluble so that it can be absorbed into the fibres to be dyed. This is carried out in deep vats, which are often buried in the ground. Cloth or yarn may be repeatedly dipped in the vats or soaked for as long as six days depending on the intensity of colour required. On removal from the vats, the dyed fibres initially appear pale yellow, but as the indigo once more becomes oxidized as it is exposed to the air it turns blue and becomes insoluble again which renders it fast against washing. To add sheen, dyed cloth may be beaten with a wooden mallet or polished with shells.

FIVE

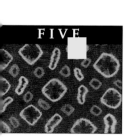

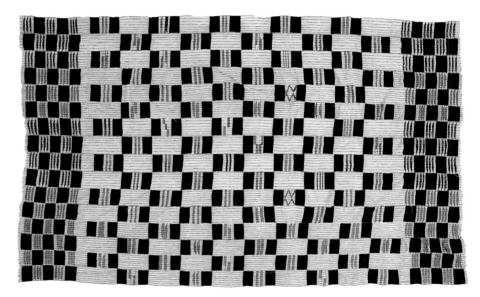

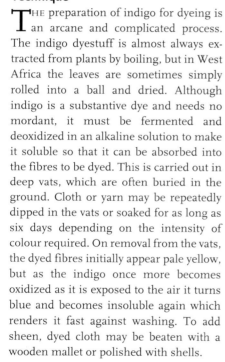

Indigo today

INDIGO dyeing remains a living art to this day, notably in West Africa and South-East Asia where indigo cloth is used for ritual purposes, to express tribal identity and to show status. Ironically, synthetic indigo is used to dye denim jeans, the common man's modern working attire.

Above: *An Ewe woman's cotton stripweave mourning cloth woven from undyed and indigo-dyed yarn, Ghana.*

Left: *Girls of the Blue H'mong tribe wearing their distinctive indigo-dyed costumes at Sapa weekly market in Vietnam. The sheen on their skirts is achieved by beating indigo-dyed cloth with a mallet.*

Top: *A woman's loincloth from Burkina Faso. The pattern was created by resisting the indigo dye with stitching.*

Opposite, above, left: *Woman's* tapis *with a warp-ikat pattern of horses, worn by the Ngada people, Flores, Indonesia.*

Opposite, below, left: *Yoruba hand-drawn* adire *cloth from Nigeria. The pattern is created by resisting the indigo with starch paste.*

Opposite, right: *A woman's stitched-resist loincloth from Burkina Faso. Strong blues are built up by repeated dippings in the indigo vat.*

Opposite, inset: *Tuaregs, the Blue Men of the Sahara, wearing the indigo-dyed veils that stain their skin blue.*

TIE AND DYE

Dye resist

DYEING only selected parts of a piece of cloth is a tricky process as dye's natural tendency is to run along the fibres of a piece of cloth. It is easier to prepare the cloth before dyeing in such a way that in certain areas the absorption of the dye is resisted. Tie and dye is one of the simplest dye-resist techniques.

Technique

IF twine is bound tightly around a bunch of fabric before it is dyed the twine will resist the penetration of the dye and upon unbinding an undyed circle will be revealed. Binding the bunch at intervals will produce concentric circles, while tying a series of independent bunches (*see diagrams on right*) will create a pattern of small rings. In India and Indonesia the cloth is poked up with the fingertip and tied. In West Africa the cloth is sometimes tied around a stone or stick to control the shape of the resist area, whereas in Japan very delicate patterns can be produced by tying tiny bunches with a grain of rice inside to hold the twine in place.

If the cloth is folded or pleated and then tied before dyeing, as is often done by the Yoruba of Nigeria, the result is a zigzag or criss-cross pattern.

Above, left: Japanese shibori *silk scarf. A border has been made at each end by tying a series of closely placed knots in a cloud pattern.*

Above: A Japanese short-sleeved, silk shibori *jacket, with a simple pattern of tiny diagonal rings.*

LEFT: TYING KNOTS FOR SEPARATE RINGS.

LEFT: TYING KNOTS FOR CONCENTRIC RINGS.

In Senegal and the Gambia a marbled effect is created by bunching up the whole cloth before binding it ready for dyeing.

By repeating the tie and dye process a number of times, using a different dye each time, a multi-coloured effect is achieved. In Indonesia this is known as *plangi* which means rainbow.

Left: Dyed cotton dress, from Hama in Syria, decorated with a simple, but striking, geometric pattern of small tie and dye rings.

Right: A Punjabi woman's shawl tie dyed at Chakwal in Pakistan. In the Indian subcontinent tie and dye is known as bandhani, *from the Hindustani word meaning 'to tie'. The demand for 'bandannas' has been so great that dyed or printed imitations are today produced as far afield as North America and Java.*

FIVE

Above: *Rabari girls, from Kutch, North-West India, one is wearing a tie and dye shawl.*

Distribution

TRADITIONAL tie and dye textiles are found in Latin America, the Middle East, the Caucasus, Africa and all over Asia. It is known as *plangi* in Indonesia, *shibori* in Japan and *bandhani* in India and Pakistan.

In the 18th century Indian *bandhani* was in such demand that 'bandanna' entered the English language as the word for a spotted kerchief. In the 1960s the technique spread to the Western world and tie and dye garments became a popular mode of dress worn by the hippies of San Francisco in North America.

Left: *A woman's silk shawl from Tajikistan. To tie the resist bindings to produce squares, the sections of fabric must be pinched up and then carefully folded or pleated before tying.*

Above: *A tie-dyed* yashmak *of loosely woven woollen cloth, worn to hide their faces by women from San'a, the capital of Yemen. Here, the cloth has been folded, pinched up and then tied in concentric circles before dyeing.*

STITCHED RESIST

Sᴛɪᴛᴄʜᴇᴅ resist, like tie and dye, prevents dye reaching parts of the cloth. In Indonesia this technique is known as *tritik* and in Nigeria as *adire alabere*. It is a commonly used technique in Japan, Indonesia and the West African countries of Senegal, Mali, the Gambia, Sierra Leone, Burkina Faso, Nigeria and Cameroon.

Technique

Tᴏ create a symmetrical pattern, and incidentally reduce the amount of work involved, the cloth to be dyed is normally first doubled up or pleated. Strong thread or raphia is sewn in and out of the fabric and then pulled very tight, causing the cloth to compress and resist the dye. The pattern is revealed in negative when the stitches are removed and the cloth opened out.

Distribution

Iɴ Sumatra and Java *tritik* is generally linear, but in West Africa a wide variety of bold patterns are produced with different arrangements of stitching. Indigo-dyed *adire alabere* textiles are produced in Nigeria, Gambia and other parts of West Africa by machine-sewing, as well as by hand.

West African stitched resist is almost always either blue or brown. Kola nut can be used for brown and the blue is obtained from either natural or synthetic indigo.

STITCHING FOLDED CLOTH.

PULLING STITCHES TIGHT.

The import of fine European mill cloth and smooth sewing threads has also meant that finer work can now be done.

In Java, Japan and Cambodia *tritik* is often combined with other methods of resist dyeing. One method is to stitch the outlines of a resist pattern, draw the threads tight, and then cover the portion of fabric within with vegetal matter, plastic or paper, which is then tacked into place. The most notable examples of this are the beautiful *selendangs* of Palembang in Sumatra which are worked on Shantung silk. As this silk is loosely woven, to save time on an arduous task, the *tritik* workers can tie them three layers at a time.

Top: *Indigo-dyed shirt from Cameroon. To produce such an elaborate pattern, the fabric has been embroidered with raphia to resist the dye and the stitches then removed to expose the undyed cloth.*

Above: *Cotton cloth, from the Gambia, stitched resist dyed in indigo. The cloth has been folded three times before stitching to ensure symmetry.*

Far left: *Tritik shawl from Palembang, Sumatra. To resist the dye, the dot patterns have been tied, but the egg shapes and linear motifs stitched.*

Left: *Indigo-dyed cloth made by the Mossi people of Burkina Faso with a pattern created by the stitched-resist technique.*

Opposite: *Dance skirt, worn by a member of the Dida tribe of the Côte d'Ivoire, made of silky raphia cloth with stitched-resist patterns.*

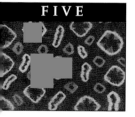

FIVE

LEHERIA AND MOTHARA

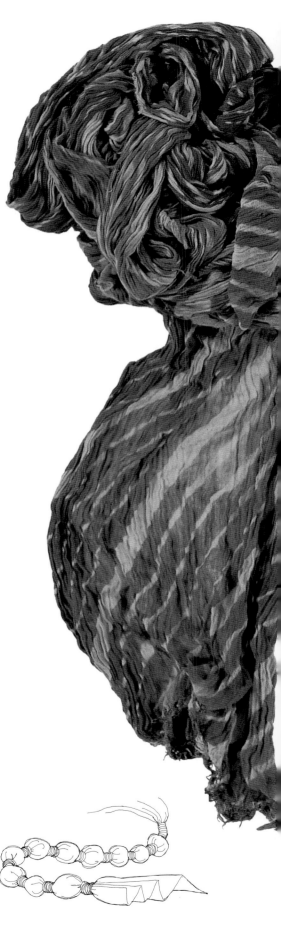

I N the 19th and early 20th centuries, the Marwaris, merchants of Rajasthan and the dominant business community of India, wore elaborately tied, brightly coloured turbans as their distinguishing mark. These turbans were made by the leheria technique ('leheria' in Hindi literally means 'waves') and this process continues to be practised in the dyeing quarters of the Rajasthani towns of Jodhpur, Jaipur, Udaipur and Nathdwara.

Technique

L EHERIA is a method of tie and dye. Fabrics, generally turbans or sari lengths, are rolled diagonally from one corner to the opposite selvedge, and then tied at the required intervals and dyed. The result is a pattern of diagonal stripes. To produce a zigzag wave pattern the fabric is folded like a fan across its width before tying.

After dyeing, the fabric may be untied, refolded or rolled, this time on the other diagonal, and retied. Fabric prepared in this way reveals a pattern of checks called mothara, named after the spaces left which are the size of a lentil ('moth' in Hindi). Further colours may be introduced with a succession of tying, dyeing in different dye baths and by bleaching back.

Colour must penetrate right through the tightly rolled cloth, so this technique can only be applied to highly permeable, thin, loose cottons or silks.

Leheria is sold with its ties still in place to show that it is the genuine article. A small end portion is unravelled to display the pattern to potential buyers.

LEFT: MAHARAJA GAJ SINGH OF JODHPUR (REIGNED 1620–38) WEARING A LEHERIA TURBAN.

Below: *A turban length, from Jaipur, Rajasthan, India, with the end untied to reveal a pattern of diagonal stripes and dots. Leheria and mothara turbans are sold with the ties still in place.*

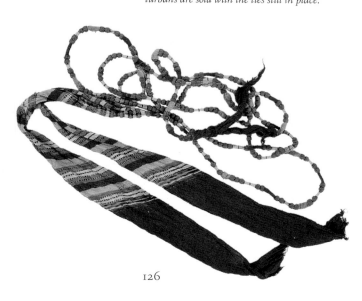

Right, from left to right: *Three leheria turban lengths from Jaipur, India. The cheap turban on the left is made of coarse, loosely woven muslin that has been stretched on one diagonal, rolled up and then tied with resists to create a pattern of simple diagonal stripes. The second is of much finer quality and has been carefully pleated before the resists have been tied in order to produce the distinctive* leheria *'wave' pattern. The third turban has been dyed like the first, the resists have been removed, and then the cloth has been stretched and rolled on the other diagonal before a new set of resists has been tied. This results in a pattern of* mothara *dots.*

Opposite, right: *Two cotton turban lengths, from Jodhpur, India, showing the result of repeated tying and dyeing in different colours.*

STARCH-RESIST BY HAND

IN Nigeria and Japan starch is used as a resist medium for designs on cloth to be dyed with indigo. In both countries it can be applied either by hand or through a stencil. In Nigeria, starch-resist is the speciality of the Yoruba people and is known as *adire eleko*.

FIVE

Above: *A Toraja banner, from the Indonesian island of Sulawesi, with panels decorated with rice-paste resist patterns.*

Below: *A saki seller's* happi *from Honshu, the largest island of Japan. In the past, indigo-dyed jackets were worn by workmen of many professions with the insignia of their employer emblazoned on the back by means of a rice starch-resist.*

Technique in Nigeria

IBADAN is the main Nigerian centre for hand-drawn adire cloth. The cloth to be dyed is always divided into squares and the designs drawn within each square. The starch used is known as *lafun* or *eko* and is made from either cassava or cornflower. It is boiled with alum and then applied to the cloth by women using a palm-leaf rib or a feather. After the starch dries, the cloth is dyed in indigo. It must be handled very carefully during the dyeing process so the starch is not rubbed off.

The cloth is dried and the starch is scraped or flaked off, leaving a pattern in negative in the same manner as Javanese batik. Because the starch does not completely resist the dye, indigo-dyed adire cloth has a pattern in light blue on a dark blue background.

Adire eleko is decorated with stylized motifs based on birds and everyday objects.

Technique in Japan

IN Japan a sheet of cotton is stretched out on a bamboo frame and a pattern is drawn on both sides using a resist paste made from rice starch. The process is

Above: *The crane and the tortoise are both symbols of longevity and appear on many Japanese textiles. Here, the patterns have been created by resisting the dye with rice starch applied with a tsutsu.*

Opposite: *Adire eleko,* from Nigeria, *with a pattern created by applying a resist-paste of cassava flour by hand. This pattern, made up of two particular motifs, conveys the messages, 'I'm getting my head together'.*

Opposite, inset: *Japanese workmen wearing traditional indigo-dyed* happi *with starch-resist insignia, while making barrels.*

known as *tsutsugaki* after the tube (*tsutsu*) with which the paste is applied. This is made from a length of bamboo with a metal tip at one end and a paper cone at the other. The cone is gently squeezed so that the starch with which it has been filled will flow out of the metal tip in a controlled line.

Indigo-dyed *tsutsugaki* cloth traditionally features designs of auspicious symbols, and figurative patterns.

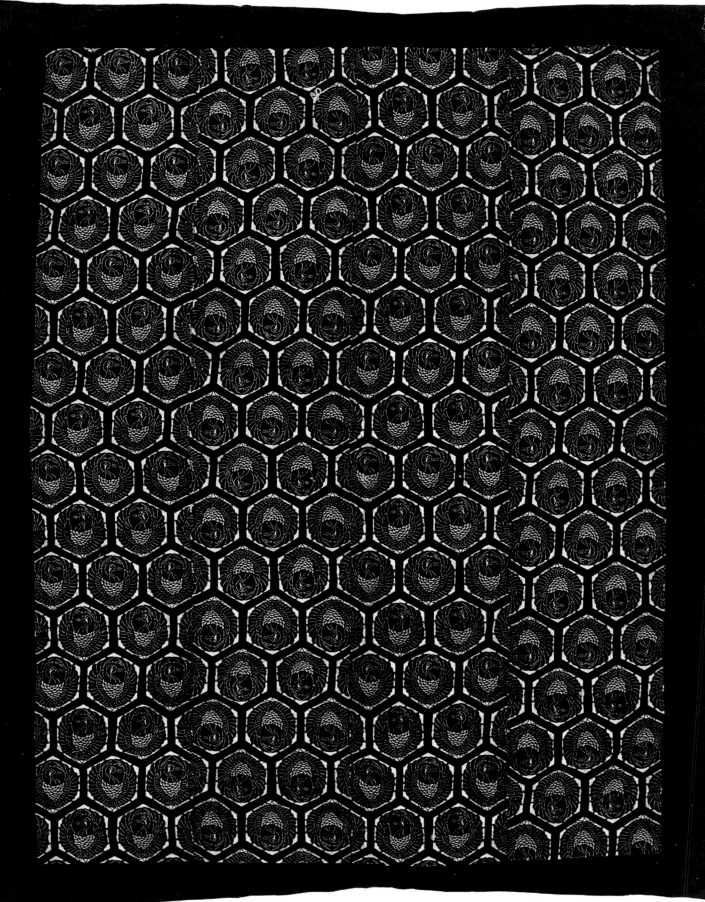

STENCILLED STARCH-RESIST

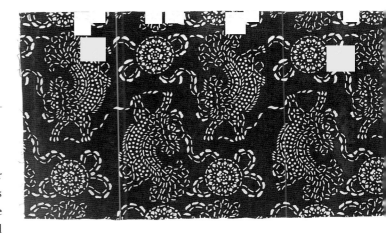

I N both Nigeria and Japan starch can be applied for resist dyeing either freehand or through a stencil. The use of stencils facilitates the precise repetition of motifs as well as making the process much quicker. In Japan several sheets of paper, made from the inner bark of the paper mulberry tree, are stuck together with well-aged persimmon juice. Patterns are then cut out accurately to ensure that the repeat design matches perfectly. Stencils with large sections of paper cut out are reinforced by sandwiching a mesh of silk threads between the layers of paper. To apply the resist, the fabric is laid out on long boards and rice starch or bean paste is spread through the stencil with a wooden spatula. After the resist paste has been dried, the fabric is dyed and the dyes are set by steaming. Finally, the rice paste is washed away.

LEFT: A KIMONO WITH STENCILLED STARCH-RESIST MOTIFS, FROM A PRINT BY KUNISADA, 1851.

RIGHT: STENCILLED JAPANESE FAMILY CRESTS OR *MON*.

Technique in Nigeria

F IRSTLY, a piece of metal is cut into a rectangle, commonly 12" x 8" (30.5 x 20.3 cm), and the required motif is cut or punched into it. The first stencils, dating back to the late 19th century, were cut out of the lead linings of tea chests and other containers.

The cloth to be stencilled is nailed flat to a table. The stencil is placed firmly on top of the cloth and cassava starch is applied and pressed into the cloth using a metal spatula. Any surplus is scraped back into a bowl. Both the stencilling and the cutting of stencils is the work of men. Abeokuta is the main centre for stencilled adire cloth.

Technique in Japan

T HE centre of the Japanese craft of stencilled resist dyeing, or *katazome*, has always been the small towns of Shiroko and Jike in Mie prefecture. It is thought to have evolved from the stencilling of armour and leather in Japan's medieval period, but is now widely used for the decoration of clothes and domestic textiles.

FIVE

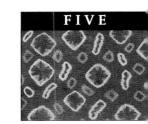

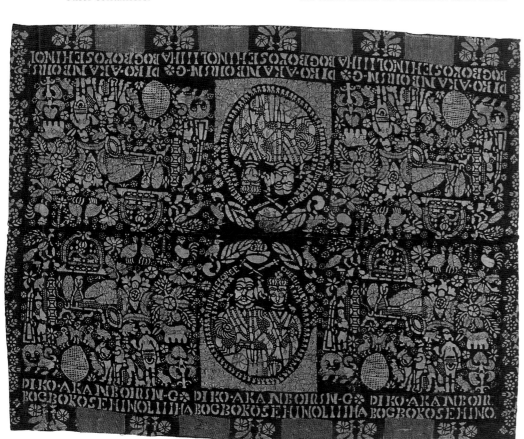

Top: *An indigo-dyed textile, from Japan, with a pattern of mythical beasts created with a stencilled starch-resist that imitates* sashiko *stitching.*

Left: *Stencilled* adire eleko, *from Nigeria, showing King George V and Queen Mary in 1935 when Silver Jubilee celebrations took place all over the British Empire.*

Right: *A Japanese trapping, tied around a horse's belly, decorated with both freehand and stencilled starch-resist patterns.*

Opposite: *A Japanese indigo-dyed futon cover with a stencilled resist pattern of cranes, a symbol of long life.*

WAX-RESIST: CHINESE KNIFE

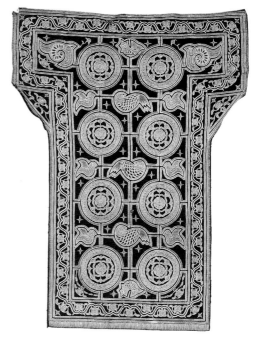

T HE oldest known example of wax-resist dates from 10th-century China. The tradition of hand-drawn wax-resist still flourishes amongst the hill tribes of South-West China. It is known as the *ladao* or wax-knife technique. The *ladao* knife consists of a bamboo handle to which two or more small triangular layers of copper are attached with enough space in between them to trap a small amount of molten wax.

Technique

N EW beeswax is mixed with wax recovered from a previous dyeing. The latter retains some blue from the indigo and makes the drawn patterns more visible. After being dipped in molten wax, the knife is held at an oblique angle to a piece of smooth cotton or hemp cloth pinned to a board. Wax is dripped from the bottom edge of the knife onto the cloth, blocking out geometric or figurative patterns. The waxed cloth is then dyed in a cold vat of indigo to prevent the wax from melting. After dyeing, the wax is removed by boiling, resulting in a pattern of white motifs against a blue ground.

The number of copper leaves on the knife determines the amount of wax that can be held; the more leaves, the larger the reserve of wax held and the thicker the line drawn. A practitioner will have a whole

Left: Tie for a baby carrier, from Guizhou, China, with a pattern of stylized birds executed with a Chinese knife.

Above, right: Indigo-dyed baby carrier, from Guizhou, China, with wax-resist patterns.

Below: Jacket from Pojao, Guizhou, China. The pattern around the neck and arms has been executed with a Chinese knife on fine cloth which is then sewn onto a coarser ground of glazed indigo.

Below, left: A design, known as 'grouped snails', popular amongst the Blue H'mong of Laos.

Left: *A baby carrier, from Laos, reinforced with coarse cotton cloth. Arranged on it are a selection of* ladao, *Chinese knives of copper and bamboo, used to draw out wax-resist patterns. Different* ladao *may be used on one textile to draw fine, broad or even multiple lines.*

Above: *A baby carrier of the type used around Sapa in Vietnam, decorated with geometric patterns drawn with a Chinese knife. Baby carriers are one of the most elaborately decorated types of textile found in Indo-China.*

Below: *A Zhao woman's skirt, from Vietnam, dyed in indigo with a striking wax-resist zigzag pattern.*

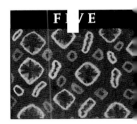

collection of *ladao* knives – ones with more leaves for drawing lines of different thicknesses and special ones for the border, dots and cross-hatching.

Distribution

THE same method of batik is practised amongst the hill tribes of Indo-China and Thailand. As in China, the women mainly work on hemp or now often on cotton cloth. The main item produced is the prized many pleated skirt.

Opposite, below, right: *Intricately patterned apron panel with wax-resists applied with a Chinese knife from Guizhou, China. Wax-resists frequently appear on the aprons, sleeves and baby carriers of women from this region.*

WAX-RESIST: CANTING

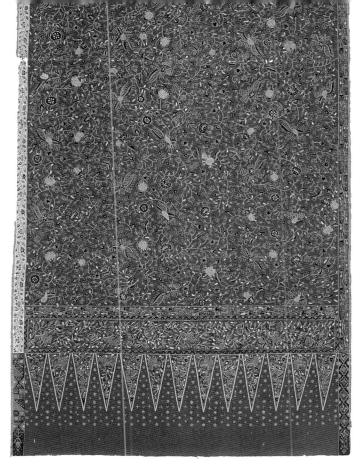

THE application of a wax-resist before dyeing to form a pattern in negative is most often referred to by the Javanese word batik. Batik is practised in India, Sri Lanka, China, South-East Asia, Turkestan and West Africa, but in Indonesia, on the island of Java, the craft has been brought to an acme of refinement. Nowhere else has wax-resist cloth been so finely detailed.

The origins of batik are obscure, but what is certain is that the Javanese invention of the *canting* waxing instrument enabled the finest hand-drawn batik to be produced.

Technique

HAND-DRAWN batik is known by the Javanese word *tulis* which means writing. The *canting* consists of a wooden handle inset into a small copper reservoir with single or sometimes multiple spouts. This is dipped into a bowl containing molten wax, which is kept at a constant temperature. The female batiker dips her *canting* into the bowl of wax and glides it over the surface of a piece of fine cotton cloth, dripping wax in a smooth continuous flow as she goes. For quality batik, the resist is always applied first to one side and then to the other. The completion of a piece of batik involves a series of stages of waxing, then dyeing, waxing fresh areas of the cloth, taking off some portions of the first waxing and then dyeing in another colour. The more complex the desired colour scheme, the more stages there are. Finally, all the wax is boiled out.

Above: *A batik* kain *from north Java. The art of hand drawing wax-resist patterns with a canting is known as* tulis.

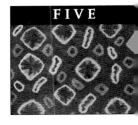

FIVE

Uses

PRODUCING high-quality, hand-drawn batik is a time-consuming, and therefore expensive, process. Some particularly fine pieces may take as long as a year to wax and dye and are therefore only worn by the wealthy. In Java, batik is traditionally worked on rectangular pieces of cotton which are not tailored, but worn by both women and men wrapped around the body as a *kain panjang*.

Opposite: *A dua negri* batik sarong *from Java. Dua negri (meaning two country) indicates that different parts of the process were carried out in two places, in this case Lasem and Pekalongan.*

Opposite, inset: *A Malay woman, from Singapore, wearing a batik sarong.*

Left: Kalligrafi *batik, based on Koranic verses, made in Cirebon, Java, to be sold in Sumatra.*

Right: *A silk sarong made in Juana, Java, intended for festive use in Bali.*

WAX-RESIST: PRINTED

I N Java in the middle of the 19th century the technique of wax-resist batik using a copper block or *cap* was developed because the supplies of European machine-printed imitation batik had been interrupted due to the economic disruption caused by the American Civil War. The structure of the *caps* was inspired by European block-printing stamps, but they were constructed according to local Chinese jewelry-making techniques.

This was truly a revolution in the making of batik. Previously a woman using a *canting* could take months to wax and dye a batik cloth, but workshops were then set up and men hired to undertake the arduous and unhealthy work. Each worker could produce up to eight batik cloths a day.

Technique

FIVE

C AP printers stand at a tightly padded-out rectangular table. Beside them on a small stove sits a circular flat-bottomed pan containing the wax. A filter made of a percolated copper plate and a fibrous mat is set in the molten wax and covered with an absorbent cloth. Any impurities in the wax are strained out by the filter. The *cap* is pressed onto the filter pad to load it with wax and then stamped onto the cloth. The

Above, right: A cap-printed selendang, from Jambi, Sumatra, with a pattern that imitates textiles from the Coromandel coast of India. These batiks were often printed with wooden blocks.

Below: A cap-printed kain, from central Java, boldly patterned with storks.

Below, right: A large silk shawl from Central Asia. The boteh motifs, familiar to Europeans through Paisley shawls, are the result of crudely printing a wax-resist with a wooden block.

worker repeats the process to leave imprints of the design all over the cloth. Changing *caps* as the design requires, he continues until the whole cloth is covered with wax. *Cap* workers are paid by the piece so work is swift.

Uses

T HE production of patterned cloth employing *cap*-printing is both quicker and cheaper than with a *canting*, so it has become possible for members of all strata of Indonesian society to afford batik textiles. In modern times European factories have begun mass-producing cheap imitation batik cloth to cash in on the demand. These days most 'batik' cloth worn in West Africa is actually machine-printed in Holland.

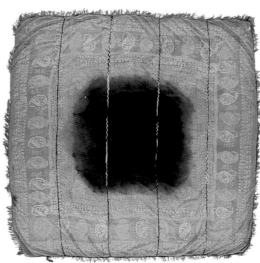

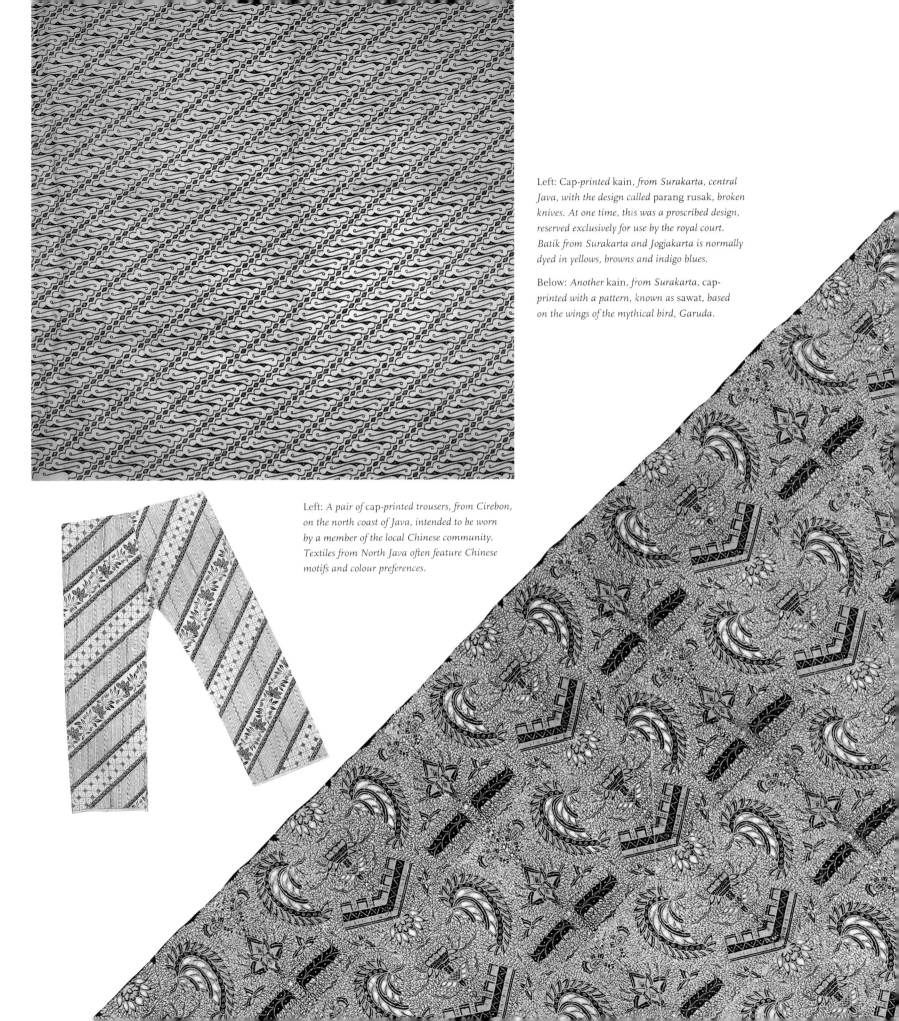

Left: Cap-*printed kain, from Surakarta, central Java, with the design called* parang rusak, *broken knives. At one time, this was a proscribed design, reserved exclusively for use by the royal court. Batik from Surakarta and Jogjakarta is normally dyed in yellows, browns and indigo blues.*

Below: *Another kain, from Surakarta, cap-printed with a pattern, known as* sawat, *based on the wings of the mythical bird, Garuda.*

Left: *A pair of cap-printed trousers, from Cirebon, on the north coast of Java, intended to be worn by a member of the local Chinese community. Textiles from North Java often feature Chinese motifs and colour preferences.*

MORDANT TECHNIQUES

A MORDANT is an agent, such as alum or urine, which is used to make an, otherwise fugitive, adjective dye permanent. Various techniques that exploit this principle have been developed for the decoration of cloth. The most basic method of all is to soak cloth in a mixture of dye and mordant or to soak it first in mordant and then in dye. This will produce an evenly distributed colour.

FIVE

Central Asian woodblock printing

IN Central Asia black dye made from an iron solution stiffened with flour or vegetable gum is printed with wood blocks onto cotton cloth that has been soaked in a mordant made from pistachio galls. An alum mordant is then printed onto the cloth which is immersed in a red-madder dye bath. The cloth is rinsed out to wash the excess dye from the unmordanted areas. The result is a pattern in black and red on a light background.

Kalamkari

IN the Indian state of Andhra Pradesh the makers of *kalamkari* cloths use a similar method. At Masulipatnam cloth which has first been bleached in a solution of dung is soaked in a mordant of myrobalan. Designs of birds and animals are then drawn or printed with mineral dyes mixed with gum which, on contact with the mordant, turn black or red. Further dyes are then painted on before being fixed by immersion in an alum solution. In the temple town of Kalahasti,

craftsmen paint religious images entirely by hand using a bamboo pen, or *kalam*, with an absorbent pad bound to the tip. The final background colours are applied by painting on a mordant solution and then immersing in dye, the reverse of the method used in Masulipatnam.

Ajrakh

A JRAKH cloth is produced by Muslim communities in the Indian regions of Kutch and Rajasthan and in the adjoining Pakistani province of Sind. The name comes from the Arabic word *azrak*, meaning blue, and refers to the dominant colour. Wooden blocks are used to print the mordant and a resist paste onto cotton. The cloth is then immersed in a red alizarin dye bath and a blue indigo vat. The mordanted areas take the red dye, the areas printed with resist remain white and the rest of the fabric is coloured by the indigo which is a substantive dye and needs no mordant. A similar, predominately red cloth called *malir* is made for Hindus in the same region.

Above: *A detail of the lining of a Turkoman woman's* chyrpy *coat. The pattern is the result of printing a resist paste of flour or mud onto cloth that has previously been soaked in mordant. On dyeing the cloth, dye is only absorbed by the unresisted areas.*

Below: *A woman's cotton shawl, from Syria, with a pattern of resists on mordanted cloth. Aniline dyes have done away with the need for mordants and in modern Syria patterns are usually printed directly in coloured dye or in negative using a resist paste made from slaked lime mixed with starch.*

Opposite, left: *Woman's cotton shawl, from Deesa, Gujarat, India, enhanced with embroidery. The light-coloured patterns are formed where a resist paste has been applied to stop dye being absorbed.*

Opposite, above, right: *Block-printed* malir *cloth, from Barmer, Rajasthan, India, made for Hindus using the* ajrakh *technique.*

Opposite, below, right: *Two* ajrakh *cloths, the one underneath is from Barmer and the other one is from Tando Mohammed Khan, Sind, Pakistan. A resist has been printed to create the white areas, then mordant has been printed on to take the red dye and the indigo blue has been absorbed by the remaining fabric.*

WARP IKAT

ABOVE, LEFT: TIED
YARN; RIGHT: DYED
YARN.

UNTIED YARN.

WARP ikat is reputed to be one of the most ancient of the resist-dyeing techniques. It is practised on the threads of cloth before it is woven, in much the same way as woven cloth can be resist dyed using the tie and dye method.

Technique

THE word ikat is derived from the Malay word *mengikat* (to tie or to bind) and is a method whereby the patterning of a textile is obtained by tying fibre resists tightly around the warp threads that have been stretched out on a frame and then immersing the tied hanks in a dye bath. If, for example, the original thread is white and the dye bath blue, the tied portions form a white pattern against a blue background. By tying up further sections of the warp threads, untying certain sections of the original tied resists, and then immersing the tied hanks in a dye bath of a different colour, a pattern emerges that is of four colours, the first of which is the original undyed colour of the warps, the second and third the colours of the successive dye baths and the final colour the hue produced by the combination of the two dyes. When the dyeing process is completed the yarn is woven up to produce a warp-faced, patterned cloth. During the 19th century Japanese craftsmen applied the *itajime* technique to yarn, a method previously employed for resist dyeing whole sheets of cloth. This involves clamping the unwoven warps between boards to resist the dye. By carving patterns into the blocks, as in block-printing, it is possible to create repeated patterns much more quickly and easily than by resist tying.

Materials

FOR climatic reasons warp ikat is usually woven on cotton, rarely on bast, although some interesting ikat textiles are woven in the Philippines from abaca fibre.

In modern times synthetic twine has been adopted for resist tying because of its excellent water-resistant properties.

Distribution

WARP-ikat textiles are produced in South and South-East Asia, Central Asia, the Near East, West Africa and Central and South America.

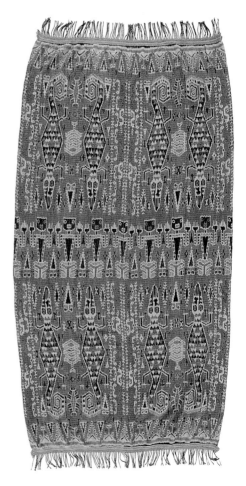

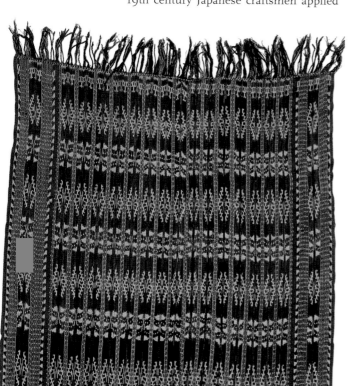

Left: *A cotton* selendang *made by the Lesser Blossom clan from the small Indonesian island of Savu. On Savu, warp-ikat textiles are made in various sizes and shapes, but normally using the same subtle colour scheme and patterns laid out in grids or rows. Geometric forms are most common, but some patterns show the influence of Dutch colonists in the use of floral and figurative motifs.*

Top right: *A warp-ikat* hinggi, *from east Sumba, Indonesia, worn by men around the waist or shoulders. Each* hinggi *is made in two halves, which are woven separately, and then sewn together along the length, selvedge to selvedge. Most often dyed in browns, reds and ochres, they feature images of monitor lizards, skeletons, chickens and sea creatures.*

Above: *An Iban woman's warp-ikat* bidang *skirt, from Sarawak, Malaysia, with lizard motifs. Iban textiles are decorated with abstract interlocking patterns inspired by local flowers and wildlife or human figures.*

Opposite: *A cotton mantle made by a group of Toraja women in Sulawesi, Indonesia.*
Inset above: *Iban woman in a* bidang *skirt.*
Inset below: *Women, from Uzbekistan, wearing ikat fabric known as* abr *or 'cloud' cloth.*

WEFT IKAT

WEFT ikat is a sophisticated process requiring more paraphernalia than warp ikat. Its origins most probably lie in the Arab world – particularly the Yemen, from whence it travelled to India and South-East Asia where the majority of its practitioners are still Muslims. Knowledge of the technique may have evolved independently in widespread locations, but it reached as far west as Majorca where a fabric called Roba de llengues, or cloth of tongues, is woven. The preferred medium is silk, but the technique can just as readily be practised on cotton or rayon. In most parts of the world weft-ikat weaving is organized on a commercial workshop or factory basis.

Technique

THE weft threads must be wound on to a simple rectangular frame that is approximately the same width as the finished cloth. This can be done by hand, but is now most usually achieved by drawing off threads from a rack containing twenty to thirty bobbins and wrapping them around a revolving frame. Threads that are to be given identical motifs are bunched together on the tying frame, and the resist patterns are then tied in using fibre or plastic thread. The tied yarn is dyed and as with warp ikat certain sections may be untied, fresh sections may be tied and further immersions in different-coloured dye baths may be carried out to produce multi-coloured yarn.

This yarn is then woven in as the weft on a plain warp using a semi-mechanized loom. Care must always be taken that each succeeding pick of the weft is correctly aligned with the preceding one.

Above: *Weft-ikat cotton sari length, from Orissa, India.*

A quicker method of producing multi-coloured weft-ikat cloth is now much practised in India and South-East Asia – different-coloured chemical dyes are daubed on sections of the yarn which are then tied over. This means the yarn only needs immersion in one dye bath. In Indonesia this is known as the *cetak* process.

Opposite: *The top right-hand textile is a vertically striped weft-ikat sarong from North-East Thailand. The other three textiles are exquisite examples of Cambodian silk weft ikat. The geometric diagonal trellis layout of the pattern is reminiscent of the fabled double-ikat weaves of Gujarat, India, which were traded widely in South-East Asia and subsequently imitated in Laos, Cambodia and parts of Indonesia.*

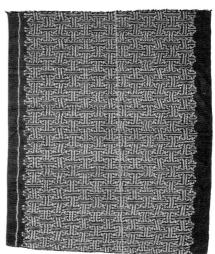

Above: *A Thai silk textile, dyed and woven with great skill into a pattern generated by small swastikas, a Buddhist good luck symbol.*

Left: Pidan, *a long figurative weaving in distinctly Cambodian style, featuring temples, dancers and elephants. This fabric is viewed on its side, with the weft running from top to bottom.*

143

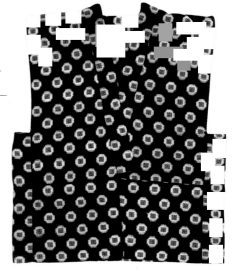

prestigious of all is *patola* – the vividly coloured and patterned, silk double ikat is now only woven by two families in Patan in Gujarat, although it was once woven in many parts of Western India and widely traded, particularly to South-East Asia where it became a symbol of royalty and was much imitated.

LEFT: DETAIL OF A JAPANESE PRINT BY UTAMARO SHOWING A WOMAN, DRESSED IN A DOUBLE-IKAT KIMONO, FOLDING TIE AND DYE CLOTH.

Technique

DOUBLE ikats are always woven on very simple looms in plain-balanced weave. *Patola*, for instance, is woven on a single-heddle, frameless loom set at an angle to catch the light. The time-consuming part of the weaving is the adjustment of each pick of the weft, so that the pattern dyed into the weft matches exactly with the pattern dyed into the warp.

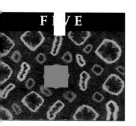

Compound ikat

WHEN both warp and weft threads are tie and dyed and then woven in plain-balanced weave the resulting fabric is known as compound ikat. Usually the warp and weft sections of patterning are in distinct areas of the textile, although sometimes they overlap to form random motifs.

Double ikat

WHEN warp and weft patterning are designed in such a way that they can be combined to form integrated motifs, the resulting textile is known as double ikat. This is without doubt the most complex and most time-consuming of all the resist-dyeing arts. Craftsmen can spend months tie and dyeing a pattern into both warp and weft threads and then painstakingly weaving the double-ikat cloth so that the pattern fits together without looking disjointed.

Double ikat is only woven in India where it is known as *patola*, on the island of Bali, in Indonesia, where it is known as *geringsing*, and in Japan where it is known as *kasuri*. In all these countries double ikat is a prestigious and expensive textile. Most

Above, left: *A cotton sari, from Orissa, India, with a warp-ikat border and panels of double ikat.*

Above, right: *A Japanese man's indigo-dyed cotton sleeveless jacket with patterns created by the* kasuri, *double-ikat, method.*

Below, left: *A double-ikat head cloth or* telia rumal, *from Chirala, Andhra Pradesh, India.*

Right: *An indigo-dyed cotton textile from Japan. The auspicious cranes are the result of weft-ikat resists (*yokogasuri *or* e-gasuri*) and the geometric motif is the result of double-ikat resists (*kasuri*).*

Opposite, above, left: *A compound-ikat textile from Guatemala. Both the warps and wefts have been resist dyed, but as the two patterns created do not interlock they create a disjointed, blurred effect.*

Opposite, below, left: *A textile from Andhra Pradesh, India. Here, it is easy to see the sections of compound-ikat pattern that have been created by weft ikat or warp ikat worked independently and the sections where the two intersect and register to create double ikat.*

Opposite, right: *Double-ikat* patola *cloth, from Patan, Gujarat, India, one of the world's most widely admired and copied textiles.*

Opposite, far right: Geringsing *from Tenganan, Bali.*

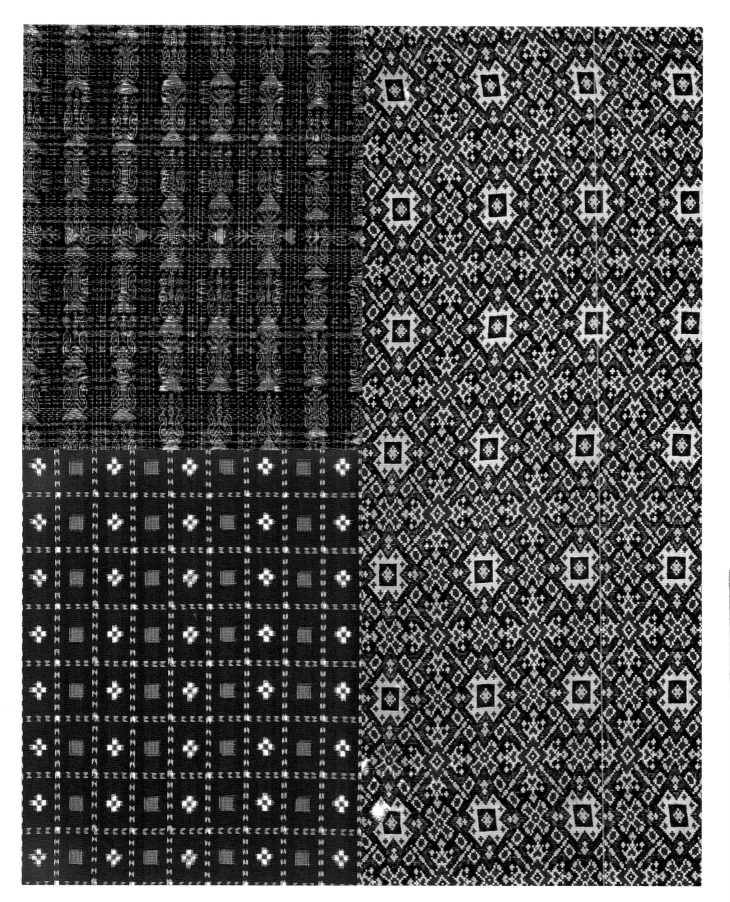

FAR LEFT: UZBEK
YURUK YASTIK
PATCHWORK FROM
AFGHANISTAN.

LEFT: PRINTED CLOTH
QUILT WITH APPLIQUÉ
MOTIFS FROM BANNI
KUTCH, INDIA.

BELOW: AN APPLIQUÉ
PANEL, FROM
TIBET, DEPICTING A
PROTECTIVE DEITY.

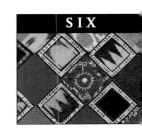

SIX

SEWING

SEWING

A<small>LL</small> loom-woven textiles are rectangular. This shape is exploited to the full and draped, gathered or tied in an enormous variety of ways for clothing and other uses. Prime examples of this are the Indian sari and the Javanese sarong. However, by cutting cloth into sections and sewing them together the range of possibilities, particularly for clothing, is greatly extended. The by-products of this tailoring are scraps and offcuts too valuable to waste.

Above: *Tailors outside a shop in the backstreets of Cairo, Egypt. Scenes like this can still be observed in many parts of the world, although the sewing machine has largely supplanted the needle.*

Above: *A cemetery on the South Sea island of Tonga where many of the graves have been decorated with lovingly sewn patchwork quilts – it was not only Christianity that missionaries introduced to the South Seas.*

Left: *A Sami mother and child from the north of Norway in 1932. These nomadic reindeer herders still decorate their colourful costume with bands of appliquéd braid.*

Right: *A Kuna Indian woman from Aligandi in the San Blas Islands off the coast of Panama. She is wearing a blouse with a mola-work panel and on her lap is a mola panel that she has just begun.*

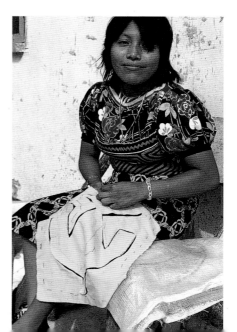

Above: *The fascination with Ancient Egypt aroused by the discovery of the tomb of Tutankhamun in 1922 provided the tent and awning makers of Cairo and Luxor with a boost to their income with demand for appliqué versions of tomb paintings.*

SCRAPS AND PATCHES

THE addition of a patch is the strongest way to mend or reinforce holes and vulnerable areas in textiles and garments. The decorative possibilities offered by adding patches of different colours quickly become obvious and over the centuries a repertoire of inventive techniques exploiting these possibilities has been built up. Textiles constructed from layers of cloth, felt or leather found in tombs at Pazyryk in the High Altai of Siberia provide evidence that sewing techniques such as appliqué were in use as long ago as the 4th century BC, if not before.

THRIFT AND POVERTY

POVERTY has lead to the recycling of old textiles and the exploitation of left-overs. From these humble origins sophisticated techniques have developed. Amongst these are *kantha* work from Bangladesh, the patchwork quilts of colonists in North America and the *molas* sewn by the Kuna Indians of Panama. In contrast, the dervishes of the Sudan, followers of the Mahdi in the 19th century, wore patchwork garments specifically to show their rejection of the material world.

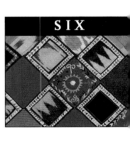

Left: *Before the First World War, an English housewife sits sewing outside her cottage in Shropshire.*

LEFT: A MEDIAEVAL EUROPEAN TAILOR MEASURING A CUSTOMER FOR A DRESS.

APPLIQUE

Applique, a technique in which pieces of material are sewn onto a ground fabric for decorative purposes, was developed out of the possibilities presented by sewing patches onto damaged cloth.

Technique

Hemmed appliqué is the simplest form of appliqué. Motifs are simply cut out of fabric and tacked onto the ground. Edges are then turned in and hemmed or slip stitched, leaving the ground fabric visible between the applied pieces.

More complicated techniques include reverse appliqué and *mola* work. The range of materials that can be employed in appliqué is considerable – including most notably cloth, felt and leather.

Uses

The bold and dramatic effects that can be achieved using appliqué have led to the adoption of the technique by martial organizations in the manufacture of uniforms and banners. The dervish army of the Mahdi in 19th-century Sudan dressed in distinctive patched robes which varied according to rank and status, while to this day the Asafo men's societies of Ghana parade spectacular flags bearing allegorical messages.

Patched cloth has also been used by many religious and mystical groups as a symbol of poverty and material renunciation. Amongst these were the Sufis who inspired the Mahdi and his dervishes.

SIX

Above: Sawtooth edging is a common appliqué device widely used for border patterns. Cuts are made at evenly spaced intervals in a strip of fabric which is tucked under to leave a row of triangular points. The strip is then neatly sewn onto the backing.

Top right: *Appliquéd dharaniyo used to cover a pile of quilts when they are not in use, from Saurasthra, North-West India. Depicted in appliqué on this cloth are a Tree of Life and elephants, lucky because of their association with the god Ganesh. Repetitive parts of the pattern are created by folding the fabric before cutting out the shapes.*

Middle right: *Chakla, or square hanging, with dense appliqué, mirrorwork and embroidery, made by Rabari shepherds in Saurasthra, North-West India. Between the ubiquitous elephants are stylized peacocks.*

Left: *A member of the Guild of the Young Folks of the Pear Garden. A Chinese male actor, playing a leading lady, dressed in a costume of boldly appliquéd cloth.*

Right: *Appliqué picture of peasants labouring in the fields in Colombia. The peasant lifestyle, however arduous for those living it, has an enduring appeal to tourists.*

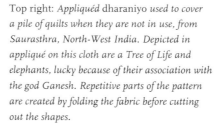

Above: *Ox-cart tent. In Rajasthan and Gujarat in Western India brides are traditionally taken to their new husband's village in a cart pulled by oxen covered with boldly appliquéd textiles. On the cart itself is a cube-shaped appliqué tent to hide the bride from prying eyes.*

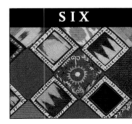

Left: *Tent hanging, Cairo. Ceramic tile patterns and appliquéd cloths are both built up from small segments and it is possible to produce similar designs in either technique. As tile work is more expensive, it is common for appliquéd tent hangings to imitate them in style and colour with arabesques and Arabic calligraphy.*

Above: *Kanduri cloth, Bahraich, Uttar Pradesh, India. The tomb of Salar Masud, a Muslim prince who died on Krishna's birthday, is a place of reverence for both Hindu and Muslim pilgrims. They buy appliquéd cloths, decorated with scenes from Indian mythology, to leave as offerings at the shrine depicted at the bottom of the cloth.*

151

Left: A Miao woman's jacket from Yunnan, South-West China. Yunnan borders Vietnam, Laos and Myanmar (Burma) and there are many similarities between the textiles of these countries, including delicate reverse appliqué work.

Below: A quilt, or ralli, from Sind in Pakistan. The patterns have been created by sewing cut-out shapes, mostly white, onto a blue base. Each shape has been folded two or three times before the cuts have been made to ensure some sort of symmetry.

REVERSE APPLIQUE

WHENEVER one shape is superimposed on another, as is the case in appliqué, a negative shape is also created by the background. This effect can be reversed if the top – superimposed – layer of fabric is regarded as the background and shapes are cut out of it to reveal the layer below. This is known as reverse appliqué or cutwork appliqué.

Technique

A LAYER of fabric is tacked onto a base layer of a contrasting colour. Cuts are made in the top layer and the edges are turned back under and sewn down with small stitches. Thread that matches the colour of the top layer is used so that the stitches will be invisible. The main pattern is thus created by exposing the bottom layer.

ABOVE: CUT EDGES ARE FOLDED UNDER AND SEWN DOWN.

Near right: *An appliqué and reverse appliqué cushion cover in the rusts and blues preferred by the Banjara of South India.*

Far right: *A woman's apron, from Yunnan, South-West China, with reverse appliqué motifs. The white fabric has been tucked under to reveal the dark spiral patterns.*

Below: *A woman's apron, from Yunnan, South-West China, with long ties. Sections of aprons or jackets are worked independently before the garment is assembled.*

Distribution

QUILTS from Sind and Rajasthan in the Indian subcontinent are often worked with bold floral and abstract patterns in a combination of appliqué and reverse appliqué. Sections of the top layer are folded and cut before sewing down to create a repetitive or symmetrical design.

Women of the hill tribes of China, Thailand and Indo-China decorate their costume and baby carriers with panels worked in reverse appliqué. These are often sewn so finely that it is almost possible to mistake them for embroidery.

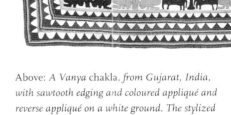

Above: *A* Vanya chakla, *from Gujarat, India, with sawtooth edging and coloured appliqué and reverse appliqué on a white ground. The stylized motifs include birds, plants, elephants and horses.*

SIX

153

MOLAS

OFF the Caribbean coast of Panama lie the beautiful San Blas islands. Here the Kuna Indian women wear blouses known as *molas* which are decorated, front and back, with appliqué designs made by a unique and very sophisticated technique. The finest *molas* are sewn for their own use, but many women now considerably supplement their incomes by selling *molas* to tourists. Kuna Indian *molas* are unique, although work that resembles them is produced by the White H'mong of Laos.

ABOVE: A *MOLA* PANEL DEPICTING A KUNA MOTHER SEWING A *MOLA*.

Opposite: *Detail of a mola,* in three layers, *depicting three stylized lizards.*

Opposite, inset: *A Kuna woman wearing a blouse with* mola *panels on the front and back.*

Technique

MOLA work is essentially reverse appliqué, but it can be worked with three or more layers of different-coloured cloth, portions of the lower layers of cloth showing through to the surface to form a multi-coloured pattern. Work begins by applying the central part of the final shape to a base and then superimposing and cutting away further layers until the final shape is revealed.

The effect can be elaborated upon by making up one layer of many colour patches which are exposed by cutting back to them on the next layer.

Cut-out cloth from the front of the *mola* is often counterchanged with cloth from the back. This results in the back and front having similar designs, although with a different colour sequence. Traditional *molas* are most often a deep red on a black base with brightly coloured layers between them.

Motifs

ALL *molas* are decorated with designs that are to some extent abstracted and stylized. Many of the most popular figurative motifs are of natural objects, flowers, birds and lizards. Some *molas* are illustrated with scenes from the everyday life of the Kuna people such as initiation, marriage and death, while others show episodes from their myths and legends. One story tells of the albino Moon Child who, during an eclipse, saves the moon when it is supposedly being devoured by the dragon-monster.

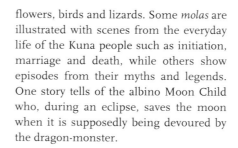

Right: *Four* mola *panels. Traditional Kuna designs depict aspects of their daily lives, such as wildlife, ceremonies and mythology. The puppy in a basket (above, right) shows the influence of the outside world.*

LEATHER AND FELT APPLIQUE

The excavation of tombs at Pazyryk in Siberia and at Noin Ula in Mongolia has shown that both leather and felt were in use in the 4th century BC for the manufacture of everyday items such as carpets and saddle covers, as well as magnificent hangings commissioned by the élite.

Leather appliqué

Leather has a naturally integrated structure so it can be cut without fear of fraying. This makes it ideal for use in appliqué and especially for the making of hard-wearing clothes and covers. Long, decorative, appliqué jackets and waistcoats are favoured by peasants in Eastern Europe, while animal and baggage covers in the same technique are widely used in Northern India and Pakistan.

Below: *A pair of* babouches, *the traditional Moroccan leather slippers, decorated with embroidery and leather appliqué.*

Above, right: *The status of this Hungu official, from Manchuria, China, is emphasized by the appliqué decoration on his coat. Similar designs were discovered in the frozen tombs of Pazyryk and Noin Ula.*

Right: *Detail of a Hungarian sheepskin coat decorated with tassels, braid, pom-poms, floral embroidery and leather appliqué.*

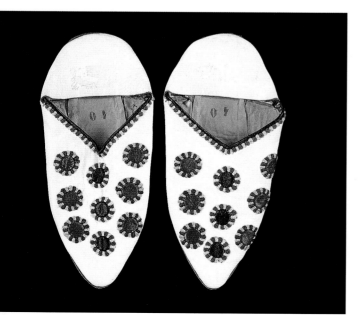

Felt appliqué

FELT is also a very suitable material for appliqué as the edges of any cut-out motif will not fray, and thus the motifs can be applied to a ground without the necessity of turning under any edges. Felt also lends itself to the art of counterchange appliqué where two different-coloured sheets of felt are laid one on top of the other to be cut. Identical motifs are cut out of both by simply cutting through both layers at once. The motifs from one felt are sewn into the voids in the other felt and vice versa. This process results in two appliquéd felt pieces of exactly similar designs, but the mirror image of each other in terms of colour.

Felt appliqué has traditionally been used by the nomadic tribes of Central Asia, such as the Turkmen and the Uzbek, in the manufacture of bags for the struts of their yurts (or tents), camel trappings and most notably for their counterchange floor coverings.

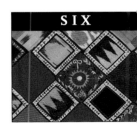

Above: *Three-coloured felt appliqué mat from Hungary. The crisp shapes have been cut out with a punch and then stitched together with a sewing machine.*

Left: *A Hungarian apron with a border of appliquéd felt strips. Women's aprons are frequently given special attention as they are thought to provide magical, as well as physical, protection.*

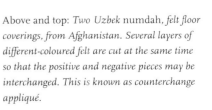

RIGHT: A FELT APPLIQUÉ MOTIF FROM PAZYRYK.

Above and top: *Two Uzbek* numdah, *felt floor coverings, from Afghanistan. Several layers of different-coloured felt are cut at the same time so that the positive and negative pieces may be interchanged. This is known as counterchange appliqué.*

157

BRAID AND RIBBON WORK

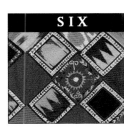

BRAIDS and ribbons are used in many parts of the world to add decorative details. The most complex and sophisticated technique is employed in China by the Miao.

Chinese braid embroidery

IN the remote mountains of Guizhou in South-West China the women of the Miao hill tribe create a unique style of embroidery, using silk braids of one or two colours couched down on rectangles of cloth. These panels are used to decorate the collar, cuffs, shoulders and lapels of the festive courting jackets that the Miao women so lovingly craft for their daughters. Folded and pleated ribbons are also employed to create dynamic designs composed of rows of triangles.

Technique

THE braids are made on a curved-top stand using weighted bobbins with eight threads of two-ply silk. The structure of the braid allows it to be manipulated into tight curves which gives it a textural appearance. The braids can either be laid flat or pleated to make a raised surface and are always stitched down with the same face of the braid showing. They may be used as either a single line, a double line or as an outline to be filled with flat or pleated braids. Two-colour braids with colour maintained as a single band on each side are not used for pleating, but solely as outlines or for zigzag filling.

Flat braids are couched down with zigzag oversewing, while pleated braids are held in place with a single stitch across the braid for each pleat. The sewing thread used is the same two-ply silk that is used to make the braids.

Opposite: *Sleeve panel, from Guizhou, China, with pleated braids and a folded-ribbon border.*

Opposite, inset left: *Miao girl in country costume, Guizhou, China.*

Opposite, inset right: *A Croatian couple with rickrack aprons.*

Native American ribbon appliqué

AFTER the introduction of commercially produced silk and satin ribbon by traders in the 1780s many tribes quickly incorporated them into their decorative repertoire. While the Apache sewed ribbons and rickrack braid directly onto their shirts and skirts, Indians of the Plains, Plateau and Woodlands developed a more elaborate style with complicated counterchange patterns built up in strips which were used to decorate women's robes and skirts. The Seminole Indians of Florida began, in the 19th century, to employ imported cotton ribbon to make patchwork borders for their clothing.

Right: *A Dong man's jacket, from Guizhou, China, decorated with overlapping strips of cloth pleated into triangles. Folding and layering is also used to work intricate silk panels for Miao costumes.*

Below: *Banjara skirt from South India. Skirts have been decorated with ribbon and braid by women from far-flung places, for instance, the Banjara of India, the Lapps of Finland and the Apache of South-West America.*

Right: *A glittering nuptial shawl, from Hyderabad, India, made of tinsel and metallic ribbon pleated and sewn onto a loose net base.*

SIX

159

PATCHWORK

PATCHWORK is a method of constructing a textile by sewing together small pieces of fabric into a geometric design. The patches are most often of identical shapes such as squares, rectangles or hexagons. Although it is most commonly used to produce the decorative top-sides of quilts, patchwork is often also used in the making of clothes, banners and other articles.

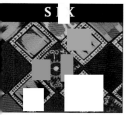

Technique

Two methods have evolved – one once widespread in Britain, the other popular in North America. With the former, now known as 'English piecing', pieces of stiff paper are cut as templates and the chosen fabric (a little larger than the template) is tacked over the paper. The separate pieces are then joined together by oversewing. Once all the pieces have been joined together the paper templates are removed.

As with the British method, the stitching of American patchwork is a relatively simple affair, the main difference being that a template is used to mark the fabric for cutting, but is not sewn onto it. The patches are joined along a plain seam using very small running stitches.

For ease of handling, patchwork is usually worked in sections, sewing together a number of patches into a block. In general, when a block is made the design is worked from the centre outwards.

Left: Rumal, *from Sind, Pakistan, sewn together from strips of cloth edged with sawtooth appliqué.*

Below, left: *English Victorian 'crazy patchwork' made from left-over scraps of material, 19th century.*

Right: *Kuba patchwork, raphia dance skirt decorated with embroidery from the Democratic Republic of Congo. The rectangular patches are made of alternately dyed and undyed raphia.*

Opposite: *A Meghwal* ralli *from Rajasthan, India. The use of geometrically shaped patches, for ease of construction, puts restrictions on the design that often lead to the creation of bold, colourful patterns.*

Opposite, inset left: *A pair of girls from Georgia doing their laundry. They are dressed in patchwork outfits made from brightly coloured Manchester cotton.*

Opposite, inset right: *A mendicant mystic, from Bokhara, Uzbekistan, in the patchwork costume of a dervish, a statement of holy poverty.*

Crazy patchwork is a method in which irregularly shaped pieces are sewn together to create a random, but hopefully attractive, effect.

Distribution

As patchwork is an ideal way to use up scraps of cloth left over from other projects it is a very economic and popular technique. Particularly in North America and Western Europe patchworking and quilting are very popular forms of needlework. As the American patchwork method lends itself to machine stitching, machine-sewn patchwork is now very common in many other parts of the world.

QUILTING

Quilting is the process of stitching layers of cloth together to form a cover of some kind. In colder climates they may be padded or stuffed with cotton waste, wool, feathers or even horse hair. In warmer climes they are often merely made up of layers of material between the surfaces. Quilts have from time immemorial been repositories for old, nearly worn-out cloth that has become surplus to requirements and quilting is often combined with patchwork and even appliqué.

Technique

The technique of quilting is basically very simple. Layers of cloth are laid on top of each other and tacked together, often incorporating padding or stuffing. Using running stitch or back stitch they are then sewn together securely around the edges and at intervals across the central area which holds the filling layers in place and gives a padded effect.

Uses

Quilting is most often used for protection from the elements – as warm bedding and clothes. However, padded and quilted garments have also frequently been worn under armour or on their own as protection against weapons. In sub-Saharan Africa both men and horses wore quilted armour.

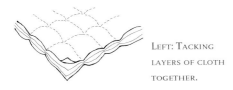

Left: Tacking layers of cloth together.

The decorative possibilities

The rows of stitching suggest their own decorative possibilities. The stitching can be sewn in patterns to give a subtle background pattern (as in the Durham quilts of North-East England) or the colour of the threads can be varied (as in the quilts of the Sindi Sami caste in east Pakistan on the border with India). Quilting has been brought to the acme of refinement in the highly figurative *kanthas* of East Bengal (now Bangladesh).

Kanthas

Kanthas are made up of layers of discarded white dhotis or saris sewn together with predominantly white thread. Where areas of pattern are required, they are outlined (usually in black chain stitch) and then filled in with running stitch in a different colour. Motifs are of animals, flowers, circus figures, scenes from rural life and even historical figures such as William Shakespeare, Queen Victoria and Lenin.

Opposite: *A distinctive* ralli *with rows of concentric stitching made by the Sami caste from Sind, Pakistan. Sami quilts are normally worked on a base of one or two strong colours and rely on the contrasting stitching to provide interest.*

Opposite, inset: *A cheerful Chinese man protected from the cold by a padded and quilted jacket of a type that has been used in the colder parts of Asia for thousands of years.*

Below: *A Banjara* rumal, *from Madhya Pradesh, India, embellished with cowrie shells. The dense quilting stitches give the cloth great strength.*

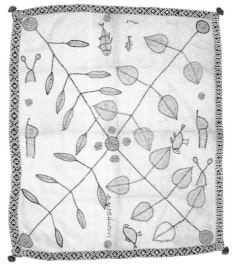

SIX

Top: *A fine kantha from Bangladesh. The patterns are picked out with coloured stitching.*

Above: *A kantha from West Bengal, India. Although this kantha appears quite plain, the background is worked intensively with white-on-white stitches.*

PATCHWORK QUILTS

A PATCHWORK quilt is a combination of patchwork, quilting and sometimes appliqué. Warm, functional and attractive, these textiles, traditionally sewn painstakingly from recycled materials, show the triumph of invention over poverty.

Technique

PATCHWORK quilts are normally built up from repeated design elements which are made from individual patches, so blocks of these are sewn up separately and stored until all of them are ready. They are then sewn up into the overall pattern and the whole fabric is attached to the filling and backing layers for quilting.

American patchwork quilts

THE patchwork quilt has a special place in the heart of Americans. Introduced by colonists from the British Isles who made a virtue out of necessity, quilts kept the early settlers warm in their log cabins, packed and cushioned the valuables of pioneers travelling west in wagon trains and acted as shrouds for the lonely graves of those who did not survive the trip.

Making up a quilt became a social event, an opportunity to catch up on news, eat, sing and even dance. Women would bring along blocks they had already made and would then collectively join them together and sew the quilting stitches. The motivation for making a quilt was sometimes charitable, but most often marked a coming of age, a wedding or the departure of a friend.

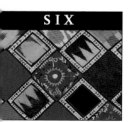

SIX

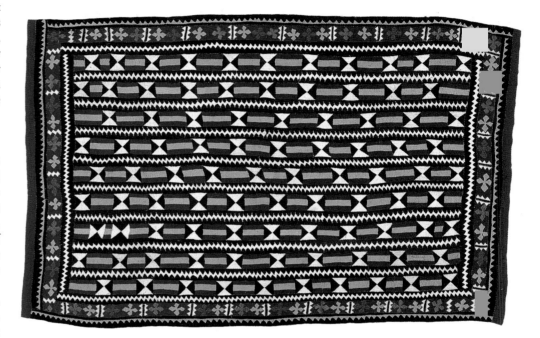

Top right: *An Amish 'diamond in a square' quilt made in Pennsylvania, North America, in 1880. The design is simple and powerful, but the feather-wreath quilting stitches are tiny and intricate.*

Above, centre and right: *Two quilts, from Sind, Pakistan, made by members of the Chauhan caste. The Chauhan use a limited colour range to create patterns with considerable visual impact.*

Above: *A tufted quilt made from patchwork squares by volunteers in Canada for the Canadian Red Cross and intended for use in English hospitals during the First World War. In North America quilting 'bees' have often provided quilts during emergencies.*

Right: *A 'log cabin' quilt made in England in 1890. The 'logs' are narrow rectangles of fabric sewn together into squares. In North America many patterns have developed based on this format. Frequently the square is divided into light and dark sections which, when separate squares are joined, form bold patterns of diamonds, zigzags and squares.*

Designs

OVER the last hundred and fifty years quilters have built up a large repertoire of patterns based on the repetition of certain motifs constructed from geometric shapes. These provide a basic design structure within which the seamstress can improvise. Popular patterns have evocative names like Log cabin, Star of Bethlehem, Tree of Life and Whig's defeat.

Distribution

STRIKING patchwork quilts are made in North-West India and Pakistan using triangles, squares and rectangles of three or four colours sewn in abstract patterns, but the most famous are those created in North America.

Stump work

STUMP work is a form of appliqué in which the applied pieces of cloth are padded out with materials such as horse hair or cotton waste to form designs in high relief. The three-dimensional effect can be enhanced with textural embroidery stitches and couching. The heyday of stump work was in England during Elizabethan times in the second half of the 16th century when stump-work boxes and other trinkets were extremely fashionable.

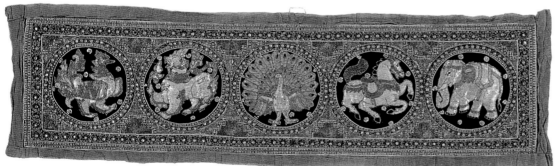

Above: *Two kalagas, from Myanmar (Burma), worked on a central field of black velvet edged with cloth saved from the discarded robes of Buddhist monks. The images of people or animals are padded and embellished with couched cords, glass studs, sequins and metal thread.*

Left: Nariyal, *a part of the wedding paraphernalia in Gujarat, India. It is made from a coconut wrapped in a bead net decorated with good luck symbols such as the swastika.*

Above, right: *Inca stuffed doll wrapped in double-weave cloth.*

Opposite, below: *A 'whimsy' made by Native Americans from the Tuscarora reservation in New York State, North America, in 1890.*

Above: *A padded Ottoman horse trapping embellished with gold thread, made in 1897 for Lord Curzon's visit to Oman.*

Whimsies

DURING the late 19th and early 20th centuries Native Americans in the Niagara Falls region considerably boosted their incomes by manufacturing 'whimsies'. These were stuffed and padded objects shaped like hearts or high-heeled boots and embellished with crystal glass beads. Their only purpose was decorative and they greatly appealed to *fin de siècle* taste.

Kalagas

IN recent times the most popular form of stump work has been the Myanmarese (Burmese) *kalaga*. Readily available to a wide tourist market in Thailand, they are smuggled across the long-porous Thai–Myanmarese (Burmese) frontier. Revived in the 1970s by aid groups, the centre of the craft is in workshops in Mandalay and Amarapura. *Kalagas* were made originally in Myanmar (Burma) from 1830 until approximately 1880, particularly during the reign of King Mindon at Mandalay, but even then they were partially an export item, though they never really caught on in 19th-century Europe. Myanmar (Burma) is a devout Theravada Buddhist land and *kalagas* are used as temple decorations. They often depict the story of the Buddha's life or feature the protective *nat* spirits or the ubiquitous Myanmarese (Burmese) elephant. *Kalagas* are padded with layers of cotton waste and the designs are picked out in lines of couched cords. Further embellishment is added with sequins and studs of glass.

LEFT: HAUSA EMBROIDERY ON A 'TWO KNIVES' SHIRT FROM NIGERIA.

ABOVE: BLUE H'MONG EMBROIDERED APPLIQUÉ COLLAR FROM SAPA, VIETNAM.

RIGHT: SATIN-STITCH SKIRT BORDER FROM ATTICA, GREECE.

BELOW: GATHERED SMOCKING ON A DRESS FROM MEXICO.

SEVEN

EMBROIDERY

EMBROIDERY

EMBROIDERY is the art of using stitches as a decorative feature in their own right. It is very versatile, does not require ponderous equipment like weaving and, unlike weaving where the patterns are perforce linear, curvilinear work is easy to achieve.

TYPES OF STITCHES

THERE are countless stitches in use by embroiderers all over the world, though they are all variations of three basic kinds – flat, knotted, and linked and looped. Flat stitches, such as running, satin and cross stitch lie on the surface of the fabric. Knotted stitches such as French and Pekin knot leave a raised or studded pattern on the surface. The classic example of a linked or looped stitch is chain stitch where the first stitch is held in place by the subsequent stitch.

Above: *A peasant girl, from the Czech Republic, wearing festive costume, which includes ribbons, lace, a printed shawl and considerable quantities of floral embroidery.*

SEVEN

Right: *A Meghwal woman, from Gujarat, India, embroidering a blouse front. In North-West India a large part of a girl's dowry consists of items embroidered by her and her family.*

Left: *In the home embroidery is usually done by women, but professionals, like this man from Pont l'Abbé in Brittany, France, have often been male.*

Right: *A Dutch girl, from Leiden, embroidering with a wooden hoop to keep the work taut.*

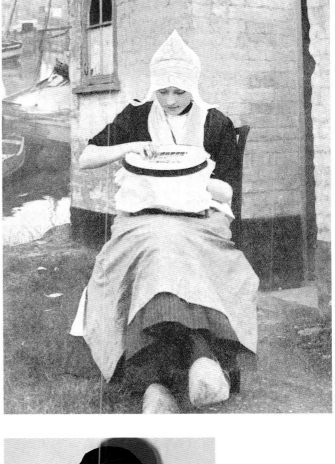

CHOICE OF STITCHES

STITCHES can be used in several ways to create different effects. They can be used to reinforce and decorate an edge (e.g., buttonhole stitch, blanket stitch and eyelet stitch), to outline a shape (e.g., running stitch, chain stitch or couched threads), to fill an area (e.g., satin stitch or leaf stitch), and finally, they can be used to create texture as is the case with French or Pekin knots.

SEVEN

Above: *Uighur women selling embroidered hats. Embroidered skull caps are worn, on their own or with a turban wrapped around them.*

Above, right: *A Meghwal woman, from Gujarat, India, drawing out embroidery patterns.*

MATERIALS

EMBROIDERY can be adapted to an enormous range of materials, but fine work requires smooth, consistent thread and a base with a balanced weave suitable for counting threads. The very finest embroidery is sewn on linen with cotton or silk thread.

RUNNING STITCH

To sew running stitch, the most basic of all the stitches, a threaded needle is quite simply passed in and out, in and out, through the ground fabric, giving the appearance of a broken line. It is a quick, easy stitch and in this form is used to tack two pieces of cloth together temporarily, to quilt layers of fabric together permanently, or to sew linear patterns. Running stitch is used for the decorative elements in the quilted *kanthas* of Bangladesh and Eastern India, and the background is often echo quilted in white on white, in running stitch.

Above: *A cotton coverlet, from Yunnan, China, sewn with white stitches on an indigo background in a crude imitation of Japanese sashiko embroidery.*

Below: *A detail of the border embroidered around the back of an Akha woman's indigo-dyed cotton jacket from North-East Myanmar (Burma). The simple geometric patterns have been sewn mainly in running stitch, with small amounts of cross stitch.*

Variations

THERE are many possible variations on running stitch, but it is most often used to make a line, sometimes solid, sometimes broken.

To sew Holbein stitch, a row of evenly spaced running stitch is worked in one direction. The direction of the needle is then reversed and a second row of stitches is worked to fill the gaps in the first row. Holbein stitch is used for embroidering geometric patterns, often in combination with cross stitch, and is the major stitch used in blackwork, an embroidery style employing black thread on a white ground

Opposite, above, left: *A kantha from Faridpur, Bangladesh. A variety of stitches are employed on* kanthas, *but the background is always densely quilted with patterns of running stitch.*

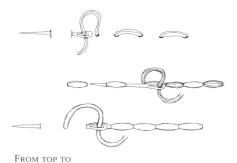

FROM TOP TO BOTTOM: RUNNING, HOLBEIN, BACK AND DARNING STITCH.

that was at its most popular in England in the 16th and 17th centuries.

Back stitch produces the appearance of a solid line on the surface of the fabric. This is achieved by taking short, 'backward' stitches on the surface and longer, overlapping stitches on the back. Two steps forward, one step back.

Darning stitch (not to be confused with the mending technique) is worked in rows of long stitches with tiny spaces between and is often used as a filler with subsequent rows worked in parallel, staggered like brickwork.

Left and above, right: *Wedding scarves, or bukhani, from Gujarat, India, worn by a Hindu bridegroom over his turban. The stylized images of elephants, parrots, flowers and gods are executed using coloured thread, in widely spaced running stitch on a lightly coloured background. Many of the motifs are intended to bring luck and protection to the wearer.*

SATIN STITCH

Sewing satin stitch.

SATIN stitch is used to sew some of the most beautiful embroideries as it produces a precise, shiny, silken effect, which is replicated on the reverse. Though simple in conception, the stitch requires much patient skill to keep the design even with a well-defined edge. The stitches must also be worked very close together to give the required satiny look. If a padded effect is wanted, the satin stitches can be worked over a base of tightly packed running or chain stitches or even over pieces of ready-shaped card. Satin stitch can be worked horizontally or diagonally.

SEVEN

Above: *Miao woman's jacket from Guizhou, South-West China. The panels of silk and the satin-stitch embroidery sewn onto the shoulders and sleeves identify this jacket as being from the east of the province.*

Above, right: *A curtain, from Rabat in Morocco, with the raised stitching typical of much satin-stitch embroidery.*

Right: *A eunuch, from Shanghai, China, before the 1911 revolution, wearing robes embroidered in satin stitch.*

Technique

THE needle is brought up on the left-hand side of the motif to be embroidered and the thread is carried across the design. The needle is then inserted in the right-hand guideline of the motif and taken under the fabric to emerge just below the beginning of the first stitch. The stitch is then repeated, making sure the stitches lie flat and parallel, touching each other.

Distribution

SATIN stitch is very characteristic of Chinese embroidery, although large areas to be covered or shaded are often worked in long and short stitch, a variant of satin stitch. It is in widespread use, being common in India, the Middle East, Europe, North Africa and Latin America.

Right: A tensifa, harem or mirror curtain, from Tétouan, Morocco. It is made of silk decorated with floral, silk embroidery worked in satin stitch. Silk thread is often used with satin stitch to imitate the smooth sheen of the petals of flowers.

Below and below, right: Sleeve panels from Miao women's jackets from Shidong in Guizhou, South-West China. Images of auspicious creatures are worked on these panels using satin stitch in a colour scheme that is predominately either red or blue. Embroiderers buy thin tissue paper templates of the motifs from local women specialists.

SURFACE SATIN STITCH

URFACE satin stitch can be used as a substitute for satin stitch. As it is only worked on the surface of the fabric, it is much more economical than satin stitch and is used to cover greater areas. It is not as smooth in appearance as satin stitch because the stitches cannot be placed so close together. Loosely stitched textiles of this type are very vulnerable to wear and tear and are usually reserved for special occasions.

Below: *Square hanging, or* chakla, *embroidered in floss silk thread by the Mahajan caste in Saurashtra, Gujarat, India. The long stitches catch easily and so these embroideries are often damaged.*

SEVEN

Technique

FIRST the needle is brought up on the right-hand side of the design outline, the thread is carried across the motif and the needle inserted at the opposite design line. A very small amount of material is picked up, so that the needle emerges just below its entry point. Then the thread is passed over to the opposite side of the motif and another tiny stitch is inserted. This process is repeated until the motif is filled in.

LEFT: SURFACE SATIN STITCH HAS A FLAT APPEARANCE, SINCE IT IS ONLY WORKED ON ONE FACE.

Above: Torans, *decorated with flowers, animals and gods, are made to hang over the windows and doors in North-West India. Elephant-headed Ganesh often appears in the centre. The outlines to be embroidered are frequently printed on with a stamp, but the Kanbi of Saurashtra prefer freehand designs.*

Opposite, far left: *Detail of a* bagh *from the Punjab, Pakistan.*

Right: *A woman's black cotton shawl embroidered with the red silk thread typical of the mountainous region of Hazara in Northern Pakistan.*

Below: *A silk* phulkari *shawl from the Punjab, India. It has embroidery covering so much of the ground that it is called a* bagh, *meaning garden. Yellow and gold are the colours most often used.*

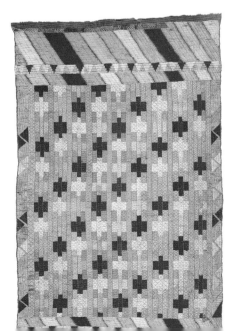

Uses

ONE of the most delightful uses of surface satin stitch is in the *phulkari* work of Punjab in the Indian sub-continent. *Phulkari* (lit. flower work) shawls were everyday wear for women in rural Punjab before Partition in 1947. Usually much of the ground cloth was exposed in the border and the field of the shawl, but for festive occasions a special kind of *phulkari*, known as a *bagh*, was made where the whole of the ground was covered with embroidery, so that the base cloth was not visible at all. On the birth of a girl, the maternal grandmother would start to embroider a *bagh*. It would take several years to complete and was embroidered with special care to be used later at the granddaughter's wedding after which it be kept as a family treasure.

Stitching ran both in horizontal and vertical directions in order to give a variation in texture. It is easy to imagine the effect light, playing upon the smooth sheen of the embroidered surface, would have on these juxtaposed sections of contrasting stitchery.

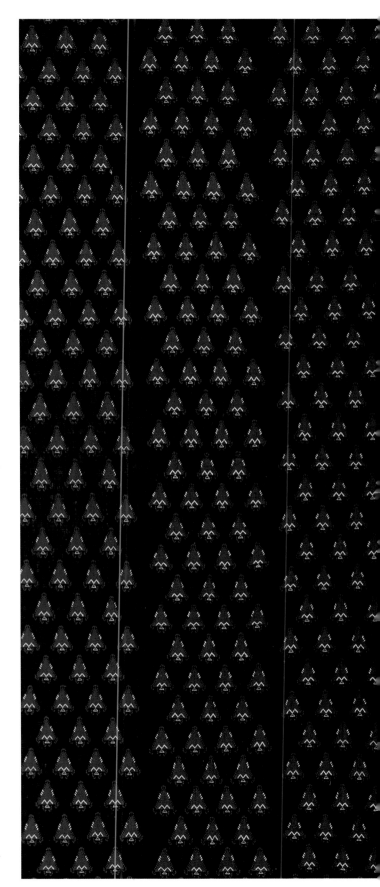

CHAIN STITCH

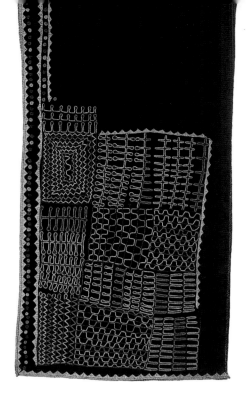

Chain stitch is a very versatile stitch with many variations and is in wide use in many parts of the world. It is often used to define lines or borders and can also be used as a filling and padding when a raised effect is required. It is ideal for linear work, effectively 'drawing in thread', so it is very popular for pictorial work such as the Kashmiri *numdahs* and Persian Resht work.

Chain stitch is one of the most ancient stitches. Examples in silk have been excavated in China and dated to the time of the Warring States period (475–221 BC) and earlier.

Technique

The needle is first brought to one side of the material, the thread is held in a loop with the thumb while the needle is inserted and brought up a short space along. The thread is then drawn through the loop, but not pulled tight, and the stitch is repeated by inserting the needle where the thread emerged from the first stitch, thus fixing this first stitch in place. As the stitch is repeated, taking care to ensure that the stitches are even, a chain appears on the surface which will show as backstitch on the underside. Chain stitch can also be worked with a tambour hook or *ari* instead of a needle.

EACH STITCH ANCHORS
THE PREVIOUS STITCH.

Above: *Wodaabe skirt from Niger. This is a superb example of the way in which chain stitch can be used to create flowing, linear designs. Great subtlety can be achieved by embroidering lines rather than solid blocks of colour.*

Uses

Because of its ease of stitchery and adaptability, chain stitch is in widespread use, along with its many variants, for the floral, bird and animal representations so beloved in rural communities for clothing and wall hangings.

Variations

Open chain is a very common and widely used variation as are double and feathered chain. Detached chain, often called lazy daisy stitch is used for floral motifs. The loops are worked independently and tacked down with a holding stitch. Chain stitch can also be combined with back stitch and when used in conjunction with coral stitch creates a laddered effect.

Above, left: *H'mong embroidery in chain stitch, from Northern Vietnam, using motifs that also appear in the wax-resist textiles of the region.*

Left: *A distinctive Hungarian style of densely worked chain-stitch embroidery known as 'Big Writing'.*

SEVEN

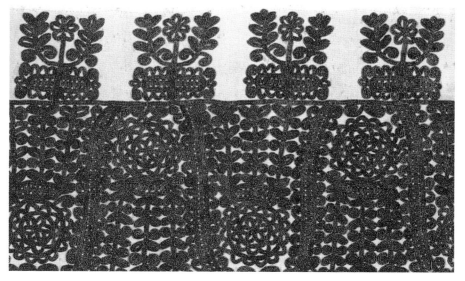

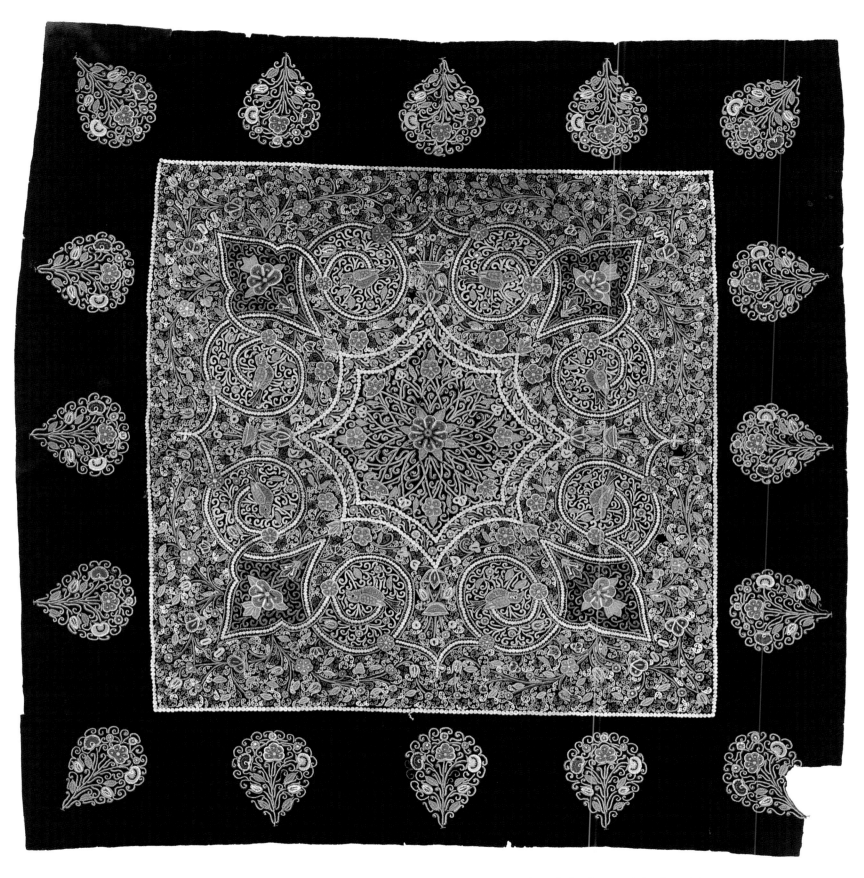

Resht work, from Iran, employing dense chain-stitch embroidery of flowers and arabesques on a ground of felted woollen cloth.

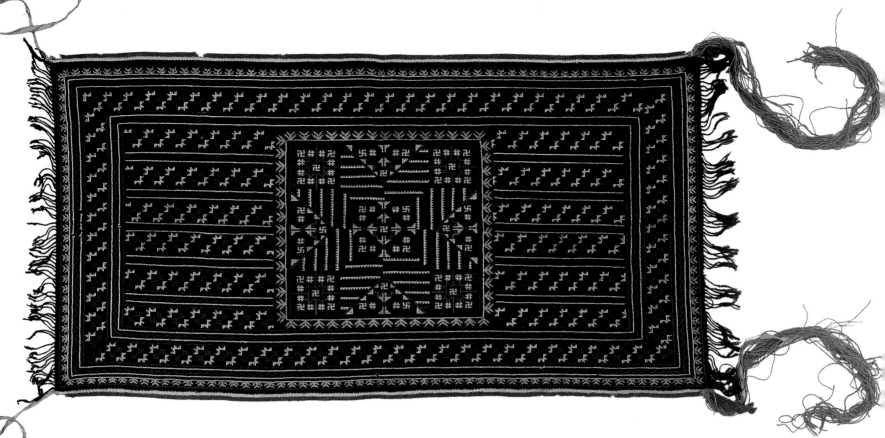

Above: *A head cloth embroidered in cross stitch worn by a Zhao bride from Vietnam. Cross stitch, having a regular, square shape, is used most often for formal and stylized designs or for patterns arranged in rows, as on this head cloth. It is also frequently employed for embroidering patterns that have first been worked out on a grid.*

Right: *Cross stitch is ideal for covering the surface of a piece of cloth as the individual stitches fit so closely together. Here, Sri Nathji, a form of the Hindu god Krishna popular in North-West India, is surrounded by worshippers and a herd of cows on a chakla from Gujarat, India. Cross stitch is a popular medium amongst the Jains of the region.*

Opposite, below, left: *A prize-winning English cross-stitch sampler. In Victorian and Edwardian times, from the middle of the 19th century to the beginning of the 20th, all young ladies were expected to learn embroidery.*

Opposite, above, right: *A Syrian woman's wedding dress, from Saraqeb, decorated with intense embroidery in cross stitch. Almost identical garments are found in Jordan, Israel, Palestine and Sinai, the main identifying feature is which part of the garment is embroidered.*

Opposite, below, right: *A wedding coat, from es-Suchne in Syria, embroidered with patterns of stylized carnation flowers.*

CROSS STITCH

Cross stitch is one of the oldest and most popular forms of embroidery. Amongst the treasures of the Victoria and Albert Museum in London are a set of delightfully naive panels of wild animals stitched in the 16th century by Mary Queen of Scots and her ladies-in-waiting in half cross or tent stitch.

Counted thread work

Many stitches, like cross stitch, are at their best when precise and regular. To achieve this they are often worked on a fabric with an even, balanced weave, such as canvas or linen, so that the threads can be counted and the needle inserted at exact intervals. Counted thread stitches are ideal for needlepoint or canvaswork.

Distribution

Cross stitch is probably the most widely used stitch of all. Ideal for neatly filling large areas with little risk of snagging, it is popular for embroidering clothing and can be found on the dresses of Bedouin women in Syria, Palestine, Israel and Jordan, the shirts and blouses of Balkan peasants and the samplers worked by young English ladies during Victorian times in the 19th century. In the Middle East cross stitch was formerly worked directly onto hand-woven cloth, but today sateen fabric is preferred which necessitates working the cross stitch over a canvas mesh. The threads of the mesh are withdrawn after the stitching is complete.

Different styles

Berlin work, popular in 19th-century England and France, is embroidered on canvas with brightly coloured German wool. Assisi, an Italian form of embroidery, uses red or blue stitches on a linen ground to cover the background and leave the pattern in negative.

Left: Cross stitch in a neat row of abutting stitches.

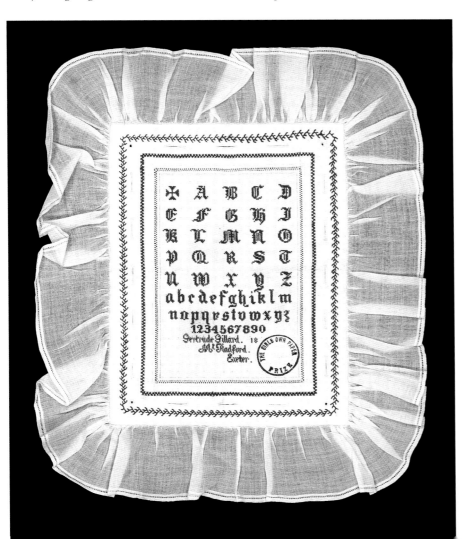

HERRINGBONE STITCH

Herringbone stitch, sometimes known as catch stitch or Russian stitch, is a very common variant of cross stitch, and has many variations.

Above: *A chakla,* from Gujarat, India, depicting Hanuman, the heroic monkey god, carrying a mountain in his right hand and a club in his left. The areas of solid colour have been embroidered in fishbone stitch.

SEVEN

RIGHT: HERRING-BONE AND CLOSED HERRING-BONE STITCH.

RIGHT: FISHBONE AND RAISED FISH-BONE STITCH.

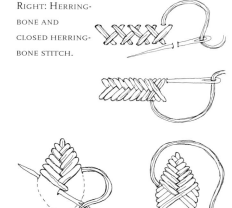

Technique

Herringbone stitch has a similar appearance to cross stitch except that the crossing over is not central, but alternates between high and low to give a trellised look. To achieve this, sewing proceeds diagonally up and down, as in cross stitch, but the needle is brought back slightly behind the previous stitch each time so that it will cross over it.

Distribution

Herringbone stitch and its variations are in widespread use. They are amongst the stitches used most frequently by the Bedouin women of Jordan, Syria, Palestine and Israel and by women living in the oases of Western Egypt, both of whom embroider patterns in red floss on their black dresses. Variants of herringbone stitch are very popular for embroidering hangings and skirts in Gujarat, North-West India. Closed herring-bone stitch is used in the Hazarajat region of Afghanistan for working bands and borders.

Variations

Closed herringbone stitch is built up by densely overlapping the individual stitches and completely covering the background which makes it good for blocking in a band of colour.

Fishbone stitch is usually employed as a filling stitch in leaf or petal motifs where the area to be covered is too wide for satin stitch. It is worked with the cross over in the middle of the motif like a spine. In raised fishbone, each stitch crosses from one edge to the other to give a raised, padded appearance. In open fishbone, the stitches only just cross the spine.

Flat stitch is worked in exactly the same way as open fishbone stitch, but with flatter diagonals.

Above: *An okbash made by the Lakai of North Afghanistan to protect the roof struts of their tents during transportation by pack animals. These bags are most often made from felt or felted woollen cloth with distinctive hooked motifs embroidered in buttonhole or chain stitch which is sometimes outlined, as in this case, with bands worked in closed herringbone stitch.*

Opposite, above: *Embroidered skirt worn by women of the Ahir herding caste of Gujarat, India. The Ahir draw on a treasury of motifs, like the flowers and stylized parrots on this skirt, filling in many of the shapes with large herringbone stitches. The more skilful and patient the embroideress, the more solid the stitches will appear.*

Opposite, below: *The border of a bridegroom's smock, from Ghazni, Afghanistan, embroidered with horizontal bands of closed herringbone stitch. The bands are sewn densely enough to rise above the rest of the embroidery. Red, green or white stitching on a white ground is typical of this area.*

Left: *Red velvet dress, from Kabul, Afghanistan, decorated with military-style metal-thread work.*

Below: *Montenegrin chieftain wearing apparel elaborately couched with gold thread. Montenegro became part of Yugoslavia in 1918.*

184

COUCHING

WHEN threads or cords are laid on a piece of fabric and stitched onto the surface this is known as couching. It is a widely used method of giving emphasis to lines and borders and is often executed with metal thread which is too abrasive for stitching in the normal fashion.

Technique

A CORD or group of threads is first laid in position on the base fabric. A needle that has been threaded with a matching or contrasting thread is then used to tack down the cord at intervals with a series of tiny stitches. The more the design curves, the more frequent the couching stitches will need to be. Sometimes the couching stitches may be worked in a more elaborate stitch, such as blanket stitch or chain stitch, for extra impact.

ABOVE: LAID THREADS ARE HELD IN PLACE WITH STITCHES.

Uses and distribution

As couching is an extremely popular way of decorating clothing, examples can be discovered on jackets, dresses and waistcoats in most parts of the world. The grandeur suggested by couched metal threads has lead to the adoption of the technique for the embellishment of ecclesiastical robes and military uniforms. The couched metal cords of the frogging on soldiers' uniforms was rapidly absorbed into the repertoire of embroiderers from Canada to Afghanistan as a result of the incursion of European imperialists in the 18th and 19th centuries.

Top: *Man's waistcoat, from Pakistan's North-West Frontier Province, with appliqué panels and couched metal-thread braids.*

Above, centre: *A jacket, from Southern Syria, with stylized floral patterns worked in couched threads.*

Near right: *A wide-sleeved dress, from the Red Sea coast of Yemen, with dense couching around the neck and on the central panel.*

Far right: *Palestinian dress panel, from Bethlehem, couched in cotton and metal threads.*

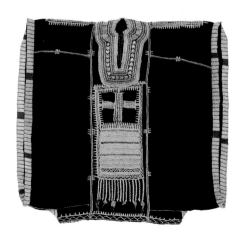

SEVEN

BOKHARA COUCHING

IN Central Asia, the walls of the palaces and hovels alike have for centuries been
hung with spectacular embroidered hangings known as *suzanis* (from the Persian
for needle). *Suzanis* are used to adorn the wedding hall, providing an awning for the
bride and groom, and to cover the bridal bed. The main filling stitch for the leaf and
petal motifs that predominate in *suzani* work is known as Bokhara couching.

Above: *Detail of a very large* suzani *from
Samarkand, Uzbekistan. An expert would draw
out the design for a* suzani *on several strips of
cloth which were then embroidered independently
by different women.*

Technique

A CONTINUOUS thread produces the
couching effect in this diagonally
worked stitch. First the needle is brought
up on the left-hand side of the motif to be
embroidered and then the thread is carried
diagonally over to the right-hand side. The
needle is inserted and the thread is drawn
through a little to the left and brought up
to make a small securing stitch over the
long stitch and then brought back to the
left of the motif to begin the next stitch.
The design is built up by repeating the
process, blocking in the whole motif with
the successive securing stitches touching
and appearing diagonally below each other.

Similar stitches

ROMANIAN couching is similar to
Bokhara couching except the couching stitches do not join up to form a
diagonal, but are normally placed to
form a regular pattern. This stitch forms
a good filling for large areas and is
employed, for example, on the large panels
of embroidered Hausa robes.

Opposite: *A* suzani, *from Shakri Sabz in
Uzbekistan, embroidered in chain stitch and
Bokhara couching. Carnations and pomegranate
flowers, symbols of fertility, worked in red on
white, are frequently the dominant images on
suzanis* from this area.

Opposite, inset: *An Uzbek woman standing in
front of an Urgut* suzani. *It has been suggested
that the swirling tendril patterns were inspired by
Chinese bat's wing motifs, symbols of happiness.*

Above: *A coverlet, from Tajikistan, with stars and
flowers worked in Bokhara couching.*

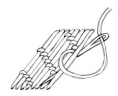

LEFT: THE COUCHING
STITCHES FORM A
DIAGONAL ACROSS
THE LAID THREADS.

Left: *An Uzbek horse blanket, from Afghanistan,
with motifs, typical of the region, which appear to
be a composite of ram's horns, flowers and sun-
wheels. Bokhara couching creates blocks of very
solid colour.*

Right: *A densely couched Urgut* fandalik, *from
Uzbekistan, for covering the brazier that heats
a room.*

Below: *A Kuba raphia skirt from the Congo (formerly Zaire). The rectangular patchwork panels are decorated with embroidered lozenges punctuated with circles worked in eyelet stitch. Kuba textiles frequently employ a number of different techniques. As well as embroidery and patchwork, this skirt also has patterns in the borders created by stitched dye-resist.*

Above: *An embroidered panel from an aska takwas, or 'eight knives', shirt, from Nigeria, worked largely in buttonhole stitch. The triangular shapes at the top represent five of the knives, the other three are embroidered at the side of the neck opening.*

Left: *Abigah, the son of the King of Lokoja, wearing an 'eight knives' shirt.*

BLANKET, BUTTONHOLE AND EYELET STITCH

BLANKET, buttonhole and eyelet stitch were all originally developed to reinforce edges and holes, but are now often exploited for their decorative value.

Blanket stitch

BLANKET stitch *(below)* is still in common use for strengthening the edges of woollen blankets. A series of stitches are made around the raw edge of the cloth, with each stitch linking through the previous one so that a line of thread is built up that will help prevent the fabric fraying. Blanket stitch is worked, often in wool, with spaces between the stitches. When used as a decorative feature it may be sewn in parallel rows or with stitches alternating between long and short.

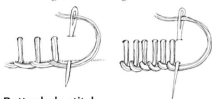

Buttonhole stitch

BUTTONHOLE stitch is worked in exactly the same way as blanket stitch except that for greater strength the stitches are packed tightly together, giving it a much more solid appearance. The hole itself is cut after the stitching has been completed. Decoratively, buttonhole stitch can be sewn to make bars, scallops and even floral motifs. Much of the fine, linear embroidery from the Hazarajat region of Afghanistan is worked in dense buttonhole stitch. Detached buttonhole stitch, which is made by working a row of stitches onto a previous row, independently of the fabric, is used for needlelace, raised elements of stump work and the neck decoration of Hausa robes.

Eyelet stitch

ALTHOUGH it is similar in appearance to buttonhole stitch, eyelet stitch *(below)* is used to pull open a hole between the threads of a fabric. In effect, a circle of stitches is worked, but between each stitch the thread is drawn from the circumference through the centre of the circle and back to the circumference to build up a sunburst effect. Algerian eye stitch is worked in radiating stitches with no ring. Eyelet stitches are common in Western Europe, North Africa and the Middle East.

Above: *A Tekke woman's* chyrpy, *from Turkmenistan. The hook and tulip motifs are embroidered in* kesdi, *a variant of buttonhole stitch.*

Below, left: Abocchnai, *or wedding shawl, embroidered in buttonhole stitch with silk thread.* Abocchnai *are made by or for women of merchant and landowning castes in the Thar Parkar, Sind, Pakistan.*

Below, right: *Panel of a man's shirt, from Ghazni, Afghanistan, embroidered in white silk on white cotton and featuring herringbone and buttonhole stitches.*

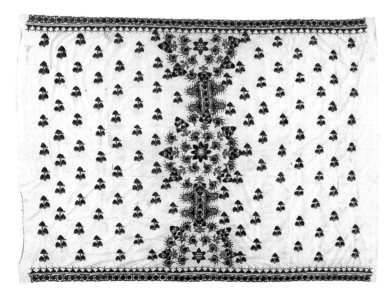

FRENCH AND PEKIN KNOTS

BOTH French and Pekin, or Chinese, knots are raised stitches employed when a textured effect is required. The size of the knot depends on the thickness of the thread and the number of times it is twisted around the needle. The embroiderer must ensure that a needle is chosen that will easily slip through the tightly coiled thread.

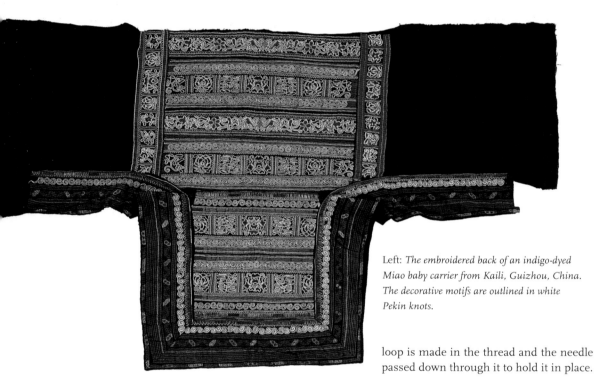

Left: *The embroidered back of an indigo-dyed Miao baby carrier from Kaili, Guizhou, China. The decorative motifs are outlined in white Pekin knots.*

loop is made in the thread and the needle passed down through it to hold it in place.

Technique

To form a French knot, the needle is first brought up through the base fabric and one or two turns of thread are taken around it before it is pulled down tightly once more into the base. Pekin knots have a neater appearance and lie flatter than French knots. Instead of wrapping the thread around the needle, a small

Uses and distribution

FRENCH and Pekin knots are used as filling stitches for relatively small areas such as the petals of a flower, or they can be used singly to provide emphasis, or where a dot is needed in the design, such as for the eye of a bird. Pekin knots are particularly used in South-West China for working linear patterns and outlines, often in white thread, on panels that will later be sewn onto clothing. The designs usually depict flowers, birds, butterflies and mythological creatures such as the phoenix. French knots are more common in Europe, for example in Sweden where knots in woollen yarn are sometimes sewn on hangings and cushions.

Other knotted stitches include bullion, coral and colonial knots.

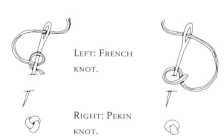

LEFT: FRENCH KNOT.

RIGHT: PEKIN KNOT.

Above: *A pair of silk-embroidered Chinese cuffs.*

Opposite: *A Miao woman's jacket from Guizhou, China. The bands of pattern, with Pekin-knot outlines, are embroidered on strips of cloth that are sewn onto the garment after completion. Baby carriers are also made in this way.*

191

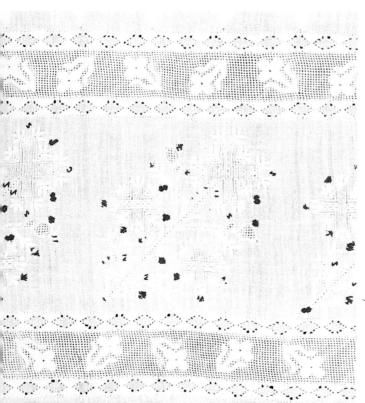

DRAWN-THREAD AND PULLED-THREAD WORK

DRAWN thread and pulled thread are two techniques whereby the structure of the fabric is changed by creating holes. Both techniques are worked on relatively loose woven fabric where threads can be counted accurately. A blunt needle must be used that will not snag on the background threads and the sewing thread must be fine enough not to show, but strong enough to hold the threads of the fabric with no danger of breaking.

Right: *A white cotton kerchief, from South Syria, with a border of multi-coloured drawn-thread work. Drawn threads are most often used to decorative effect in borders.*

Drawn-thread work

IN drawn-thread work threads of the ground fabric are actually pulled right out. The threads remaining are then pulled tightly together with stitches to create an open, lace-like effect. As this leaves the fabric weakened, the technique is most often used to work margins and borders on decorative items.

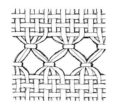

DRAWN THREADS.

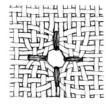

PULLED THREADS.

Pulled-thread work

THIS technique results in a much more durable fabric as no threads are removed. Instead, groups of counted threads are pulled together out of their original alignment by gathering them with stitches, thus creating small holes.

Distribution

TEXTILES worked with drawn and pulled threads are to be found in the repertoire of embroiderers in Europe, Latin America and many parts of Asia.

Opposite, above: *A drawn-thread sampler, from Mexico, showing the range of patterns that can be worked in this technique with the introduction of colour.*

Opposite, below, left: *The end of a Greek towel on which the rectangular border shows the netted effect typical of drawn-thread work.*

Opposite, below, right: *A Russian pulled-thread towel-end in which ties of red thread have been employed to create a pattern of horsemen.*

Left: *A textile made in Cyprus in about 1850 in which pulled-thread work has been used to create a geometric pattern of openwork shapes. Some of the solid areas have been highlighted with satin-stitch embroidery.*

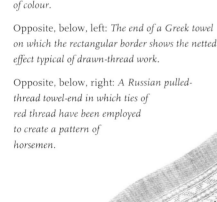

SEVEN

NEEDLEWEAVING

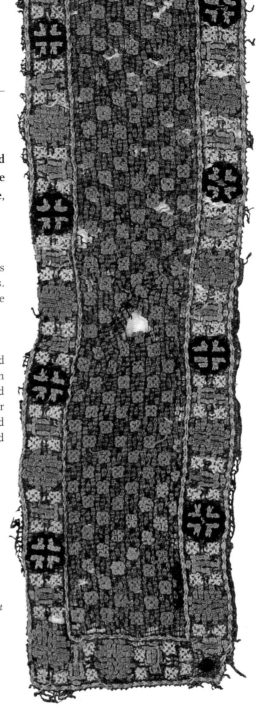

NEEDLEWEAVING, sometimes called Swedish weaving, is a variant of drawn-thread work and is used most often to make decorative bands or borders around the edges of linen or cotton cloth. Sometimes, to increase the range of effects possible, the weaving is carried out with thread of a contrasting colour.

Technique

THREADS lying lengthways along the section of cloth in which the border is to be worked must first be cut and drawn. Then the exposed edges are hemstitched which reinforces them and also divides the remaining threads into groups.

Using a blunt needle, or the wrong end of a needle, the top section is worked, weaving two groups of threads together at a time, passing the needle back and forth, over and under.

When all the groups of threads in the top section have been woven in pairs, the work moves down to the next section, and proceeds in the same way, only this time staggering the groups to be woven together.

When working on a large area it is possible to build up openwork designs. With the introduction of colour, quite complex patterns can be produced.

Distribution

NEEDLEWEAVING has been used to decorate shawls and table linen in many parts of Eastern Europe and Russia, most often worked in one colour only. Multi-coloured work can be found in the Middle East, Sumatra, China and even Mexico.

Right: *A decorative border from a Russian cotton towel featuring a checkered field and stylized floral border executed in coloured needleweaving. Needleweaving was also a feature of traditional Russian peasant costume.*

Below: *A cotton border made in England in about 1910. A variety of techniques have been used, including cutwork, pulled threads, drawn threads and needleweaving. The cruciform motifs that appear in diagonal lines at intervals along the textile were worked in needleweaving.*

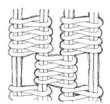

ABOVE: NEEDLEWEAVING.

SEVEN

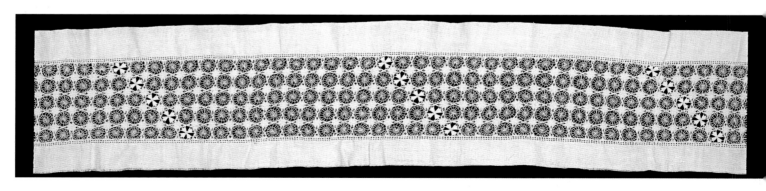

194

Above: *The end section of a Russian cotton towel. As needleweaving is worked around the warps and wefts of a textile's ground structure, which form a grid, it has often been employed to decorate the ends and borders of textiles with simple geometric patterns of lattices and crosses.*

Right: *A Chinese kerchief from West Sumatra. The ground cloth is an Indian tabby-weave plaid woven in Chennai (Madras) which has been embellished by drawing threads from the border and needleweaving a multi-coloured, abstract pattern of stars.*

WHITEWORK

WHITEWORK is a general term covering a myriad of techniques. The unifying factor is that, independently or in combination, the techniques can all be worked on white fabric with white thread. Whitework may be carried out on an opaque surface, such as linen or cotton, or, for particularly fine work, on sheer fabrics, such as muslin or net.

Techniques

THERE are three main techniques used in whitework.

Openwork relies on drawn or pulled threads to create holes that will appear dark in contrast to the white ground.

In cutwork, shapes are actually cut into the ground and then hemmed with buttonhole stitch to prevent fraying. Stitches of needlelace are often used to fill the spaces left by cutwork.

Classic whitework employs white stitchery to create heavy or padded shapes which cast grey shadows.

Above: *A man's embroidered smock front, from Ghazni, central Afghanistan, decorated with an exquisite combination of mirrors and subtle white-on-white stitches.*

Opposite: *A whitework panel from a christening robe sewn in Ayrshire, Scotland, utilizing embroidery and pulled threads.*

Opposite, inset above: *French women, from Valence, wearing whitework aprons.*

Opposite, inset below: *A Kabyle girl from Algeria. Whitework creates interest through the use of texture.*

Above and below: *Two examples of* chikan *work from Lucknow, Uttar Pradesh, India. Chikan is a form of whitework using predominately floral patterns on a net of loosely woven cotton muslin. A raised effect is achieved by executing the patterns in a variety of techniques including appliqué, pulled- and drawn-thread work and embroidery.*

Styles of whitework

WHITEWORK has been produced for hundreds of years all over the world and has developed many distinctive styles using different combinations of techniques. Hardanger is a Norwegian style using satin stitch and blocks of drawn threads or cutwork. Cutwork styles range from the dainty holes of broderie anglaise to the floating shapes of Italian reticella in which the amounts of background that are cut away are so large it can often be mistaken at first glance for lace. Styles of whitework sewn on net or gauze include the Scottish Ayrshire, Irish Carrickmacross, Dresden from Germany and *chikan* from the Indian city of Lucknow.

Uses

WHITEWORK has long been popular for decorating cuffs, collars and bonnets. In Europe, the finest work has been reserved for ecclesiastical vestments, bridal wear and christening robes.

SEVEN

197

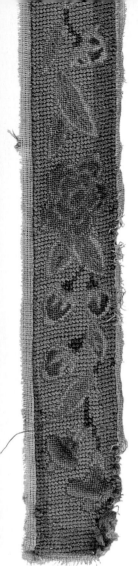

NEEDLEPOINT

Nᴇᴇᴅʟᴇᴘᴏɪɴᴛ, or canvaswork, is very ancient in origin. Sometimes called needlework tapestry because of its similarity to woven tapestry, it is used to embroider figurative designs in counted-thread embroidery stitches that completely cover the fabric on which it is worked.

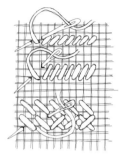

Fʀᴏᴍ ᴛᴏᴘ ᴛᴏ ʙᴏᴛᴛᴏᴍ: Tᴇɴᴛ ꜱᴛɪᴛᴄʜ ᴏʀ ᴘᴇᴛɪᴛ ᴘᴏɪɴᴛ, ɢᴏʙᴇʟɪɴ ᴏʀ ɢʀᴏꜱ ᴘᴏɪɴᴛ, ᴀɴᴅ ᴄʀᴏꜱꜱ ꜱᴛɪᴛᴄʜ.

Materials

Fᴏʀ centuries the preferred base for needlepoint was linen, but now the most popular base is canvas, a fabric woven mainly from hemp (the Italian for hemp is *canavaccio*). In the West, two different kinds of fabric are used as a base – one, a canvas woven of single threads, the other, Penelope canvas, is made up of double threads. Both come in a variety of fine and coarse grades. Historically, the threads used most often were wool and silk, but cotton has long been in vogue.

Needlepoint stitches

Nᴇᴇᴅʟᴇᴘᴏɪɴᴛ stitches resemble those used in other embroidery, but they are worked densely and must, therefore, be regular. Canvas is the ideal base for this sort of work as the threads can be counted easily to ensure that the entry and exit points of the needle are precisely spaced.

The basic stitches of many embroideries are the diagonal tent stitch, sometimes referred to as petit point, and the longer gobelin stitch, also called gros point. Longer still is the Byzantine stitch which resembles a diagonal satin stitch and is used to cover large areas quickly. Cross stitch is the best known of all needlepoint stitches and many books of patterns fill the shelves of European and American bookshops. The other major stitches are those worked vertically. These include the straight gobelin stitch and the longer Florentine or Irish stitch.

Types of needlepoint

Mᴀɴʏ styles of needlepoint exist, among them are Berlin work, which employs tent and cross stitch and wool yarn (the best used to come from Berlin), and Bargello work which uses vertical stitches in patterns of subtly coloured zigzags.

Far left: *English 19th-century upholstery fabric with a textured finish produced by embroidering in a combination of gobelin and tent stitch.*

Near left: *English Bargello work. Bargello, sometimes called flame work or Florentine work, has distinctive patterns of zigzags worked in long or short vertical stitches.*

Above: *Afghan* sai goshas *embroidered in cross stitch and used for decorating rolled-up bedding during the day.*

Below: *An English Berlin-work bag. In the 19th century the most colourful yarn was dyed in Germany.*

Opposite: *A dress panel, from Hazarajat, Afghanistan, embroidered with silk thread in a densely worked brick stitch. The lozenge patterns and bright colours are diagnostic of the embroideries of this region.*

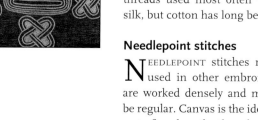

SEVEN

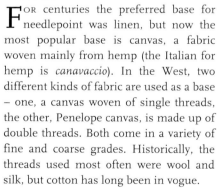

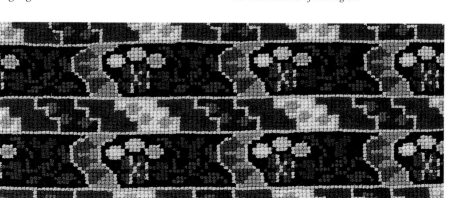

SMOCKING

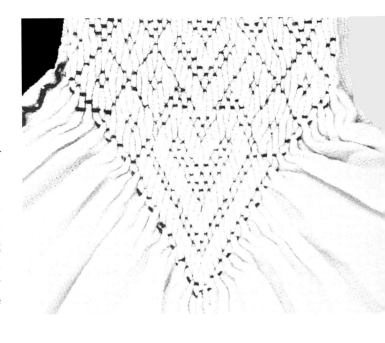

SMOCKING is a term originally applied to the technique used in the construction of the linen smock-frocks worn by agricultural workers in parts of England and Wales in the 19th century. These were loose-fitting garments gathered to fit around the chest by means of smocking stitches. The layers of cloth and heavy embroidery on vulnerable places were not only decorative, but also made the smock very hard-wearing. The patterns of stitches employed have often been interpreted as identifying a man's place of origin and trade. Such a garment, frequently made by specialists, could cost as much as a week's wages. Smocks were normally white, although they were sometimes blue, brown or olive green. The stitching was usually the same colour as the base cloth.

Technique

HORIZONTAL rows of dots must first be marked out on a piece of cloth three times the required width. A needle and thread is passed in and out of these dots and pulled tight so that the fabric is drawn into small, vertical pleats (these threads are later removed). A variety of stitches that are either decorative in their own right or pull the pleats out of alignment to form raised patterns of waves, diamonds or honeycombs are then sewn.

Uses

TODAY, in Britain, smocking is most often used on clothing for children as it is not only attractive, but also flexible. Clothing for special occasions, such as Christening robes and party frocks, has often been lovingly sewn for small children by doting mothers.

The use of smocking is also widespread in Europe and the Americas.

Smock-like garments

SMOCK-LIKE garments are found in many cultures. In Nuristan, Eastern Afghanistan, men wear loose, white, cotton shirts embroidered with black thread. The stitches create an amazingly diverse array of vertical bands of pattern between ridges caused by tight stitching.

Above: A narrow-necked bag from Portugal. Although the embroidery on the bag and handle is comparatively crude, the join between them is beautifully worked with tightly gathered smocking.

Opposite: A fragment of a smock, from Gloucestershire, England, with chain- and feather-stitch embroidery on the collar and shoulder and a panel of tight smocking on the chest.

Opposite, inset: The last man in Worcestershire, England, to wear a traditional smock, once the distinctive costume of many English and Welsh agricultural labourers.

SMOCKING IN
DIAMOND STITCH.

SEVEN

Left: A man's smock from the Hindu Kush, Afghanistan. The vertical bands of delicate black stitching pull the fabric into long ridges. Usually the neckline alone is embroidered with pink thread.

TAMBOUR WORK

TAMBOUR work was developed in the East as a quick method of producing embroidery in a style resembling chain stitch. In the late 19th century it became popular in the West for sewing beads onto fabric.

Tambour beadwork

WHEN the tambour is used for beadwork, the fabric is mounted with the reverse side up. Beads or sequins are threaded on and one by one are pulled up tight to the fabric as each loop is hooked up in the usual way.

Uses

As it is so quick and versatile, tambour-work embroidery continues to be a commonly used method of working linear designs on clothing and decorative textiles.

The Mochi cobbler caste of Kutch and Saurasthra in Northern India, who have been credited with the invention of this technique, use the tambour frame and the *ari* to embroider skirts, blouses and hangings in silk thread on satin. The designs are of parrots, peacocks, flowers and human figures.

In the region around Bokhara, in Uzbekistan, fine, white, cotton textiles, called *suzanis*, are embroidered, often using the tambour, as part of a girl's dowry. These exquisite hangings and coverlets are adorned with subtly coloured trellises of carnations and pomegranate blossoms.

Left: *A section of a silk* choli, *or blouse, embroidered in silk thread with a tambour and hook, by Mochi embroiderers in Kutch, North-West India.*

Below: *A large tambour-work* suzani *made as part of a bride's dowry in the Bokhara area of Uzbekistan.*

Opposite: *Detail of a skirt embroidered by Mochi embroiderers in Kutch, North-West India. It is the men of the Mochi cobbler caste who are professional embroiderers.*

Technique

TAMBOUR comes from the French word for a drum – in this form of embroidery fabric has to be stretched over a drum-like frame. Instead of a needle, a special hook or *ari*, rather like a fine crochet hook, is used to pull loops of thread through the fabric. As one loop lies on the surface, another loop is hooked through it. By repeating this process a chain of stitches is built up which can be made to meander around the fabric according to the desires of the embroiderer. This simple, but ingenious, technique led ultimately to the invention of the sewing machine.

SEVEN

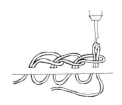

LEFT: LOOPING STITCHES TOGETHER WITH AN *ARI* HOOK.

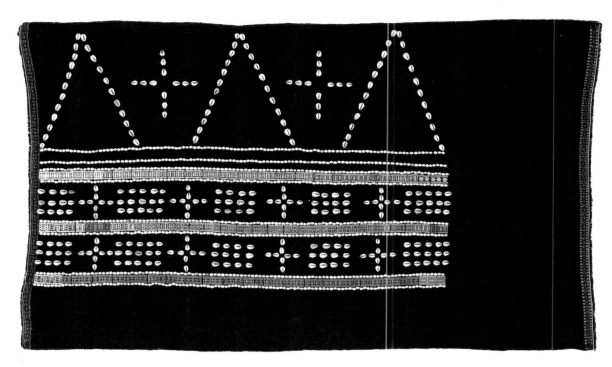

FAR LEFT: *OYA* BORDERS FROM THE AEGEAN COAST OF TURKEY.

ABOVE: A SHAWL FROM NAGALAND, EASTERN INDIA, WITH METAL AND COWRIE SHELL DECORATION.

LEFT: A *CHAKLA* FROM SAURASHTRA, INDIA, EMBELLISHED WITH MIRRORS AND EMBROIDERY.

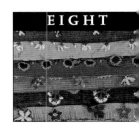

EMBELLISHMENT

EMBELLISHMENT

T HE coveting of shells, beads and shiny objects with which to adorn clothing and the body for reasons of superstition or vanity has led to the setting up of trade routes and the establishment of diplomatic relations between many different countries and cultures. Beads and trinkets were the essential luggage of the traveller or explorer for centuries.

SOCIAL IDENTITY

D IFFERENT styles of clothing are often worn as uniforms and are frequently enhanced with signs of rank, whether military, clerical or occupational. Metal thread is very popular for this purpose as it is opulent and eye-catching. Buttons, beads and medallions that glitter and sparkle similarly set the wearer above the common herd suggesting importance, wealth or power.

On a less formal level, humbler objects may be used to identify the allegiance or achievements of an individual – for instance, the scallop shell worn by medieval pilgrims, the white cockade worn by Jacobites in their bonnets or the eagle feathers, awarded for bravery, worn by the Native Americans of North America.

Left: *A Kiowa woman from the southern Plains of North America. Her finery has been embellished with wool and buckskin fringes, tassels, metal concha discs and bead embroidery. On her blouse are seven rows of elk teeth.*

Above: *Chief Ben Charles, a Blackfoot Indian, in North America, wearing a costume featuring a feathered war bonnet and bead embroidery.*

Left: *A Meghwal woman, from the Rann of Kutch, North-West India, wearing a choli decorated with rickrack braid, embroidery and mirrors.*

Left: *Using scissors to cut a sheet of mirrored glass into pieces suitable for* shisha *work at Limbdi, Gujarat, India. Shisha or* abla *mirrors are now made at several sites in Gujarat.*

Right: *An Indian beadworker in Rajkot, Gujarat. In India interlooping rows of threaded beads is the most common way of making a beaded structure.*

MAGIC AND SUPERSTITION

MANY objects believed to have magic powers may be attached to clothing to protect the wearer from evil spirits or to ensure fertility. Shiny items such as coins are commonly sewn on to avert the evil eye, while objects with shapes suggesting genitalia are considered to promote fertility and potency. In Central Asia amulets resembling ram's horns are widely used because of their association with vitality and power.

Right: *Detail of the bottom of a cap, from Samokov in Bulgaria. Many materials and techniques have been used to embellish this cap, including fringes, beads, coins, metal chains, shells and buttons. Bits and pieces are often attached to clothing, particularly the hats of children, to give magical protection.*

Far right: *An inhabitant of Mangareva, the largest islet of the Gambier group in the South Pacific. In the South Pacific shells are readily available in many colours and are used in the construction of a wide range of beautifully patterned adornments.*

VANITY

THE desire to attract the admiration of others is as common to every part of the globe as the need to feel beautiful or important. In the cause of vanity enormous amounts of time and effort are expended, cost becomes a minor consideration, anything goes. The search for new and different items with which to adorn oneself has led to amazing invention and creativity – not always with the greatest subtlety.

METAL THREAD

I<small>N</small> many cultures precious metals have a long history of being used to adorn prestigious textiles. Whether for court or religious use, or merely for ostentation, the use of gold and silver threads is used to show wealth and importance on ceremonial occasions.

Above: *Couched metal-thread panel on the back of a jacket from Guizhou, China. The metal thread used here is a long flat strip which means that only angular and not curved patterns are possible. The tassels are also made of metal-wrapped thread.*

Below: *Hama brocade shawl from Syria. A striking effect has been achieved by enhancing the black woven ground with supplementary gold-wrapped threads.*

Opposite, above, left: *The front panel of an embroidered wedding blouse, or* guj, *from Sind, Pakistan, decorated with spiralling floral patterns of couched, flat metal thread.*

Metal-thread manufacture

T<small>RADITIONALLY</small>, gold or silver is drawn through a series of dies until very fine thread is obtained. This can be hammered flat and either used to embroider as it is, or in ribbon form, in purl, or else wound round a silken core to make thread. Nowadays, in most cases very thin ribbons of shiny base metal or copper-wire silver gilded by electrolysis are wrapped around cotton thread. Plastic may even be substituted for metal.

Above: *The end of a Turkish towel decorated with trees and flowers embroidered in a combination of silk and metal thread.*

Metal-thread embroidery

W<small>HATEVER</small> the origin of the metal thread the techniques of embroidery remain the same. Most professional metal-thread work is done by men who, by and large, sew in workshops using a frame as this keeps the fabric taut and leaves the embroiderer with both hands free. Women use metal thread for folk embroidery extensively in the Balkans, the Islamic world, in India and South-East Asia and mainly embroider without using a frame.

EIGHT

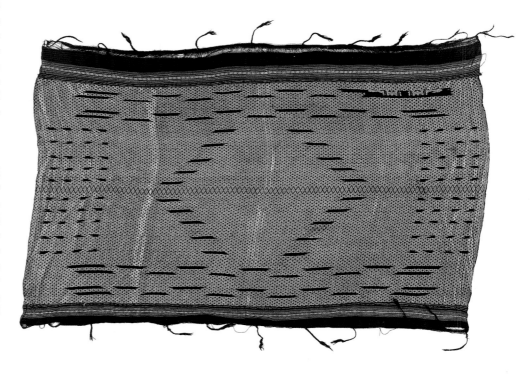

Right: *A tulle scarf made from beaten silver tinsel yarn on a net base, with patterns of lozenges, plants and dancing figures, from Baalbek, Lebanon.*

Right, inset: *A Palestinian woman from Bethlehem wearing a bodice and jacket embroidered with silk and couched metal threads.*

Metal threads are laid on a background and couched down with stitches in a matching or contrasting colour. To add bulk, the metal threads may be laid over a base of cotton threads or even wrapped around a cardboard shape before sewing down. Purl, a very fine, long coil of metal, cut into sections and stitched on like a flexible bead, is often used for borders.

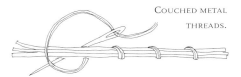

COUCHED METAL
THREADS.

Distribution

METAL-THREAD embroidery worked on costly materials such as velvet, silk and satin is used for vestments and hangings in churches, mosques and temples, and for court costume and furnishings for ceremonial umbrellas and banners and for animal trappings. It is also used in moderation to embellish the dress of the rich and wealthy.

Certain styles originating in the Islamic world have spread to India and South-East Asia and have their counterparts in Christian Europe and Africa. China has its own style of metal-thread work, which has spread to South-East Asia. The New World had no indigenous tradition of metal-thread work, until the Spanish introduced it for church and court use.

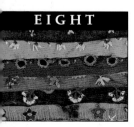

Above, inset: *A Rabari shepherdess, from Morvi District, Gujarat, India, wearing a mirrorwork marriage shawl.*

Above: *Meghwal girl's embroidered wedding choli from Sind, Pakistan.*

Right: *A mirrored Rajput toran for decorating a doorway from Kutch, North-West India.*

MIRRORS

MIRRORWORK embroidery seems to have originated in the Indian subcontinent. The heartland of the technique is the Indian states of Gujarat and Rajasthan and the adjoining province of Sind in Pakistan. All are arid desert areas where water is consequently scarce. The profusion of mirrors, known as *shisha*, used to embellish marriage and festival costume brings to mind the delight the people of this area feel at the sight of light on water. Although the abundant use of mirrors is a result of past trade with Europe (trading ships used shards of mirrored glass as ballast), the original reflective material used in embroidery was pieces of mica which can be found in the Sind desert.

Technique

THE mirrored glass made in great spheres at Kavadganj in Gujarat is shattered into hand-sized pieces and distributed to the small market towns of Kutch and Saurashtra. There, women of the peasant and pastoral communities take it home and cut it up with scissors into small, roughly square, circular or triangular shapes.

As the mirrors have no holes through which they can be tacked to the background cloth, they are normally first held in place with two vertical and two horizontal threads. The object is then to hold the mirror firmly and decoratively in place by the surrounding threads. The tension of these base stitches is important as they get pulled towards the edges of the mirror by the top stitching – if they are too loose or if the holding stitches are too close to the edge, the mirror will fall out. The top stitching can be of the *shisha* stitch, buttonhole, herringbone or cretan stitch, but there are numerous variations.

Distribution

APART from in the north-west of the Indian subcontinent, the technique of mirrorwork is found in a number of other locations, most notably amongst the Banjara people of the Indian Deccan plateau, in Afghanistan and amongst the Melayu people of Eastern Sumatra, disseminated no doubt by trade and migration.

Top: *A mirrored skirt worn by a woman of the Ahir herding caste from Kutch, North-West India.*

Above: *The leg of a pair of drawstring trousers, salwar, from Kutch, India, embroidered with mirrors and motifs of peacocks, parrots and flowers.*

Below: *The bodice of an Afghan dress decorated with couched metal threads and mirrorwork.*

Above: *A Banjara* galla, *or neck decoration, from South India, decorated with mirrors, embroidery and a cowrie-shell border. The Banjara normally use a muted range of colours in their embroidery.*

Right: *An intensely mirrored* toran *embroidered by the Rabari shepherd caste, from Kutch, North-West India, decorated with stylized flowers, parrots and trees.*

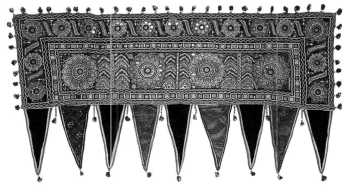

DECORATIVE FINISHING STITCHES.

TACKING DOWN MIRRORS.

COINS AND SEQUINS

Above: *A chakla,* from Gujarat, India, decorated with plain and coloured sequins.

Left: *One of a pair of Chinese panels, from Sumatra, which is so densely encrusted with gold thread and gold sequins that it gives a three-dimensional effect.*

Below: *A child's tunic, from Turkmenistan, decorated with talismans to avert evil and misfortune. These include discs, bells, beads, cowrie shells, amulet cases, containing texts from the Koran, and two rows of coins.*

Coins

SINCE money was invented by the ancient peoples of Anatolia coins have been worn as jewelry and sewn onto clothing as a form of decoration. Not only is this a convenient way for valuables to be safeguarded, but it is also a way of displaying one's wealth. Young brides and small children are still often bedecked with coins as in many cultures the sparkling and flashing is believed to confuse and avert the 'evil eye'.

Sequins

THE sequin was a small, gold, Venetian coin in use from the early 17th century. During the 19th century the name was given to small spangles used to decorate dresses. Made of very thin metal or plastic, lighter than coins and more resilient than glass, sequins are an inexpensive way of making a costume or textile eye-catching and glamorous, although, used in excess, the effect can be cheap and tawdry.

Uses and distribution

SEQUINS are normally round with a hole either in the middle or near the edge which makes it possible to sew them onto fabric. Coins, with a few exceptions, need to have a hole drilled in them or to be welded onto a metal loop. Sequins and coins are sometimes sewn on independently, as around the edges of Syrian headscarves, but they are frequently applied like miniature chainmail in overlapping rows. Some of the most common images depicted on the *kalagas* of Myanmar (Burma) are horses and

Above: *An apron, from Guizhou, China, with densely sewn, multi-coloured sequins.*

Far left: *A woman's cap, from Hungary, adorned with embroidery, tubular beads and sequins.*

Left: *Knitted money pouch, or* monedero, *from Bolivia, with attached coins.*

elephants which appear metallic due to the way in which they are encrusted with sequins.

One of the most outrageous uses of sequins is on hangings worked in the Karachi region in Pakistan which sparkle as if spangled with whole constellations of stars.

Right: *Spangled wedding hanging, from Karachi, Pakistan, with a base of cotton cloth worked in reverse appliqué.*

Top: *A Balouch* juval *for storing and transporting a family's belongings. The yarn of the tassels has been threaded through blue beads and seashells.*

Left: *A dress from the Siwa oasis in Egypt. Although Siwa is isolated and a long way from the sea, shells are still a common costume accessory.*

Right: *A Kailash woman's headdress, from Chitral, Pakistan, decorated with cowrie shells.*

SHELLS

SINCE prehistoric times shells have been used for jewelry and the embellishment of clothing. Whether whole, as beads or cut into discs, they have been employed for decoration in virtually every corner of the globe and have sometimes travelled vast distances from their places of origin as trade items. Many different shells have been used, but a few are worthy of special comment.

Cowrie shells

THE shell of the cowrie, *Cypraea moneta*, which is abundant in the Indian Ocean, has been used in parts of Africa and Southern Asia as a form of currency for 4,000 years, partly because of its intrinsic beauty and convenient size, but mainly for magical reasons. The aperture of the cowrie is considered to resemble a woman's sexual parts and therefore, according to the theory of sympathetic magic, the carrying or wearing of the shells should ensure fertility. The shape of the shell has also been interpreted as resembling an eye and eye-shaped beads and talismans are considered capable of averting the force known as the evil eye. Cowries are in use on textiles as far from the ocean as Tibet.

Mother-of-pearl

THE innermost layer of a shell, the nacreous layer, is made up of many thin coats of crystals. The softly reflective nacre of three shells in particular is so beautiful that it is known as mother-of-pearl. These three shells are the pearl-oyster, *Pinctada margaritifera*, and two univalve shells, *Trochus niloticus* and *Turbo marmoratus*.

Mother-of-pearl is surprisingly tough and can be cut, ground, polished or drilled. Many artefacts have been decorated with it, but its most common use is in the form of pearl buttons which are not only used as fastenings, but are also sewn onto textiles purely as decoration in many countries. They have been employed by such diverse groups as the Pearly Kings of London and the hill peoples of Kohistan in Pakistan.

Wampum

WAMPUM beads were used by the indigenous peoples of North America as currency four hundred years ago, if not before. Belts woven with different arrangements of wampum were also used to keep records and send messages. The most commonly used shells were the Quahog clam, *Mercenaria mercenaria*, prized for its purple colour, whelks and, in California, the iridescent abalone, *Haliotis*. With the coming of settlers and traders from Europe, wampum were gradually superseded by glass 'pony' beads.

Top: *A Bilaan blouse from Mindanao in the Philippines. The patterns are made up from hundreds of pearly sequins cut and ground from the lustrous nacreous layer of seashells.*

Above: *A Banjara* chakla, *from South India, embroidered with eye-dazzling zigzag patterns. Banjara textiles frequently make use of cowrie shells in fringes and tassels or sometimes sewn down to form a row or, as on this* chakla, *a rosette.*

Left: *A choli made by the Chauhan caste of carters from Sind, Pakistan, embellished with mirrors and hundreds of tiny shells.*

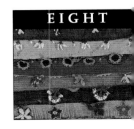

EIGHT

215

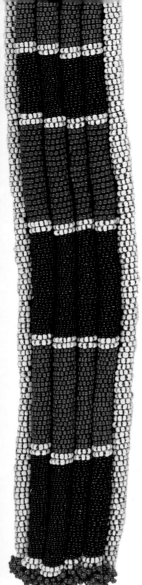

BEAD EMBROIDERY

BEADS made of stone and animal teeth found at La Quina in France have been dated back to 38,000 BC. The use of beads is found in every inhabited place on earth and every conceivable material has been used in their manufacture including glass, metal, wood, shell, plastic, seeds, clay and resin. Beads are most commonly used for making jewelry, but are frequently used in embroidery or even woven into a form of fabric on a loom.

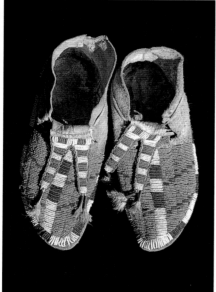

Far left: A Zulu bead belt, from Southern Africa.

Near left: Sioux moccasins made in about 1890. After the arrival of white traders in North America, European glass beads quickly replaced porcupine quills and shell beads as decoration on the clothing of Plains Indians.

Right: The beaded cap and waistcoat of a Sarakat shepherd boy from the Macedonian region of Greece.

Technique

THERE are three main ways to embroider with beads. Firstly, each bead may be sewn on individually by passing a threaded needle through it and then through the backing. The second method is to use lazy stitch which involves passing the needle through several beads before passing a stitch through the backing. Finally, a couching stitch may be used to tack down a thread onto which a number of beads have already been strung.

Densely sewn, bead-encrusted textiles are common in Africa south of the Sahara, Indonesia and Polynesia.

Distribution

GLOBAL disparity in the availability of materials, the development of diverse techniques in different regions and the

BACK STITCH.

LAZY STITCH.

COUCHING STITCH.

Magic

IN many places the embellishment of a textile with beads is considered to be auspicious. Blue beads in particular are considered good protection against the evil eye and are commonly used as edgings in the Middle East and in Central Asia. Red is the colour of life and red beads are therefore widely used to ensure fertility and vitality.

vagaries of local taste have meant that beads have been one of the most widely traded commodities of all time. Gold and ivory from Africa, precious stones from India, amber from the Baltic, glass from Venice, jade from the East, lapis lazuli from Afghanistan and many other prized substances have travelled thousands of miles and influenced the rise and fall of empires. Manhattan island, the site of New York City, was acquired from the Mohawk Indians for a handful of trade goods which included Venetian glass beads.

A Bilaan jacket, from Mindanao in the Philippines, decorated with white beads.

Opposite: A panel of embroidered glass beadwork, from Hardanger, worn on the bodice of the Norwegian national costume as shown in the inset.

BEAD WEAVING

A<small>N</small> alternative to sewing beads onto a backing is to weave with them. This decorative technique is a popular method of working decorative belts and bands in East Africa, particularly amongst the Kikuyu and the Masai who work mainly with white and red. This is also how wampum and decorative beadwork was constructed by the indigenous peoples of North America. It is possible to construct a beaded fabric purely with a needle and thread, but to facilitate the task a bead or bow loom can be employed.

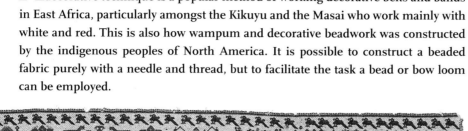

The bead loom

A<small>NUMBER</small> of warp threads are strung on the loom according to the width required. The frame of the loom is bent like a bow to keep the warps taut. The weft is threaded with beads and passed underneath so that one bead lies between each pair of warps. Using a needle, the weft is then passed back through the beads, but this time above the warps. This process is repeated, back and forth, varying the sequence of the beads to build

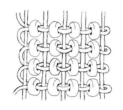

LEFT: LOOM-WOVEN BEADS.

Above, left: *Mahajan beadwork from Gujarat, India.*

Above, right: *Woven beadwork bag from Timor.*

Right: *A beadwork sash of about 1900, possibly Apache, woven in New Mexico on a loom.*

Below, left: *Mahajan beaded* ganeshtapan *from Gujarat, India.*

Below: *Bohemian knitted beadwork purse.*

up the pattern. Although the structure dictates a geometric arrangement, an astounding variety of representational and symbolic designs can be found.

Other techniques

ONCE beads have been threaded up, it is actually possible to employ a large number of techniques to construct a fabric incorporating them. The ground structure can be woven, netted, crocheted, knitted, looped or knotted.

Above, right: *A Basuto girl in the beaded costume once worn by Basuto and Zulu women in Southern Africa.*

Above, far right: *Two Zulu or Xhosa woven bead aprons from South Africa. Part of the courtship ritual of the Zulus was the weaving of beaded 'love letters' by teenage girls which were given to young men. The arrangement and colouring of the beads was used to convey an allegorical message.*

Below: *Beadwork* bidang *skirts and shellwork jackets worn by Taman women from Putussibau, Upper Kapuas River, Kalimantan, Indonesia.*

Right: *A Kenyah Dyak bag, from Sarawak, Malaysia, beaded with the convoluted monster motifs that appear on weavings, carvings and paintings of the region.*

EIGHT

FEATHERS

APART from skins, hides and wool, many parts of animals are used in the construction and decoration of textiles – bones, teeth, claws, hair, beetles' wing cases and feathers. Featherwork is widespread and although it is at its most colourful in the tropical and equatorial regions of the world, such as New Guinea and the Amazon rain forest, where the plumage of birds is most brilliant, the technique is at its most refined in New Zealand and North America. Even in the British Isles, feathers have often been in great demand as a fashion item and in Victorian times in the 19th century the popularity of feather muffs brought about the virtual extinction of the bittern. Today, the threat to bird life continues, for instance, in New Guinea where birds of paradise are endangered because of their beautiful plumage.

Techniques

LARGE and distinctive feathers have often been used in the construction of headdresses to show status and achievement – as amongst the Sioux Indians of the North American Plains or the Ayoreode of Bolivia, but the more subtle techniques developed by the Native Americans of California include gluing, stitching, appliqué and weaving. The Hupa and Yurok used whole woodpecker skins and glued them to deerskin to make headbands, while in central California individual feathers were sewn together in strips to form bands. The Pomo Indians also made baskets and even blankets in which feathers were incorporated into the structure by twining or weaving.

Maori feather cloaks

FOR centuries the Maoris of New Zealand have woven rain capes from the leaves of *Phormium tenax*, New Zealand flax, which are similar to those made by the Japanese from rice straw. Cloaks incorporating feathers into the borders were sometimes made, but it was not until the late 19th century that they began to weave cloaks entirely covered in the feathers of kiwis and other indigenous birds. These garments are called *Kaha Hururhuru* by the Maori.

Weaving is a secretive process amongst the Maoris and has not only survived the deprivations of colonization, but has also been enjoying a revival along with other traditions including wood carving and the Maori language. A foundation cord is stretched between two wooden pegs and warps are suspended from it. The wefts are then twined from left to right around the warps in a variety of ways, using the fingers. The quills of feathers are twined in as weaving progresses and secured by bending the ends over and twining that in too. An average feather cloak may take a year to make.

Above: A Sioux chief, from North America, and his wife in full regalia, including an impressive, eagle-feather war bonnet.

METHODS OF ATTACHING FEATHERS IN PERU (ABOVE, LEFT), NEW GUINEA (ABOVE, RIGHT) AND NEW ZEALAND (LEFT).

Above, left: A Plains Indian eagle-feather head decoration from about 1850, of a type favoured by the Apache.

Opposite: Kaha Hururhuru, a Maori feather cloak from New Zealand. The ground structure of this cloak is a weft-twined fabric of Phormium tenax fibres.

Opposite, inset above: 'Te Kawau and his nephew Orokai', by George French Angas, published in 'New Zealanders Illustrated', 1847.

Opposite, inset below: Two Maori girls wearing feather cloaks.

BELOW, RIGHT: AZTEC FEATHER WORKERS, FROM A 16TH-CENTURY CODEX.

EIGHT

PORCUPINE QUILLS

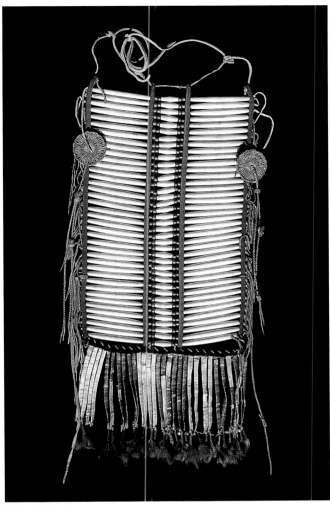

BEFORE the introduction of glass beads by white traders and settlers porcupine quills were one of the major decorative accessories of the indigenous North American peoples, particularly on the Plains and in the woodlands of the north-east, where the American porcupine lives. The quills, which are usually about two or three inches long, may be dyed before use as decoration for clothing, footwear, pouches or animal trappings.

Techniques

OCCASIONALLY porcupine quills may be woven together, but more often they are stitched onto brain-tanned leather, plaited or wrapped around a rawhide thong. The two latter techniques are normally used for decorating objects and utensils rather than textiles. Traditionally, immediately prior to use, the quills are softened in the mouth before being flattened by pulling between the teeth.

Embroidery

THE basic technique used in porcupine-quill embroidery is to sew down the quill and then fold it back to hide the stitch. The quill is bent back and forth and sewn down at each fold. This will produce a texture of bands or zigzags depending on whether the quill is folded back over or under itself. By introducing different-coloured quills at strategic intervals, a geometric pattern can be built up.

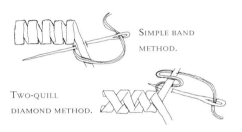

SIMPLE BAND METHOD.

TWO-QUILL DIAMOND METHOD.

Right: *A Sioux breast ornament of bone 'hair-pipe' beads, once made from the centre of conch shells. The fringe is made of rawhide strips wrapped in dyed porcupine quills.*

Below: *The quill-wrapped rawhide fringe of a Teton Sioux pipe bag.*

Opposite: *Teton Sioux porcupine-quill embroidery on buckskin couched in the simple band method using sinew for thread, North America.*

Opposite, inset above: *An old Stoney Indian couple from Banff, Canada. They are dressed in buckskin embellished with porcupine quills and ermine tails.*

Opposite, inset below, left: *A Blackfoot Indian from the reservation in Montana, North America, with quillwork panels and roundel on his shirt.*

Opposite, inset below, right: *The hood of a Sioux baby carrier, from North America, made in 1860 and decorated with linear patterns of quillwork.*

EPHEMERA

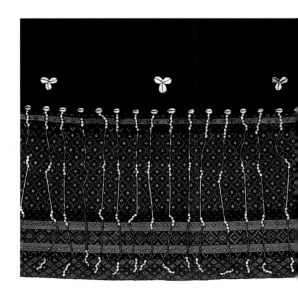

WE take many objects for granted, viewing them from a familiar, functional standpoint. It is only when they are taken out of context that we recognize their intrinsic appeal. Items rejected and thrown away in our consumer-based society are often the unconsidered trifles snapped up eagerly in the Third World. The teeth of dismembered zips are considered an attractive edging by the occupants of the Hindu Kush as are British naval buttons and plastic beads, while flattened Coca-Cola cans and bottle tops are much sought after in New Guinea for the decoration of personal attire.

Natural objects

SINCE time immemorial people have bedecked themselves with flowers. Worn in the hair, tucked into a hat or pinned to a jacket, flowers add a touch of passing beauty, and also convey messages of love, availability or, as in the case of Scottish Highlanders before the adoption of specific clan tartans, affiliation to a social group.

Many other natural objects have been exploited for adornment. Some, like seeds such as Job's Tears, may last for years, but others, like the iridescent wing cases of beetles, are fragile and last only a short time.

Above, left: *Scalp, North America, 1850. The Plains Indians used enemy scalps to decorate clothing, weapons and horse trappings.*

Above, right: *Ch'in apron, from Myanmar (Burma), with tassels made from sardine tins.*

Right: *A Siberian shaman, his shirt decorated with metal objects such as bells, coins and nails.*

Below, left: *Woman's* jumlo, *from Kohistan, Pakistan, decorated with embroidery, beads and buttons.*

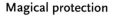

Magical protection

THE most fruitful hunting ground for incongruous ephemera is on clothing for children, notably in the mountainous valleys of Kohistan in Pakistan. In the attempt to protect the young and vulnerable from evil forces, all manner of talismans may be attached to hats, dresses or shirts and any shiny object, glass, coin or button, may be used to reflect and avert the evil eye. Even the metal medallions from bottles of Brut aftershave have been found sewn on children's clothes.

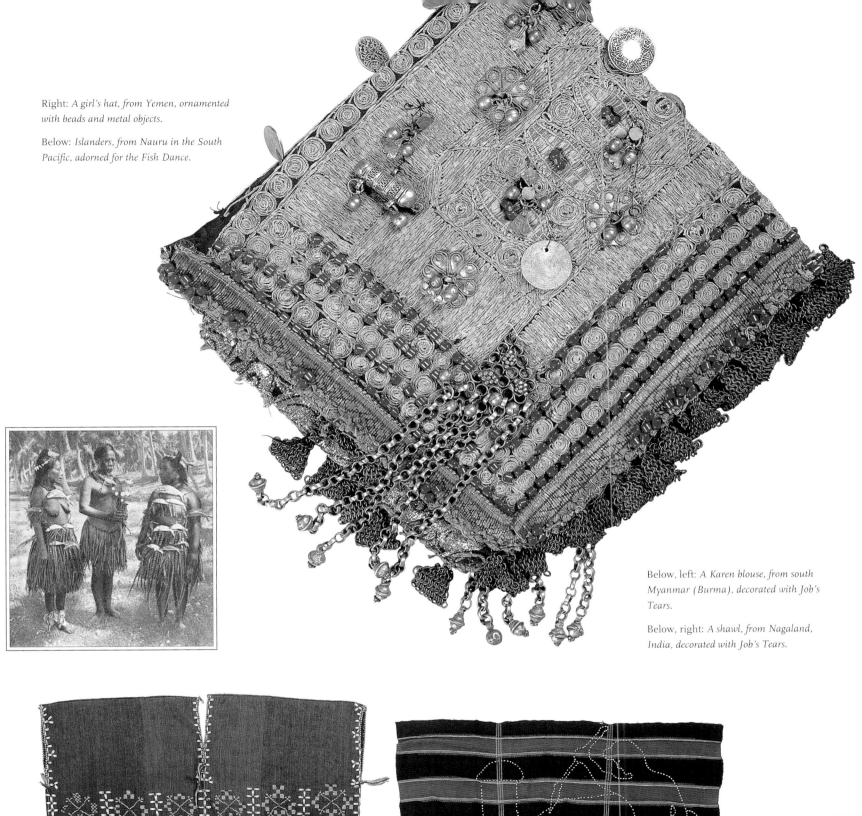

Right: *A girl's hat, from Yemen, ornamented with beads and metal objects.*

Below: *Islanders, from Nauru in the South Pacific, adorned for the Fish Dance.*

Below, left: *A Karen blouse, from south Myanmar (Burma), decorated with Job's Tears.*

Below, right: *A shawl, from Nagaland, India, decorated with Job's Tears.*

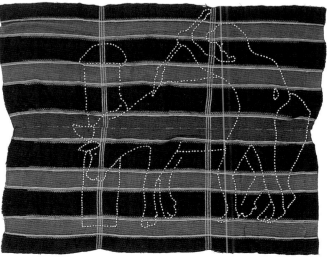

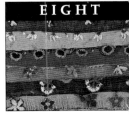

FRINGES

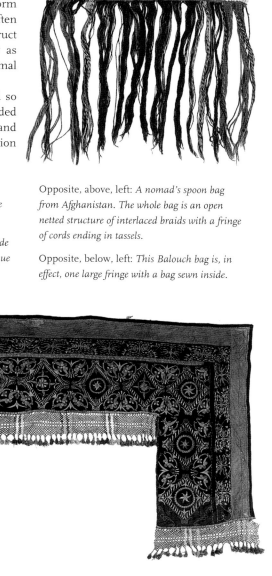

FRINGES have been in popular use for thousands of years and appear in the Babylonian stone carvings of the 8th century BC. In Java they are so popular that the effect is often simulated on the batik shawl, or *selendang*, worn by all Javanese women.

Techniques

WHEN any woven textile is taken from the loom, a fringe of warp strands that have not been bound in by the weft remains. This can be quite attractive, but the weft is vulnerable to unravelling with wear and so more elaborate ways of securing the ends of textiles have evolved. The simplest and most common method is to tie groups of warps into knots and trim the loose ends to the same length, thus creating a row of tassels.

A more sophisticated method is to divide the loose end of each tassel and tie one half to the adjoining half of its neighbour on the left and the other half to half its neighbour on the right. This can be repeated ad infinitum to create a net-like effect. In Central Asia a more elaborate technique is employed in which the groups of warps are not finished in a knot, but in a braid which is either plaited or worked in sinnet as in macramé. Sometimes these braids are interlaced with each other obliquely and can be extended downwards indefinitely to form a net. In fact, this technique has often been used in its own right to construct bags for carrying spoons and purely as decoration for dwellings and animal trappings.

On occasion, a fringe is considered so desirable that extra threads are added to the ends or sides of textiles and garments specifically for the construction of fancy fringes.

Above, right: *A Montangard loincloth, from Vietnam, with a simple, loose, unknotted fringe anchored by a supplementary weft border.*

Below: *A hanging, from Kirghizia, for the inside of a nomad's yurt with an added fringe of oblique interlacing terminating in tassels.*

Opposite, above, left: *A nomad's spoon bag from Afghanistan. The whole bag is an open netted structure of interlaced braids with a fringe of cords ending in tassels.*

Opposite, below, left: *This Balouch bag is, in effect, one large fringe with a bag sewn inside.*

BELOW, RIGHT: AN 8TH-CENTURY BC BAS-RELIEF CARVING IN STONE, FROM THE PALACE OF SARGON, DEPICTING AN ASSYRO-BABYLONIAN GENIE IN HEAVILY FRINGED ROBES.

EIGHT

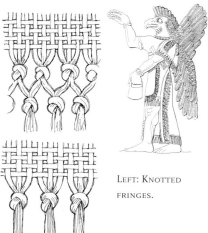

LEFT: KNOTTED FRINGES.

Above: An Uzbek yurt hanging. Suspended from a piece of warp-faced weaving is a loosely netted structure embellished with tassels.

Right: A Native American woman wearing a buckskin dress and skirt. Fringes were often cut directly into the bottom of garments.

EIGHT

TASSELS

THE ultimate extension of a fringe is a tassel – an ending becomes a flourish. A tassel adds a third dimension to a textile. Its swish and sway give the excitement of movement, making it a popular feature of costume and animal trappings.

Techniques

THE simplest form of tassel is made by tying a bunch of warps in an overhand knot.

A more elaborate tassel can be made by knotting a bundle of threads, twice the required length, in the middle, folding both ends down and then tying the two bunches together. The head of the tassel is sometimes enlarged by wrapping it over a piece of cloth or wood.

The pom-pom is a spherical tassel made from yarn. To make a pom-pom two rings of card are placed back to back and yarn is wrapped around both passing through the hole in the middle. When the hole is choked and it is impossible to thread any more yarn through, a cut is made around the circumference so a knot can be tied tightly between the two rings. The card is then pulled off, allowing the yarn to spring out into a fluffy ball. Tassels are often further embellished with beads, knots, embroidery or wrapped cords.

228

Far left: *Three silk and mother-of-pearl tassels from China.*

Left, centre: *A Bolivian festival bag, from Lake Titicaca, embellished with dangling multi-coloured pom-poms.*

Near left: *Peruvian hair ties, from Cuzco, made from narrow, tightly woven bands with fringes formed from unwoven warps strung with beads.*

Opposite, below, left: *Red Zhao girls, from Sapa in Vietnam, wearing headdresses of woollen tassels.*

Opposite, right, from left to right: *Afghan tassels with wrapped cords and Josephine knots; tassels, from Sinai, with wrapping and beads; Afghan wrapped tassels worn in the hair.*

Opposite, above, right: *An itinerant musician wearing a tasselled leather satchel made by Hausa craftsmen in Nigeria.*

Distribution

Tassels are used wherever textiles are made, not only to provide a secure hem for a textile, but also as a decorative feature. They are used all around the world on rugs, clothing, bags, domestic decorations and animal trappings. One imposing tassel on its own is sometimes considered sufficient, but frequently a whole mass are used to emphasize the swish and sway of clothing or beasts of burden.

Elaborate tassels are made in many countries, but the most sophisticated are probably those made in China and Japan.

Above: *Three French tassels for embellishing curtains and drapes. The heads of two of them have been exaggerated by tying the cords over a piece of turned wood and building up stitched decoration over the top.*

GLOSSARY

aba A tunic-shaped dress worn over trousers by Muslim women.

abocchnai Embroidered wedding shawl made by merchant castes in Thar Parkar, Sind, Pakistan, and also Banni Kutch, India.

abr (Persian for cloud) Fabric dyed in Central Asia using the ikat technique.

adinkra cloth Fabric from Ghana covered in symbolic designs printed using stamps carved from calabash shell.

adire Yoruba for resist-dyeing in indigo.

adire alabere A West African tie and dye technique in which the dye is resisted using stitching.

adire eleko A West African method of dyeing in indigo in which a resist paste is painted or stencilled onto the fabric.

adjective dye A dyestuff that has to have a mordant to make it permanent.

ajrakh Cloth from North-West India which is printed with mordants and resist paste before dyeing.

aniline dyes Chemical or synthetic dyes derived originally from coal tar.

ari A small notched awl or hook used in tambour work.

babouche Leather slippers worn in Morocco.

back-strap loom A loom that is tensioned by the weaver leaning back against a strap or backrest.

bagh A special kind of Punjabi shawl, *phulkari*, densely covered with silk embroidery.

bandhani Gujarati for tie and dye.

bast Fibre obtained from the stems of certain herbaceous plants.

batik The Javanese method of resist-dyeing using wax.

bidang Tubular skirt worn by the Dyak tribes of Borneo.

billum A bag from New Guinea with a structure of interconnected looping.

binding system The method used to interweave the elements of a loom-woven textile – can be tabby, twill or satin weave.

blackwork Embroidery worked in black thread on a white ground, once popular in England.

bogolanfini Black and off-white 'mud' cloth from Mali.

bolim posh Canopy held over a bride and groom in Central Asia.

bukhani Scarf or sash worn by a bridegroom in Kutch and Saurashtra, North-West India, and Sind, Pakistan.

cable A raised area on a knitted fabric bearing a resemblance to rope.

canting An instrument for drawing batik patterns with a reservoir for containing hot wax.

cap A copper block for printing wax onto cloth during the batik process.

carding The separation and cleansing of wool fibres by stroking them between two blocks covered with bent wire teeth.

cetak The application of chemical dyestuff directly onto sections of yarn as a short cut in the ikat technique.

chakla A square hanging from North-West India.

chikan An Indian form of whitework consisting of white floral embroidery on a net ground.

chintz Printed and painted cloths produced in South India for export.

choli A backless blouse worn by women in Rajasthan and Gujarat, Western India.

chullo A knitted hat from the Andes.

chumpi A woven belt worn in the Andes.

chyrpy An embroidered coat with vestigial sleeves worn by Turkoman women.

'cisele' velvet Velvet on which a pattern is created by the contrast in texture between areas of cut and uncut pile.

combing Method of separating long wool strands for weaving fine worsted cloth.

complementary warp or weft Extra structural elements incorporated into a woven textile to create patterns.

dhoti A length of cloth tied around the waist by Hindu men to form loose trousers.

drawloom A hand loom capable of raising individual warps and therefore suitable for weaving complicated patterns.

dye A colouring agent that soaks into the fibres of cloth or yarn.

end An individual warp thread.

float Where the warp or weft is not woven into the ground weave, but floats across the surface.

galla Embroidered cloth worn over the back of the neck by Banjara women from South India.

ganeshtapan Indian pentagonal embroidered hanging depicting the Hindu god Ganesh.

ger Mongolian nomad dwelling with collapsible trellis walls covered in felt, known in Central Asia as a yurt.

geringsing Double-ikat cloth woven in Bali.

ghudjeri An Uzbek horse blanket made from narrow woven strips sewn together.

gin A mangle used to remove seeds and impurities from cotton.

goncha Woollen robe worn by men and women in Tibet and the Himalayas.

guj An embroidered wedding blouse or dress from Kutch, North-West India, and Sind, Pakistan.

happi Japanese short, cotton coat.

heddle A device for lifting a group of warp ends to open a shed.

hinggi A man's ikat-woven mantle from the Indonesian island of Sumba.

huilpil Short poncho worn by women in Central America.

Jacquard loom An automated system of raising heddles in a programmed order using punched cards.

jamawar A Kashmiri tapestry-weave shawl.

juval A woven bag used for storing and transporting belongings in Central Asia.

kaha hururhuru A Maori cloak covered with feathers.

kain A rectangle of cloth wrapped around the body in Indonesia.

kalaga Padded temple hanging from Myanmar (Burma) decorated with glass, couched cords and sequins.

kalam A pen with a reservoir of felt or wool to hold dye, used in South India to draw the outline of *kalamkari*.

kalamkari A textile, from South India, usually decorated with religious images. The lines are drawn with a pen, or *kalam*, made from a stick with an absorbent wad of cotton bound to the tip.

kanduri Appliquéd cloths given as offerings by pilgrims at the shrine of Salar Masud in the state of Uttar Pradesh in India.

kantha Quilted and embroidered cloths made from recycled fabric in Bihar, West Bengal and Bangladesh.

kasuri The Japanese ikat technique.

katazome Japanese for dyeing with a stencil.

kente **cloth** Stripweave cloth from Ghana.

khes Double-weave cloth from India and Pakistan.

kilim/*kelim* A rug constructed in tapestry weave.

kinkhab Silk and metal brocade woven in India.

ladao The copper-tipped 'Chinese knife' used to apply wax-resist in South-West China.

mashru Satin-weave fabric with silk warp and cotton weft.

mechita A Colombian bag made of string.

monedero A knitted purse used in the Andes to carry coins.

mordant A metallic salt which combines chemically with the dyestuff to fix the dye permanently.

nariyal A decorated coconut carried at Hindu weddings.

numdah A Central Asian felt rug.

odhni A shawl worn by women in North-West India and Pakistan.

okbash A bag used by Central Asian nomads for protecting the ends of a yurt's roof poles during transportation.

par A painted hanging depicting the adventures of Pabuji, a Rajasthani folk hero.

patola Double-ikat textile woven in Gujarat, Western India.

phulkari Punjabi wedding shawl decorated in surface satin stitch or darning stitch.

pick A single passage of the weft from one selvedge to the other.

picot A decorative loop on the edge of a piece of tatting, macramé or embroidery.

pigment A colouring agent, usually mineral in origin, that adheres to the surface of a fabric.

pis A cotton kerchief from the Philippines.

plangi (Indonesian for rainbow) The name for tie and dye in Indonesia.

ply The number of spun threads twisted together to make yarn, i.e., two threads twisted together are called two ply.

pojagi A Korean wrapping cloth.

ralli A North Indian or Pakistani quilt.

rawhide Tough, untanned animal skin.

Resht work Chain-stitch embroidered textiles named after the Iranian city of Resht.

retting Soaking plant stems to soften them in the preparation of bast fibres.

rolag Roll or bundle of wool or cotton from which the fibres are drawn out during spinning.

rumal An Indian kerchief or square cloth.

sai gosha Chevron-shaped embroidered textiles used in Uzbekistan to cover bedding when stacked away.

sari A length of cloth worn by Indian women wrapped around the waist and over the shoulder.

sarong An untailored rectangle of cloth wrapped around the waist in Indonesia.

sashiko Japanese textiles quilted with running stitch (also a technique).

selendang A long, narrow, multi-purpose cloth used by women in Indonesia as a shawl, for carrying babies, wrapping shopping and so on.

selvedge The edge of a woven fabric where the weft begins its return run.

serape Central American shawl.

shed An opening between the warps through which the weft can be passed whilst weaving.

shibori Japanese for tie and dye.

shigra Bag, made of interlooped plant fibre, used in the Andes.

shisha Mirrored glass used in Indian embroidery.

sinnet/sennet Macramé cord created by tying reef knots or granny knots around a core of twine.

songket Indonesian brocade woven with silk or metal thread.

soumak A method of weft wrapping used in the manufacture of bags and rugs.

substantive dye A dye that does not require the use of a mordant to make it permanent.

suspension loom A loom where the warps have weights attached to them to maintain the tension.

suzani (Persian for needle) A large embroidered cover or hanging from Central Asia.

tambour A drum-shaped frame used for holding fabric taut whilst embroidering with a tambour hook or *ari*.

tanning Soaking skins in acidic substances to make them supple and prevent decay.

tapa Polynesian barkcloth made from the paper mulberry tree.

tapis Sarong worn by women in Sumatra.

tensifa An embroidered Moroccan curtain.

toran A embroidered door hanging from Gujarat, India.

tritik Indonesian for stitched resist.

tsutsugaki The Japanese technique of applying starch-resist paste through a bamboo tube.

tulis Javanese batik in which the wax-resist has been drawn on by hand using a *canting*.

vertical loom Loom on which the warps are stretched vertically rather than horizontally.

wampum Shell beads made by Native Americans from the North Atlantic coast.

warp The fixed longitudinal elements stretching the length of a woven fabric.

weft The transverse elements of a woven fabric.

weft inlay The process of weaving a supplementary weft in with the ground weft.

whitework A combination of sewing and embroidery techniques using white thread on a white ground.

worsted Fine-quality fabric in which long, combed wool fibres are used.

yurt The circular dwelling of many Central Asian nomads which consists of a wooden lattice and strut frame covered in felt.

FURTHER READING

All of the books listed were published in London or New York unless otherwise stated.

Materials
Baines, P., *Linen Hand Spinning and Weaving*, 1989
Balfour-Paul, Jenny, *Indigo*, 1998
———, *Indigo in the Arab World*, 1992, 1997
Burkett, M. E., *The Art of the Felt Maker*, Kendal, 1979
Burnard, Joyce, *Chintz and Cotton*, 1994
Dixon, M., *The Wool Book*, 1979
Feltwell, John, *The Story of Silk*, Stroud, 1990
Gibson, Thomas, *Feather Masterpieces of the Ancient Andean World*, exhibition catalogue, Thomas Gibson Fine Art, London, 1990
Sandberg, Gösta, *Indigo Textiles*, 1989
———, *The Red Dyes, Cochineal, Madder and Murex Purple: A World Tour of Textile Techniques*, Asheville, North Carolina, 1997
Saul, M., *Shells*, 1974
Scott, Philippa, *The Book of Silk*, 1993

Techniques
Bühler, A., and Fischer, E., *Clamp Resist Dyeing of Fabrics*, Ahmedabad, 1977
Burnham, D. K., *A Textile Terminology: Warp and Weft*, 1981
Cave, O., and Hodges, J., *Smocking: Traditional and Modern Approaches*, 1984
Clabburn, Pamela, *Beadwork*, Aylesbury, 1980
Clark, Hazel, *Textile Printing*, Aylesbury, 1985
Collingwood, P., *The Techniques of Ply-split Braiding*, 1998
———, *The Techniques of Sprang*, 1974
———, *The Techniques of Tablet Weaving*, 1982
———, *Textile and Weaving Structures: A Source Book for Makers and Designers*, 1987
Dyrenforth, Noel, *The Technique of Batik*, 1988
Embroiderers Guild Practical Study Group, *Needlework School*, 1984
Emery, I., *The Primary Structure of Fabrics, An Illustrated Classification*, Washington, D.C., and London, 1980, reprinted 1994
Farrell, Jeremy, *Socks and Stockings*, 1992
Fuhrmann, B., *Bobbin Lace*, 1985
Hecht, A., *The Art of the Loom*, 1989
Heinbuch, J., *A Quillwork Companion*, Liberty, Utah, 1990
Hooper, Luther, *Hand-Loom Weaving: Plain and Ornamental*, 1979
Larsen, Jack, Bühler, Alfred, and Solyom, Garret, *The Dyers Art*, 1976
Leadbeater, Eliza, *Spinning and Spinning Wheels*, Princes Risborough, 1979, reprinted 1985
Morrell, Anne, *The Techniques of Indian Embroidery*, 1994
Nicholls, E., *Tatting: Technique and History*, Toronto, 1962
Oelsner, G. H., *A Handbook of Weaves*, 1975
Puls, H., *The Art of Cutwork and Appliqué, Historic, Modern and Kuna Indian*, 1978
Reigate, E., *An Illustrated Guide to Lace*, Woodbridge, 1986
Ryan, M. G., *The Complete Encyclopaedia of Stitchcraft*, 1981

Seward, L., *The Country Quilter's Companion*, 1994
Stillwell, Alexandra, *Cassell Illustrated Dictionary of Lacemaking*, 1996
Storey, J., *The Thames and Hudson Manual of Textile Printing*, 1974
Swain, Margaret, *Ayrshire and Other Whitework*, Princes Risborough, 1982
Thurstan, T., *Dye Plants and Dyeing, A Handbook*, 1973
———, *The Use of Vegetable Dyes*, Leicester, 1975

History
Anton, F., *Ancient Andean Textiles*, 1987
Clabburn, Pamela, *Samplers*, Princes Risborough, 1977
Coe, R. T., *Sacred Circles: Two Thousand Years of North American Indian Art*, exhibition catalogue, Arts Council of Great Britain, 1976
D'Harcourt, Raoul, *Textiles of Ancient Peru, and their Techniques*, 1962
Geijer, Agnes, *A History of Textile Art*, 1979
Hall, Rosalind, *Egyptian Textiles*, Aylesbury, 1986
Harris, Jennifer, *5000 Years of Textiles*, 1993
Humphrey, C., *Samplers*, Cambridge, 1997
Stone-Miller, Rebecca, *To Weave for the Sun, Ancient Andean Textiles in the Museum of Fine Arts, Boston*, 1994
Thurman, C. C. M., *Textiles in the Art Institute of Chicago*, Chicago, 1992
Volbach, Fritz, *Early Decorative Textiles*, 1969

North America
Amsden, Charles, *Navaho Weaving, Its Technic and History*, 1991
Crews, Patricia Cox, and Naugle, Ronald C., *Nebraska Quilts and Quiltmakers*, 1991
Dockstader, Frederick, *Weaving Arts of the North American Indian*, 1993
Feest, Christian F., *Native Arts of North America*, 1980, rev. ed. 1992
Horse Capture, George P., *Robes of Splendor*, 1993
Hughes, Robert, *Amish, The Art of the Quilt*, 1990, 1994
Oakes, Jill, and Riewe, Rick, *Our Boots, An Inuit Women's Art*, 1996
Smith, Monte, *The Technique of North American Beadwork*, 1983
Whiteford, A. H., *North American Indian Arts*, Wisconsin, 1970
Wien, C. A., *The Log Cabin Quilt Book, Complete Patterns and Instructions for Making All Types of Log Cabin Quilts*, 1984
Wildschut, William, and Ewers, John, *Crow Indian Beadwork*, 1959

Central America
Cordy, Donald and Dorothy, *Mexican Indian Costume*, 1968
Deuss, Krystyna, *Indian Costumes from Guatemala*, 1981
Kapp, Kit, *Mola Art*, 1972
Parker, A., and Neal, A., *Molas Folk Art of the Cuna Indians*, 1977
Pettersen, Carmen L., *Maya of Guatemala, Their Life and Dress*, Seattle, 1976
Puls, H., *Textiles of the Kuna Indians of Panama*, Princes Risborough, 1988
Sayer, Chlöe, *Mexican Textile Techniques*, Aylesbury, 1988
———, *Mexican Textiles*, 1990
Schevill, Margot Blum, *Evolution in Textile Design from the Highlands of Guatemala*, 1985
Start, Laura, *The McDougall Collection of Indian Textiles from Guatemala and Mexico*, Pitt Rivers Museum, Oxford, occasional paper, 1980

South America

Davies, Lucy, and Fini, Mo, *Arts and Crafts of South America*, 1994

D'Harcourt, Raoul, *Textiles of Ancient Peru and their Techniques*, 1962

Feltham, Jane, *Peruvian Textiles*, Aylesbury, 1989

Frame, Mary, *Andean Four-Cornered Hats*, exhibition catalogue, Metropolitan Museum of Art, New York, 1990

Meisch, L. A. (ed.), *Traditional Textiles of the Andes: Life and Cloth in the Highlands*, The Jeffrey Appleby Collection of Andean Textiles, exhibition catalogue, Fine Arts Museums of San Francisco, 1997

Stone-Miller, Rebecca, *To Weave for the Sun, Ancient Andean Textiles in the Museum of Fine Arts, Boston*, 1994

Villegas, Liliana and Benjamin, *Artefactos, Colombian Crafts from the Andes to the Amazon*, 1992

Europe

Bossert, H., *Peasant Art in Europe*, 1927

Cheape, H., *Tartan, the Highland Habit*, Edinburgh, 1995

Johnstone, Pauline, *A Guide to Greek Island Embroidery*, 1972

Kasparian, Alice, *Armenian Needlelace and Embroidery*, McLean, Virginia, 1983

Morris, B., *Victorian Embroidery*, 1962

Proctor, M., *Victorian Canvas Work, Berlin Wool Work*, 1972

Taylor, Roderick, *Embroidery of the Greek Islands and Epirus*, 1998

Wardle, P., *A Guide to English Embroidery*, 1970

Yefimova, L., and Belogorskaya, R., *Russian Embroidery and Lace*, 1987

Africa

Adler, Peter, and Barnard, Nicholas, *African Majesty, The Textile Art of the Ashanti and Ewe*, 1992

————, *Asafo! African Flags of the Fante*, 1992

Carey, Margaret, *Beads and Beadwork of East and South Africa*, Princes Risborough, 1986

Clarke, Duncan, *The Art of African Textiles*, San Diego, 1997

Eicher, Joanne, *Nigerian Handcrafted Textiles*, Ife, 1976

Fagg, William, *Yoruba Beadwork, Art of Nigeria*, 1980

Jereb, James, *Arts and Crafts of Morocco*, 1995

Lamb, Venice and Alastair, *Au Cameroun, Weaving, Tissage*, 1981

————, *Sierra Leone Weaving*, 1984

Lamb, Venice, *West African Weaving*, 1975

————, and Holmes, Judy, *Nigerian Weaving*, 1980

Mack, John, *Malagasy Textiles*, Princes Risborough, 1989

Picton, John, *The Art of African Textiles, Technology, Tradition and Lurex*, 1995

————, and Mack, John, *African Textiles*, 1979, 2nd ed. 1989

Reswick, Imtraud, *Traditional Textiles of Tunisia and Related North African Weavings*, Los Angeles, 1985

Spring, Christopher, *African Textiles*, 1989

————, and Hudson, Julie, *North African Textiles*, 1995

Stone, Caroline, *The Embroideries of North Africa*, 1985

The Middle East

Baker, Patricia, *Islamic Textiles*, 1995

Johnstone, Pauline, *Turkish Embroidery*, 1985

Kalter, Johannes, Pavaloi, Margareta, and Zerrwicke, Maria, *The Arts and Crafts of Syria*, 1992

Rajab, Jehan, *Palestinian Costume*, 1989

Stillman, Yedida Kalfon, *Palestinian Costume and Jewelry*, 1979

Taylor, Roderick, *Ottoman Embroidery*, 1995

Weir, Shelagh, *Palestinian Costume*, 1989

————, and Shahid, Serene, *Palestinian Embroidery, Cross-stitch Patterns from the Traditional Costumes of the Village Women of Palestine*, 1988

Central Asia

Ferrier, R. W., *The Arts of Persia*, London and New Haven, 1989

Fitzgibbon, Kate, and Hale, Andy, *Ikat, Silks of Central Asia, The Guido Goldman Collection*, 1997

————, *Ikats, Woven Silks from Central Asia, The Rau Collection*, 1988

Harvey, Janet, *Traditional Textiles of Central Asia*, 1996

Hull, Alastair, and Barnard, Nicholas, *Living with Kilims*, 1988

Kalter, Johannes, *The Arts and Crafts of Turkestan*, 1984

————, and Pavaloi, Margareta, *Uzbekistan, Heirs to the Silk Road*, 1997

Phillips, E. D., *The Royal Hordes, Nomad Peoples of the Steppes*, 1965

Wulff, Hans, *The Traditional Crafts of Persia, their Development, Technology, and Influence on Eastern and Western Civilizations*, London and Cambridge, Massachusetts, 1966

South Asia

Adams, Barbara, *Traditional Bhutanese Textiles*, Bangkok, 1984

Askari, Nasreen, and Crill, Rosemary, *Colours of the Indus, Costume and Textiles of Pakistan*, exhibition catalogue, Victoria and Albert Museum, London, 1997

Barnard, Nicholas, *Arts and Crafts of India*, 1993

Bühler, Alfred, Fischer, Eberhard, and Nabholz, Marie-Louise, *Indian Tie-dyed Fabrics*, Ahmedabad, 1980

Cooper, Ilay, Gillow, John, and Dawson, Barry, *Arts and Crafts of India*, 1996

Crill, Rosemary, *Indian Ikat Textiles*, 1998

Fisher, Nora (ed.), *Mud, Mirror and Thread: Folk Traditions of Rural India*, Ahmedabad and Middletown, New Jersey, 1993

Gillow, John, and Barnard, Nicholas, *Traditional Indian Textiles*, 1991

Gittinger, Mattiebelle, *Master Dyers to the World: Technique and Trade in Early Indian Dyed Cotton Textiles*, Washington, D.C., 1982

Guy, John, *Woven Cargoes, Indian Trade Textiles in the East*, 1998

Hitkari, S. S., *Phulkari, The Folk Art of Punjab*, New Delhi, 1980

Irwin, John, *The Kashmir Shawl*, 1973

————, and Hall, Margaret, *Indian Embroideries*, 1973

————, *Indian Painted and Printed Fabrics*, 1971

Jacobs, Julian, *The Nagas: Hill Peoples of Northeast India, Society, Culture and the Colonial Encounter*, 1990

Konieczny, M. G., *Textiles of Balouchistan*, 1979

Krishna, Rai, Anand and Vijay, *Banaras Brocades*, 1966

Levi-Strauss, Monique, *The Cashmere Shawl*, 1987

Lynton, Linda, *The Sari*, 1995

Mohanty, B. C., *Brocaded Fabrics of India*, 1984

Murphy, Veronica, and Crill, Rosemary, *Tie-Dyed Textiles of India: Tradition and Trade*, 1991

Nabholz-Kartaschoff, Marie-Louise, *Golden Sprays and Scarlet Flowers, Traditional Indian Textiles from the Museum of Ethnography* [Basel, Switzerland], Kyoto, 1986

Sarabhai, Mrinalini, and Dhamija, Jasleen, *Patolas and Resist-Dyed Fabrics of India*, 1988

Stockley, Beth (ed.), *Woven Air*, exhibition catalogue (of Bangladeshi textiles), Whitechapel Art Gallery, London, 1988

Talwar, Kay, and Krishna, Kalyan, *Indian Pigment Paintings on Cloth*, Ahmedabad, 1979

Zaman, Niaz, *The Art of Kantha Embroidery*, Dhaka, 1993

South-East Asia

Campbell, Margaret, *From the Hands of the Hills*, Hong Kong, 1978

Connors, Mary, *Lao Textiles and Tradition*, 1996

Conway, Susan, *Thai Textiles*, 1992

Fraser-Lu, Sylvia, *Handwoven Textiles of South-East Asia*, Oxford and Singapore, 1988

Gavin, Traude, *The Women's Warpath, Iban Ritual Fabrics from Borneo*, 1996

Gillow, John, and Dawson, Barry, *Traditional Indonesian Textiles*, 1992

Gittinger, Mattiebelle, *Splendid Symbols, Textiles and Tradition in Indonesia*, 1979, 1984

———, and Lefferts, Leedom, *Textiles and the Thai Experience in Southeast Asia*, Washington, D.C., 1992

Haddon, A. C., and Start, L. E., *Iban or Sea Dayak Fabrics and their Patterns, a Descriptive Catalogue of the Iban Fabrics in the Museum of Archaeology and Ethnology, Cambridge*, 2nd ed., 1982

Hauser-Schaublin, B., Nabholz-Kartaschoff, Marie-Louise, and Ramseyer, Urs, *Balinese Textiles*, 1991

Hitchcock, Michael, *Indonesian Textiles*, 1991

Lewis, Paul and Elaine, *Peoples of the Golden Triangle, Six Tribes in Thailand*, 1984

Mallinson, J., Donelly, N., and Hang Ly, *H'mong Batik*, Chiang Mai, 1988

Maxwell, Robyn, *Textiles of South-East Asia, Tradition, Trade and Transformation*, Oxford and Melbourne, 1990

Pastor-Roces, Marian, *Sinaunang Habi, Philippine Ancestral Weave*, 1991

Selvanayagam, Grace Inpam, *Songket, Malaysia's Woven Treasure*, Oxford and Singapore, 1990

Veldhuisen, Harmen, *Batik Belanda, Dutch Influence in Batik from Java*, 1993

Warming, Wanda, and Gaworski, Michael, *The World of Indonesian Textiles*, Tokyo, 1981, 1991

Warren, William, and Invernizzi Tettoni, Luca, *Arts and Crafts of Thailand*, 1994

The Far East

Benjamin, Betsy, *The World of Rozome, Wax-Resist Textiles of Japan*, London and Tokyo, 1996

Faulkner, R., *Japanese Stencils*, Exeter, 1988

Gao, Hanyu, *Chinese Textile Designs*, 1992

Garrett, Valery, *Chinese Clothing: An Illustrated Guide*, Oxford and Hong Kong, 1994

Kennedy, Alan, *Japanese Costume, History and Tradition*, Paris, 1990

Middleton, Sheila Hoey, *Traditional Korean Wrapping Cloths*, Seoul, 1990

Minick, Scott, and Ping, Jiao, *Arts and Crafts of China*, 1996

O'Connor, D., *Miao Costumes from Guizhou Province, South West China*, exhibition catalogue, James Hockney Gallery, W.S.C.A.D., Farnham, 1994

Rathbun, W. J., *Beyond the Tanabata Bridge: Traditional Japanese Textiles*, exhibition catalogue, The Art Institute of Seattle, Washington, 1993

Tsultem, N., *Mongolian Arts and Crafts*, 1987

Wada, Yoshiko, Kellogg Rice, Mary, and Barton, Jane, *Shibori, The Inventive Art of Japanese Shaped Resist Dyeing, Tradition, Techniques, Innovation*, Tokyo, 1983

Wang, Loretta, *The Chinese Purse*, 1991

Wilson, Verity, *Chinese Dress*, 1986, 1990

The Pacific

Clunie, Fergus, *Yalo i Viti, a Fiji Museum Catalogue*, Suva, 1986

Hemming, Steve, and Jones, Philip, *Ngurunderi, An Aboriginal Dreaming*, exhibition catalogue, South Australian Museum, Adelaide, 1989

Kooijman, Simon, *Polynesian Barkcloth*, Princes Risborough, 1988

———, *Tapa on Moce Island, Fiji, a Traditional Handicraft in a Changing Society*, Leiden, 1977

Ling Roth, H., *The Maori Mantle*, Bedford, 1979

Neich, R., and Pendergrast, M., *Traditional Tapa Textiles of the Pacific*, 1997

Pendergrast, M., *Kakahu, Maori Cloaks*, Auckland, 1997

———, *Te Aho Tapu, The Sacred Thread*, Auckland, 1987

General

Faegre, T., *Tents, Architecture of the Nomads*, 1979

Hull, Alastair, Barnard, Nicholas, and Luczyc-Wyhowska, José, *Kilim, The Complete Guide*, 1993

Paine, Sheila, *Embroidered Textiles, Traditional Patterns from Five Continents with a Worldwide Guide to Identification*, 1990, paperback 1995

Thompson, Jon, *Carpets from the Tents, Cottages and Workshops of Asia*, rev. ed. 1988

COLLECTIONS

AUSTRALIA
Adelaide
National Textile Museum of
Australia
Urrbrae House
Fullarton Road
Urrbrae
Adelaide
South Australia (5064)
Collections: Worldwide textiles

South Australian Museum
North Terrace
Adelaide
South Australia (5000)
*Collections: Aboriginal, Oceanic
and South-East Asian textiles*

Canberra
Australian National Gallery
Lake Burley Griffin
Canberra City
A.C.T. (2600)
*Collections: South-East Asian
textiles*

AUSTRIA
Vienna
Museum für Völkerkunde
Neue Hofburg
Heldenplatz
A-1014 Vienna
*Collections: African and
Oceanic textiles*

BANGLADESH
Dhaka
National Museum
Junction of New Elephant
Road and Mymensingh Road
Dhaka
Collections: Kantha quilting

BELGIUM
Antwerp
Ethnology Museum
International Zeemanshuis
Falconrui 2
2000 Antwerp
*Collections: African, South
Asian and South-East Asian
textiles*

Brussels
Musée du Costume et de la
Dentelle
6 rue de la Violette
1000 Brussels
Collections: Lace

Musées Royaux d'Art et
d'Histoire
10 Parc du Cinquantenaire
1040 Brussels
*Collections: European, American
and Far Eastern textiles*

Tervuren
Musée de l'Afrique Centrale
Royal
13 Steenweg op Leuven
3080 Tervuren, Brabant
Collections: Congolese textiles

BOLIVIA
La Paz
Museo Nacional
Calle Tihuanacu 93
La Paz
Collections: Bolivian costume

National Museum of Folklore
Calle Ingani 942
La Paz
Collections: Bolivian costume

BRAZIL
Rio de Janeiro
Museu do Indio
Rua Mata Machado 127
20000 Rio de Janeiro
*Collections: Brazilian Indian
costume*

São Paulo
Folklore Museum
Pavilhao Garcez
Parque Ibirapuera
01000 São Paulo
*Collections: Brazilian folk
costume*

BRITISH ISLES
Bath
Museum of Costume
Assembly Rooms
Bennett Street
Bath BA1 2QH
*Collections: English period
costume*

Bradford
Cartwright Hall Art Gallery
Lister Park
Manningham
Bradford BD9 4NS
*Collections: Indian and
Pakistani textiles*

Bristol
City Museum and Art Gallery
Queens Road
Bristol BS8 1RL
*Collections: Asian, African and
North American textiles*

Cambridge
University Museum of
Archaeology and
Anthropology
Downing St
Cambridge CB2 3DZ
*Collections: Worldwide
ethnographic textiles, including
major holdings of Iban and
Naga tribal textiles*

Durham
Oriental Museum
University of Durham
Elvet Hill, Durham DH1 3TH
Collections: Asian textiles

East Molesey
Embroiderers' Guild
Collection
Apartment 41
Hampton Court Palace
East Molesey
Surrey KT8 9AU
*Collections: Worldwide
embroidery*

Edinburgh
Royal Museum of Scotland
Chambers Street
Edinburgh EH1 1JF
*Collections: European and
Asian textiles*

Halifax
Bankfield Museum
Boothtown Road
Halifax HX3 6HG
*Collections: Worldwide
ethnographic textiles*

Honiton
Allhallows Museum
High Street
Honiton, Devon EX14 8PE
Collections: English lace

Horsted Keynes
The Forge North American
Indian Museum
Horsted
West Sussex RH17 7AT
*Collections: Native American
textiles*

Leicester
Leicestershire Museum and
Art Gallery
New Walk, Leicester LE2 0JJ
*Collections: Indian and
Pakistani textiles*

London
British Museum
Great Russell St
London WC1B 3DG
*Collections: Worldwide
ethnographic textiles*

Horniman Museum
100 London Road
Forest Hill, London SE23 3PQ
*Collections: Worldwide
ethnographic textiles*

Victoria and Albert Museum
Cromwell Road
London SW7 2RL
*Collections: The most extensive
holdings from Europe and Asia*

Manchester
Gallery of English Costume
Platt Hall, Rusholme
Manchester M14 5LL
*Collections: British, Indian and
Pakistani textiles*

Whitworth Art Gallery
University of Manchester
Oxford Road
Manchester M15 6ER
*Collections: Worldwide
ethnographic textiles*

Nottingham
Lace Centre
Severns Buildings, Castle
Road, Nottingham NG1 6AA
*Collections: Costume,
embroidery and lace*

Museum of Costume and
Textiles
43–51 Castle Gate
Nottingham NG1 6AF
*Collections: European and
Asian textiles*

Oxford
Ashmolean Museum of Art
and Archaeology
Beaumont Street
Oxford OX1 2PH
*Collections: European and
Asian textiles*

Pitt Rivers Museum
University of Oxford, South
Parks Road, Oxford OX1 3PP
*Collections: Worldwide
ethnographic textiles*

BRUNEI
Begawan
Brunei Museum
Kota Batu, Banda Seri
2018 Begawan
*Collections: South-East Asian
textiles*

BULGARIA
Sofia
Etnografski institut s muzej
kam Balgarska akademija
na naukite (National
Ethnographic Museum
of the Bulgarian Academy
of Sciences)
ul Moskovska 6a, 1000 Sofia
*Collections: Bulgarian folk
costume*

CAMEROON
Yaounde
National Museum
Direction des Affaires
Culturelles, Yaounde
*Collections: Cameroon folk
textiles*

CANADA
Ottawa
National Museum of Natural
Sciences
MacLeod and Metcalfe Sts
Ottawa, Ontario K1A 0M8
*Collections: Worldwide
ethnographic textiles*

Toronto
Canadian Museum of Carpets
and Textiles
585 Bloor St West
Toronto, Ontario M6G 1KT
*Collections: Central Asian and
Canadian textiles*

Royal Ontario Museum
100 Queen's Park
Toronto, Ontario M5S 2C6
*Collections: European and
Asian textiles*

CHINA
Beijing
Museum of the Cultural
Palace of National Minorities
Changan Street
100 000 Beijing
*Collections: Hill-tribe textiles,
embroidery, batik and weaving*

Giuyang
Guizhou Provincial Museum
Beijing Rd
Guiyang
550 000 Guizhou
*Collections: Miao, Dong and
Shwe tribal textiles*

Kunming
Yunnan Provincial Museum
2 May Day Road
Dongfeng St
Yuantong Shan Hill
Kunming
650 000 Yunnan
Collections: Hill-tribe costume

COLOMBIA
Bogotá
Museo Etnografico de
Colombia
Calle 34, No 6–61 piso 30
Apdo. Aéreo 10511
Bogotá
Collections: Colombian costume

THE CONGO (formerly ZAIRE)
Kinshasa
Museum of Ethnology and
Archaeology
Université National du Congo
B.P. 127
Kinshasa
Collections: Congolese textiles

235

CYPRUS
Nicosia
Folk Art Museum
Archbishop Kyprianos Square
PO Box 1436
Nicosia
*Collections: Cypriot folk
costume*

CZECH REPUBLIC
Prague
Náprstkoro Muzeum
asijskych, africkych a
americkych kultur
(Náprstkoro Museum of
Asian, African and American
Culture)
Betlemské nám 1
11000 Prague
*Collections: Asian, African and
American textiles*

DENMARK
Copenhagen
National Museum of
Denmark
Ny Vestergade 10
Copenhagen
*Collections: Greenland, North
American, African, Indonesian
and Oceanic textiles*

EGYPT
Cairo
Arabic Museum
Midal Babel-Hkalk
Cairo
Collections: Islamic costume

Cotton Museum
Egyptian Agricultural Society
Khediv Ismael St
PO Box 63
Cairo
*Collections: History of cotton
growing in Egypt*

FIJI
Suva
Fiji Museum
Thurston Gardens
PO Box 2023
Suva
*Collections: Fijian tapa (bark
cloth)*

FRANCE
Lyon
Musée des Tissus et des Arts
Décoratifs
30–34 rue de Charité
69002 Lyon
*Collections: Historical European
and Middle Eastern textiles*

Mulhouse
Musée de l'Impression sur
Etoffes
3 rue des Bonnes-Gens
68100 Mulhouse
*Collections: European and
Asian block-printed textiles*

Paris
Musée de l'Homme
17 place du Trocadéro
75016 Paris
*Collections: Worldwide
ethnographic textiles*

Musée National des Arts
Asiatiques Guimet
19 avenue d'Iéna
75116 Paris
Collections: Asian textiles

Musée National des Arts
d'Afrique et d'Océanie
293 avenue Daumesnil
75012 Paris
*Collections: African and
Oceanic textiles*

GERMANY
Berlin
Museum für Indische Kunst
Staatliche Museen zu Berlin –
Preußischer Kulturbesitz
Lansstrasse 8
14195 Berlin
Collections: Indian textiles

Museum für Völkerkunde
Staatliche Museen zu Berlin –
Preußischer Kulturbesitz
Lansstrasse 8
14195 Berlin
*Collections: Worldwide
ethnographic textiles*

Pergamonmuseum Staatliche
Museen zu Berlin –
Preußischer Kulturbesitz
Bodestrasse 1–3
Museumsinsel
10178 Berlin
*Collections: Worldwide
ethnographic textiles*

Cologne
Rautenstrauch-Joest-Museum
für Völkerkunde der Stadt
Köln
Ubierring 45
50678 Cologne
Nordrhein-Westfalen
*Collections: Asian, American
and African textiles*

Dresden
Staatliches Museum für
Völkerkunde Dresden
Japanisches Palais, Palaisplatz
01097 Dresden
*Collections: Indian and South-
East Asian textiles*

Frankfurt am Main
Museum für Völkerkunde
Schaumainkai 29
60594 Frankfurt am Main
*Collections: Worldwide
ethnographic textiles*

Krefeld
Deutsches Textilmuseum
Krefeld
Andreas-markt 8
47809 Krefeld
Nordrhein-Westfalen
Collections: European textiles

Stuttgart
Linden-Museum Stuttgart-
Staatliche Museum für
Völkerkunde
Hegelplatz 1
70174 Stuttgart
*Collections: Central Asian and
Oceanic textiles*

GHANA
Accra
Ghana National Museum
Barnes Rd
PO Box 3343, Accra
*Collections: Ghanaian kente
cloth*

GREECE
Athens
Museum of the Greek
Folklore Society
12 Didotou St, Athens

National History Museum
13 Stadiou St, Athens
Collections: Greek folk costume

GUATEMALA
Ciudad de Guatemala
Museo Nacional de Artes
e Industria Populares
Avenida 10 No. 10–70
Zona 1 Ciudad de Guatemala
*Collections: Guatemalan folk
costume*

HUNGARY
Budapest
Magyar Nemzeti Múzeum
(Hungarian National
Museum)
Múzeum Körút 14–16
1088 Budapest
*Collections: Hungarian folk
costume*

Néprajzi Múzeum
(Ethnographic Museum)
Kossuth Lajos tér 12
1055 Budapest
*Collections: Hungarian folk
costume*

INDIA
Ahmedabad
Calico Museum of Textiles
Retreat, Shahi Bagh
380004 Ahmedabad, Gujarat
*Collections: The most important
holding of Indian textiles in
India*

Bhuj
Madansinghji Museum
The Palace, Bhuj
Collections: Kutchi embroidery

Calcutta
Indian Museum
27 Jawaharlal Nehru Rd
700016 Calcutta, West Bengal
*Collections: Indian and
Myanmarese (Burmese) textiles*

New Delhi
Crafts Museum
Pragati Maidan, Bhairon Road
110001 New Delhi
*Collections: Indian folk textiles
and saris*

INDONESIA
Jakarta
Museum Textil
Jl. K. Satsuit Tuban 4, Jakarta
*Collections: Batik, ikat and
plangi*

ISRAEL
Jerusalem
Sir Isaac and Lady Edith
Wolfson Museum
Hechal Shlomo
Rehov Hamelekh George 58
91073 Jerusalem
Collections: Jewish textiles

ITALY
Milan
Museo di Arte Estremo
Orientale e di Etnografia
(Museum of Far Eastern Art
and Ethnography)
Via Mosé Bianchi 94
20149 Milan
*Collections: Chinese, Indian
and Myanmarese (Burmese)
textiles*

Rome
Museo Nazionale Preistorico
Etnografico Luigi Pigorini
(Luigi Pigorini Museum of
Prehistory and Ethnography)
Viale Lincoln 3
00144 Rome
*Collections: Worldwide
ethnographic textiles*

JAPAN
Osaka
Kokuritsu Minzokugaku
Hakubutsukan
(National Museum of
Ethnology)
17–23 Yamadaogawa Suita-
Shi, Osaka
*Collections: Asian and Oceanic
textiles*

Museum of Textiles
5–102 Tomobuchi-Cho
1–Chome, Miyakojima-Ku
Osaka
*Collections: Worldwide
ethnographic textiles*

LAOS
Vientiane
National Museum
Saysettha District
PO Box 67, Vientiane
Collections: Laotian weaving

MADAGASCAR
Tananarive
Museum of Folklore
Parc de Tsimbazaza
PO Box 434, Tananarive
Collections: Madagascan textiles

MALAYSIA
Kinabalu
Sabah State Museum
1239 Gaya St
Kota Kinabalu
Collections: Dyak textiles

Kuala Lumpur
Muzium Seni Asia
(Museum of Asian Art)
Universiti Malaya
Kuala Lumpur
*Collections: South-East Asian
textiles*

National Art Gallery
109 Ampang Road
Kuala Lumpur
*Collections: South-East Asian
textiles*

National Museum
Jl. Damansara
Kuala Lumpur
*Collections: South-East Asian
textiles*

Kuching
Sarawak Museum
Jl. Tun Haji Openg
Kuching
Collections: Dyak ikat, bark cloth, bead and shell work

MALI
Bamako
National Museum of Mali
Rue de Général Leclerc
PO Box 159
Bamako
Collections: Mali textiles

MEXICO
Mexico City
Museo Nacional de Historia
Castillo de Chapultepec
11580 Mexico City
Collections: Mexican and European textiles

NETHERLANDS
Amsterdam
Tropenmuseum
Mauritskade 63
1092 AD Amsterdam
Collections: Indonesian and South-East Asian textiles

Delft
Nusan Tara Ethnographical Museum
Agatha Plein 4
2611 HR Delft
Collections: Indonesian and South-East Asian textiles

Leiden
Rijksmuseum voor Volkenkunde (National Museum of Ethnography)
Steenstraat 1
2300 AE Leiden
Collections: Indonesian and South-East Asian textiles

Rotterdam
Museum voor Volkenkunde (Museum of Geography and Ethnology)
Willemskade 25
3016 DM Rotterdam
Collections: Indonesian and South-East Asian textiles

NEW ZEALAND
Auckland
Auckland Institute and Museum
The Domain
Auckland
Collections: New Zealand and Oceanic textiles

Wellington
Museum of New Zealand
PO Box 467, Wellington
Collections: New Zealand, Hawaiian and Oceanic textiles

NIGERIA
Lagos
Nigerian Museum
PO Box 12556, Lagos
Collections: Nigerian textiles

PAKISTAN
Karachi
National Museum of Pakistan
Burns Garden, Karachi
Collections: Pakistani folk textiles

PAPUA NEW GUINEA
Port Moresby
National Museum and Art Gallery
Waigini, Port Moresby
Collections: Papua New Guinea costume

PERU
Lima
Museo Amano
Calle del Retiro 160
Miraflores, Lima
Collections: Pre-Columbian weaves

Museo Nacional de Antropologia y Arqueologia
Plaza Bolivia s/n
Pueblo Libre, Lima
Collections: Peruvian folk and historic costume

PHILIPPINES
Manila
National Museum of the Philippines
P. Burgos St, Rizal Park
1000 Manila
Collections: Philippine folk and tribal costume

POLAND
Warsaw
Muzeum Azji i Pacyfiku (Asia and Pacific Museum)
ul. Solec 24
(00–467) Warsaw
Collections: Asian and Oceanic textiles

PORTUGAL
Lisbon
Museu Etnográfico
Rua Portas de Santo Antao
100 Lisbon
Collections: Asian, African and South American textiles

ROMANIA
Bucharest
Muzeul national de istorie al Romaniei (Museum of Popular Art)
Calea Victoriei nr. 12
79740 Bucharest
Collections: Romanian folk costume

RUSSIA
Moscow
Museum of Oriental Art
ul. Obucha 16, Moscow
Collections: Asian textiles

St Petersburg
Peter the Great Museum of Anthropology and Ethnology
nab Universitetskaja 3
St Petersburg
Collections: Asian textiles

Staatliche Eremitage (Hermitage Museum)
Dworzowaja Nabereshnaja 34–36, St Petersburg
Collections: Russian and historical textiles

State Museum of Ethnography
ul. Inzenernaya, 4–1
St Petersburg
Collections: European and Asian textiles

SINGAPORE
National Museum
93 Stamford Road
0617 Singapore
Collections: South-East Asian textiles

SOUTH AFRICA
Cape Town
South African Cultural History Museum
49 Adderley St, PO Box 645
Cape Town
Collections: African, Asian and European textiles

SPAIN
Barcelona
Museu Etnològic
Parque de Montjuic
08038 Barcelona
Collections: Worldwide ethnographic textiles

Madrid
Museo Nacional de Etnologia
Alfonso XII, 68
28014 Madrid
Collections: Worldwide ethnographic textiles

SWEDEN
Gothenburg
Etnografiska Museet
Norra Hamngatan 12
41114 Gothenburg
Collections: African, South American, South-East Asian and Lappish textiles

Stockholm
The National Museum of Ethnography
Djurgardsbrunnsvägen 34
10252 Stockholm
Collections: Worldwide ethnographic textiles

SWITZERLAND
Basel
Museum für Völkerkunde und Schweizerisches Museum für Volkskunde Basel
Augustinergasse 2
4001 Basel
Collections: Asian, African and Oceanic textiles

St Gallen
Völkerkundliche Sammlung
Museumstrasse 50
9000 St Gallen
Collections: European textiles

Zürich
Völkerkundemuseum der Universität Zürich
Pelikanstrasse 40
8001 Zürich
Collections: Worldwide ethnographic textiles

TAIWAN
Taipei
Taiwan Museum
2 Siangyang Rd
Taipei
Collections: Chinese court textiles and Taiwanese folk costume

THAILAND
Bangkok
National Museum
Bamlampu
Bangkok
Thai court and folk costume

TURKEY
Istanbul
Topkapi Sarayi Müzesi (Topkapi Palace Museum)
Sultanahmed
Istanbul
Collections: Turkish court costume

UNITED STATES OF AMERICA
Berkeley
Lowie Museum of Anthropology
Kroebber Hall, Bancroft Way
University of California
Berkeley, CA 94720
Collections: Worldwide ethnographic textiles

Boston
Museum of Fine Arts
465 Huntingdon Ave
Boston, MA 02115
Collections: Worldwide historic textiles

Cambridge, Mass.
Peabody Museum of Archaeology and Ethnology
Harvard University
11 Divinity Ave
Cambridge, MA 02138
Collections: Worldwide ethnographic textiles

Chicago
The Art Institute of Chicago
111 S. Michigan Ave at Adams St
Chicago, IL 60603-6110
Collections: Chinese, Greek and Turkish textiles

Field Museum of Natural History
Roosevelt Rd at Lake Shore Drive, Chicago, IL 60605
Collections: Worldwide ethnographic textiles

Cincinnati
Cincinnati Art Museum
Eden Park
Cincinnati, OH 45202-1596
Collections: Asian textiles

Cleveland
The Cleveland Museum of Art
11150 East Boulevard
Cleveland, OH 44106
Collections: European, North American and Asian textiles

Denver
The Denver Art Museum
100 West 14th Ave, Parkway
Denver, CO 80204
Collections: European, North American and Asian textiles

Detroit
The Detroit Institute of Arts
5200 Woodward Ave
Detroit, MI 48202
Collections: European and Asian textiles

Indianapolis
Indianapolis Museum of Art
1200 West 38 St
Indianapolis, IN 46208
Collections: Asian textiles

La Jolla
Mingei International
Museum of Folk Art
4405 La Jolla, CA 92037
*Collections: Worldwide
ethnographic textiles*

Los Angeles
Fowler Museum of Cultural
History
University of California
405 Hilgard Ave
Los Angeles, CA 90024
*Collections: Reserve collection of
worldwide ethnographic textiles*

Los Angeles County Museum
of Art
5905 Wilshire Boulevard
Los Angeles, CA 90036
Collections: Asian textiles

Newark
The Newark Museum
49 Washington St
Newark, NJ 07101-0540
*Collections: Asian and African
textiles*

New York City
American Museum of Natural
History
79th St and Central Park West
New York, NY 10024
*Collections: African and
American textiles*

The Brooklyn Museum
200 Eastern Parkway
New York, NY 11238-6052
*Collections: Worldwide
ethnographic textiles*

Cooper-Hewitt National
Museum of Design
Smithsonian Institution
5th Ave at 91st St
New York, NY 10128
*Collections: Asian and
European textiles*

The Metropolitan Museum
of Art
1000 Fifth Avenue
New York, NY 10028
*Collections: Worldwide
ethnographic textiles*

Philadelphia
Philadelphia Museum of Art
26th St and Benjamin
Franklin Parkway
Philadelphia, PA 19130
*Collections: European and
Asian textiles*

Salem
Peabody Essex Museum
East India Square
Salem, MA 01970
Collections: Asian textiles

San Francisco
The Fine Arts Museums of
San Francisco
M.H. de Young Memorial
Museum
Golden Gate Park
San Francisco, CA 94118
*Collections: Asian and
European textiles*

Santa Fe
Museum of International
Folk Art
706 Camino Lejo
Santa Fe, NM 87505
*Collections: Central American,
South American and Asian
textiles*

Seattle
Historic Costume and Textile
Collections
University of Washington
Seattle, WA 98105
*Collections: Italian and Balkan
textiles*

National Museum of Natural
History
Seattle Art Museum
Volunteer Park
Seattle, WA 98122
*Collections: African and Asian
textiles*

Washington
National Museum of Natural
History
10th St and Constitution Ave,
N.W
Washington, DC 20560
*Collections: Worldwide
ethnographic textiles*

Textile Museum
2320 S Street, N.W
Washington, DC 20008
*Collections: Reserve collection of
worldwide ethnographic textiles*

SOURCES OF ILLUSTRATIONS

The following abbreviations have been used: *a*, above; *b*, below; *c*, centre; *i*, inset; *l*, left; *m*, main picture; *r*, right; *t*, top.

All drawings are by Bryan Sentance

All studio photography is by James Austin unless otherwise stated.

Janet Anderson, 27*ar*, 207*bl*; Elizabeth Andrews 206*bl*; Auckland War Museum, New Zealand, 221*ia*; Jenny Balfour-Paul, 118*bl*; Nicholas Barnard, 43*br*, 102*bl*, 119*cr*; Brian Brake, 221*m*; Ilay Cooper, 210*i*; Sian Davies, 30*b*, 31*al*, 70*l*, 75*l*, 107*a*, 107*b*, 110*br*, 122*br*, 143*ar*, 144*al*, 144*bl*, 162*m*, 177*bl*, 205*ar*, 224*tr*, 225*br*; Barry Dawson, 37*c*, 67*b*, 68*a*, 85*bc*, 85*br*, 108, 112*ar*, 113*b*, 119*tr*, 119*cl*, 119*bl*, 119*br*, 135*br*, 136*ar*, 136*bl*, 166*bl*; Mark Farrell, 120*bl*, 228*bl*; John Gillow, 5, 43*bl*, 68*bl*, 69*b*, 103*a*, 103*c*, 103*bl*, 103*br*, 118*al*, 118*r*, 123*al*, 128*ar*, 131*br*, 141*ib*, 148*cr*, 158*il*, 171*bl*, 187*i*, 219*bl*; Nicky Grist, 22*bl*; Caroline Hart, 102*br*; Iles photo, New Zealand, 221*ib*; India Office Library, 18*bl*; Sheila Paine, 197*c*, 197*bl*; Jennie Parry, 170*r*, 171*br*, 207*al*, 207*ar*; Herta Puls, 148*br*, 155*i*; Bryan Sentance, 59*tr*, 83*al*, 83*ar*, 83*bl*, 83*br*, 91*br*, 104*al*, 106*al*, 122*al*, 137*t*, 147*b*, 167*b*, 216*ac*, 218*br*, 220*l*, 222*m*, 222*ir*, 223*al*, 223*b*, 224*al*; Ron Simpson, 164*tr*; Ian Skelton, 112*l*, 202*al*; South Australia Museum, Adelaide, 21*br*; Roddy Taylor, 167*a*, 193*b*, 204; Andrew Turner, 82*l*, 82*r*; Janet Willoughby, 68*br*.

ACKNOWLEDGMENTS

We should like to thank the following for their kind help, for the loan of textiles and photographs and for their advice: Janet Anderson, Elizabeth Andrews, Tim and Ferelith Ashfield, The Auckland Museum, James Austin, Jenny Balfour-Paul, Nicholas Barnard, Ishwar Singh Batti, Ave and Beryl Behrens and Patrick Watson, Dawn Berry, Virginia Bond, Bungo, Mrs Muriel Cass, Peter and Elizabeth Collingwood, Ilay Cooper, Dennis Cope, Caroline Crabtree, Anna Crutchley, Kate Curtis, Barry Dawson, Marjolien and Tony Dibden and family, Joyce Doel, Eve Eckstein, Dave Edmonds, Mark Farrell, Rosie Feesey, Rosie Ford, Jim and Diane Gaffney, Polly Gillow, Seth Gillow, Nicky Grist, Lindsay Hardingham, Peggy Harper, Caroline Hart, Janet Harvey, Sally Hirons, Molly Hogg, C. J. Howlett-Jones and Emma Hubbard, Hiroko Iwatate, Anthea Jarvis, Jessica King, Heidi Kleinschmidt, Raymond Lau, Sue Leighton-White, Alysn Midgelow-Marsden, Claudia Mills, Anne Morrell, Colleen and Bill Morrow, Lucy Moss, Sein Win Myint, Roger Neich, Deryn O'Connor, Sheila Paine, Jane Page, Michael Pak, Dave and Carolyn Phillips, Herta and Oscar Puls, Benonia Puplampu, Barbie Rich and Toshio Okomura, Clare Rose, Alan and Joan Sentance, Paul and Christine Sentance, Ron Simpson, John Smith, Rupert Smith, South Australia Museum, the late Montse Stanley, Marsha Stanyukovich, Christine Sterne, Caroline Stone, the late Marianne Straub, Karun Thakar and Roy Short, Judy and Andrew Taylor, Roddy Taylor, Goodie Vohra, Peter Wallin, Janet Willoughby, Marina Yedigaroff, Ann-Marie Young and once again Alastair Hull for the use of his photographic facilities and Jennie Parry for so thoroughly investigating the techniques of Chinese braid embroidery upon whose original research that section of this book is based. We are much indebted to them all and to the nameless craftsmen and women from all over the globe who created the wonderful textiles that illustrate this book.

INDEX

Figures in *italic* refer to pages on which illustrations appear

abaca fibre 37, 140; *37*
Abeokuta 131
adinkra printing 110; *103, 110, 111*
adire 131; *121*
adire alabere 124
adire eleko 128; *129, 131*
adjective dyes 118
Afghanistan 52, 92, 102, 182, 185, 189, 201, 211, 216; *23, 25, 28, 45, 52, 54, 78, 97, 114, 147, 157, 182, 183, 184, 186, 189, 197, 198, 199, 201, 211, 227, 228*
agave fibre 56
Ahmedabad 113; *12, 103, 107, 110*
Ainu people 33; *33*
ajrakh print 139; *119, 138, 139*
Akha hill tribe *172*
Alaska 64, 68
Aleppo 74
Algeria 189; *196*
alpaca 23, 48; *53*
alum 118, 128, 139
Amazonia 220; *43*
Amish *164*
Anatolia 65; *24*
Andes 14, 27, 48, 52
aniline dyes 119; *139*
Apache 159; *159*
appliqué 12, 149, 150–51, 154, 156–57, 163, 164, 166; *7, 14, 20, 21, 25, 38, 147, 148, 149, 150, 151, 156, 157, 169, 185*
Aran islands 23, 50; *50*
Arizona 69
Armenia 74
Ashanti people 30, 89, 92, 110; *31, 68, 93*
Astrolabe Bay 33; *101*
Atayal tribe *36*
Atlas mountains 27
Australia *12, 21, 102*
Ayrshire 197; *196*
Aztecs 20

back stitch *172, 216*
Baffinland *114*
Bagobo tribe *117*
Bali 85, 91, 144; *91, 119, 135, 145*
Balkans, the 181, 208; *35*
Balouch 92; *214, 227*
Balouchistan 65
bandhani 70, 122
Bangladesh 149, 163, 172; *163, 173*
Banjara tribe 211; *37, 153, 159, 163, 211, 215*
Bargello work 198; *198*
bark cloth 11, 32–33, 105; *11, 16–17, 19, 32, 33, 101, 102, 104, 106, 115*
Basques *18*
bast fibres 34, 36–37, 140; *19, 36, 37*
Basuto people *219*
batik 12, 128, 133, 135, 136, 226; *119, 134, 135, 136*

bead work 104, 167, 202, 206, 216–17, 218–19; *20, 48, 166, 206, 207, 214, 216, 217, 218, 219, 224, 225*
Belgium 62; *13*
Benares 13, 91
Bengal 37; *90, 163*
Berlin work 181, 198; *198*
Bethlehem *185*
Bhutan 88, 98–99, *110*
Bilaan tribe *215, 216*
blackwork *172*
blanket stitch 171, 185, 188–89; *188, 189*
block printing 110, 112–13, 136, 139; *12, 70, 110, 112, 113, 119, 136, 139*
bobbin lace 62; *42, 62*
body-tensioned loom 68, 85; *68*
Bokhara couching 186–87; *186, 187*
Bolivia 48, 52, 95, 220; *23, 27, 53, 55, 65, 78, 95, 213, 229*
Borneo 37
braid embroidery 158–59; *158, 159, 206*
braiding 43, 54–55
British Isles 51, 119, 160, 164, 201, 220, 224; *95; see also England, Ireland, Scotland, Wales*
Brittany *42, 171*
brocade 12, 13, 90–91; *31, 67, 83, 90, 91, 99*
broderie anglaise 197
Bulgaria 35, 52, 58, 91, 207
Burkina Faso 124; *2, 120, 121, 124*
Burma *see* Myanmar
buttonhole stitch 171, 188–89, 197; *188, 189*

Cairo 113; *148, 149, 151*
calico 28
Calicut 28, 70
California 73, 220
Cambodia 124; *142, 143*
Cameroon 124; *19, 32, 124*
Canada 11, 64, 95, 185; *54, 165, 222*
Canary Islands 38
canting 134–35; *134, 135*
cap 136; *119, 136, 137*
Carpathian Mountains *21*
cashmere wool 23
Caucasus 65, 123; *15*
Central Africa 30, 33, 38
Central America 42, 140
Central Asia 25, 48, 75, 113, 139, 140, 157, 207, 226; *96, 136*
chain stitch 163, 170, 171, 178–79, 185, 202; *178, 179, 187, 200*
Channel Islands 23, 48
Chiapas 28
chikan 197; *197*
Ch'in tribe 224
China 15, 30, 65, 82, 91, 110, 120, 132, 133, 135, 136, 159, 175, 178, 190, 194, 209, 229; *24, 30, 36, 39, 45, 77, 83, 91, 118, 132, 133, 137, 150, 152, 153, 156, 159, 162, 172, 174, 175, 190, 191, 208, 212, 213, 229*

Chinese knife 132–33; *118, 132, 133*
Chitral 23, *214*
choli 202, 206
cochineal 118; *117*
coins 212–13; *212, 213*
Colombia 56; *56, 106, 150*
complementary warps 78
compound ikat 144–45; *70, 144, 145*
Congo, the (formerly Zaire) 13, 38, 96–97; *3, 16–17, 33, 38, 97, 104, 116–117, 160, 188*
Copts 48, 76; *77*
Côte d'Ivoire 38, 102, 105; *125*
cotton 11, 28–29, 34, 47, 48, 61, 74, 91, 108, 110, 126, 132, 139, 143, 166, 167, 171, 194, 197; *18, 28, 29, 35, 36, 40–41, 44, 47, 48, 59, 79, 100–01, 106, 112, 118, 124, 127, 140, 141, 143, 144, 177, 194*
couching 171, 184–85, 186–87, 216; *184, 185, 186, 187, 208, 209, 216*
counted-thread embroidery 181, 198; *35, 70*
counterchange appliqué 157; *157*
cowrie shells 215; *205, 215*
Croatia 158
crochet 43, 46–47, 219; *43, 46, 47*
cross stitch 170, 172, 180–81, 198; *34–35, 180, 181*
cutwork 197
Cyprus 62; *193*
Czech Republic 19, 170, 218

Damascus 82; *75*
damask 82–83; *82, 83*
Dani tribe 44
darning stitch 172; *172*
daubed textiles 104–05; *104, 105*
denim 73
Denmark 56
Dida tribe 125
double ikat 144–45; *119, 144, 145*
double weave 94–95; *94, 95*
drawloom 82
drawn-thread work 192–93, 197; *192, 193, 197*
Dubrovnik 46
dyes 116–45; *116–45*

East Africa 218
East Indies 120
Ecuador 95; *44, 45, 106*
Egypt 10, 34, 48, 61, 76, 120, 182; *77, 148, 149, 214*
elm-bark fibre 33; *32*
embroidery 12, 70, 168–203; *3, 20, 21, 22, 34, 35, 39, 70, 97, 168–203, 206*
England 62, 112–13, 160, 163, 166, 172, 181, 201, 215; *15, 26, 40–41, 42, 46, 47, 48, 50, 51, 58, 59, 62, 70, 83, 96, 149, 160, 165, 181, 194, 198, 200*
Ersari tribe 117
Ewe people 89, 92; *66–67, 69, 92, 120*
eyelet stitch 171, 188–89; *188, 189*

Fante tribe 28
featherwork 220–21; *206, 220, 221*
felt 10, 11, 24–25, 150, 156, 157; *25, 157*
Fiji 11, 33; *32, 115*
Finland 159
fishbone stitch 182; *182*
flat stitch 182
flax 34, 70; *10, 18, 34*
Flores 121
Florida 14
Former Yugoslavia 62; *46, 184*
France 62, 82, 181; *18, 42, 43, 48, 63, 171, 196, 229*
French knot stitch 170, 171, 190–91; *190, 191*
fringes 226–27; *226, 227*
Fulani people 92

Gambia, the 122, 124; *10, 124*
gauze weave 65; *64, 65*
Georgia *161*
geringsing 144; *145*
Germany 95, 197
Ghana 30, 89, 92, 110, 150; *9, 28, 31, 66–67, 68, 69, 92, 93, 103, 111, 120*
Ghazni 183, 189, 197
ginning 28; *18*
Greece 61; *10, 34–35, 52, 53, 61, 62, 98–99, 169, 192, 216*
Guatemala 56; *52, 70, 79, 88, 89, 145*
Guernsey 23, 48, 51
Guizhou 159; *24, 31, 36, 118, 132, 133, 158, 159, 174, 175, 190, 191, 208, 213*
Gujarat 14, 113, 144, 182, 211; *12, 15, 65, 70, 103, 107, 110, 112, 138, 145, 151, 153, 166, 170, 171, 173, 176, 180, 182, 183, 207, 210, 212, 218*

hair 22–23, 166; *43, 65*
Hama 122, 208
Hani tribe 45
Hardanger 197; *35, 81, 217*
Harris Island 73; *72*
Hausa people 189; *168–69, 186, 228*
Hebrides 42, 73; *72*
hemp 37, 70, 132, 198; *19, 36, 45*
Herat 102; *28, 114*
Herringbone stitch 182–83; *182, 183, 189*
H'mong hill tribe 120, 132, 169, 178
Hokkaido 33
Holbein stitch 172; *172*
Holland 136; *171*
Homer 10
Honshu 128
Hungary 21, 156, 157, 178, 213
Hunza 46

Ibadan 128
Iban tribe 18, 140, 141
Ifugao tribe 38
ikat 12, 75, 140–41, 142–43, 144–45; *11, 70, 74, 81, 97, 140, 141, 142, 143, 144, 145; see also warp ikat and weft ikat*
Incas 166

India 13, 14, 15, 28, 30, 37, 61, 70, 74, 76, 91, 107, 108, 110, 112–13, 120, 122, 123, 126, 135, 143, 144, 148, 153, 156, 163, 165, 172, 175, 182, 202, 208, 209, 211, 216; *6, 9, 12, 15, 17, 18, 22, 26, 31, 37, 43, 47, 60, 61, 65, 70, 74, 75, 77, 90, 94, 102, 103, 106, 107, 109, 110, 112, 113, 114, 117, 118, 119, 123, 126, 127, 136, 138, 139, 143, 144, 145, 147, 150, 151, 153, 159, 161, 163, 166, 170, 171, 173, 176, 177, 180, 182, 183, 197, 202, 203, 205, 206, 207, 210, 211, 212, 218*
indigo 118, 119, 120–21, 128, 139; *2, 10, 29, 78, 120, 121, 124, 128, 129, 130, 133, 139, 144, 172, 190*
Indo-China 133, 153; *133*
Indonesia 33, 38, 85, 92, 98–99, 122, 123, 124, 135, 143, 144, 216; *11, 67, 85, 87, 119, 121, 128, 140, 141, 216, 219, 135, 144*
Indore 103
Inuit 11; *114*
Iran 76, 108, 113, 178; *73, 108, 113, 179*
Iraq 28, 70
Ireland 23, 197; *50*
Israel 180, 181, 182; *181*
itajime 140
Italy 30, 58, 62, 95, 181, 216; *42, 62*
Itneg tribe 87
ivory 13

Jacquard loom 82
Jaipur 126; *126*
Japan 33, 61, 114, 120, 122, 123, 124, 128, 131, 144, 220, 229; *32, 114, 122, 128, 129, 130, 131, 144*
Java 124, 135, 136, 148, 224, 226; *68, 119, 122, 134, 135, 136, 137*
Job's tears seeds 224; *225*
Jodphur 126; *103, 113, 126, 127*
Jogjakarta 119
Jordan 181, 182; *181*

Kach'in tribe 89
kalagas 167, 212; *166*
kalamkari 108, 113, 139; *102, 108, 109*
Kalimantan 37, 219
Kanchipuram *31*
Kano 6, 81, 92
kantha 149, 163, 172; *163, 173*
Kashgar 118
Kashgaria 25
Kashmir 76, 178; *5, 73, 77*
kasuri 144; *144*
katazome 114, 131
kente cloth 92; *9, 31, 68, 93*
Kenya 103
kesdi stitch 189
khes 95; *94*
kilim 76; *22*
kinkhab brocade 91
Kirghizia 25, 226
Kirman 73
knitting 42, 43, 48–49, 50–51, 52–53, 219; *9, 12, 18, 26, 27, 42, 43, 48, 49, 52, 53*

239

Kohistan 215, 224; *224*
Korea *82*
Kuba people 38, 96–97; *3, 17, 33, 38, 39, 97, 116–17, 160, 188*
Kulu *77*
Kuna tribe 149, 154; *14, 148, 154, 155*
Kutch 107, 139, 202; *9, 47, 75, 106, 119, 123, 147, 202, 203, 206, 210, 211*

lace 62–63; *62, 63, 170*
Ladakh *22*
Lakai *182*
Laos 86, 154; *86, 87, 89, 132, 133, 143, 152*
Lapps 68; *159*
Latvia *18, 94*
lazy stitch *216*
leather 20, 21, 150, 156, 223; *20, 21, 156, 222, 223*
Lebanon *209*
leheria 126–27; *126, 127*
Lhasa *26*
linen 10, 11, 34–35, 37, 171, 181, 194, 197, 198, 201; *34, 35, 37*
linking 44–45; *44*
llama wool *48*
Lombok *67, 87, 119*
looms 42, 43, 68–99, 218; *10, 13, 68, 69, 218*
looping 44–45, 209; *44, 45, 219*
Luzon *38, 86*

macramé 43, 58–59, 226; *40–41, 58, 59*
Madagascar *38*
madder 118, 139; *117*
Majorca *143*
Malaysia *11, 18, 140*
Mali 92, 102, 124; *92, 93, 102, 105*
Malta 62; *63*
Mandalay *167*
Mandaya tribe *37*
Manila *14*
Maoris 64, 220; *65, 221*
mashru 19, 74–75; *74, 75*
metal-thread work 208–09; *184, 185, 208, 209*
Mexico 194; *11, 12, 28, 41, 44, 48, 64, 76, 80, 87, 169, 192, 218*
Miao hill tribe 159; *6, 31, 36, 152, 158, 159, 174, 175, 190, 191*
Middle East 75, 82, 123, 175, 181, 189, 194, 216; *74*
milkweed *37*
Minangkabau people *91*
Mindanao *6, 37, 117, 215, 216*
mirrorwork 210–11; *7, 197, 205, 206, 207, 210, 211*
Moi tribe *86*
molas 149, 150, 154–55; *14, 148, 154–55*
Moluccas *85*
Mongolia *10, 156*
Montenegro *184*
mordants 108, 113, 118, 120, 138–39; *138, 139*
Morocco 21; *20, 97, 156, 174, 175*
Mossi people *2, 124*
Mosul *28, 70, 97*
mothara 126–27; *126, 127*

mother-of-pearl 215; *215*
mud cloths 104; *102, 105*
Murshidabad *90*
muslin 28, 197; *101, 197*
Myanmar (Burma) 167, 212; *29, 71, 76, 89, 152, 166, 172, 224, 225*

Nagaland *6, 205, 225*
Native Americans 55, 104, 159, 167, 206; *167, 206, 227*
natural dyes *119*
Navaho tribe *13, 69*
Nazca desert *67*
Near East *58, 140*
needle lace 62, *197*
needlepoint 181, 198–99; *62, 198, 199*
needleweaving 194–95; *194, 195*
Nepal 50, 61; *51, 101*
netting 37, 43, 44–45, 219; *44, 45*
New Guinea 45, 220, 224; *44, 220*
New Mexico *218*
New York *216*
New Zealand 64, 220; *221*
Nigeria 14, 19, 21, 38, 68, 122, 124, 128, 131; *6, 78, 81, 92, 121, 128, 129, 131, 168–69, 188, 228*
Noin Ula 10, 156; *156*
Normandy *63*
North Africa 25, 27, 86, 175, *189*
North America 23, 33, 37, 38, 42, 55, 73, 95, 104, 149, 159, 160, 164, 165, 167, 206, 209, 215, 216, 218, 220, 223; *14, 55, 69, 95, 104, 165, 167, 206, 216, 220, 222, 223, 224, 227*
Norway 52, 68, 197; *35, 81, 148, 217*

Oman *167*
openwork 197; *197*

padded work 166–67; *166, 167*
painting 70, 106–07; *106, 107*
paisley *136*
Pakistan 14, 19, 28, 56, 95, 123, 139, 156, 163, 165, 211, 213, 215, 224; *7, 14, 20, 23, 31, 46, 57, 72, 106, 122, 138, 152, 160, 162, 164, 177, 185, 189, 209, 210, 213, 214, 215, 224*
Palembang 124; *124*
Palestine 180, 181, 182; *34, 90, 185, 209*
Panama 149, 154; *148*
Pandanus fibre *45*
Papua New Guinea 33; *101*
patchwork 12, 160–61, 163, 164–65; *3, 14, 38, 146–47, 148, 160, 161, 164, 165, 188*
patola 144; *145*
Pazyryk 24, 149, 156; *156, 157*
Pekin knot stitch 170, 171, 190–91; *190, 191*
pen work 108–09; *108, 109*
Peru 10, 48, 95; *27, 28, 67, 68, 95, 166, 220, 229*
Philippines 37, 140; *37, 38, 76, 87, 117, 215, 216*

Phormium tenax 220; *65, 220*
phulkari 177; *177*
plangi 122, 123
ply-splitting 60–61; *60, 61*
Poland *95*
polychrome woodblock printing 112–13; *112, 113*
Polynesia 33, 216; *207*
porcupine quills 222–23; *222, 223*
Portugal *39, 201*
pulled-thread work 192–93, 197; *15, 192, 193, 197*
Punjab 95, 177; *122, 176, 177*
pygmies *16–17, 104*

quillwork 104, 222–23; *222, 223*
quilting 12, 153, 162–63, 164, 165; *152, 162, 163, 164, 165*

Rajasthan 61, 107, 126, 139, 153, 211; *26, 43, 60, 61, 103, 107, 113, 114, 117, 118, 126, 151, 161*
Ramallah *34*
ramie fibre *36, 82*
raphia 13, 18, 38–39, 96–97, 124; *3, 17, 19, 33, 38, 39, 116–17, 124, 125, 160, 188*
rawhide 20; *104, 223*
Resht 177; *179*
resist dyeing 122, 140, 144; *29, 70, 119, 139, 145*
reticella *197*
reverse appliqué 150, 152–53, 154; *152, 153*
ribbon embroidery 158–59; *158, 159*
roghan work 107; *106*
Romania *27*
Romanian couching *186*
running stitch 163, 170, 171, 172–73; *172, 173*
Russia 62, 194; *45, 63, 96, 192, 194, 195*

Salish tribe *23*
Samarkand *186*
Sam Neua 86; *86*
Samoa 11; *19, 32*
San'a *123*
San Blas Islands 154; *148*
San Francisco *123*
Sarakat nomads *52, 61, 216*
Sarawak 11, 18, 140, 219
sashiko stitching *131*
satin 202, *209*
satin stitch 170, 171, 174–75, 176–77, 197; *30, 169, 174, 175, 176, 177*
satin weave 69, 74–75, 78; *74, 75*
Savu *140*
Scotland 15, 42, 52, 73, 95, 112–13, 119, 197, 224; *26, 49, 51, 58, 72, 73, 196*
screen printing *114*
seeds *224*
Seminole Indians 159; *14*
Senegal *122, 124*
sequins 212–13; *212, 213*
sheepskin *21*
shellwork 206, 214–15; *205, 207, 214, 215, 219*
Shetland Islands 52; *26*
shibori 123; *122*

Siberia 24, 149, 156; *11, 224*
Sicily *107*
Sierra Leone 124; *79*
silk 11, 30–31, 47, 74, 75, 82, 91, 114, 126, 140, 143, 171, 202, 209; *17, 30, 31, 34, 36, 71, 75, 82, 83, 86, 91, 122, 123, 135, 142, 174, 175, 189, 199, 208, 209*
Silk Road, the *9, 30*
Sinai *181, 228*
Sind 14, 95, 139, 153, 163, 211; *7, 20, 57, 106, 138, 152, 160, 162, 164, 189, 209, 210, 215*
Singapore *135*
sisal *38*
smocking 200–01; *15, 169, 200, 201*
Sokoto *21*
songket brocade 91; *91*
soumak 65; *22, 64, 65*
South America 23, 25, 65, 76, 86, 123, 140, 175, 193, 209
South-East Asia 33, 76, 91, 108, 120, 135, 140, 143, 144, 208, 209
South Pacific *207, 225*
Spain 38, 58, 95, 98; *14, 47, 59, 96*
spangles *212*
spinning 11, 23, 26, 27; *13, 26, 27*
sprang 43, 56–57; *56, 57*
Sri Lanka *135*
starch resist 128–29, 130–31; *128, 129, 130, 131*
stencilling 114–15, 131; *32, 114, 115, 130, 131*
stitched resist 124–25; *2, 3, 116–17, 124, 125, 188*
stripweave 92–93; *6, 31, 66–67, 81, 92, 93*
stuffed work 166–67; *166, 167*
stump work *166*
substantive dyes 118, *120*
Sudan *149, 150*
Sulawesi 98–99; *128, 141*
Sulu Islands *76*
Sumatra 91, 124, 194, 211; *91, 124, 135, 136, 195, 212*
Sumba 85, 92; *1, 85, 140*
Sumeria 23; *23*
supplementary warp 12, 84, 85, 96; *84, 85*
supplementary weft 12, 86–87, 88–89, 91, 92, 96; *26, 80, 86, 87, 88, 89, 91, 92*
surface weft packing *89*
suzani 186; *186, 187, 202*
Swat *31*
Sweden *190*
Syria 74, 82, 181, 182, 212; *11, 74, 75, 84, 100–01, 122, 139, 181, 185, 193, 208*

tabby weave 69, 70–71, 144; *68, 70, 71, 195*
tablet weaving 98–99; *98, 99*
Taiwan *36*
Tajikistan 75; *7, 123, 186*
tambour hook 178, 202; *202*
tambour work 202–03; *202–03*
Tanimbar Islands *38*
tapa cloth 33, 105; *19, 33, 104, 115*
tape lace 62; *63*
tapestry weave 12, 76–77, 89; *5, 6, 67, 73, 76, 77, 89*

tartan 15, 73
tassels 226, 228–29; *206, 224, 226, 228–29*
tatting 62; *62, 63*
Thailand 133, 153, 167; *80, 142, 143*
Tibet 15, 54, 107; *22, 26, 54, 81, 147*
tie and dye 122–23, 126, 140, 143, 144; *7, 70, 117, 122, 123, 126, 127*
Timor 85; *85, 86, 218*
Tonga 33, 105; *33, 43, 102, 104, 148*
Toraja people *128, 141*
tritik 124; *124*
tsutsugaki 128; *128*
Tuaregs *121*
Turkestan 135; *25*
Turkey 15, 61, 74, 212; *34, 55, 59, 65, 98–99, 167, 204–05, 208*
Turkmenistan 157; *71, 117, 139, 157, 189, 212*
tussar silk *17*
tweed cloth 73; *72, 73*
twill weave 69, 72–73; *72, 73*
twining 64–65; *64, 65*

Uganda *11, 71*
Uighurs *171*
Ukraine *21*
Urgut *187*
Uzbekistan 75, 92, 157, 202; *11, 22, 97, 141, 146–47, 157, 161, 186, 187, 202, 227*

velvet 96–97, 209; *96, 97*
Venice 216; *42*
vicuña 23, 48; *53*
Vietnam 86, 120, 133, 152, 169, 178, 180, 226, 228

Wales 95, 201; *12*
wampum 215, 218
warp-faced weave 78, 79, 98–99; *78, 79*
warp ikat 37, 140–41, 143; *11, 37, 121, 140, 141*
wax resist 132–33, 134–35, 136–37; *118, 132, 133, 134, 135, 136, 137*
weft-faced weave 80–81; *80, 81*
weft ikat 142–43; *80, 119, 142, 143, 144*
West Africa 37, 38, 54, 92, 120, 122, 124, 135, 140
whimsy 167; *167*
whitework 196–97; *196, 197*
wild-orchid fibre *37, 44*
woad *120*
Wodaabe tribe *178*
woodblock printing 110–11; *110, 111*
wool 11, 22–23, 24, 25, 26–27, 47, 48, 198; *22, 23, 25, 26, 27, 35, 47, 48, 49, 50, 51, 52, 53, 65, 70, 72, 81*
worsted cloth *26*
wrapping 64–65; *64, 65*

Yemen 143; *12, 99, 123, 185, 225*
Yoruba people 14, 19, 68, 122, 128; *29, 78, 121*
Yunnan 45, 152, 153, 172

Zulus 10, 216, 219

D1389738

M42 ESO/J. Emerson/VISTA. Acknowledgment: Cambridge Astronomical Survey Unit

VOYAGER

VOYAGER

101 WONDERS BETWEEN EARTH AND THE EDGE OF THE COSMOS

Atlantic Books
London

A journey through
space and time   08

01	Earth	18
02	The Moon	20
03	Venus	22
04	Mercury	24
05	The Sun	26
06	Mars	28
07	Phobos	30
08	Eros	32
09	Comet Holmes	34
10	Jupiter	36
11	Io	38
12	Europa	40
13	Saturn	42
14	Mimas	44

15	Enceladus	46
16	Titan	48
17	Hyperion	50
18	Iapetus	52
19	Neptune	54
20	Triton	56

0 Light Seconds

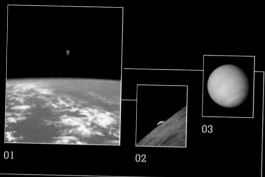

01

02

03

04

05

06

07

08

09

10

11

12

13

14

15

16

17

18

19

20

DUN LAOGHAIRE-
RATHDOWN LIBRARIES

DLR20001008296

BERTRAMS 29/10/2012

£25.00

EA

WITHDRAWN FROM
DÚN LAOGHAIRE RATHDOWN COUNTY
LIBRARY STOCK

21	Rho Ophiuchi	62
22	T Tauri	64
23	Helix Nebula	66
24	Snake Nebula	68
25	Witch Head Nebula	70
26	Vela Supernova	72
27	Cygnus Loop	74
28	Medusa Nebula	76
29	Orion Molecular Cloud	78
30	Orion Nebula	80
31	Horsehead Nebula	82
32	NGC 1999	84
33	M78	86
34	Pelican Nebula	88

35	Elephant Trunk	90
36	NGC 2264	92
37	Cat's Eye Nebula	94
38	Soap Bubble Nebula	96
39	Butterfly Nebula	98
40	Lagoon Nebula	100
41	Crescent Nebula	102
42	Rosette Nebula	104
43	Trifid Nebula	106
44	Cat's Paw Nebula	108
45	NGC 3582	110
46	Crab Nebula	112
47	Eagle Nebula	114
48	Tycho's Supernova	116

49	Carina Nebula: Eta Carinae	118
50	Carina Nebula: The Mystic Mountain	120
51	War & Peace Nebula	122
52	Cassiopeia A	124
53	Thor's Helmet	126
54	Omega Centauri	128
55	Skull & Crossbones	130
56	NGC 3603	132
57	V838 Monocerotis	134
58	Milky Way Core	136
59	Sagittarius A*	138
60	M72 Globular Cluster	140

460 Light Years

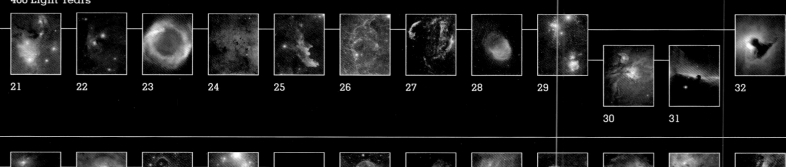

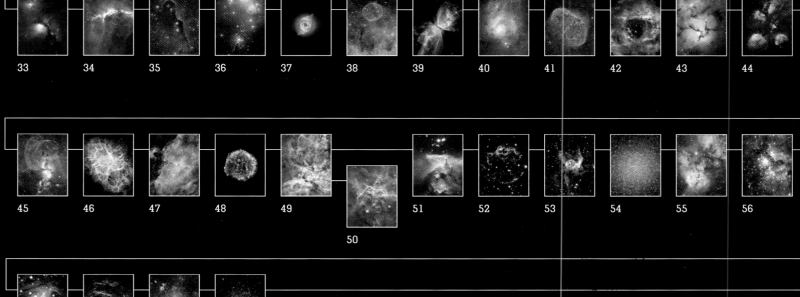

21 22 23 24 25 26 27 28 29 30 31 32

33 34 35 36 37 38 39 40 41 42 43 44

45 46 47 48 49 50 51 52 53 54 55 56

57 58 59 60

61	LMC	146
62	Tarantula Nebula	148
63	NGC 346	150
64	Andromeda Galaxy	152
65	Triangulum Galaxy	154
66	Sagittarius Dwarf Irregular Galaxy	156
67	Centaurus A	158
68	Bode's Galaxy	160
69	Cigar Galaxy	162
70	NGC 4449	164
71	Pinwheel Galaxy	166
72	Sombrero Galaxy	168
73	Whirlpool Galaxy	170
74	Spindle Galaxy	172
75	Antennae Galaxies	174
76	NGC 1427A	176
77	NGC 1672	178
78	NGC 4522	180
79	NGC 1300	182
80	NGC 1316	184
81	HCG 90	186
82	NGC 4696	188
83	Perseus A	190
84	Norma Cluster	192
85	The Mice	194
86	3C 75	196
87	Stephan's Quintet	198
88	AM0644-741	200
89	NGC 1132	202
90	NGC 4921	204
91	Hercules Cluster	206
92	Tadpole Galaxy	208
93	Hoag's Object	210

160 Kilo Light Years

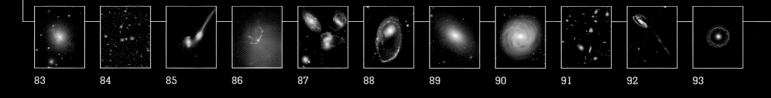

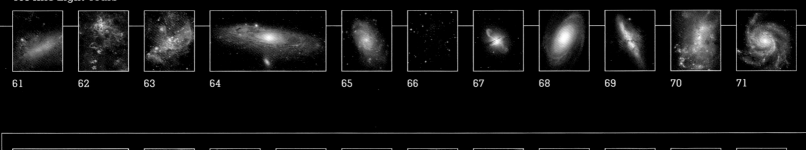

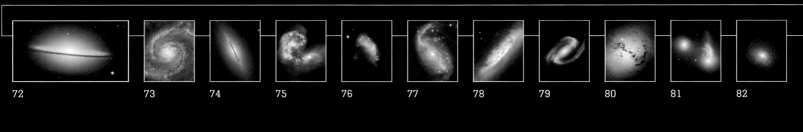

94	2MASS Survey	216
95	The Sloan Great Wall	218
96	Abell 315	220
97	Abell 1689	222
98	Bullet Cluster	224
99	Cl 0024+17	226
100	Hubble UDF	228
101	WMAP Survey	230

Glossary	232
Index	238
Credits	240

1 Giga Light Year

94   95   96   97   98   99   100   101

This is a journey through space and time. The Universe that surrounds us is vast beyond comprehension and a testament to both titanic forces and cosmic timescales. From the simplest of beginnings to the complex tapestry of celestial objects that surrounds us now, space is filled with wonders. On this journey we will encounter grandeur on an astonishing scale, beauty in the most unexpected places, and the most shocking natural violence.

We will see sand dunes weaving across the northern plains of Mars, driven by the winds of Martian spring and the icy surface of Enceladus cracking like an egg to blast geysers of water into space, feeding Saturn's rings. We will soar above alien cloudscapes of fluorescing gases, and burrow into the secret nests of new stars hidden within. We will marvel at the way stars sweep themselves into graceful spiral forms across vast tracts of space, and how galaxies string themselves into filaments to create a cosmic web that stretches from one side of the Universe to the other.

___The journey is organized into four distinct sections each representing a cosmic dominion: interplanetary, interstellar, interglalactic and finally, intertemporal. As we move from zone to zone, so the pace of our journey increases. Our first interplanetary steps are measured in light seconds, our final strides in the intertemporal zone are measured in giga light years. The transition from zone to zone also represents a leap in scale where we see how the components of the previous zone band together to create an altogether more monumental assemblage. What is striking about each zone is that it possesses its own character. Each is a unique realm that functions almost like an ecosystem in its own right, with hierarchies populated by dominant and subservient celestial objects, cycles of life and death, and evolution on the long scale of cosmic time.

___We start on Earth, in orbit around the Sun, a typical middle-aged star. At 4.6 billion years old, it is about halfway through its lifespan and comfortably stable in both the light it puts out and the magnetic activity that spits giant gouts of its superheated atmosphere into space.

___We shelter from this rain of particles on the Earth, protected by our magnetic field, while we watch the rest of our sibling planets. From the furnace of rocks on Mercury's airless wastes to the ephemeral clouds of Saturn's upper atmosphere, they exhibit different temperaments and personalities just like the brothers and sisters of a human family. Yet all were born from the same cloud of dust and gas that surrounded the young Sun.

___There are rocky planets like the Earth, with surfaces to be explored and in some cases clouds to soar through, and there are bloated giants with soupy atmospheres and no appreciable solid surfaces. These are alien dominions that strike few resonances with what we think of as a planet based on the world around us.

___There are ten times as many moons in the Solar System as planets, and that means ten times more worlds of wonder to behold. Jupiter's moons have a special place in history, as they were the first to be discovered beyond our own moon, and are wildly divergent from one another. Io and Europa are worlds of fire and ice respectively with the sulphur volcanoes of Io contrasting with the ice floes of Europa.

___These days the planets live in isolation – like neighbours that never talk – unless it is to exchange the odd meteorite. Interspersed with the planets and moons are the asteroids and the comets. Smaller, mountain-sized worldlets, they remind us of the formation of the Solar System, when a prodigious number of these objects formed the building blocks of the bigger things. They smashed together, melting into one another and solidifying into the planets of today.

___Each object in interplanetary space is unique and striking, but one stands out above all the others. To our knowledge, it is the one place in the Universe where matter organized itself well enough for conscious minds to be able to peer out across the heavens and attempt to comprehend it all. It is our home and the start of our journey, Earth.

___How did Earth become so privileged that life became widespread across its surface? Its distance from the Sun and its size certainly play a part, but how life actually started and whether these conditions have been replicated elsewhere in the Universe are questions that tantalize.

___In the interstellar zone, the planets disappear from view and are replaced by the burning orbs of light that are the stars. The Sun's soft yellow glow blends with the light from its companions. Around each star, there may well be planets but for now they are mostly lost to our view on this scale. Here the stars are the individuals, with differences in brightness, colour and activity to distinguish them.

___Unlike planets, stars can be identical twins. The defining property of a star is its mass. This determines how fast the nuclear reactions run in its core, and therefore how much energy it produces. In turn, the energy determines the surface temperature and brightness of the star. So two stars with the same mass will have the same brightness.

___The unit of currency used to compare stars is the solar mass: 2×10^{30} kg. The Sun is outshone millions of times by the Galaxy's most massive stars. With masses of ten times or greater that of the Sun, and surface temperatures higher than 10,000°C, these heavyweight stars consume

galaxies, and sometimes in galaxies of different shapes and sizes such as giant elliptical collections or even poorly stocked, irregularly shaped assemblages.

___As these other galaxies come into range, so the Milky Way begins to lose its overwhelming importance. This is a dizzying height from which to contemplate the Universe, and we can catch our first glimpse of the true scale of creation.

___The Milky Way is just one participant in a small collection of thirty or so galaxies. Beyond the 'Local Group' lie other collections of galaxies, some bigger, others of similar size. Many galaxies cluster together in this way, whilst others are loners; between a third and a half of them are content to wander the intergalactic void in isolation. Those in groups and clusters tend to accumulate into even larger groupings, forming superclusters that stretch tens of millions of light years across space.

___Within these giant flocks, the galaxies all rotate whilst circling each other. Occasionally they will clash, igniting ferocious conflicts in which the galaxies pit themselves against one another for gravitational supremacy. During these bouts, they rip each other's stars out, tussling for control of the stellar cargo because each new influx promises to make the winning galaxy larger and more powerful. They persist until one or the other, or sometimes both, are destroyed, leaving behind a wrecked assemblage of confused stars.

___As at all the scales of the Universe, there are new questions to be answered. What sets the spiral pattern of arms going? Can galaxies recover from direct hits from other galaxies? Is the rotation of each galaxy driven by a form of invisible matter as yet undiscovered in Earthly laboratories?

___At the greatest scales, space and time become intertwined. This is what we have termed the intertemporal zone, where the galaxies themselves are the grains of sand. There could more galaxies in the Universe than stars in the Milk Way: hundreds of billions or even more. Trillions of galaxies, in fact, many gathered into clusters, which themselves assemble into superclusters. Nature has strung these superclusters out into filaments, stretched across the Universe like bunting. In between the filaments are gigantic voids, intertemporal deserts with only the odd galaxy acting as an oasis of light.

___With each step taking us billions of light years further from home, whole clusters of galaxies are now the building blocks, and the galaxies themselves are reduced to mere

pinpricks of light. You would be forgiven for thinking that you were looking at single stars but no, these are stellar metropoli containing millions or billions of individual stars.

___On these scales, things can easily become confusing. You cannot rely on time as you do in the everyday world because the presence of matter slows it down. This means that time must be travelling more slowly in the superclusters than in the giant voids. Truly we run into the concept of space and time as conjoined realities: where you are in space affects how time runs. They are flipsides of the same coin rather than entirely separate entities.

___There is movement here, too. In the spaces between the clusters of galaxies, space itself is expanding like a never-ending piece of elastic. If space is growing ever bigger, it means that the Universe must have been smaller in its earlier days. Running the cosmic clock backwards tells us that everything we can see today would have been concentrated into a single point-like mass about 13.7 billion years ago. So this is assumed to be the age of the Universe, and the event that gave birth to it is called the big bang.

___No one knows what happened during the big bang, it is the ultimate enigma. Our knowledge of physics has yet to be developed sufficiently. However, at that time, something created all matter and energy, space and time, and sent it hurtling across space. The expansion of space is a remaining vestige of the magnificent fury unleashed during this extraordinary creation event.

___Light is our messenger for scanning the heavens. It is a wave of energy that rolls through space, just like a wave of water rolls across the sea. Matter creates light and matter absorbs light. It does this by juggling the positions of the outer particles in its atoms, allowing them either to expel excess energy or to absorb a new delivery. If the matter doing the absorption happens to be in the retina of our eyes, so we perceive the light and see the object. These days, telescopes act as our proxy eyes. They can be much larger than our biological ones, having mirrors 10 metres across compared to our pupils of a few millimetres.

___They are sited in high places, on mountaintops and plateaux above most of Earth's thick atmosphere that blurs the images of the celestial objects. This is where the Hubble Space Telescope reigns supreme. Although modest in size, just 2.4 metres across, it is in orbit above the turbulent atmosphere.

___There is a lot more to light than meets the eye.

We are all familiar with the rainbow spectrum of visible light, but it forms only a tiny band in the middle of the overall electromagnetic spectrum. Most light exists in forms that are invisible to us, our human eyes having evolved to see just the most plentiful wavelengths given out by the Sun. Across the Universe as a whole, objects radiate in all the other wavelengths, and we need mechanical eyes to help us see.

___The names of these other wavelengths are familiar: radio waves, microwaves, infrared, ultraviolet, X-rays and gamma rays. All are fundamentally the same as visible light, which lies between infrared and ultraviolet on the spectrum, but with longer or shorter wavelengths. All carry energy and are one of means by which widely separated concentrations of matter can communicate with each other, because all atoms have the ability to absorb or emit light of these various wavelengths.

___Without the help of artificial eyes sensitive to the hidden wavelengths of electromagnetic radiation, most of the Universe would remain invisible to us. It would be the equivalent of approaching a city at night and seeing only the streetlights, while the main bulk of the buildings remained invisible all around us.

___Using specialized telescopes we can tease out the hidden messages from the celestial objects. In the same way that a bat detector transforms ultrasonic utterances into chirps that human ears can register, so we have to colour-code invisible radiations – be they radio or X-rays – into visible images. In all cases, the longest wavelengths are coloured red and the shortest blue, to mimic the sweep of the rainbow.

___The most plentiful form of electromagnetic radiation is at microwave wavelengths. There are a billion photons of microwave energy for every single atom; they were created during the fireball of the big bang, and now they bathe all of space in a perpetual sleet.

___As we delve ever deeper into the Universe, so we will be travelling back through time. This is because light travels faster than anything else through space. Racing at almost 300 million metres a second, it could circumnavigate the Earth's equator seven and a half times in that second. And it never tires. Light will always travel at this speed through space, regardless of the distance it has covered, or the colour it contains. Truly light is the fleet-footed messenger of the heavens, carrying with it most of the knowledge we can gather about the Universe.

At this speed, it can cross approximately 9.5 trillion kilometres every year. So, this is the distance called a light year. For example, our nearest large galactic neighbour, the Andromeda Galaxy is 22 million trillion kilometres or 2.3 million light years away. In our everyday world, light travels so quickly it can be thought of as travelling instantaneously from one place to another. In the Universe at large, however, the distances can be so vast that even light will take millions or billions of years to cross the firmament and deliver its cargo of information. So we see celestial objects the way they appeared when they released their light, which is not necessarily as they would look now. We see the Andromeda Galaxy as it was 2.3 million years ago, and won't know what it looks like right now for another 2.3 million years.

___Like an archaeologist digging down through successive rock strata, this means that the further we peer into space, the further we look back through time because it has taken longer for the light to reach us.

___We will measure our journey against light speed, giving us an easy way of judging both distance and this look-back time. A distance in light units, be they seconds, minutes, hours or years, instantly tells us how far back in time the object is located. Across the interplanetary realm we will measure our journey in light seconds and light minutes. These are but small steps through our cosmic garden. Within interstellar space, our yardstick will become the light year. As we press on into intergalactic space, the ruler extends to millions of light years – mega light years. Eventually we reach the billions of years light – giga light years – that correspond to the intertemporal zone and the effect of look-back time will become extreme.

___Most of the objects we see in this realm are long gone today, evolved into new forms, or rendered extinct by the changing universal environment. Many of them are just distant memories; they exist now only as long as light carries their song across space. By studying this light, we can chart the course of celestial evolution.

___This new image from the European Space Agency's spacecraft Planck shows all of creation [1]; from the very first microwave light to enter the Universe to the very latest created just a few scant light years away.

___The oldest light appears at the top and bottom of the image as the mottled pattern of magenta, gold and purple. It reveals subtle

pervaded the whole Universe just 00,000 years after the big bang. This gas was composed of the atoms that we now see corralled into planets, stars and galaxies. Where the microwave background radiation is densest, in the gold spots, so the likelihood of galaxies forming is greatest. The opposite is true for the purple patches, where the gas was sparse. In short, this pattern represents the cosmic blueprint for the web of galaxies found today.

___Across the middle of the image, superimposing themselves on top of the ancient light, are the braided filaments of cold dust that thread the Milky Way. Our Galaxy is a flat twist of stars 100,000 light years across, when viewed from above. Situated in one of the spiralling arms, we view the Galaxy as a thin band of stars that crosses the night sky. This view is echoed in microwaves but with embellishments. The pink band is the disc of the Galaxy, suffused with dust and then streamers of dust-laced gas reach upwards and downwards to surround us with a 'cat's cradle' of matter.

___The dust itself exists at a temperature of –261°C, only about 12 °C above absolute zero. At such frigid temperatures, it is sluggish and almost completely at the mercy of gravity. Almost.

___To the right of the image, just below the main disc of the Galaxy is the mighty Orion cloud of molecular gas. Surrounding this region is an arc of pink light, which is the shockwave of a star that exploded 2 million years ago. It has snowploughed dust in its path, creating the bubble. Other areas show similar activity, such as the arcs that sit above and below the plane of the Galaxy, just to the left of Orion. These mark the region of the Vela supernova, another exploded star. Over on the opposite side of the Galaxy, much smaller pink bubbles show younger stellar explosions. These cataclysms keep the dust moving, stirring the Galaxy and ensuring that gravity does not have its own way all the time.

___Resting in space, between the Milky Way and the background radiation are over hundred billion other galaxies. A few of them show up in this image. The nearest are the two knots of white light below the centre right of the image. These are the small nearby galaxies, known as the Magellanic Clouds. The Andromeda Galaxy shows up in the lower left quadrant of this image as a diagonal sliver of microwave light. At 2.3 million light years away, it is the most distant object he unaided eye can resolve from the surface of the Earth, with

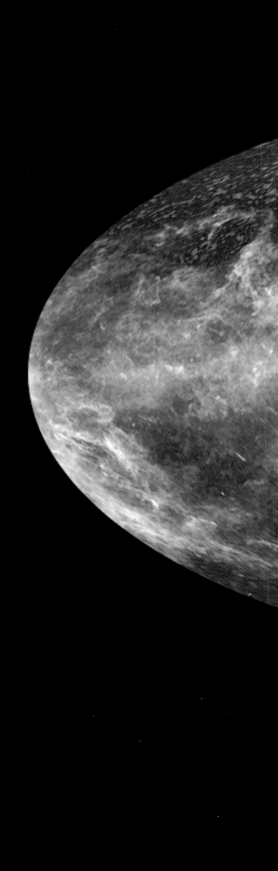

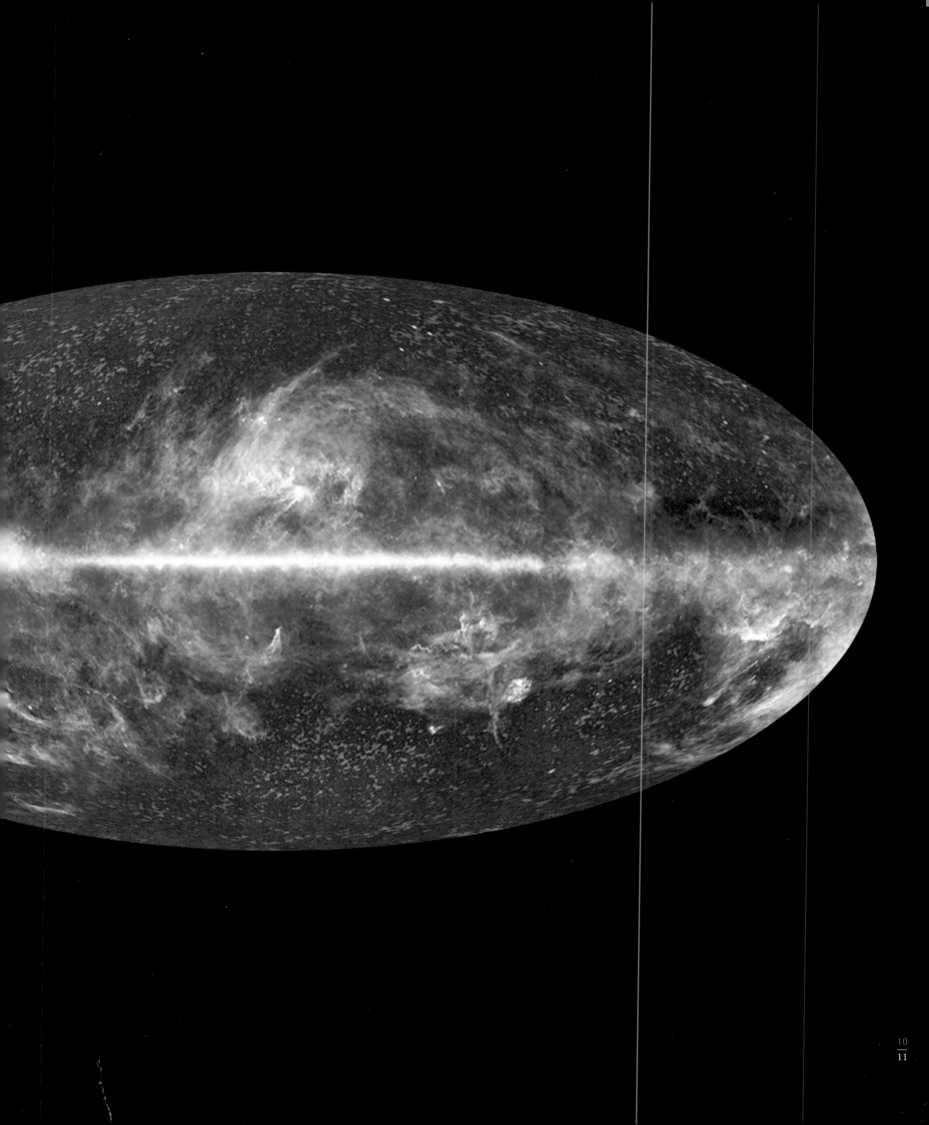

___The bright diagonal stream to the upper right of the centre is the active galaxy Centaurus A, 11 million light years away. Here two mature spirals have collided, one scything into the other. Copious quantities of matter have been forced into the clutches of a supermassive black hole. These lurking gravitational ogres are destroyers, gripping nearby celestial objects and crushing them out of existence. In the process, they wring out energy from the captured atoms and the outpouring of X-rays catapults other matter to safety. What is shining here is the ejected dust, now rapidly cooling off in the frigid depths of intergalactic space.

___If light is the messenger, then gravity is the architect. In absolute terms, gravity is the weakest of the forces of nature but it does have the longest range. Created by every object that has mass, its real strength lies in the fact that it is purely attractive. Gravity never repels. It helps to sculpt the great sweep of the Universe on its grandest scales and provides much of the details on the finer scale too.

___All celestial objects are formed because of the action of gravity pulling matter together while other forces rise to challenge its supremacy. At the smallest end of that scale, planets and asteroids are the result. Here the amounts of matter squeezed together are small enough that the strength of chemical bonds is able to halt gravity in its stride. The atoms in the rocks cast themselves into a crystalline lattice that provides an unbreakable scaffolding to prevent further collapse.

___On the interstellar scale, gravity can break these bonds. It squeezes larger volumes of matter together and heats them as it does so. As the temperature rises, so solid chunks of matter are vaporized; even molecules of gas are ripped apart. All the while, gravity is squeezing the matter into a smaller and smaller volume of space. It ends when the temperature of the gas cloud reaches around 15 million °C. At that point collisions between hydrogen atomic nuclei are so fast they fuse together.

___This unleashes energy from the nuclei, which starts to fight its way out through the surrounding mass of matter. As it repeatedly collides with atoms on its outward journey, so it provides support, helping to shore up the collapsing matter from the relentless pull of gravity. This is the situation inside a star; it is a delicate balance of light versus gravity and, for as long as the star has fuel to fuse, it will remain a stable celestial object.

___At the end of a star's life, gravity will triumph.

The object's complement of matter will be pulled ever denser, until either the atoms are compressed into a new stable configuration – such as a neutron star – or it collapses completely into that most mysterious of objects: a black hole. No one truly knows what happens to the matter inside a black hole. Can it really disappear out of existence? It remains an enduring celestial conundrum.

___A journey through the Universe, from familiar shores to distant realms is the perfect way to explore space because the history of astronomy has been one of ever-expanding horizons. Every great advance in our understanding has been at the price of divesting the Earth of another level of assumed importance and each time this has happened, the reward has been a greater cosmic perspective over a wider Universe.

___For two millennia, from the time of the ancient Greeks until the 16th century, Earth was considered to be the centre of the heavens, the focus of creation. Yet, while trying to understand the movement of the planets through the night sky, Copernicus and Kepler were forced to demolish this cherished view. The former proposed that the Sun was the centre of everything and Kepler made the system work by showing that the planets did not all follow perfect circular orbits, as had been assumed, but elliptical paths.

___The next great leap was into the stellar universe, when the true distance of the stars was finally revealed in the 19th century. Now, clearly shown to be tens of thousands of times further away than the planets, the stars were unmasked as anything but fixed in space in the way the apparently immortal constellations had suggested. Instead all stars move through space and our Sun is not even near the centre of rotation but just one of the massed ranks out in the boondocks of the Galaxy. In time, the constellations will deform as the stars move.

___The greatest leap outwards took place during the early 20th century, when indistinct smudges of light revealed themselves in the telescopes of the day as whole galaxies. The Universe was not only larger than we had imagined, it was vastly larger than we could imagine, stretching for some 90 billion light years in diameter. Fortunately, this was the moment in human history when Albert Einstein developed General Relativity, the mathematical tools by which we can investigate the Universe as a whole. It was the moment we realized all of space was expanding, driving clusters of galaxies ever further away from each other

and forever banishing the idea that the Universe was eternally static.

___Today, we are grappling with the very largest scales of the Universe and realizing that, at such enormous distances, space and time become inextricably linked both through the concept of look-back time and the way gravitational fields make time pass more slowly. As well as living in a cosmic landscape, we may also be living in a cosmic timescale, with time running at different speeds in different parts of the Universe.

___Take your own journey across these fascinating reaches. There are billions of light years of space represented here, flip through, stop anywhere that takes your fancy. The book can be read in any order but, taken sequentially, it works from the Earth outwards. The positions of the objects have been frozen in time on 25 December 2010. This particularly affects the Solar System objects, and specifically those closest to Earth, as they doggedly follow their orbits. If our growing understanding of the Universe has taught us anything, it is that the Universe is a dynamic place of perpetual movement.

___Every second, the Earth covers 34 more kilometres in its orbit around the Sun, which itself speeds 269 kilometres in its orbit around the centre of the Milky Way, whilst the whole Galaxy moves 121 kilometres closer to the Andromeda Galaxy. The Local Group, containing the Milky Way and Andromeda, have moved away from the nearby Virgo cluster of galaxies by 965 kilometres in that second.

___Over the average human lifespan of 70 years, the Sun will have carried you on a journey 500 billion kilometres through the Galaxy, and the Galaxy will have taken you 267 billion kilometres closer to Andromeda.

___Yet these are small steps in the grand scale. Over its lifetime, the Sun has completed around 21 orbits of the centre of the Galaxy, each turn taking some 200 million years. Although these distances and times sound vast, from interplanetary space outwards the slow clockwork of the Universe will make little difference if you are reading this a year, a decade or a century from publication. But don't dally too long. The grand sweep of the Universe will not last forever!

___Perhaps the biggest of the cosmic mysteries, if indeed there is something more to it than just random chance, is that there will never be a better time to see the Universe than in the next billion years or so. This is its heyday.

___It has taken 13.7 billion years to finesse itself to this standard but it will not last much longer. The rate of star formation is dropping as reserves of gas run out and the clusters are gradually destroying their individual galaxies in favour of much larger, less elegant conglomerations. And even the superclusters are doomed.

___They could perhaps have survived the gradual expansion of space for aeons yet to come. However, with space accelerating constantly, they will be torn apart, their galaxies orphaned and then shredded as the dark energy of expansion builds up its strength. There may not be any end to this acceleration. As time passes, it might simply grow stronger and stronger.

___In this nightmare scenario, stars are the next to disintegrate, then planets, people and eventually even the atoms themeselves will surrender to the boundless rise of dark energy.

___Its ultimate battle will be with black holes. These all-powerful destroyers were once thought to be impervious to external forces. But if the cosmic acceleration just keeps growing, how soon before even the black holes are ripped to shreds? We simply have no idea.

___But enough of the speculation, there is enough real wonder in the heavens that humankind will never run out of targets for its telescopes. Take the stars in our Galaxy. Two hundred billion incandescent orbs, each one tens or hundreds of times larger than our home planet. Yet each one reduced to a mere speck in our cameras [1].

___Now jump to the largest scales and the pattern repeats itself only this time the specks are not individual stars but mammoth collections of hundreds of billions of stars: whole galaxies in their own right [2]. There are as many galaxies in the Universe as there are stars in the Galaxy. And every galaxy is creating new stars at a rate of between one and a thousand per year and each star is waiting for us to know it.

___This book is a journey into these extraordinary realms. You start here, on Earth, nestled in the Orion Spur of the Milky Way Galaxy, near the centre of the Local Group, gravitationally bound to the Virgo Supercluster, but the entire night sky is now yours to explore. You have 45 billion light years to travel and 13.7 billion years of time to traverse. So, with the clock set to zero, let the journey commence!

1

2

LIGHT SECONDS
LIGHT MINUTES
LIGHT YEARS
KILO LIGHT YEARS
MEGA LIGHT YEARS
GIGA LIGHT YEARS

01

INTER
PLANETARY

The worlds of the Solar System provide the stepping-stones for the first stage in our journey. Each world, be it a planet or moon, although often mixed from a common set of ingredients has its own unique characteristics. From the airless hunk of Mercury to the toxic atmosphere of Jupiter, from the barren magnificence of the Moon to the ice mountains of Mimas, the landscapes are all expressions of possibility. It seems as if all of nature's myriad permutations occur somewhere.

There is a remarkable dichotomy of planetary types. In the inner regions, the four planets are closer together. Mercury, Venus, Earth and Mars share properties in common. They are relatively small, made predominantly of dense material such as rock, and possess relatively thin atmospheres, if any at all. These are called the terrestrial worlds or simply the rocky planets.

___In the outer Solar System, the type of planet changes dramatically. Taking Jupiter as their role model, Saturn, Uranus and Neptune are much larger worlds. They are made largely of gases with extensive atmospheres sitting on cores of crushed rocks and metal. These solid hearts are buried so deeply beneath their atmospheres that these planets have no solid surfaces of which to speak. They are known appropriately as the gas giants.

___Then there are the vagabonds: the asteroids and the comets. These are the smallest of the celestial objects, just hunks of rock and ice hurtling through space. The majority of the asteroids are made of rocks and metal, and shepherded within a wide belt around the Sun between Mars and Jupiter. The comets on the other hand have free range. They wheel through the Solar System, swooping from above or climbing from below to dart briefly round the Sun like birds hunting on the wing. They mark their paths with trails of dust and gas that were once part of these small bodies. Eventually they deplete themselves so much that they disintegrate, or they develop a layer of carbonaceous scarring that seals in the remains of the ice. In either case, the comet fades from further view.

___And, at the centre of it all, presiding over this retinue is the Sun. It accounts for 99 percent of the mass in the Solar System and provides the gravitational hub around which everything turns. Its energy drives the atmospheres of the planets, conjuring impressionistic storms and vortices, cloud belts and blankets of chemical smog. It launches a constant wind of particles that flows past the planets, sparking dancing aurorae on those planets with any atmosphere.

___The worlds of the Solar System follow a hierarchy. In the kingdom of the Sun, there are eight fiefdoms, each belonging to one of the orbiting planets. In each of these domains, the planet exerts control over its moons. These smaller celestial bodies orbit the planets, as the planets orbit the Sun. The moons are as individualistic as the planets.

___There is infernal Io, which is in a perpetual state of catastrophic eruption; twilight Titan with dense clouds that prevent most sunlight reaching its surface; and hypnotic Hyperion, which tumbles through its orbit with no predictable pattern to its day and night cycle.

___Jupiter itself is so large that it extends its dominion over the asteroid belt as well as its moons. Although the asteroids go around the Sun rather than circling the giant planet, nevertheless Jupiter's gravity keeps them in regimented orbits, allowing some gatherings but dispersing others.

___Then there are the dwarf planets, such as Pluto. These are worlds that orbit the Sun yet cannot muster the gravity to control their wider environments. In the case of Pluto, a swarm of smaller asteroid-like objects called the plutinos share similar but independent paths. Pluto even blurs the definition of what should be considered a planet and a moon because its largest companion, Charon, is half its size, prompting some to think of them as a double dwarf planet system, rather than a planet and moon. In the asteroid belt, the biggest member is called Ceres. At 975 km in diameter, it too is a dwarf planet.

___The segregation of the planets, from rocky worlds to gas giants, lends itself to a simple formation scenario in which the planets coalesced from a rotating disc of matter that was heated from the centre to the edge by the nascent Sun. Such a disc would be formed naturally as a gas cloud fell together, because of the way the cloud's rotation resisted the collapse around its equator.

___In the inner portion of the disc, where the temperatures would have been greatest, only the high temperature chemicals such as silicon and iron would have found it possible to solidify. The more volatile material such as water ice would have been forced to remain in gaseous form. So the planets in the inner Solar System would have had a restricted diet from which to feed. This is now reflected in their composition and relatively small sizes.

___Further out the temperature of the disc dropped, creating a 'snow line' beyond which water and other volatile chemicals such as ammonia and methane could become . solid. These increased both the amount and variety of the building blocks available to the embryonic gas giants, ensuring their magnified size. Occasionally one of the icy building blocks slid through the inner Solar System, creating

the first rain of comets that helped fill the oceans of the inner planets. Venus, Earth, Mars – all would have received their quota. Yet only Earth jealously protected it, hiding it under a shield of magnetism from the ravages of the Sun's young light. Now, of course, Earth is the only world that retains an abundance of liquid surface water. Venus and Mars show evidence of formerly being lush, but Mercury displays no signs of ever having been hydrated. This is probably due to its ringside seat by the Sun.

___As the matter thinned out with ever-increasing distance, so the icy worlds of Pluto, Charon and myriad other dwarf planets that probably exist at extreme distances from the Sun, could form. Only a handful of these distant outposts have been found so far. Many may have been exiled there by gravitational slingshots during close encounters with the gas giants billions of years ago.

___As sensible as this pattern of planets appears to be, we know it is not the only possible one. Planets around other stars, known as exoplanets, have been sensed by the way they cause their parent stars to wobble. Of the 400 plus that have been detected, most are gas giants locked into orbits even tighter than Mercury's around the Sun; some much tighter. The closest planets whip around their stars in just a few days, making Mercury's 88-day orbit look leisurely.

___It is thought that such gas giants form far from their sun as expected but then migrate inward as the pressure of their remaining natal clouds sap them of orbital energy. As they begin the long march towards their star, they sweep ahead of them any smaller planets that get in the way. One by one these are forced into the fires of the central orb and lost forever, as the gas giant manoeuvres into its final resting orbit.

___Given the proximity of these gas giant exoplanets to their stars, the input of heat would be enormous, rousing storms of immense ferocity. Winds up to 10,000 km/h power through the atmosphere as blistering gas races from the glare of the star to the night-time side of the planet.

___While, in time, we may well find solar systems similar to our own, at the moment it remains a unique crown bedecked with a diverse array of planetary jewels.

Right: the Sun rises behind the International Space Station

16
17

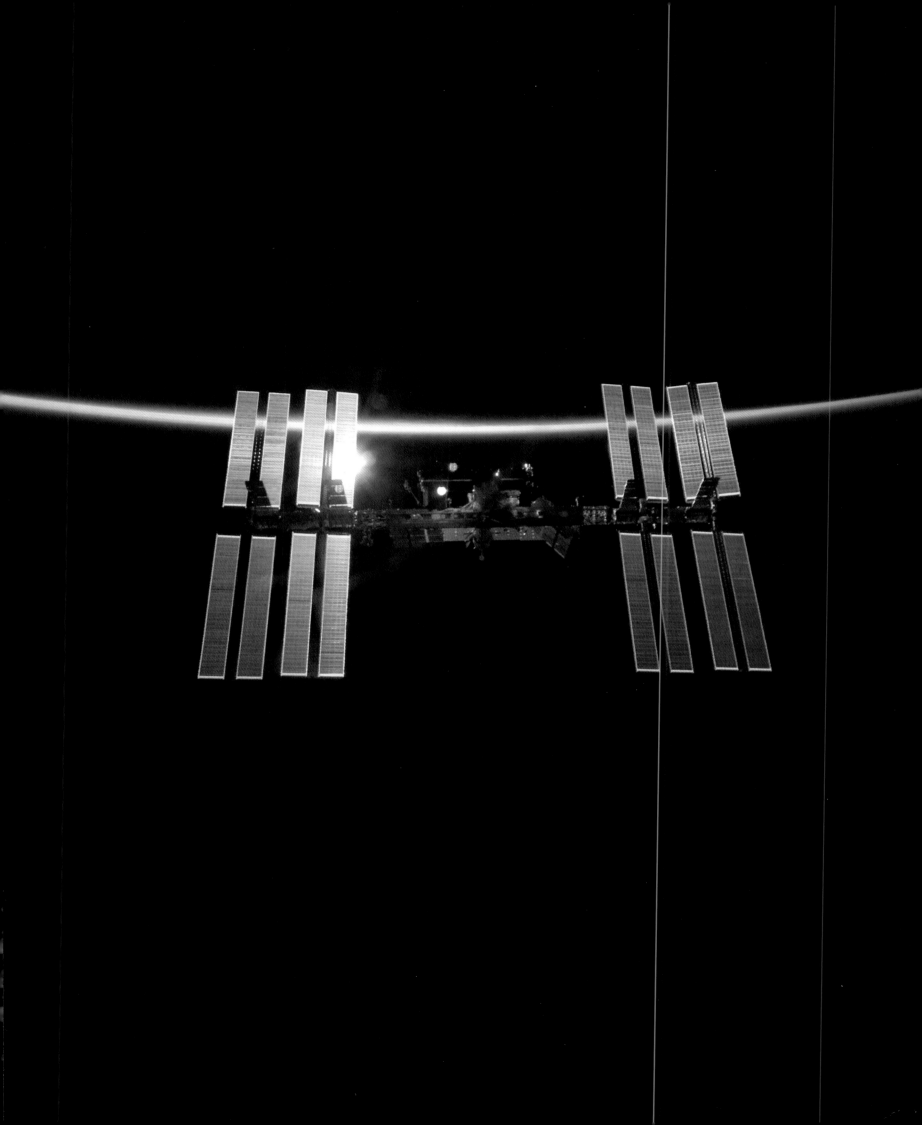

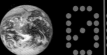

LIGHT SECONDS
LIGHT MINUTES
LIGHT YEARS
KILO LIGHT YEARS
MEGA LIGHT YEARS
GIGA LIGHT YEARS

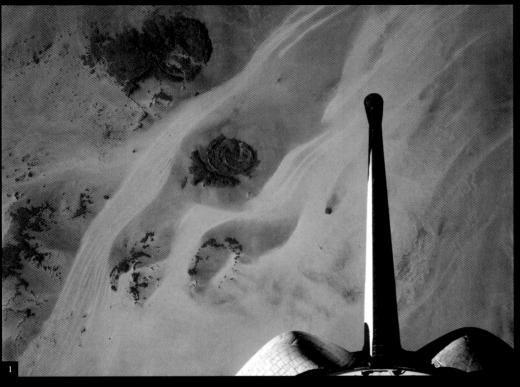

1

2

A planet called home

We live on a world of many hues and many faces:
from the lush green of the forests to the burnt ochre
of the deserts; from the silver tint of stone and metal in
the cities, to the gleaming white of the Arctic wastes.
Yet from space, one colour overwhelms them all: blue.

'How inappropriate to call this planet Earth when it is quite clearly Ocean', said the science fiction author Arthur C Clarke. It is a sentiment easy to concur with from space. More than seventy percent of Earth's surface is covered in water. The restless bulk of the great seas ebbs and flows in synchrony with the Moon, lapping at the shoreline and stirring our adventurous hearts.

___The molecular basis of life depends so much on water, maybe the oceans stirred life into the Earth in the first place. On the sea floor there are powerful volcanic vents that jet scalding water into the otherwise frigid depths. The dissolved chemicals and abundant microbes clustering around these today suggest they may have been good sites for early life. But exactly what transforms a

collection of chemicals into life is something that continues to elude us.

___Earth is the largest rocky planet in the Solar System, and our home. Its great age is measured at 4.6 billion years, or about one third of the total age of the Universe. Yet our tenure on this world has so far been but the merest blink of a cosmic eye. Humans became distinct from their genetic ancestors some 200,000 years ago, emerging from the African savannah.

___Life transforms our planet into a vibrant, changeable place yet it is not omnipotent. Today, large swathes of the planet are excluded from our habitation, and they always have been. The mighty desert wastelands offer barren comfort to humans but glorious sights from space [1]. The swirling

hurricanes of water vapour that grip the atmosphere every year terrorize us but take on a serenity from on high [2].

___Taken over the sweep of cosmic time, only a tenth of a percent of the planet's entire lifespan will afford what we think of as habitable conditions. Nevertheless, Earth is all we have. No other place in the Solar System comes close to replicating its 'Goldilocks' nature: not too hot, not too cold, but just right. The more we look into the Universe, the more we realize our luck.

___In the same way that the early mariners were inspired to cross the oceans, so our celestial observations draw our minds upwards. Where once it was the promise of distant continents that lured us, now it is the stars that are our destination.

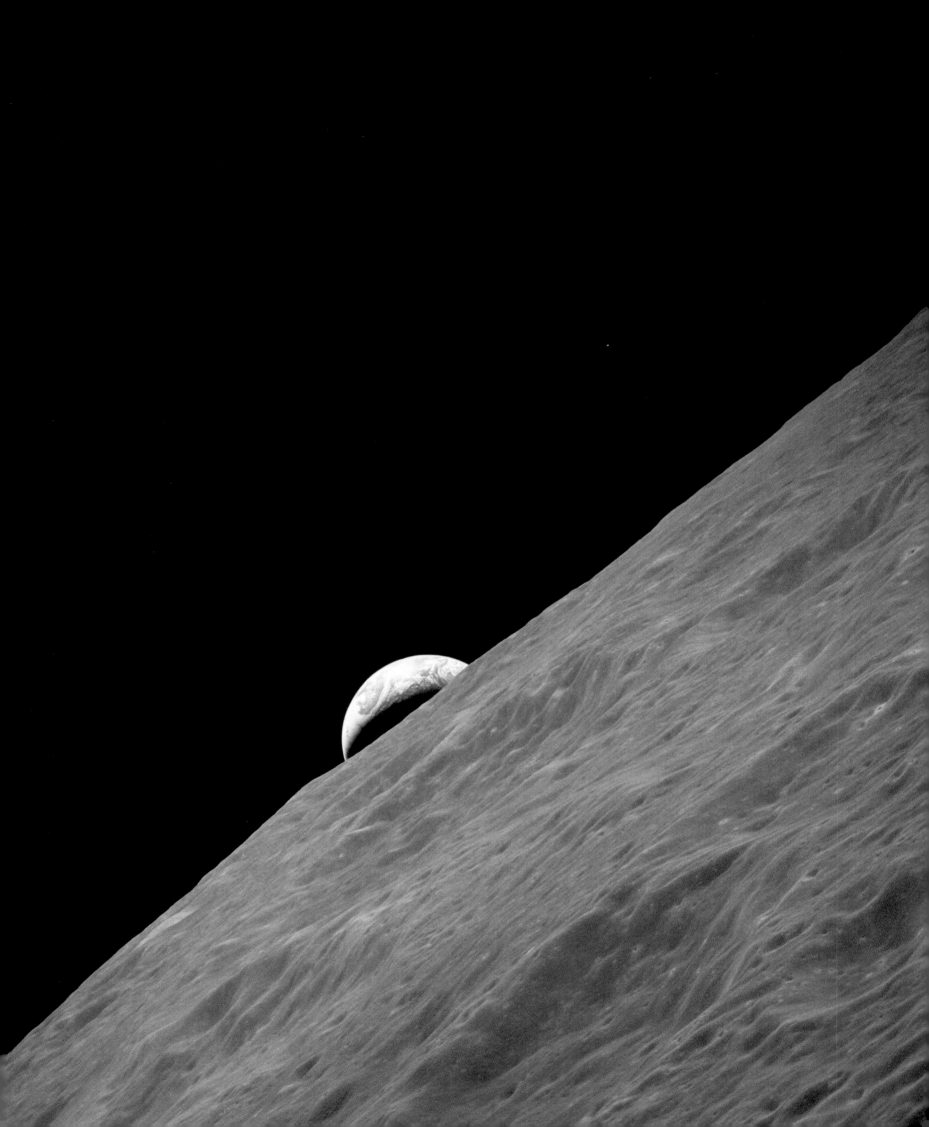

LIGHT SECONDS
LIGHT MINUTES
LIGHT YEARS
KILO LIGHT YEARS
MEGA LIGHT YEARS
GIGA LIGHT YEARS

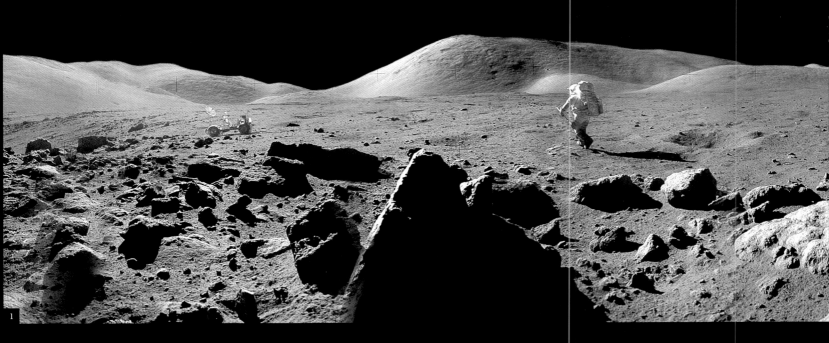

1

One small step

<u>Earth's fixed companion, the Moon sits on our cosmic doorstep. Yet it took millennia of human technological development to get us there in rocket ships. Now awaiting our return, the Moon may hold the secret to why there is life on Earth.</u>

The surface of the Moon is pure in a way that no stone on Earth can ever be. Untouched by wind or rain, there is nothing to alter the lunar rocks in any way. The face that we see today, the ridges and the craters, and the solidified lava seas, are all the same as they were billions of years ago.

___Our Moon is by no means the largest in the Solar System. It ranks only fifth, but it is the largest moon in relation to its parent planet, containing about one eightieth of the mass of the Earth. Now the Moon watches over us, stirs our oceans into tides with gravity, and keeps her silent counsel.

___Time has stood still for the Moon, giving us a snapshot of forces no longer at play in the Solar System. In particular, the craters mark the final act of formation, speaking of a nightmarish era when mountain-sized rocks rained down on the newly forged worlds.

___Today little hits the Moon, or any other celestial body in the Solar System. The leftovers from the era of planetary formation have largely been mopped up. Go back 4 billion years and the environment was entirely different. The nascent Solar System swarmed with asteroids, colliding with the planets and the moons, blasting out titanic impact craters. Through it all, the Moon endured.

___On Earth, this bombardment brought with it the raw chemical ingredients that went on to form life. Today, the evidence is long gone from our planet: either transformed into life, eroded away by the weather, or melted into the planet's depths by the movement of the continents. Not so on the Moon.

___Until the six Apollo landings [1], the Moon's silver surface had lain virtually untouched for aeons. Although the astronauts did not find these most ancient of rocks, future lunar missions could finally reveal the chemical building blocks supplied to Earth that made life possible. It is a tantalizing possibility, perhaps even the best reason to return to our nearest celestial neighbour.

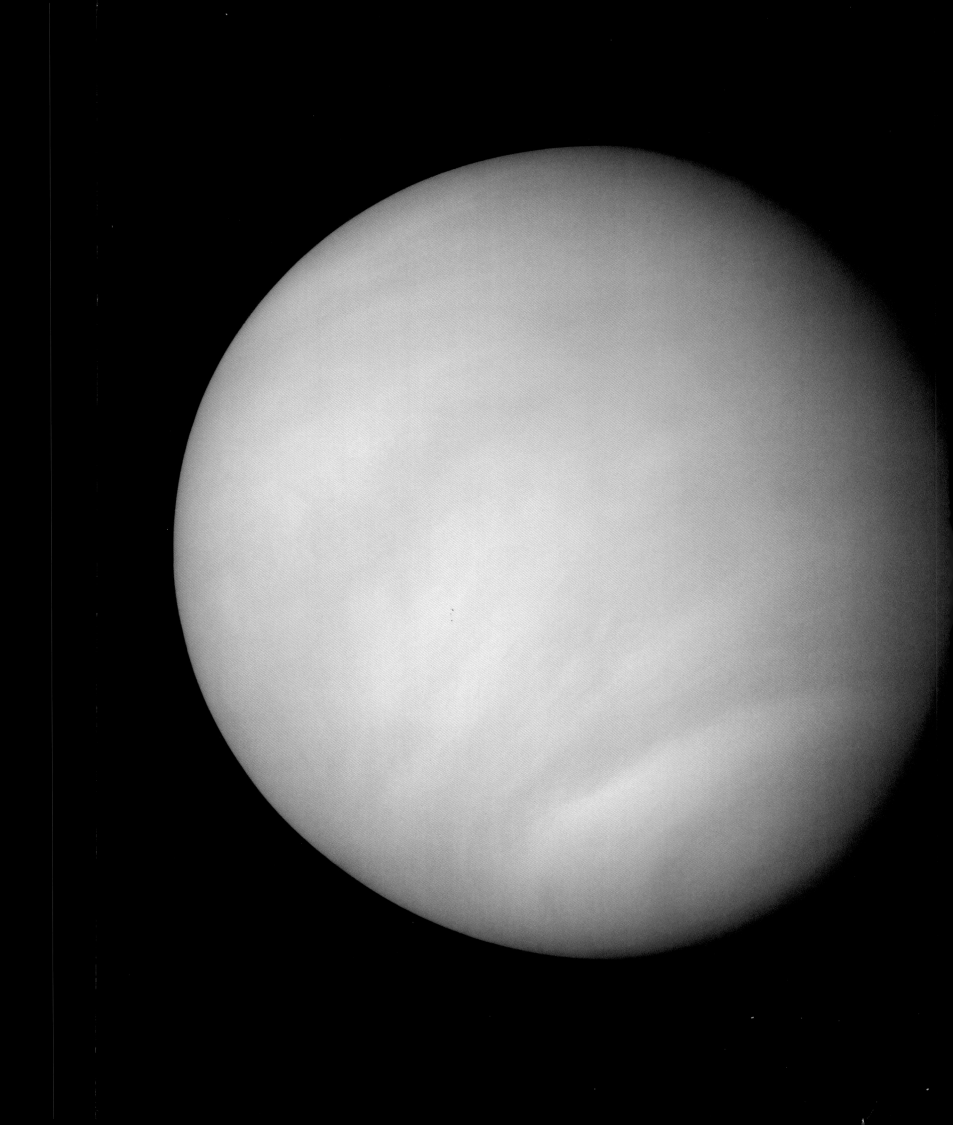

Venus
PLANET
DIAMETER: 12,100 KM

008.0
LIGHT SECONDS
LIGHT MINUTES
LIGHT YEARS
KILO LIGHT YEARS
MEGA LIGHT YEARS
GIGA LIGHT YEARS

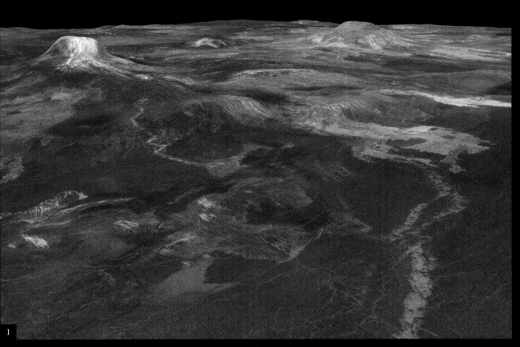

1

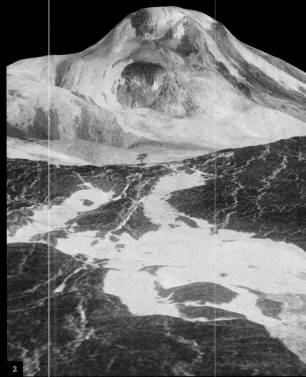

2

Welcome to hell?

<u>Venus is hell: hotter than a kitchen oven, sulphuric acid rain, and winds that tear through the atmosphere at 400 km/h. Yet despite all that, Venus is the only other place in the Solar System where pockets of Earthly conditions prevail. Forget Mars, Venus is the place to search for extraterrestrial life.</u>

Of all the planets, Venus is the one most reluctant to yield its secrets. Despite drawing closer to Earth than any other planet, a mere 38 million kilometres, its blankets of cloud mask the surface from direct view. Only by using radar can we see the ground from orbit [1].

___Occasionally sky watchers have reported glimpsing an 'ashen light' from the night-time side of the planet. While the reality of this phenomenon is debated, if true it could be caused by lightning in the Venusian atmosphere, or temporary partings in the clouds, allowing the light from the hot rocks below to escape.

___The surface is littered with volcanoes like Maat Mons [2], some thought to be still active and belching plumes of sulphur dioxide into the atmosphere. Lava flows have been spotted that look remarkably young, maybe even created in the recent past. While such volcanoes are another fitting contribution to

the Hadean landscape, drift upwards into the atmosphere and remarkable changes begin to occur.

___First, things get even worse. There are the clouds of sulphuric acid that drape themselves across the atmosphere. But above these, the conditions become more familiar, clement even.

___Between 50 and 60 km above the hellish surface, sunlight is streaming in providing a source of ready energy. The atmospheric pressure is the same as at sea level on Earth, and the temperature lies between 0–100 °C, in other words within the range where liquid water droplets could condense. And, perhaps crucially, all the chemicals necessary for life on Earth are also found here in the atmospheric gases: nitrogen, carbon, oxygen, and hydrogen.

___The only problem is the wind. At the surface, it is little more than the lightest of

breezes but it picks up relentlessly with altitude until at this otherwise clement height, it is tearing past you at 360 km/h.

___Nevertheless, this layer of the Venusian atmosphere is the only other place in the Solar System that replicates the life-bearing conditions of Earth – minus the surface of course. Not even Mars is this similar: it is too cold, the atmospheric composition isn't right and the pressure is too low. There is no guarantee that life is present in the atmosphere of Venus but it is surely worth a look. Some have even suggested that the dark swathes seen in ultraviolet images of Venus are concentrations of airborne bacteria, harvesting the ultraviolet light from the Sun and using it to metabolize chemicals for food. Most believe that these markings are ultraviolet absorption by molecules in the atmosphere but, until we visit the atmosphere with scientific equipment, we cannot be sure one way or another.

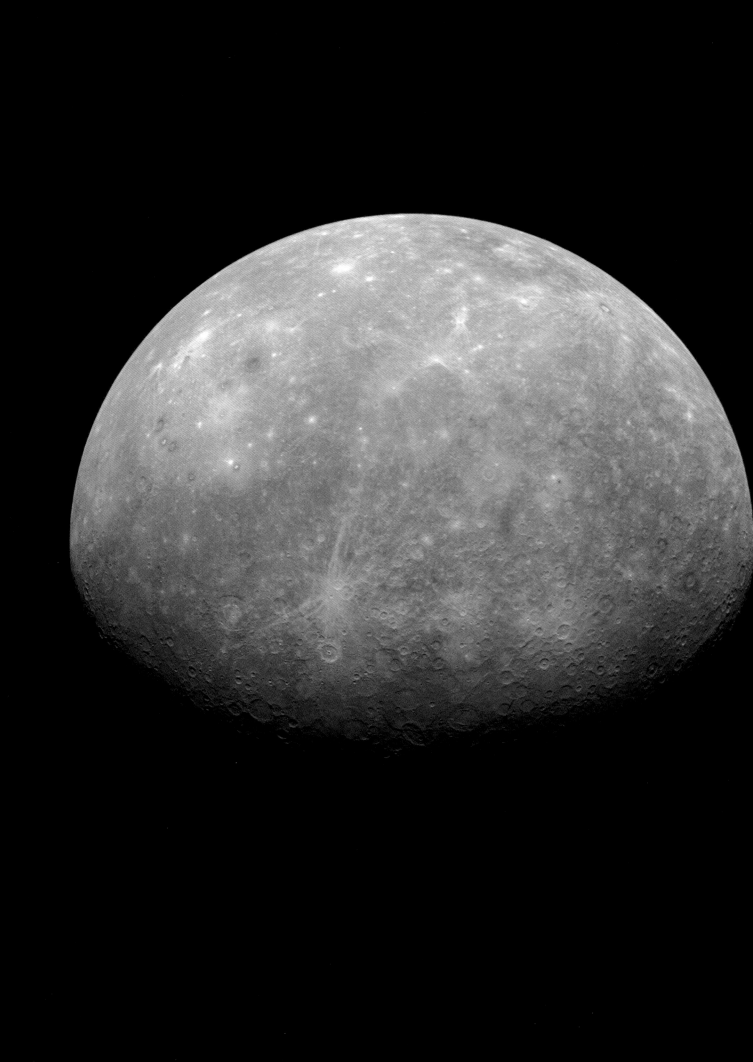

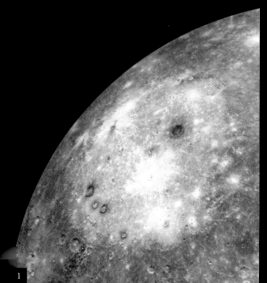

1

2

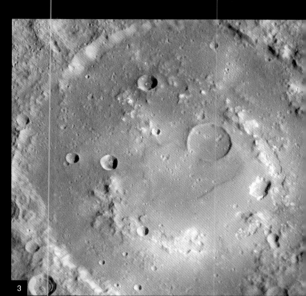

3

Mystifying Mercury

At first glance, you'd be forgiven for thinking we have returned to the Moon with its silver grey landscape of barren desolation. But look closer: no dark lava plains. This is Mercury, a world that does not make sense.

Perhaps Mercury should have been called Icarus. Lying closer to our Sun than any other planet, by mid afternoon Mercury's temperature has soared higher than 350 °C, hot enough to melt lead. Then at night, with no blanketing atmosphere, the temperature plunges to –200 °C.

___Up near the poles, there are deep craters where the Sun's burning rays can never penetrate. Inside these dark traps, the ground is so cold that it will snare any passing water molecule, creating a permanently icy floor. But that's not what makes Mercury a mystery.

___Icarus lost his wax and feather wings by lying too close to the Sun. Mercury may have lost its entire outer layers of rock, irradiated away by the fearsome light from the newborn Sun. The clues lie hidden inside the planet.

___Mercury is the smallest planet but it possesses a metal heart larger than that of Mars. This swollen core accounts for 40 percent of the planet's volume, more than twice the percentage taken up by the Earth's core, and signals that Mercury may once have been twice its present size. If the planet pulled itself together quickly, then the young Sun's X-ray birth pangs may have been sufficient to evaporate half of it away.

___Or perhaps the impacts that scarred the Moon were so much worse at Mercury that they blasted away the outer rocky layers, allowing the original core to dominate. There is certainly good evidence of calamity.

___The Caloris Basin [1] is a giant impact scar measuring 1,550 km across. On the other side of Mercury, directly opposite, is a region of chaotic terrain. It is as if a giant has scooped up a handful of the planet, crushed it and patted it back into the ground. In this case, the giant was the Caloris Basin impact, sending shockwaves ricocheting through Mercury's body. When they reached the other side, they pulverized the surface layers. Huge fault lines disect the surface [2] and sunken pits tinged with yellow minerals hint at past volcanic episodes [3].

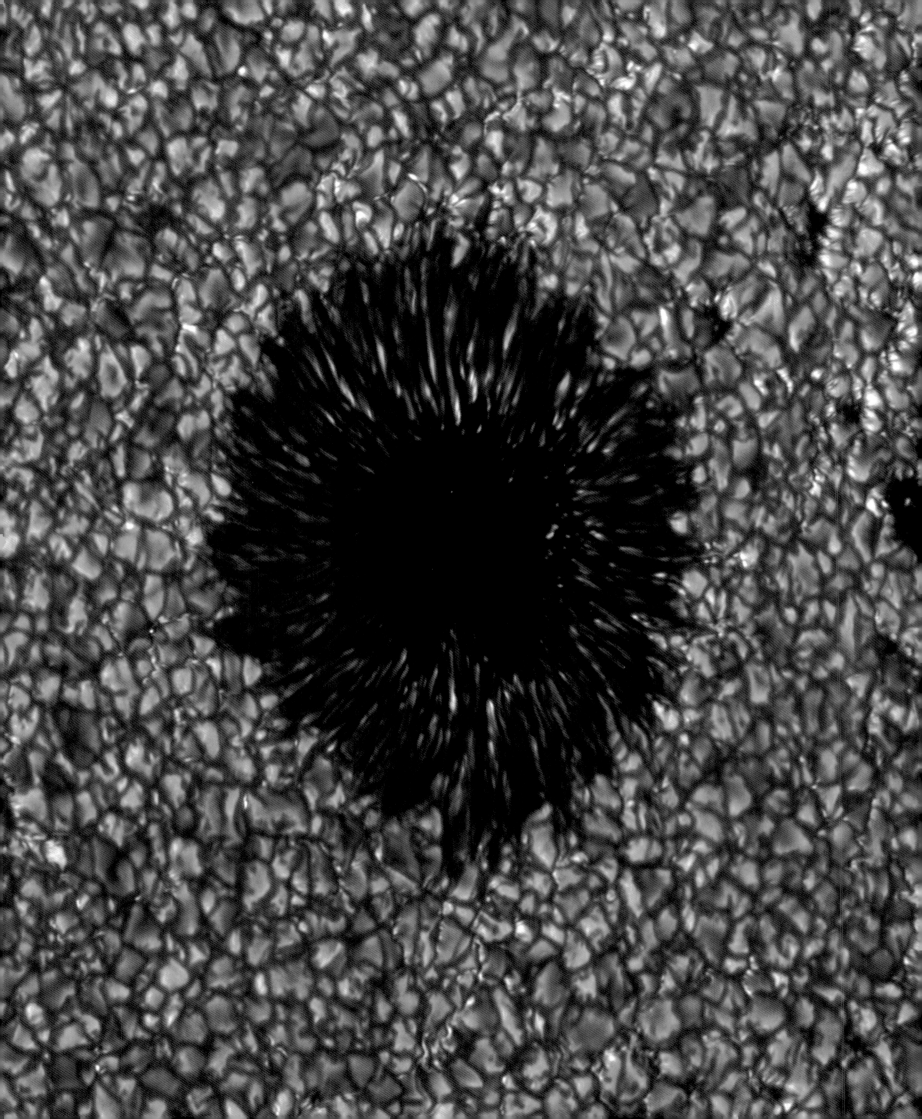

LIGHT SECONDS
LIGHT MINUTES
LIGHT YEARS
KILO LIGHT YEARS
MEGA LIGHT YEARS
GIGA LIGHT YEARS

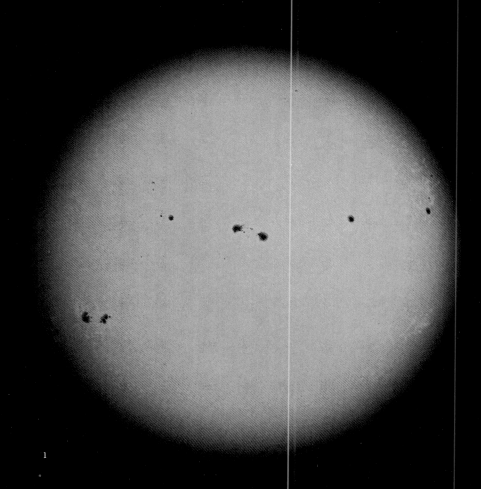

1

Brilliant fury

It is the heart of our Solar System. The Sun is both the hub around which the planets orbit, and the furnace that creates the energy for life on Earth. Millions of tonnes of matter are transmuted into energy every second but the sunlight reaching Earth is hundreds of thousands of years old. Where has it been?

Talk to an astronomer and they are likely to tell you that the Sun is an unremarkable, middle-aged star orbiting in a stellar backwater of the Galaxy. But we know better. The Sun is the beating heart of our existence. It provides the gravitational glue to keep the planets in orbit and the energy to maintain life on Earth.

___No wonder then that it was once thought a god, its divine radiance cascading into space. Now we know that the fire is generated in a nuclear furnace, concealed in the very heart of the Sun. At these great depths, 522,000 km from the surface, the crushing weight of the Sun's outer layers raises the temperature higher than 13 million °C and the density to 150 times that of water. At these extremes, atoms are first stripped of electrons, their outermost particles,

and then the nuclei are slammed together.

___The pummelling drives many nuclei to overcome their mutual repulsion and they fuse with one another. Once joined, they transform into a new chemical species, releasing floods of energy. Inside the Sun, it is the creation of helium from hydrogen that keeps the energy pouring out.

___Released initially as gamma rays, this powerful radiation is swiftly absorbed by other nuclei within the dense surroundings. But they cannot contain their newly found energy and so hand it on, shooting the rays back out into the gas in random directions where they are absorbed again, this time by other, nearby atomic nuclei. This chaotic absorption and re-emission takes place repeatedly, sapping

the gamma rays of energy and working them into visible rays of light.

___The torturous journey from core to surface takes hundreds of thousands of years. The surface is a roiling mosaic of convection cells heated to 6,000 °C, spotted with cooler dark blemishes, or sunspots [1], where giant magnetized arcs puncture the surface. Free at last, light catapults from the surface at breakneck speed, covering 300 million metres every second.

___If it happens to be heading for Earth, it arrives just over eight minutes later. Each Earthly dawn, we bathe in the energy of the Sun, but it is old stock, manufactured hundreds of thousands of years ago deep in the Promethean heart of our central star.

LIGHT SECONDS
LIGHT MINUTES
LIGHT YEARS
KILO LIGHT YEARS
MEGA LIGHT YEARS
GIGA LIGHT YEARS

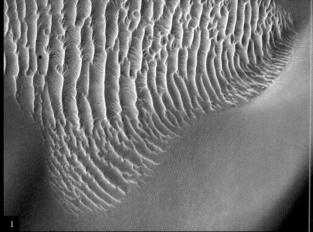

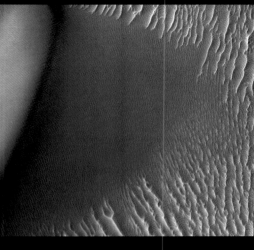

1

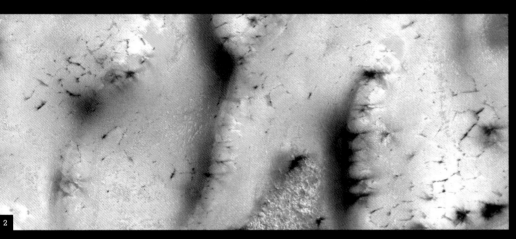

2

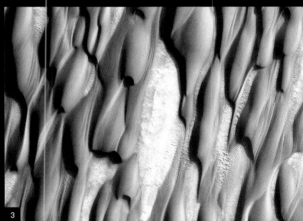

3

Sands of Mars

Alien trees seem to sprout upwards from the Martian sand dunes. But look again: these tendrils run not upward but downhill. They are mini landslips caused by the planet belching out frozen gases as the atmosphere stirs from its winter hibernation.

Winters are harsh on Mars, so cold that they sap the planet's atmosphere, leaving the surface exposed to the vacuum of space. Mars's atmosphere, which is tenuous at best, freezes to the surface, binding into the planet's fine sands [1] and covering them in a frosty pink layer that looks eerily organic [2].

___As spring dawns in the northern hemisphere, so the temperature begins to climb from a low of –150 °C, to a Martian balmy –17 °C, and the frozen atmosphere stirs back into life. Composed chiefly of carbon dioxide, which has a melting point at –78 °C, the atmosphere thaws, turning straight from ice into gas.

___The bubbles of gas burst upwards through the sands, creating dark spots across the dunes

into the atmosphere, revealing the true colour of the Martian sand. Where these blisters break on slopes, they push the sand tumbling down, creating the streaks. By summer, these dunes will all be as dark as the streaks and spots, and the atmosphere will be returned to its gaseous state, veiling the planet.

___As the gas liberates itself, like invisible mayflies escaping their cocoons, so it rushes to populate the entire atmosphere. It whips across the surface of the planet at speeds of several hundred kilometres per hour and lifts the fine sand into the air creating billowing clouds of dust and setting columns of dunes marching across the Martian plains [3].

___In the most extreme cases, the entire planet can become smothered in the dust. Even the

reaches up many kilometres into the atmosphere. As the summer months progress, so the dust settles again and one by one the volcanoes come back into view. Then the smaller peaks, the craters and the rifts all materialize once more. The planet settles, morning mist hugs the slopes, the polar caps shrink away and Mars bathes in the sunlight.

___But it is temporary respite. As the planet climbs away from the Sun, so the temperature drops again. The atmosphere becomes sluggish and the molecules sink to the ground. The dune fields in the far north and the icy plains of the south become cold traps, instantly freezing any gas that touches the surface, and the seasons start all over again.

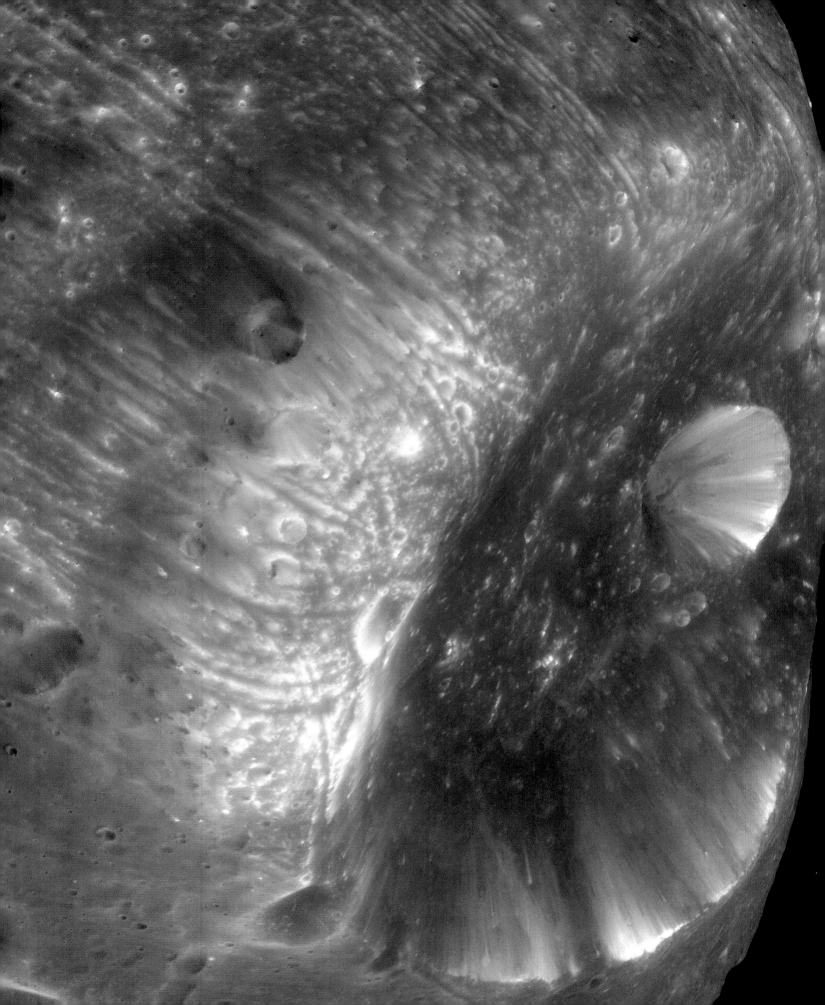

LIGHT SECONDS
LIGHT MINUTES
LIGHT YEARS
KILO LIGHT YEARS
MEGA LIGHT YEARS
GIGA LIGHT YEARS

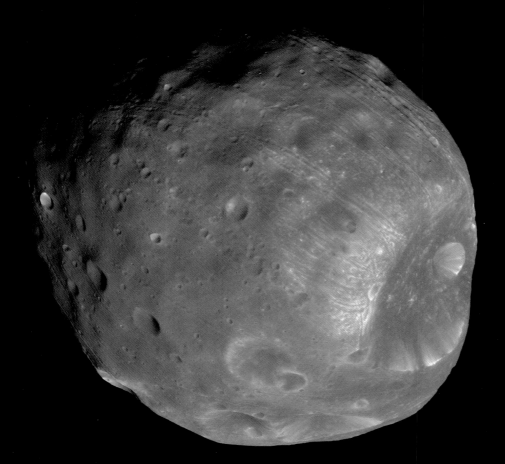

1

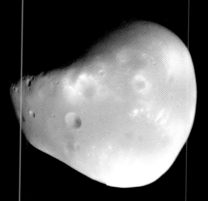

2

Puzzling Phobos

It is Mars's largest moon but don't let that fool you, Phobos is still little more than an asteroid. Just two-billionths of the Earth's mass, it has no atmosphere and hardly any gravity. Yet it could be an easier destination for exploration than our own Moon.

Phobos [1] is an elongated rock measuring just 26.8 x 22.4 x 18.4 km. Its sister moon, Deimos [2], is even smaller at 15 x 12.2 x 10.4 km. Both resemble asteroids and so can be thought of as just that: small space rocks that wandered too closely and were captured by the gravity of Mars.

___Phobos is dark, almost black, absorbing more than 90 percent of the sunlight that strikes its surface and resembling the meteorites known as carbonaceous chondrites. These ancient celestial objects are thought to originate in the furthest parts of the asteroid belt, a couple of times more distant from the Sun than Mars itself. The same is true for Deimos.

___But there is a sticking point: the orbits these moons follow are nothing like those expected

for captured asteroids. Both Phobos and Deimos follow paths that lie close to the equatorial plane of Mars. Had they been captured, they would be orbiting on randomly inclined paths.

___Equatorial orbits imply that the moons formed in situ, from the same coalescing cloud that became Mars. But, if this is the case, then the moons' composition makes no sense; Phobos and Deimos should resemble Martian rock, not carbonaceous chondrites.

___The only clue may be that Phobos is not a single chunk of solid rock. Its density is so low that there are probably vast empty spaces inside. This could mean that a giant impact on Mars long ago threw big chunks of debris into orbit that retain their ancient façade today,

even though the planet below them has evolved. The chunks then settled against one another at haphazard angles to form the conglomeration we now call Phobos.

___More excitingly, it could be the staging post humankind needs for exploring the Solar System. Phobos is so small that it generates only a weak gravitational field. Upon arrival in Martian orbit, landing and launching from Phobos would require only the smallest of impulses. In those terms, it is cheaper and easier to send a robotic spacecraft to distant Phobos than it is to send one to the surface of our own Moon, where landers have to fight against the lunar gravity.

___On these terms alone, Phobos is an ideal destination.

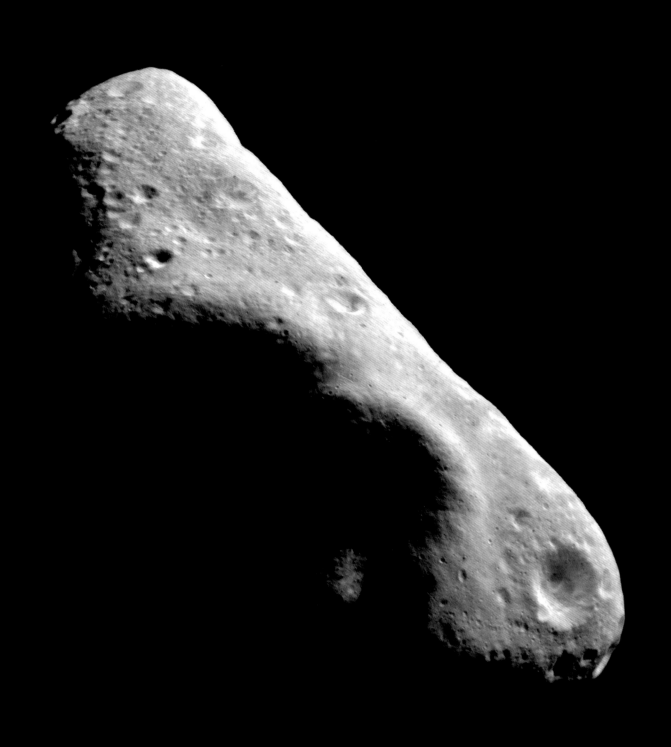

LIGHT SECONDS
LIGHT MINUTES
LIGHT YEARS
KILO LIGHT YEARS
MEGA LIGHT YEARS
GIGA LIGHT YEARS

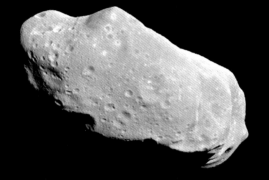

1

2

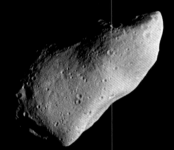

3

Stony messengers

The detritus of the Solar System's formation still surrounds us in the form of millions of asteroids. Most of them are safely tucked away in the asteroid belt between Mars and Jupiter – but not all. Some draw close to Earth, providing both tempting possibilities and a threat of global annihilation.

Sixty-five million years ago, life on Earth changed irrevocably. An asteroid or similar body smashed into the Earth, travelling in excess of 11 km/s. It hit just off the coast of Mexico, in the Yucatan peninsula, creating a flash of light brighter than a thousand suns. Giant tsunamis rolled across the seas, the blast wave circled the Earth several times and a fountain of shattered earth was thrown into the atmosphere. Immediately there was a climate disaster as the sunlight was blocked from the surface, and the temperature fell away. For the dinosaurs, it was the final straw, their death knell and exit from the tapestry of living creatures.

___Asteroids continue to swing by Earth to this day. This particular irregular lump of natural space junk is called Eros. It circles the Sun but loops around it, following a highly elliptical path. At 33 km long, Eros is 10 times larger than the asteroid that wiped out the dinosaurs.

___Despite spending most of its time much further away, Eros can sometimes approach our world to within just 75 light seconds. Yet it is not the most dangerous of the known asteroids. Even at its closest approach, in astronomical terms it is a safe distance away.

___Most asteroids are stony mountains such as Ida and its moon Dactyl [1]. Mathilde resembles Phobos in that it is partly hollow [2]. Gaspra [3] may once have been part of a larger body.

___The asteroid to really keep an eye on is Apophis. It will next go by Earth in 2013 but during 2029 it will approach within a cosmic hair's breadth of less than a tenth of a light second. This will be nearer than the geostationary satellites that handle our communications. Ironically, this close pass will take place on 13 April, which just happens to be a Friday.

___Like a shark preparing to launch an attack, an asteroid will tend to swing near to a planet before it strikes. Indeed, it is the unwitting planet's own gravity that blindly nudges the asteroid onto the final collision course, if the asteroid passes through a specific volume of space, known as a keyhole. Within the keyhole, gravitational forces conspire to set the asteroid on its fateful last orbit.

___Even when beyond these keyholes, the orbits of the asteroids and comets are not immutable. They can evolve with time, pushed and prodded by the faint gravity of the planets, changing their orbits and commanding constant vigilance.

LIGHT SECONDS
LIGHT MINUTES
LIGHT YEARS
KILO LIGHT YEARS
MEGA LIGHT YEARS
GIGA LIGHT YEARS

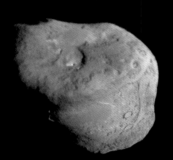

1

2

Ghost writers

Something really got under the skin of Comet Holmes.
During 2007, the usually shy comet made a true spectacle
of itself. It brightened 500,000 times more than usual and
expanded to almost three quarters the size of the Sun.
So where did all this ambition suddenly come from?

Comets are the icy heralds from a bygone epoch. When the Solar System was forming these icy leftovers brought water to the inner planets. Now they are merely ghostly messengers who write their stories in dust; each statement costs the comet dearly.

___The Sun's heat works on the comet as it draws closer to the sultry realms of the inner Solar System. The comet's icy surface evaporates away, diminishing it but producing an arcing tail that can stretch through space. Eventually the comet will fade into obscurity when it has no ices left to give up, or it will simply fall to pieces as the icy glue evaporates from the rocky honeycomb.

___Comet Holmes, however, was determined to go out in style. Between October 23–24 2007 it flared up. Comets have been seen to rally before, but not like this. While the central nucleus remained constant at around 3.4 km across, the debris cloud grew to a diameter of a

million kilometres, which is about 70 percent of the Sun's width. The mass distributed throughout this vast volume remained minuscule, only a little denser than the vacuum a good laboratory could produce using modern air pumps, but it caught the sunlight and reflected it all across space.

___Either a meteorite struck the comet or perhaps the Sun's warmth wheedled its way inside where it blew open a cavity of ice, ejecting the contents into space. Still to this day, nobody knows what caused it.

___A comet's natural habitat is in the deepest, darkest regions of the Solar System, way beyond the planets, and part way to the nearest stars. There could be a trillion of these icy asteroids out there, all slung away by Jupiter's mighty gravity early in the evolution of the Solar System. Lofted to their great distances, most comets are now only occasional visitors to the inner regions.

By substantially reducing the threat of impacts Jupiter has safeguarded our world and our neighbours.

___This magnanimity comes at a price though; from time to time Jupiter takes a hit itself. In 1994, it snared a passing comet, crushed it into pieces and then took blow after blow as the fragment struck the planet's bloated body. The resulting explosions created smoke palls that drifted in the atmosphere for weeks and smothered areas larger than Earth. Other smaller impacts have been observed on Jupiter since.

___But impacts are not always one-way. In 2005, NASA's Deep Impact probe struck comet Tempel 1 [1 & 2], excavating a crater approximately 100 meters wide and 30 meters deep. The probe's spectrometer revealed the presence of silicates, carbonates, clays, metal sulfides (like fool's gold) and polycyclic aromatic hydrocarbons.

LIGHT SECONDS
LIGHT MINUTES
LIGHT YEARS
KILO LIGHT YEARS
MEGA LIGHT YEARS
GIGA LIGHT YEARS

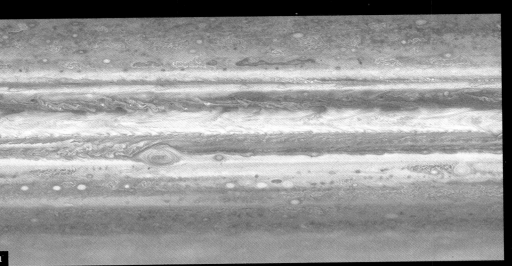

1

2

Stellar aspirations

Jupiter is the colossus of the Solar System. A giant
stormy world that outweighs all other planets together
by more than twice. Its pull of gravity diverts asteroids
and comets from their paths and controls a retinue of
moons. How then can Jupiter be thought of as a failure?

Condensed out of the same cloud that gave
birth to the planets, giant Jupiter has more in
common with the Sun than the rocky planets.
This is because it is composed of the same
gases as our central orb. Hydrogen and helium
contribute 98 percent of its bulk. All the other
elements that seem so familiar to us on Earth,
the silicon in the rocks, the calcium in our
bones, the iron in our blood, and all the other
elements of the periodic table, comprise no
more than a meagre two percent of Jupiter.

___Though vast by planetary standards,
317 times more massive than the Earth, Jupiter
remains slight in stellar terms. Less than one
thousandth the mass of the Sun, for all its

a planet – and this marks it as a failed star.
___Only by adding some 80 times more
mass to the planet, would the nuclear core
be crushed to the point of igniting under its
own weight. In that instant, the planet would
transform itself into a star, but a lowly one.
It would become a red dwarf, the smallest,
dimmest stellar minnow possible.

___Nevertheless, Jupiter does release some
small measure of energy from its interior. It is
generated because Jupiter is shrinking by about
2 cm per year. It is a habit left over from the
planet's formation, when it was twice its current
size. In the 4.5 billion years since, gravity has
been pulling the planet ever denser and, as it

As this escapes through the planet, it stirs the
atmosphere into the perpetual storm belts that
we see today [1]. The brightly banded layers
of Jupiter stretch around the planet, sometimes
deepening with a ginger flush, at other times
fading away into the creamy background.

___Jupiter is more than ten times wider than
the Earth. Our entire planet could get lost in
the storms that swirl across its face – and none
are larger than the Great Red Spot [2]. This
giant anti-cyclone rises about 8 km above the
surrounding clouds and rotates once every six
days. Most impressive of all, this storm system
has been stable for centuries. No one knows
how old it is, nor how long this 'perfect storm'
will endure.

LIGHT SECONDS
LIGHT MINUTES
LIGHT YEARS
KILO LIGHT YEARS
MEGA LIGHT YEARS
GIGA LIGHT YEARS

1

Infernal Io

Forget the myriad volcanoes of Earth, the veiled vents of Venus, and the possibly extinct peaks of Mars. If there is a volcanic heart in the Solar System, this tiny moon of Jupiter is the place.

Io reinvents itself every thousand years or so. The catastrophically volcanic moon is constantly spewing lava onto its surface, painting itself a new face, and producing the youngest surface in the Solar System. Io has been driven into this volcanic frenzy by the tormenting pull of Jupiter, which gives rise to extreme tidal forces. On Earth, the tide from the Moon drives the oceans to lap the shoreline but, on Io, Jupiter's gravity forces the moon to turn itself inside out.

___The tidal force occurs because gravity weakens with distance, even across the width of a relatively small moon such as Io. With gravity pulling on one side of the moon harder than on the other, the moon is pulled into an elongated shape. This shape changes as Io follows its elliptical orbit around Jupiter, altering the strength of the gravitational force

it experiences. In this way, Io's innards are squeezed and stretched like a concertina and melted by the friction.

___Io does not produce molten rocks as Earth's volcanoes, but sulphur compounds that gush from plutonic depths. They rise to the surface through vents in the floor of paterae, flat-floored depressions bounded by steep walls. Some eruptions take place with such force that the lava is ejected high into the sky, reaching 200 km into space [1] before raining back to the surface in a hellish downpour.

___The lava results in the yellow stain that covers the moon. It gradually turns darker under the influence of the Sun's ultraviolet light. The eruptions surround Io in a thin fog of sulphur dioxide. While this is enough to constitute an atmosphere, it varies greatly both in temperature and density according to the

time of day and the ferocity of the volcanic eruptions.

___As well as the volcanoes there are extensive mountain peaks on Io, forced upwards by compression of the crustal rocks. Io eschews the long ranges favoured by Earth and prefers its mountains as isolated individuals. The tallest can be found at South Boösaule Montes. Reaching upwards for some 17.5 km, this extraordinary mountain is more than twice the height of Everest on Earth. Most of the mountaintops on Io are flat, each one stretching for kilometres to form rugged mesas. And all of the mountains are collapsing, mostly being dragged back down from the edges by the moon's gravity.

___The moon is constantly changing. So don't waste time mapping Io; it is a never-ending job – just enjoy the spectacle.

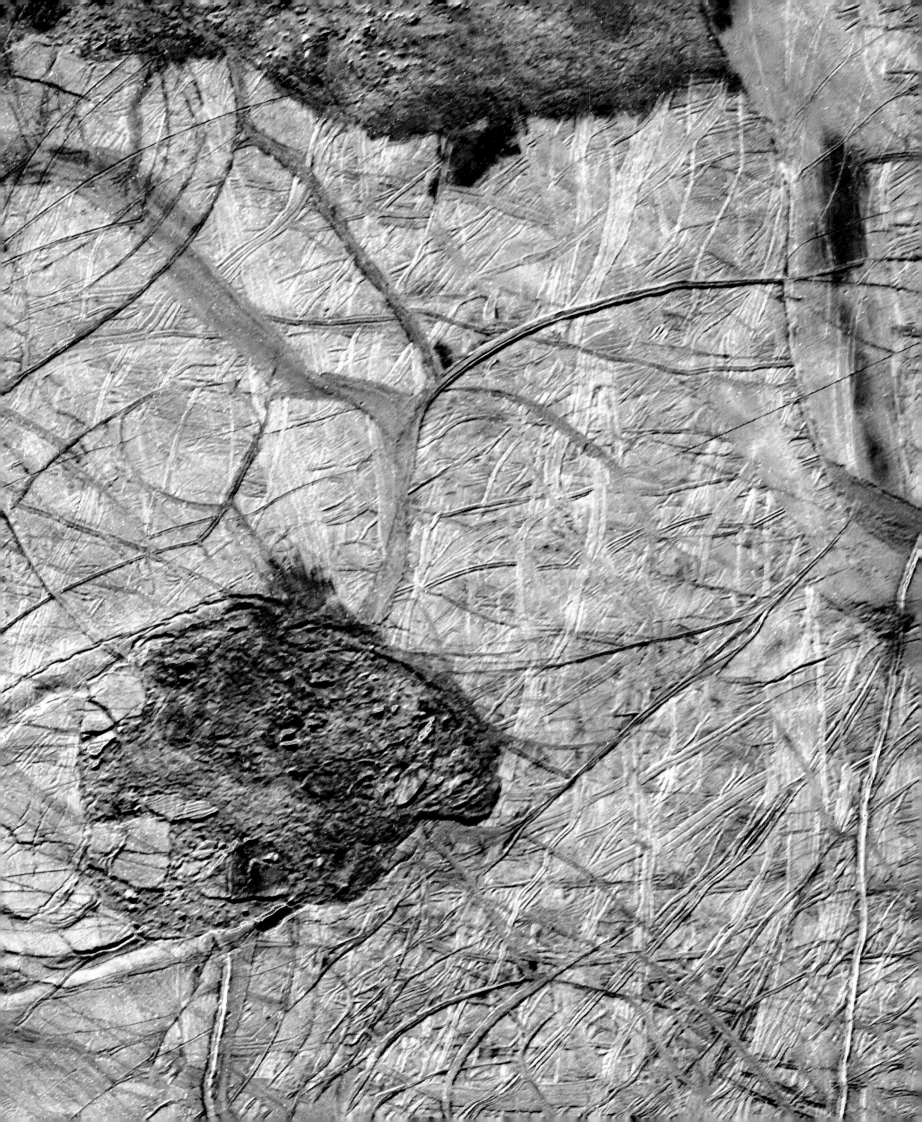

LIGHT SECONDS
LIGHT MINUTES
LIGHT YEARS
KILO LIGHT YEARS
MEGA LIGHT YEARS
GIGA LIGHT YEARS

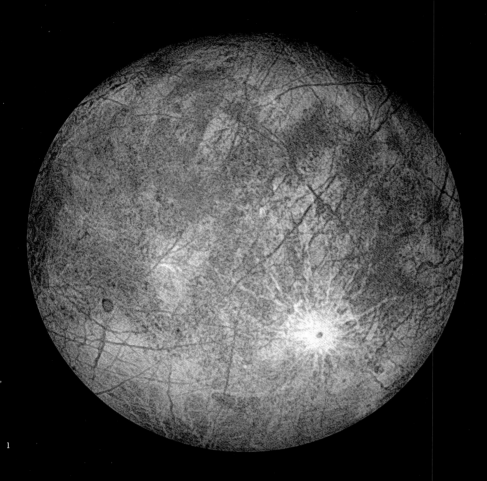

1

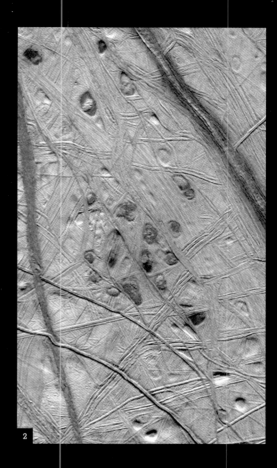

2

Dark eden

The same gravitational forces that have condemned Io to a state of constant flux, may just have endowed its sister moon with an unlikely oasis. If so, it is a dark oasis and we are going to have to burrow kilometres underground to find it.

Europa orbits Jupiter one and a half times further out than Io. Here, the vice-like grip of the planet has been loosened somewhat. The friction that its tidal forces engender may be enough to melt some of the moon's icy mantle, but not the rocks and chemicals themselves.

___Europa could possess an ocean tens or even hundreds of kilometres deep, trapped beneath an icy crust that is measured in thickness between 1 and 10 kilometres. If this is true, there could well be more liquid water on tiny Europa than on the entire Earth.

___Evidence for this ocean is found on the surface in the malleable formations there. Giant cracks riddle the surface [1], split by the tidal forces and tinted by the upwelling of mineral-bearing waters from below. In other

places, called chaos regions, the ice sheets appear to have broken up into giant bergs, briefly formed a floe and then re-frozen into a new position. Now they look like a giant's abandoned jigsaw puzzle. Ruddy freckles [2] mark regions where warm ice has risen from the ocean below.

___All these are signs that the ice crust is sitting on something mobile; a softly churning ocean would fit the bill. But this unknown ocean is pitch black, with no sunlight penetrating the icy layers. Nevertheless there is energy for life here.

___The energy absorbed from Jupiter may drive ocean vents, where hot water gushes up into the surrounding ocean. On Earth, such thermal vents may have been the birthplace of life, and today they maintain ecosystems that

owe nothing to the Sun for their survival. Could the same be true on this moon of Jupiter?

___To find life on Europa, or indeed elsewhere in the Solar System would have major ramifications for our understanding of biology. For example, would it be based on DNA? If so, could it be an offshoot of Earthly life carried from our world to there, or vice-versa? If it is not based on DNA, how does this alien life form pass on its genetic information?

___Life could have arisen once in our Solar System as the result of a random fluke, but twice would indicate there's something easier about the process than we think. If we were to find a second architecture of life, it would indicate that we should expect living things to be widespread throughout the cosmos.

LIGHT SECONDS
LIGHT MINUTES
LIGHT YEARS
KILO LIGHT YEARS
MEGA LIGHT YEARS
GIGA LIGHT YEARS

1

2

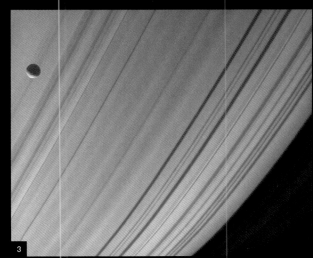

3

Gravity's rainbow

<u>Delicate grandeur greets the eye at Saturn. The pastel shades of its atmosphere and the graceful sweep of its rings speak of a place of serene beauty. Yet below the clouds, titanic forces are lurking, ready to break out and cause havoc.</u>

No other planet can compete with Saturn. Its sublime rings, menagerie of moons and opalescent complexion [1] make it a world of staggering beauty. The rings themselves span 1,000,000 km but edge on they are just 1 km thick [2]. Despite their gossamer beauty, they are little more than rubble – icy rocks and pebbles that shine brightly in the sunlight. So brightly, in fact, that they must have been placed there relatively recently.

___Perhaps a moon was destroyed by a stray asteroid or comet, and the debris was corralled by gravity into the rings. That would explain why they are still so bright, as the icy material tends to discolour over time. Based on their reflectivity, Saturn's rings are estimated to have formed just a few hundred million years ago, at a time when dinosaurs were ruling the Earth.

___So it could be that mankind is simply lucky to share its existence with Saturn's rings, or it could be that the rings are a moon-recycling plant. Maybe they are constantly replenished as moons are destroyed, and perhaps they are even capable of forming new moons – if sufficient ring material were to fall together.

___However they were formed, the tapestry of rings is woven by the gravity of Saturn's many moons. Gaps both small and large divide the rings, and each gap can be attributed to the gravitational pull of a moon. Any ring particle that strays into a gap will be nudged back out by its lunar shepherd. Some gaps, such as the Encke Division and the Cassini Division span hundreds or thousands of kilometres, whereas others impart little more than textures that appear as ripples on the rings. The moon Pan

carves out the Encke Division, from its orbit inside the gap, whereas Mimas [3] controls the Cassini Division from afar.

___Below the rings lie the cloud tops, a subtle boundary of pastel beauty. Saturn guards its privacy and most of its weather takes place below these cloud tops, hidden from our view. But occasionally the planet shows its true temperament. Giant storms, usually pearl white and always larger than the entire planet Earth, can burst through the upper cloud decks. They bring with them violent bursts of radio waves and lightning. Peculiarly, these storms often appear at the same latitude in the planet's southern hemisphere, dubbed storm alley. They hint at the titanic forces at play within this beguiling gas giant.

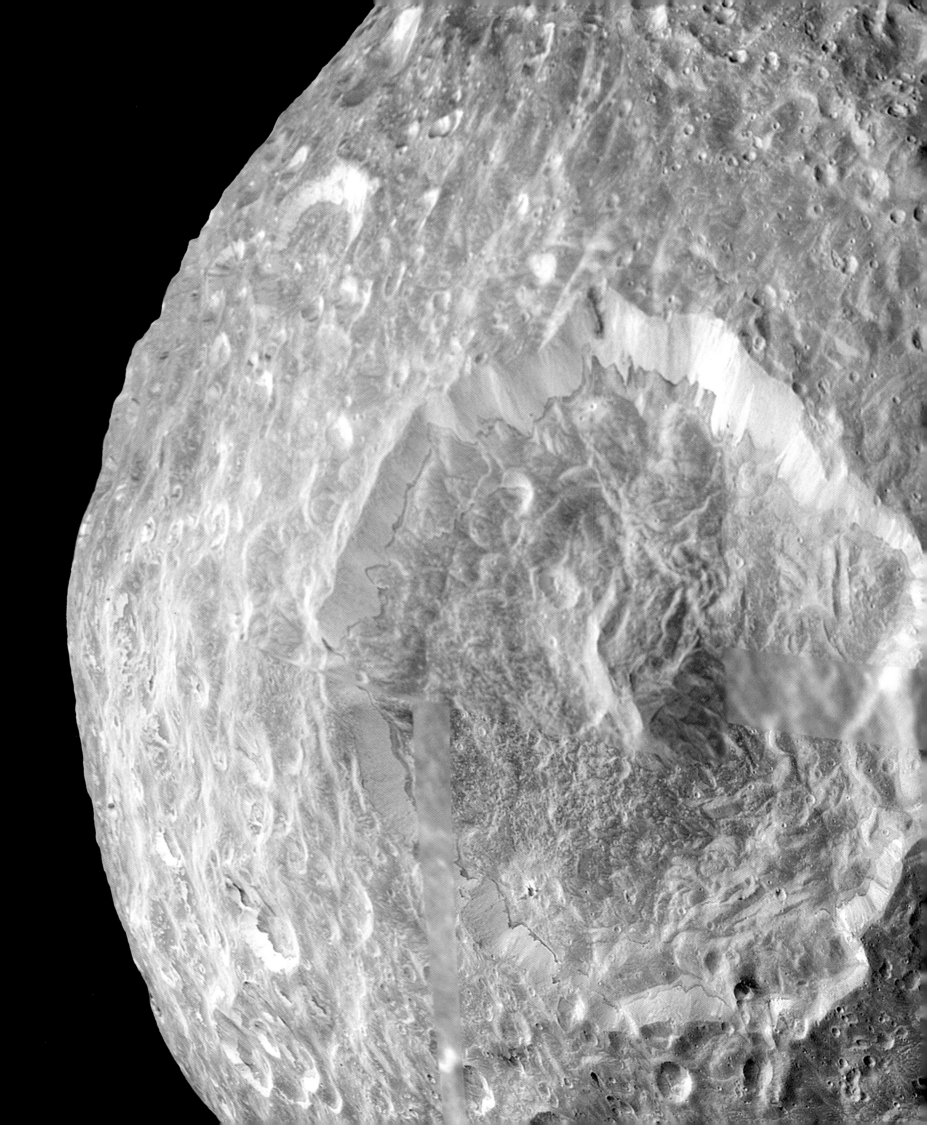

LIGHT SECONDS
LIGHT MINUTES
LIGHT YEARS
KILO LIGHT YEARS
MEGA LIGHT YEARS
GIGA LIGHT YEARS

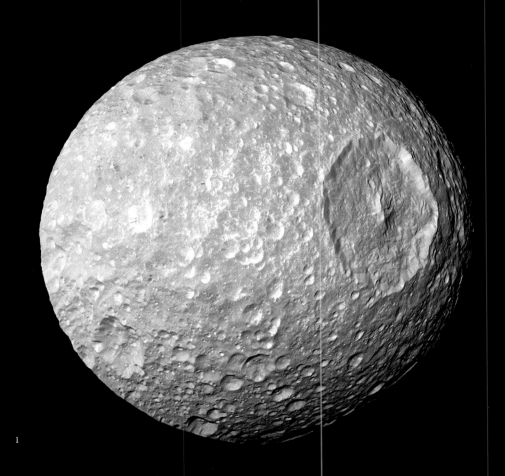

1

Breaking the ice

The icy surface of Mimas is representative of its interior.
There is hardly any rocky material in this moon, just ice
frozen solid by the frigid temperature of outer space:
Mimas is an iceberg in space.

At just three-hundredths of the diameter of
Earth, Mimas is one of the smallest bodies in
the Solar System to have pulled itself into a
round shape. It has been battered over the
course of its history by smaller asteroids and
meteorites, and now displays the scars as
craters [1].
___No crater can be more impressive than its
Herschel Crater. At 130 km across it is almost
one-third of the moon's total diameter. Its walls
tower 5 km into the air and parts of the floor
sink to 10 km below the rest of the surface.
In the centre of the crater, like the solidified
rebound by a giant water droplet, the central
peak of the crater rises higher than 6 km.
___The impact that created the Herschel Crater
may have come close to shattering the moon

because, in the opposite hemisphere, the
surface is riddled with fractures. These are
probably the result of seismic waves that rolled
through the moon following the impact and
ruptured the ice in their wake.
___The surface temperature of Mimas reveals
a dilemma. As it is heated by the Sun, so its
equator should be hotter than its poles.
But if anything the reverse is happening.
The equatorial temperatures plunge as soon
as the Sun has passed by overhead but the
higher latitudes continue to heat up well into
the Mimantean afternoon. It is as weird as if
you were to stand on Earth's equator and
experience the afternoon temperature on a
cloudless day suddenly plunge to its lowest
night-time level.

___This behaviour is probably the result of
highly conductive impurities in the ice at the
equator. As these absorb sunlight, they channel
the heat down into the interior and so the
surface temperature appears to drop quickly.
Nearer the poles, these impurities are not in
the ice and those areas retain their heat.
But why there should be differences in
the surface composition is unknown.
___And finally: yes, the similarity in
appearance between Mimas and the Death
Star from Star Wars has been noticed. It is
entirely coincidental. Hershel Crater was
discovered in 1979, two years after the first of
the science fiction blockbusters was released.

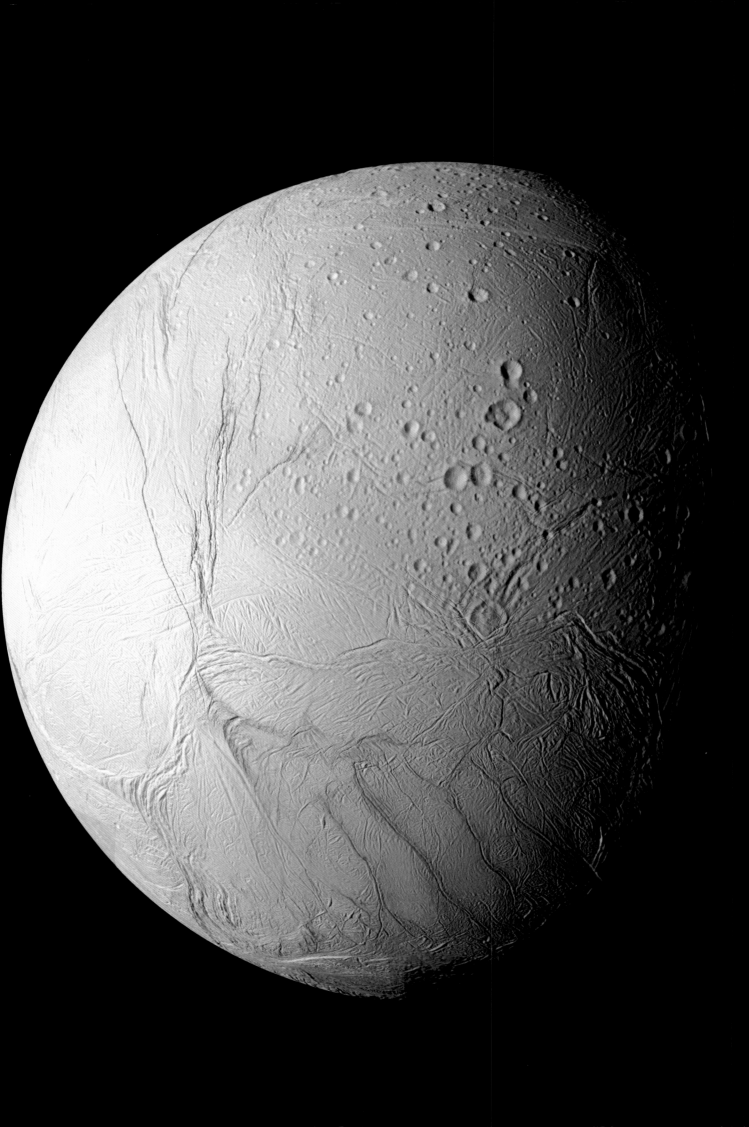

Enceladus
MOON of SATURN
DIAMETER: 504 KM

LIGHT SECONDS
LIGHT MINUTES
LIGHT YEARS
KILO LIGHT YEARS
MEGA LIGHT YEARS
GIGA LIGHT YEARS

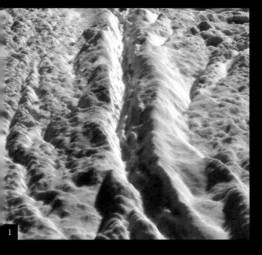

1

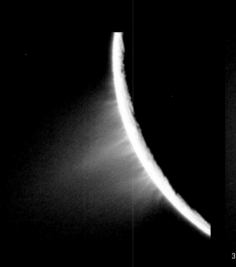

2

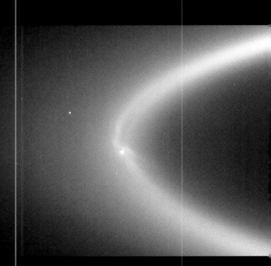

3

Tiger-stripes

Bright and shiny Enceladus is the most reflective body in the Solar System. It bounces 90 percent of the light that strikes its icy surface right back out into space. And that's not the only thing the moon spurns: jets of water burst from the south pole, never to return.

Containing almost the same surface area as the countries of France and Germany combined, Enceladus is a special place. It is one of only three moons in the Solar System wracked by volcanic activity.

___Geologically, it is a place of variety. There are at least five different types of terrain on the moon including smooth plains, cratered regions, cracks and ridges. Warmth from within may be melting the plains smooth, erasing millions of years of history from the surface.

___The most intriguing of the features are the 'tiger stripes', sinuous coloured markings that snake across the moon's southern pole. They are cracks leading to Enceladus's restless depths [1] and the origin of strange fountains of water that reach high into the black sky [2]

– but never fall back to the ground. The plumes are stunning examples of cryo-volcanism, so called because they take place only in frigid realms where molten lava is replaced by liquid water.

___To feed the geysers on Enceladus, it is imagined there must be misty caverns partly filled with water existing beneath the thick icy surface. These natural reservoirs hold water seeping up from below through the cracks, and then explode it into space because, in the airless environment, the water turns straight to vapour. It jets out of Enceladus like steam from a kettle. The moon's gravitational pull is just a hundredth of that on Earth so the water does not fall back down. Instead, it launches into space where Saturn's gravity catches the

microscopic particles and confines them to Enceladus' orbit, creating the tenuous E ring that girdles the giant planet [3]. Although spanning a million kilometres in width, the ring would decay to nothing in between 10,000–1,000,000 years, if it were not for the constant replenishment from Enceladus's alien geysers.

___The water rushing from the moon is unlikely to be freshly melted ice because it contains sodium salts, leached from the rocks where it had prolonged contact. A similar mechanism makes Earth's oceans salty.

___The conclusion is inescapable: far down in Enceladus a deep ocean must rest unseen, as one does at Europa around Jupiter, halfway back towards the Sun.

Titan
MOON of SATURN
DIAMETER: 5,200 KM

LIGHT SECONDS
LIGHT MINUTES
LIGHT YEARS
KILO LIGHT YEARS
MEGA LIGHT YEARS
GIGA LIGHT YEARS

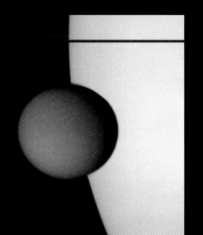

1

2

3

The twilight zone

Out around Saturn, 10 times further from the Sun than the Earth, Titan receives just one hundredth of the warmth that permits widespread life on our world. But don't write off Titan; it could be humankind's lifeboat in aeons to come.

Of all the moons in the Solar System, Titan stands out because it is the only one with a thick, hazy atmosphere [1&3]. Despite being just one-third the size of Earth, Titan has more atmosphere than our planet. The gases press down on its surface 1.5 times harder than on ours, and are mostly nitrogen, with a noxious mixture of methane and hydrogen adding some chemical piquancy.

___The valleys and hills of Titan's surface present a familiar landscape, but it is all built from an alien chemistry. Water ice takes the place of rocks, frozen to granitic strength by the –180 °C daytime temperature. When it rains on Titan, liquid methane and ethane torrent through the ravines that twist down the moon's hillsides into lakes where it glints in the dawn Sun [2].

___Methane and ethane are not the only things to fall from the sky. A gentle snow of tarry particles also drifts down. They are produced in the upper atmosphere where ultraviolet light breaks up methane molecules, which then grab any chemical they can get their molecular hands upon. The resultant particles rain out, coating the surface with a grimy hydrocarbon layer.

___With all that said, Titan might actually be giving us a glimpse into our own past, an inkling of what the Earth was like before life began. Stuck out in the celestial deep freeze, Titan has preserved its primordial atmosphere whereas ours has been changed irrevocably with the passage of time. Perhaps all Titan needs to develop into a pleasant, though smaller world, is a little bit of extra heat.

In a few billion years, that might be exactly what it receives.

___In that distant future, the Sun will begin to exhaust its stock of hydrogen. This will trigger a sequence of events inside our star that bloats it into a red giant. At that point it will grow so large that it will engulf the inner planets, including Earth. But Titan stands to gain.

___The red giant Sun will be much brighter than our present day luminary, and could supply Titan with enough energy to shrug off its frigid complexion. If it develops a clement aspect, it could become a safe haven for any humans still around.

___So Titan is a fixer-upper, a place full of potential but in need of time and energy. Luckily for the moon, the Sun has plenty of both.

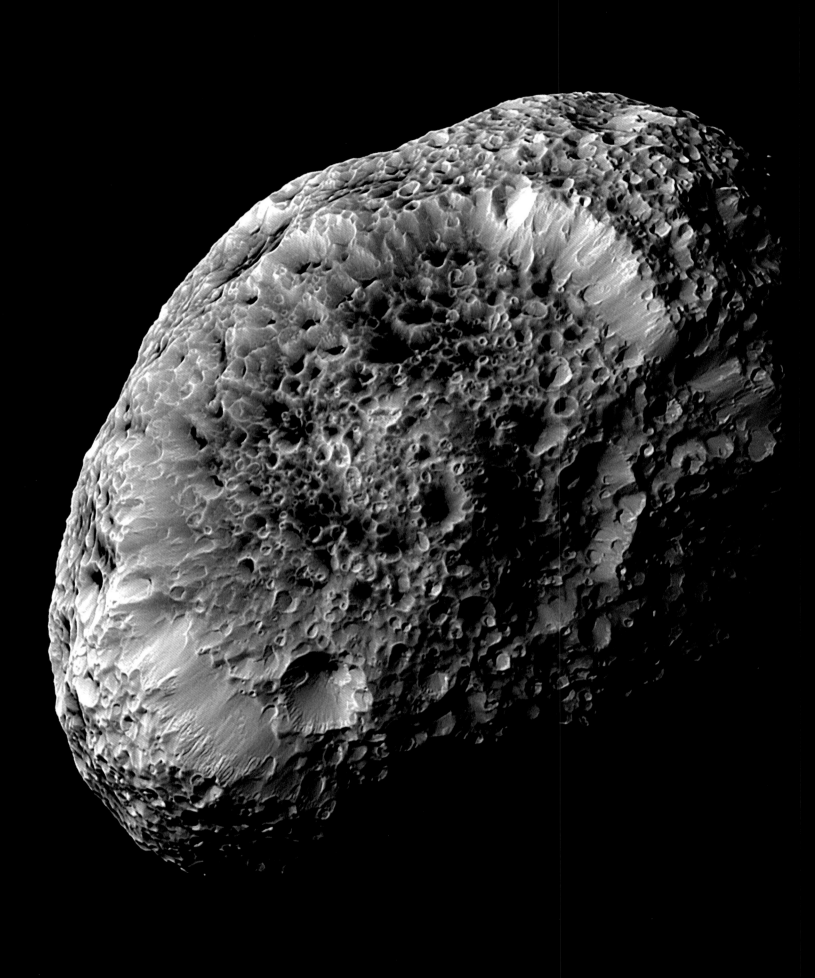

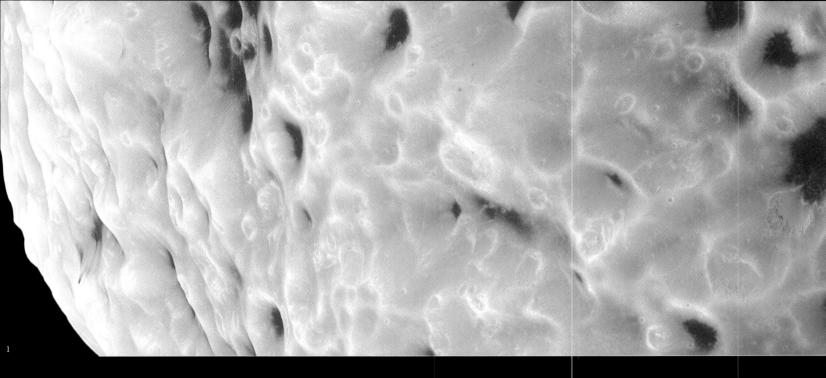

1

Caverns of Hyperion

Imagine being on a world and not being able to predict the time of sunrise or the length of the coming day. Nothing you can measure will let you be certain of these fundamental quantities; they change chaotically every day. Welcome to Hyperion.

Looking like a giant sea sponge in space, Hyperion spins unpredictably as it follows an eccentric orbit around Saturn. It is not just the period of rotation that changes but the imaginary spindle around which the moon rotates as well. One day, the Sun – visible only as an intensely bright star from Hyperion's distance – will simply bob its head over the horizon, another day it will rise and stay overhead for hours. On yet another day, it will begin to set and then rise again before dipping below the horizon.

___This moon's out-of-control rotation is the result of a conspiracy of factors. The first is its irregular shape, the second is its elongated orbit and the third is its occasional proximity to the large moon Titan. All of them unsettle Hyperion, which tries to respond to the myriad gravitational fields acting on it, and their ever-changing strengths based on its distance from Saturn and Titan.

___The cratering is dense on Hyperion [1], perhaps a product of its chaotic rotation as every surface is repeatedly laid open for assault. Even so, one impact stands out. It is a behemoth measuring 120 km across, while the average radius of the moon is only 135 km. Gouged to a depth of more than 10 km deep, how could such a giant impact not shatter Hyperion into a billion fragments?

___Perhaps the secret lies in Hyperion's interior. In common with many of Saturn's moons, it is more ice than rock but the secret is that, rather than being a solid lump, Hyperion is a honeycomb. Up to 40 percent of the moon could be empty, with vast caverns stretching through the interior. It may not even be a single object, just a pile of celestial rubble that has been pulled together by gravity. But the gravity is insufficient to crush the rock and ice together into a single, solid body.

___This porosity acts as a crumple zone, allowing Hyperion to absorb the energy of an otherwise fatal impact. So, when Hyperion suffered the mighty strike, it collapsed inwards producing not so much a crater as a dent, but otherwise remained intact – or as intact as a celestial rubble pile can ever be.

Iapetus
MOON of SATURN
DIAMETER: 1,400 KM

LIGHT SECONDS
LIGHT MINUTES
LIGHT YEARS
KILO LIGHT YEARS
MEGA LIGHT YEARS
GIGA LIGHT YEARS

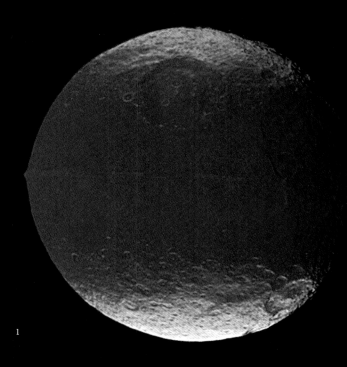

1

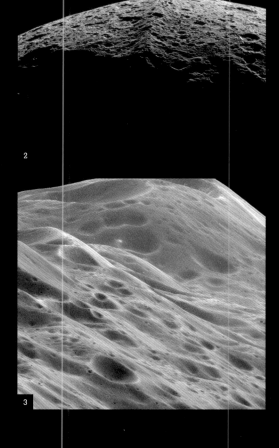

2

3

Cosmic graffiti

Something has painted Iapetus but not finished the job.
While one hemisphere of this Saturnian moon shines
with gleaming ice, the other is distinctly saturnine.
Stenciled with grime, it begs the question: who is the
cosmic graffiti artist?

By all rights, Iapetus should be just another icy moon. All indications are that it is composed mostly of ice with just a fifth of its interior made from rock. On its surface there are the usual mix of craters and other markings but one feature stands out. It is unique amongst the many worlds of the Solar System.

___One hemisphere of Iapetus is stained with a dark material [1], which absorbs more than 95 percent of the light that falls on it. The other face is bright ice with a sharp boundary between the two colours.

___The black powder itself is a mix of carbon-bearing molecules that resemble the organic material found in comets and some meteorites. These molecules represent the chemical building blocks that made life possible on Earth. In the frigid, airless wastes of Iapetus, however, they are preserved for all to see.

___As they built up, so they absorbed more sunlight, warming that hemisphere of the moon and driving the bright surface ice to escape. This loss further darkened the hemisphere, leading to its current midnight complexion. But why did it accumulate on just one hemisphere?

___The first clue is that the gleaming hemisphere is the trailing one. Saturn has trapped Iapetus into always turning the same face to the planet, exactly the same as the Earth has done to the Moon. This means that one half of Iapetus always faces forwards while the other looks behind, and it is the forward-facing hemisphere that is caked in the dark deposits. So the stuff is in Iapetus' orbit. Now, how did it get there?

___The culprit is Phoebe, another of Saturn's moons and 9.5 million kilometres further out. This chunk of a moon is just 100 km across, little

more than a glorified comet, and it is coming apart at the seams. Spewing dust into space, Phoebe has surrounded Saturn and the visible ring system with an almost invisible girdle of sooty particles. Reaching from the orbit of Phoebe across millions of kilometres of space, the dusty particles litter Iapetus's orbit, which are then splattered onto the moon as Iapetus ploughs through the grimy cloud.

___It is not just Iapetus that suffers; Hyperion also receives a share of Phoebe's grime. Though because of its chaotic rotation, the particles have accumulated more evenly across Hyperion's tumbling surface.

___But Iapetus is more that a painted face, an equatorial spine of mountains runs 1,300 km around the moon [2]. More than 10 km tall, these peaks are the Himalaya of Iapetus [3], but their origin remains mysterious.

LIGHT SECONDS
LIGHT MINUTES
LIGHT YEARS
KILO LIGHT YEARS
MEGA LIGHT YEARS
GIGA LIGHT YEARS

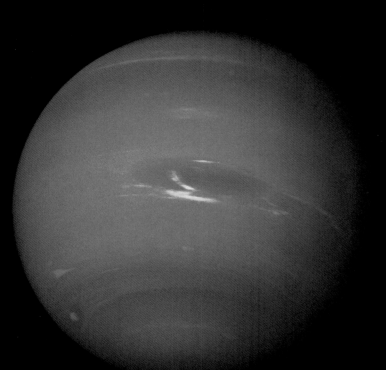

1

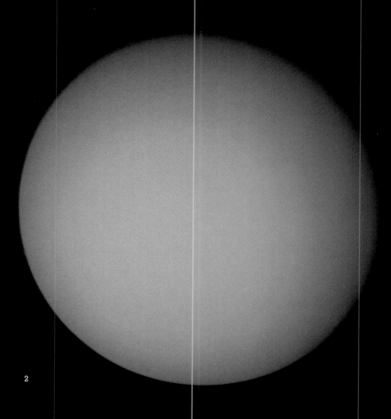

2

The ice giants

Something is stirring the clouds of Neptune. Whereas
its planetary brother, Uranus, presents a glassy
appearance, devoid of activity or markings, Neptune
is a dynamic world of storms – possibly the result of
an indigestible dinner.

Uranus and Neptune are strikingly similar in terms of composition. Mostly composed of light gases such as hydrogen and helium they both possess a noticeable component of methane, ammonia and water vapour in their atmospheres. This reflects the fact that these planets formed in the further expanses of the Solar System, where the strength of sunlight was so low that ices found it easier to condense into planetary material.

___But these planets probably did not form as far out as we see them today. Uranus sits 15 times further from the Sun than the Earth, and Neptune doubles that to 30 times. That's a puzzle because, at those distances, and certainly that of Neptune, there simply should not have been enough material to build a planet 17 times the mass of the Earth.

___Instead, Neptune most probably formed

significantly closer and then migrated to its current orbit as gravitational forces exerted themselves between the planets, and moved them into some state of equilibrium.

___Neptune is a dynamic world of storms and cloud systems. The Great Dark Spot on Neptune was discovered in 1989 and measured to be large enough to swallow the Earth [1]. Unlike the Great Red Spot on Jupiter, however, it proved to be a transitory feature, disappearing by 1994. In its place other storms have occasionally appeared, providing a continual reminder that all has not settled inside the planet.

___Uranus on the other hand, does not show any signs of atmospheric shenanigans; even spotting clouds on the planet is almost impossible [2]. This is strange because Uranus receives four times the amount of sunlight that

Neptune does, yet seems to do nothing with it. Something must be driving Neptune's weather from the inside.

___The solution may be the early safari that the planet took to reach its current orbit. This would have swept Neptune through a swarm of dwarf planets, similar to Pluto, also jockeying for position. If Neptune drew sufficiently close to one of these, it could conceivably have swallowed it whole, as a snake devours its prey. Maybe the subsequent release of energy, as it digests this planetary mouthful, continues to this day, stirring the atmosphere.

___Yet it is peaceful Uranus that displays the most peculiar attribute of this pair of giants: it has fallen onto its side, spinning over and over rather than round and round, and receives more solar heat at its polar regions than at its equator.

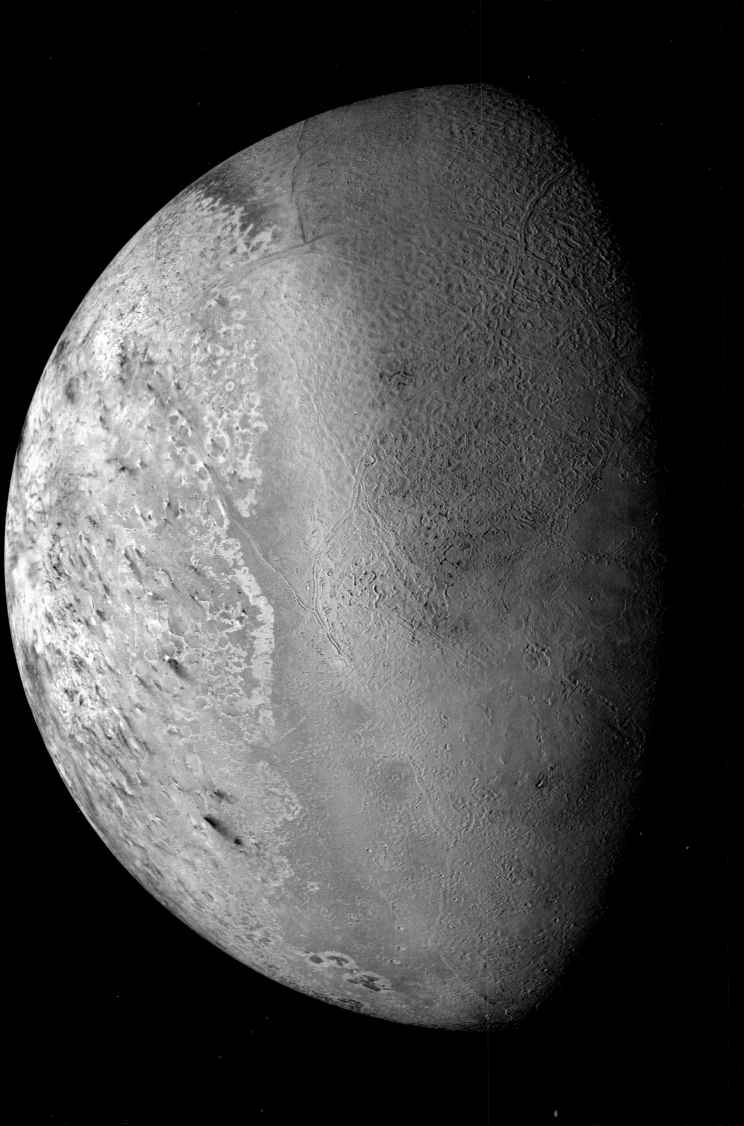

Triton

MOON of NEPTUNE

DIAMETER: 2,700 KM

LIGHT SECONDS
LIGHT MINUTES
LIGHT YEARS
KILO LIGHT YEARS
MEGA LIGHT YEARS
GIGA LIGHT YEARS

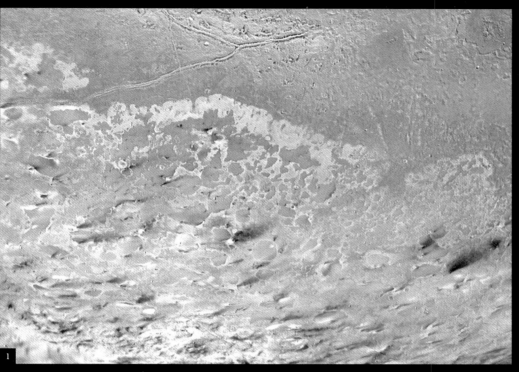

1

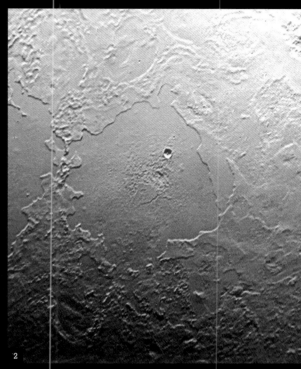

2

Kidnapped moon

Neptune's largest moon Triton defies easy description.
Its pink south pole receives a constant stream of sunlight
from the Sun. Although weak because of distance, this
illumination is somehow enough to spark volcanic
activity in this icy outpost of the Solar System.

Neptune's largest moon must somehow have been kidnapped by the large planet, snagged by its gravity and hoisted into orbit. A naturally occurring moon would follow an orbit more-or-less around the parent planet's equator, travelling in the same direction as the planet spins. Triton, however, opts for the difficult life: a backward path around the planet, and so inclined it sweeps within easy sight of Neptune's polar regions.

___Triton's seasons are dominated by the slow march of Neptune around the Sun, which takes 165 years to complete an orbit. This means that a season on the moon lasts some four decades. Triton is currently holding its southern hemisphere sunward, and this is driving a bizarre form of volcanic activity on it.

is a chilly –235 °C. Nonetheless, black streaks mark out a volcanic region [1]. This is where the icy surface is being heated by the distant Sun, forcing geysers of invisible nitrogen gas to erupt upwards to an altitude of 8 km. As the gas blasts skyward, it carries with it dark dust blown by a faint breeze. Falling downwind, the dusty particles daub the surface.

___Once an eruption starts it can last for up to a year, spraying debris across 150 km downwind of the geyser. This behaviour may be similar to that happening in Mars's polar regions during the spring months.

___The atmosphere itself amounts to nothing more than a tenuous collection of gases, 20,000 times lower in pressure than the Earth's, and during the long winter it will freeze to

___Craters are gradually healed on Triton as the internal warmth of the moon allows the ice to flow and slowly fill its wounds, erasing them over millions of years [2].

___Were Triton to be magically released from Neptune's clutches, it would resume an orbit around the Sun, and be sufficiently large to be proclaimed a dwarf planet in its own right. The dwarf planets are a newly classified group that includes Pluto. There are a handful of examples known so far. These include Ceres, the largest asteroid, the distant worldlet of Eris and the fancifully named Haumea and Makemake. There could be many more, perhaps hundreds or even thousands that lie, yet to be observed, in the distant reaches of the Solar System.

56

57

INTER STELLAR

Leaving the planets behind, we see them swiftly shrink to pinpoints and disappear into the glare of the Sun. Now we are truly in deep space. There is nothing but blackness, and the misty light of the Milky Way beckoning to us, urging us on.

Somewhere around us are a trillion comets, all but invisible because their dirty icy surfaces are reflecting nothing but the feeble starlight. This tenuous shell of leftovers from the planets' formation was scattered into these exiled realms by the gravity of the giant planets. They are a lost resource: the mountains of Iapetus that never were, the plateau of Titan that missed its mark, and the inland sea that never found its way to Earth.

___They no longer concern us, we have more luminous targets in sight but to reach them we will have to lengthen our stride. The stars in our part of space are separated by light years, and to visit the marvels that adorn our Galaxy we will have to cover tens of thousands of them.

___On the puny time scale of a single human lifetime, the stars are immutable, fixed and constant. But taken across the entire sweep of the Milky Way, they are a varied population covering all stellar races and ages.

___At the smallest end of the scale are red dwarf stars. These celestial minnows are the misers of the Galaxy. They have little fuel and what they do have they are determined not to fritter, so they produce a weak glow of red light that burns for 100 billion years. At the opposite end of the scale are the spendthrift blue supergiants. These furious dynamos burn themselves away in just a few million or a few tens of millions of years.

___The lifespan of each star is governed by the interplay of gravity against pressure. Gravity tries to squeeze the star into an ever more compact configuration, while radiation pressure tries to blow it apart. The harder gravity squeezes, the faster the nuclear reactions in a star's core occur and the more energy they produce. This is why we experience the seemingly paradoxical situation that the smallest stars, with the lowest fuel stocks, live the longest, while the profligate massive stars live fast and die young.

___At the heart of each star is an alchemist's furnace capable of turning plentiful hydrogen and helium into rare heavier chemical elements. With each transmutation, so energy is produced to keep the star shining and alive. When the star eventually dies, either in a graceful flowering of its outer layers or

in the calamity of a supernova, it bequeaths the newly created elements back into space, enriching the interstellar medium with the seeds of future stars and planets.

___Mature stars often come in pairs or more. These groupings are for life. Once joined at birth, nothing can part them. Fully half the stars in the Galaxy are partnered in one way or another; they pull each other into pirouettes that can take decades to complete or just mere hours.

___But as brilliant as the stars are, it is the beautiful nebulae that attract the most attention; they blossom from the great bulk of the giant molecular clouds that drift through the Galaxy. Each colossal nimbus has stitched itself together out of the disparate wisps of dust and gas found in interstellar space, gradually sealing off its interior from view. In these secret realms, the process of stellar gestation can take place.

___Shrouded in utter darkness, it is only when these stellar embryos are close to being born that they begin to burst with light. And not only light, for magnetic windows can open in their atmospheres out of which a wind of particles blows. These streaming stellar winds begin to carve a way out of the nebula for the star. In the case of the largest stars they are assisted in their task by the welter of ultraviolet radiation they exude.

___All of this combines to open a cavity around the star, pushing ever-greater quantities of dust and gas away until ultimately the leading edge of the bubble reaches the outer surface of the cloud. Now, the cavity opens up to view, and a magnificent luminous cavern is revealed in which dwell young stars, ready to take their place on the galactic stage.

___There is an embarrassment of these celestial jewel boxes close to the Solar System. From the radiant beauty of Orion to the towering pillars of the Eagle Nebula, by way of the hydrogen waves of the Lagoon Nebula and the misty mountains of creation in Carina, each one is riddled with embryonic stars.

___We quickly encounter more of these regions than we might otherwise expect because the Sun sits in the middle of a mysterious ring of star formation called Gould's Belt. It is inclined

from the stars of the Milky Way by 20 degrees and the Sun is misplaced from its centre by 325 light years. This sparkling necklace was formed some 60 million years ago and is now responsible for some of the most recognizable constellations in the sky. Gould's Belt supplies bright stars for Orion, Scorpius and the Southern Cross amongst others.

___What set this giant ripple in motion is not well known. It could have been a giant molecular cloud dive-bombing the Galaxy, or a similar collision with a clump of the hypothetical particles known as dark matter.

___Theories of galaxy formation postulate that this, as yet undetected, stuff must surround every galaxy in a giant sphere, termed a halo. Each one is more than ten times wider than the visible portion of the galaxy, contains at least ten times more mass than the stars and is clumpy rather than smooth. These clumps are the last vestiges of all the smaller halos that the galaxy has swallowed in order to grow to its present size.

___Regardless of its origin, Gould's Belt is now 3,000 light years in diameter, and contains a few thousand high-mass stars as well as hundreds of thousands of low-mass stars.

___Pressing onward, no journey through space would be complete without a visit to the dark heart of our Galaxy. Situated 26,000 light years from Earth, the centre of the Milky Way is the dwelling place of a supermassive black hole. It is the kernel around which the Galaxy originally formed; the black hole itself may even be the original seed. Now cloaked in the blinding fog of X-rays from a spiralling whirlpool of doomed matter, it sits feeding on anything that passes.

___Finally as we turn our sights upwards to soar out of the Galaxy, we pass the spherical bulks of the globular clusters. With populations in the millions, these ancient stellar metropoli have seen it all; they are the silent witnesses to the Galaxy, having been present for its formation and its subsequent 10 billion years of evolution.

Right: M27, aka the Pleiades or the Seven Sisters, a cluster of hot blue stars some 440 light years away

LIGHT SECONDS
LIGHT MINUTES
LIGHT YEARS
KILO LIGHT YEARS
MEGA LIGHT YEARS
GIGA LIGHT YEARS

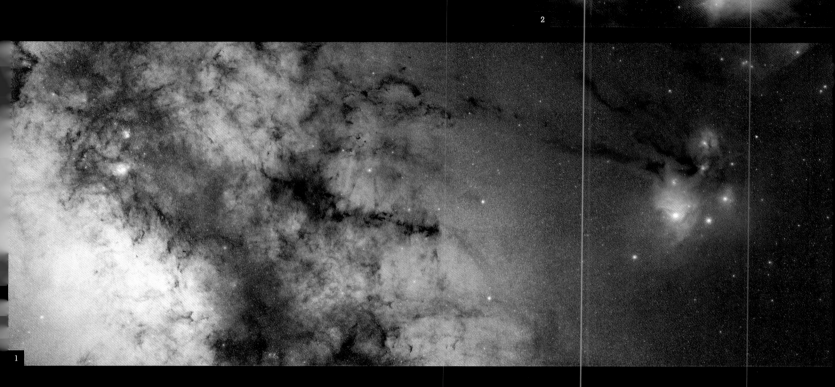

First impressions

<u>Sitting towards the centre of the Galaxy is a cornucopia of stars, big and small, young and old. Wrapped in vibrant dust clouds, the combined starscape resembles a canvas from an impressionist master.</u>

This particular canvas is huge, 10 light years across. Although it appears to hang on display just above the crowded galactic core [1], it is actually much nearer to us.

___The medium used to create this masterpiece is dust and gas – amounting to 3,000 solar masses of the stuff – and fortuitous alignment. The giant star of Antares sits towards the bottom of the image, just to the left of M4, a mass of stars known as a globular cluster. M4 is seen through a rare window in the cloud. It is much further away and takes no part in the business of the cloud.

___Antares is another interloper, more than a hundred light years behind the dust cloud. Outshining our Sun by 10,000 to 1 at visible wavelengths, and by 65,000 times at infrared,

its light punches through the dusty realms. Were Antares to magically replace our Sun, it would engulf the inner Solar System, reaching to the asteroid belt. Its extremities are thousands of times less dense than water and it exhibits a lazy pulsation that follows no particular pattern in brightness or period.

___But the centrepiece is Rho Ophiuchi, a pair of blistering stars, embedded in the white orchid just above the centre of the image. Each one is a giant, eight and nine times the mass of the Sun and blazing with surface temperatures of around 20,000 °C. The stars keep their distance, circling each other at 400 times the distance between Earth and the Sun, shifting their bulks through their conjoined orbits only once every 2,000 years.

___All the stars in this complex are between 100,000 and 1,000,000 years old. They include nearly 200 almost formed T Tauri stars and more than 400 condensations that are on their way to becoming stars. In the infrared [2], the youngest stellar objects reveal themselves as bright points, mimicking the stars they will one day become.

___Radiating away from the whole complex are black fingers of unilluminated dust. They stretch off for hundreds of light years into space, perhaps connecting this region to other hotbeds of star formation throughout the Milky Way.

___In the epoch to come, the cloud will be utterly consumed by these burgeoning stellar fires, and replaced by a gleaming star cluster.

LIGHT SECONDS
LIGHT MINUTES
LIGHT YEARS
KILO LIGHT YEARS
MEGA LIGHT YEARS
GIGA LIGHT YEARS

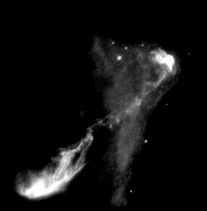
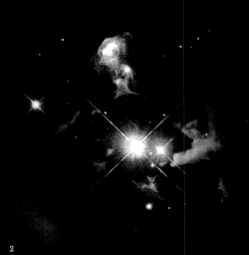
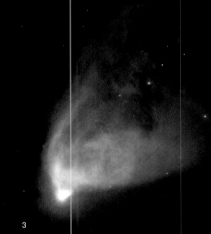

1   2   3

Stellar dawn

Stars are born in darkness, richly swaddled inside cocoons of dust and gas. Just as in the insect kingdom on Earth, the first task of the stellar newborn is to break free of its protective swathes. It does it with an early act of rebellion.

By strict definition, the shining object at the centre of this view, surrounded by veils of dust, is not even a star. T Tauri, as it is known, has yet to achieve the core temperature and pressure necessary to ignite its nuclear furnace and thus generate its own energy. But it is already shining brightly.

___Its secret power source is that it is still contracting: pulling itself together by dint of the gravity its mass creates. As it shrinks, so it squeezes out energy from the movement of the atoms and this allows it to shine, giving it the outward appearance of maturity, like a child dressing up and pretending to be adult. All of this play-acting should take place behind the veils of dust but somehow the star has managed to emerge.

___Before the discovery of nuclear fusion, contraction was thought to be the means by which all stars shone. But if that were true, stars would live truncated lives, burning themselves out in a million years or less. The only force that can keep so many stars shining in the Universe is nuclear.

___How T Tauri and other stellar newborns emerge from their cocoons is still mysterious. The first stirrings of nuclear fusion are thought to pour radiation into the surrounding clouds, pushing them away and rending holes to peer through.

___Nuclear ignition does not start smoothly. The hallmark of a nuclear engine stuttering into life are million km/h jets of gas launched trillions of kilometres into space [1]. They inflame the surrounding cloud, causing knots of gas to fluoresce brightly [2]. Such distinctive stellar blowtorches are known as Herbig-Haro Objects.

___These tantrums excavate increasingly large conical cavities [3] and starve the protostar of matter, stunting any further growth. In T Tauri's particular case, it is destined to become a star similar to the Sun, although orbited by two other stars. These two siblings are still too young to be readily visible, having failed to emerge yet from their cocoons. No one knows whether there are planets around any of these stars.

___T Tauri has become so influential in the study and the understanding of young stars that it now gives its name to a whole class of stellar show-offs: the T Tauri stars. Each one is about a million years old and readying itself for the big wide cosmos.

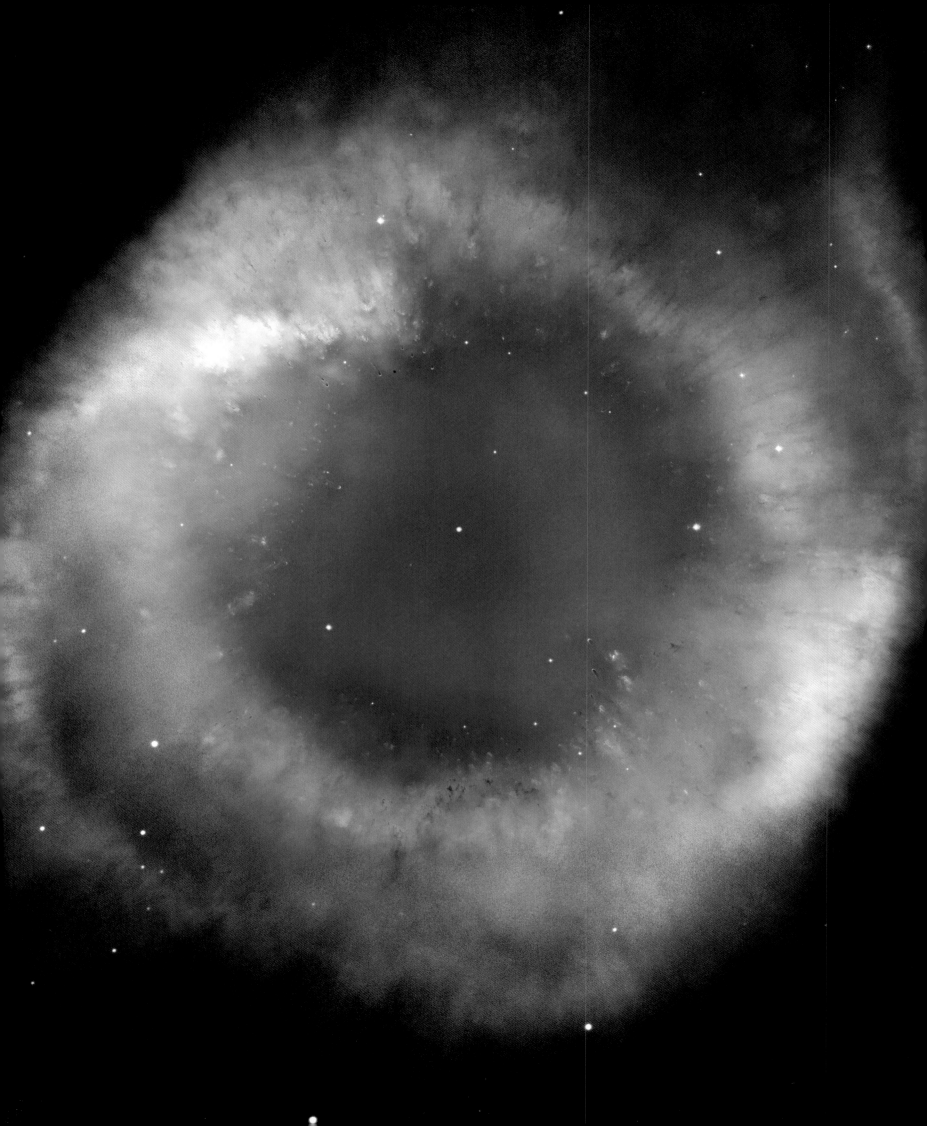

LIGHT SECONDS
LIGHT MINUTES
LIGHT YEARS
KILO LIGHT YEARS
MEGA LIGHT YEARS
GIGA LIGHT YEARS

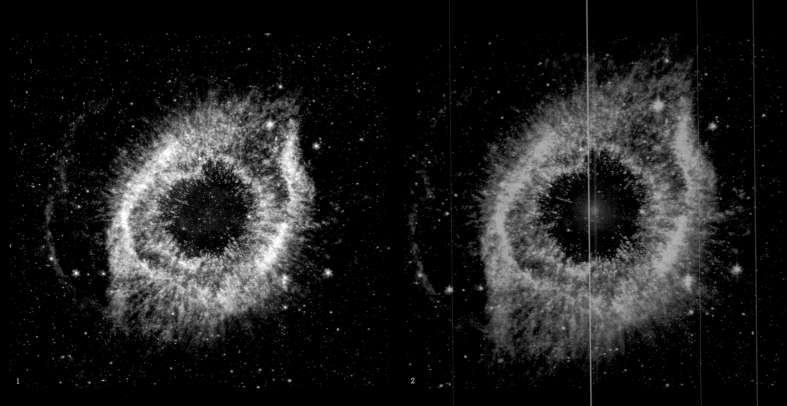

1

2

Death spiral

While the double helix of DNA is one of the secrets of life on Earth, this single celestial helix shows us the secrets of stellar death – and offers some clues about the next generation of stars.

This is how stars die, not in faded senescence but rather at their most beautiful. Around 12,000 years ago, there would have been nothing to distinguish this star. It would have been a bulging red giant, shining with ruby lustre. Now, it is a fluorescent bloom. As the nuclear fusion in its core faltered, so the star blossomed, discharging its outer layers to the mercy of space.

___Contrary to appearances, the Helix is not a spiral but a tunnel of glowing gas that we happen to be looking into. And we catch it early in its formation. Stellar flowers such as these bloom for just 50,000 years before they disperse into the more tenuous interstellar dust and gas all around them.

___The death throes are governed by the fusion of helium inside the star. It is a highly temperature-dependent affair, with small

changes in a star's core temperature leading to large variations in the rate of energy output. These palpitations cause dramatic changes, blasting the outer layers away into space and creating a planetary nebula.

___The term 'planetary nebula' is a misnomer from the 18th century when William Herschel thought that these celestial blooms bore a faint resemblance to his recent discovery, the planet Uranus. He guessed they signified the construction of solar systems, rather than their destruction. Despite their true nature becoming apparent as knowledge increased, the name has stuck.

___In the Helix Nebula, thousands of tentacles appear to be reaching back towards the central, dying star. This is an illusion. At the head of each tendril is a knot of dust and gas, previously ejected from the Helix Nebula's

central star. Now the knots are getting in the way of the other streaming gases, deflecting them and giving rise to these filaments. In the infrared [1] the tentacular nature of the nebula is emphasized. At even longer wavelengths the Helix fixes the cosmos with a baleful red eye made from the dust of immolated comets [2].

___Planetary nebulae are instrumental in changing the composition of the Galaxy. Inside red giant stars, turbulent currents of roiling gas dredge up the heavier elements synthesized in the nuclear core during the star's lifetime, including life-giving carbon and oxygen. As the outer layers lift off into space, so these elements are transported along with them. They enrich the gas and dust in interstellar space forming the building blocks of the next generation of stars.

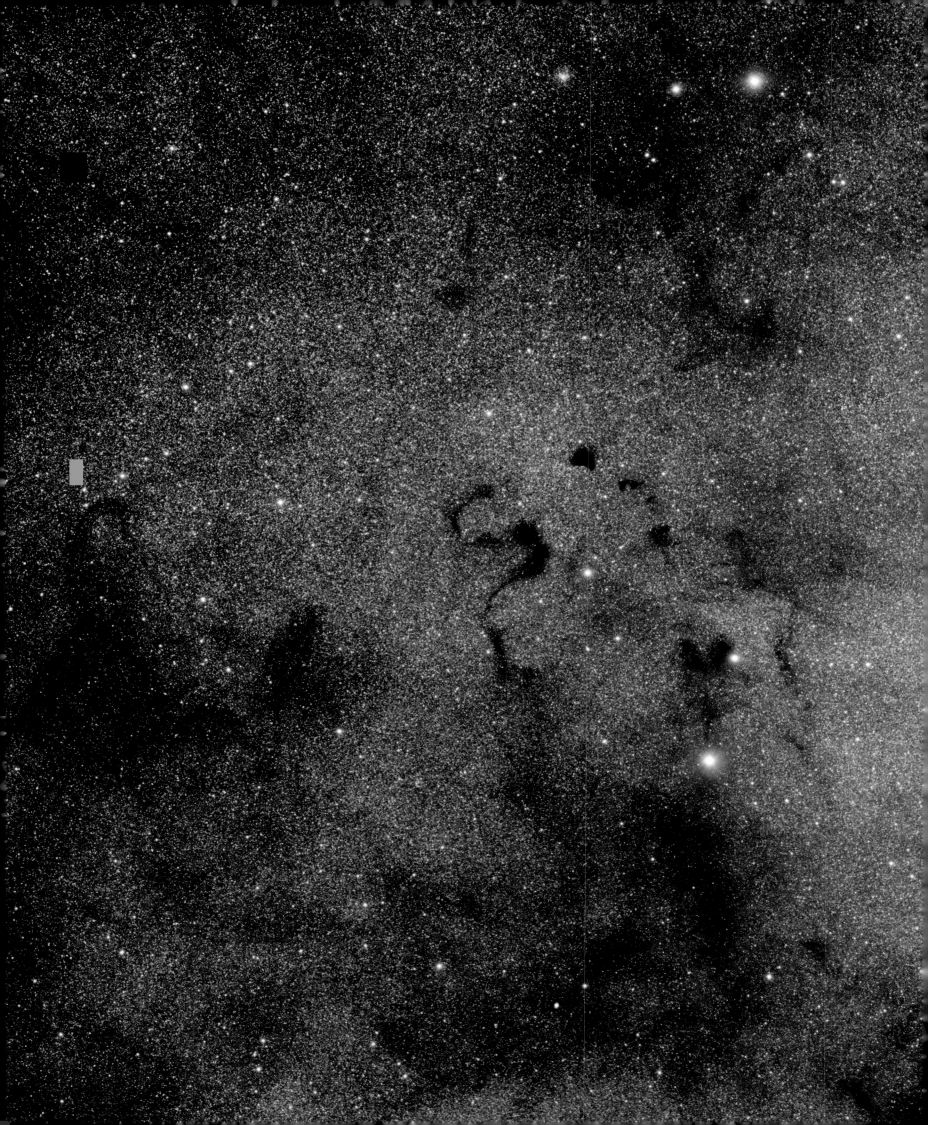

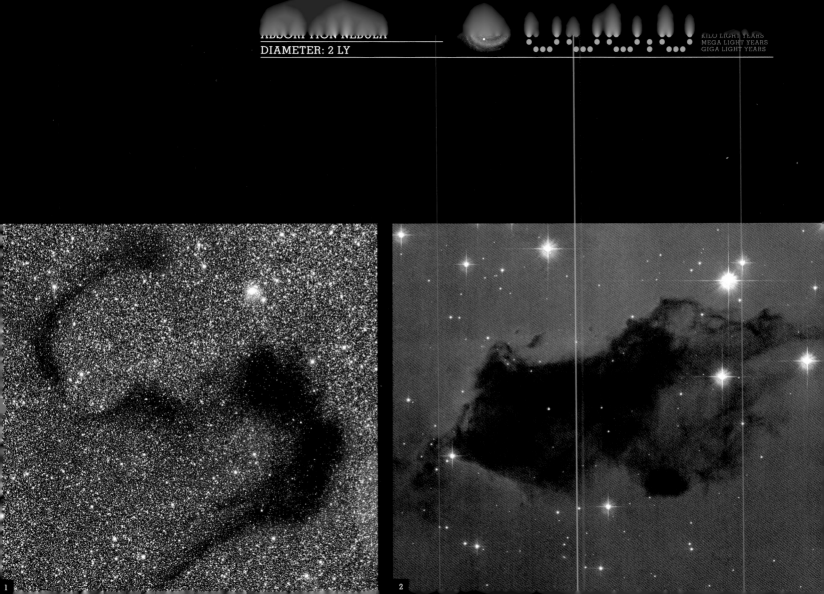

ABSORPTION NEBULA

DIAMETER: 2 LY

KILO LIGHT YEARS
MEGA LIGHT YEARS
GIGA LIGHT YEARS

1

2

684.0 LIGHT SECONDS
LIGHT MINUTES
LIGHT YEARS
KILO LIGHT YEARS
MEGA LIGHT YEARS
GIGA LIGHT YEARS

1

2

The blue witch

**Look closely at this tumble of interstellar dust and gas.
With a touch of imagination it resembles a witch's head
in profile, with pointy nose and chin. As strange as it
may seem, this ethereal blue glow is conjured up for
the same reason Earth's daytime sky is blue.**

Light does not always travel in straight lines through space. Occasionally it can be diverted from its path by collisions with dust particles. This is exactly what is happening here, light is streaming into this cloud of dust and gas from the nearby bright star Rigel, which denotes the right shoulder of Orion, the Hunter. The star itself is not visible on this image, resting just beyond the top right-hand edge.

___While the majority of Rigel's light passes straight through cloud, a small percentage collides head-on with myriad dust grains and is scattered in all directions. Some of that light happens to bounce towards Earth, allowing us to make out the cloud where otherwise we would see nothing.

___But why does this cloud show only blue light when Rigel releases all the colours of the rainbow? It is because not all colours respond to the dust in the same way. The shorter wavelengths of light, which we perceive as blue colours, are far more susceptible to bouncing off the dust grains. Whereas the longer, redder wavelengths find it easier to bypass the grains of dust.

___We exploit this property of light on Earth, by using orange streetlights that penetrate fog more successfully than white lights. It also gives rise to our blue skies and red sunsets.

___At noon, about fifty percent of the sunlight is scattered around the sky, mostly at blue wavelengths. The remaining light from the Sun appears with a yellowish tinge. In space, the Sun appears to give out more of a white light; hence there was no yellow tint on the airless lunar landscape photographed by the Apollo astronauts.

___On Earth, as the evening approaches and the Sun sinks to the horizon, it takes on a roseate hue. This is because its light is shining through more layers of atmosphere, as it runs parallel to the ground and so more of its blue light is being bounced out of its beams.

___In space, blue is the characteristic colour of reflection nebulae, as shown by the Corona Australis Complex [1], and IC 4592 surrounding the star Nu Scorpii [2].

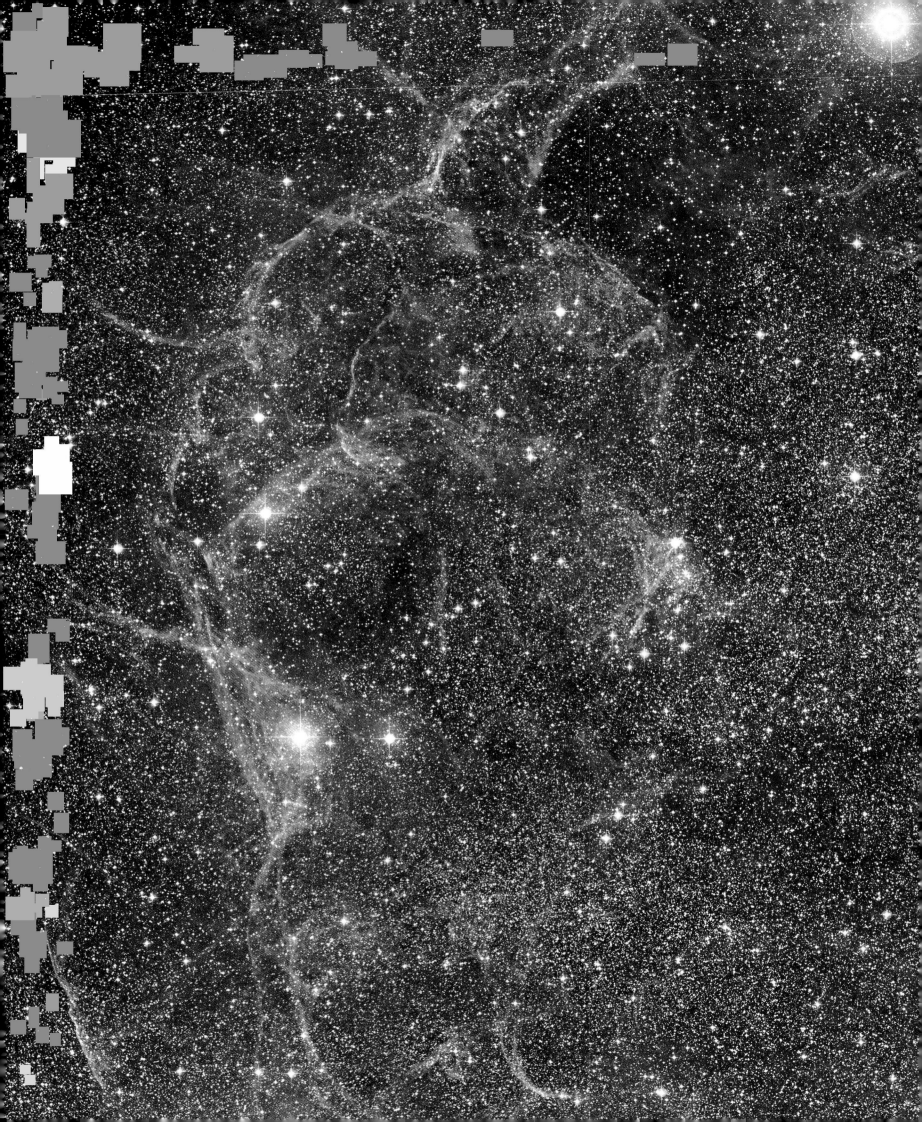

LIGHT SECONDS
LIGHT MINUTES
LIGHT YEARS
KILO LIGHT YEARS
MEGA LIGHT YEARS
GIGA LIGHT YEARS

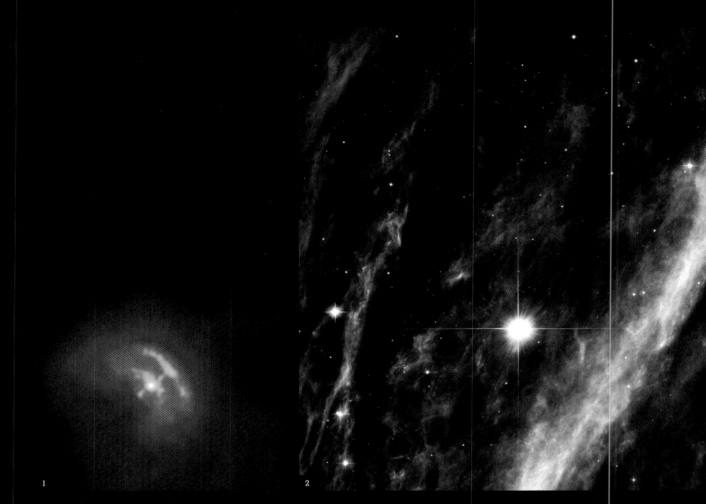

1

2

Celestial tsunami

The fury of the heavens is never more obvious than during a supernova. Each of these catastrophic stellar detonations unleashes celestial tsunamis that plough through space, ripping apart atoms in their wake. In the constellation of Vela, the havoc began 11,000 years ago; it's still going on – and it's heading our way.

It took little more than a single day for this star to die and then 11,000 years for it to sculpt these extraordinary filaments of gas. For millions of years of life before its demise, the star's nuclear heart had been furiously generating energy, smashing atomic nuclei together to feed its rapacious appetite for energy.

___Energy is all that stands between any star and death. Without the constant outrush of power to provide support, gravity would crush it utterly. As long as the nuclear furnace can be maintained, the star can live. But inevitably the fuel runs out.

___When a massive star begins to build iron in its heart, its fate is sealed. Its remaining lifetime can be measured in hours.

___Iron cannot fuse easily and so builds up like the ash at the bottom of a fire, robbing the centre of the star of the energy it needs for support. It take just a day for a star to build an iron core roughly the size of Earth and containing almost one and a half times the mass of the Sun. At such proportions, the core can no longer fight gravity and spontaneously implodes.

___In microseconds, it is crushed together by its own weight to become a tiny, ultra-dense neutron star no bigger than an asteroid [1]. This robs the star of its foundations, and the overlying layers come crashing down, triggering the supernova: an explosion that cannons gas in all directions throughout space.

___In Vela, this cataclysm took place 11,000 years ago. The leading edge of the shock wave has now reached 200 light years into space [2], and although it has slowed a little from its original velocity of 35 million km/h, still the violence of its passage is enough to shred atoms as it passes, leaving them to light up space as they recombine in its wake. And it's heading our way.

___It has already covered 200 light years and has some 600 left to go. However, by the time it arrives, in around 24,000 AD, its power will have diminished so much that it will pack no further punch. Nevertheless, such waves contribute to the general turbulence of the interstellar gas, helping to determine how easy it is for new stars to form.

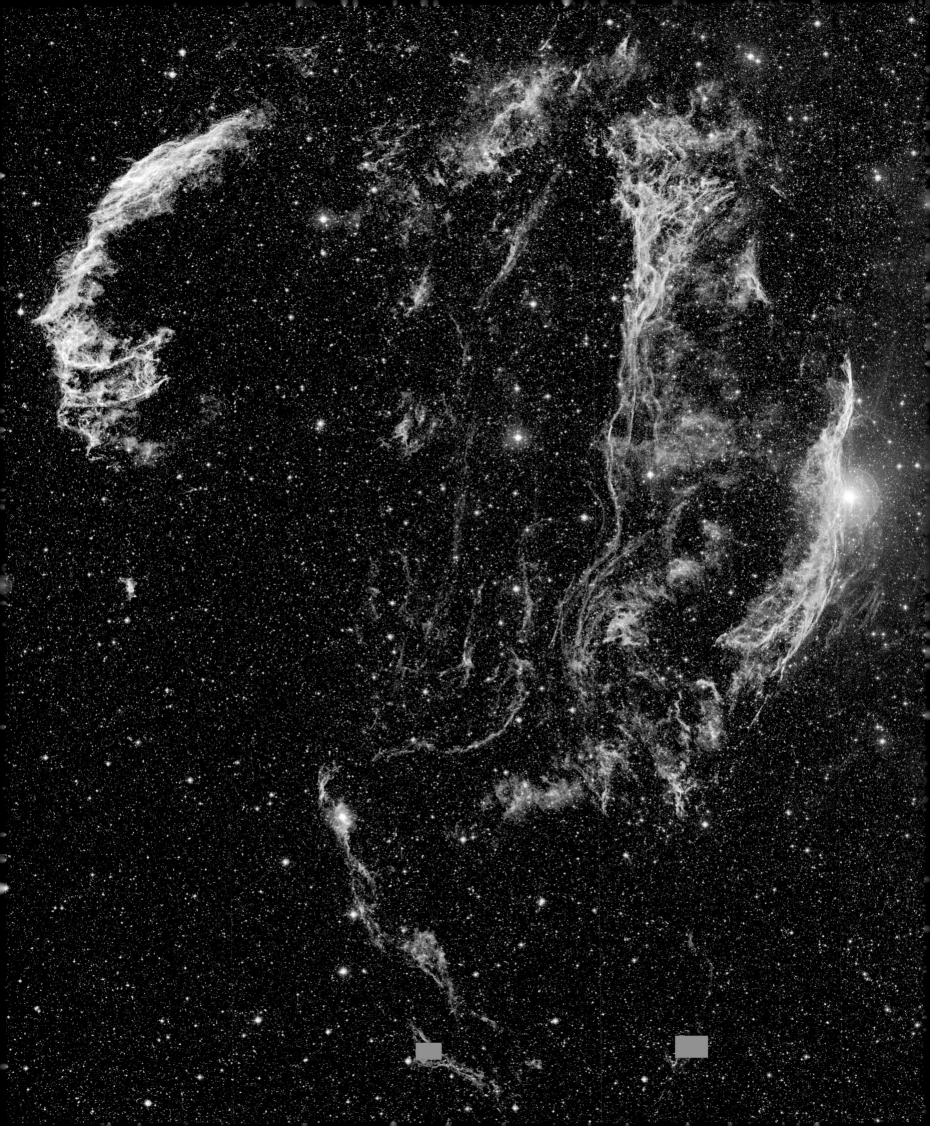

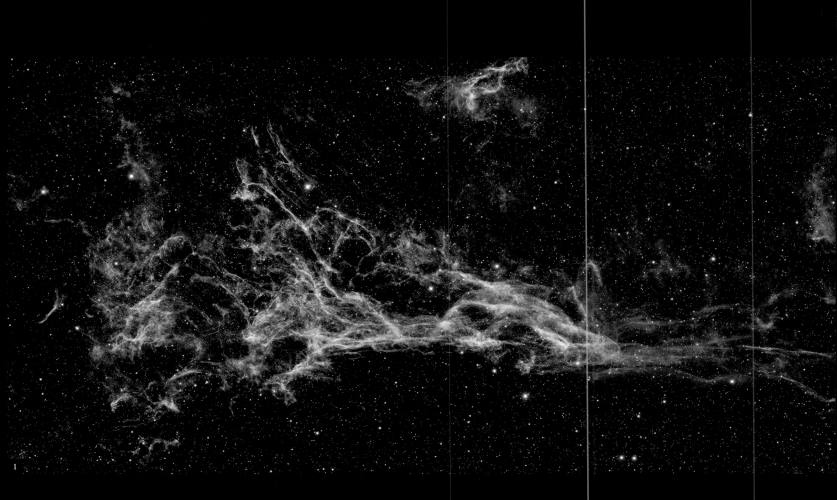

LIGHT SECONDS
LIGHT MINUTES
LIGHT YEARS
KILO LIGHT YEARS
MEGA LIGHT YEARS
GIGA LIGHT YEARS

1

Dusty demise

Supernovae are fleeting but dramatic. Our Galaxy should produce one such celestial suicide every 50–100 years. But something is wrong. These spectacular explosions seem to have stalled in our Galaxy because no one has seen one here since 1604.

The Cygnus Loop is not the celestial conflagration it once was. Now 10,000 years old, it is beginning to lose its power. It can no longer be traced as a continuous loop in the sky and in another 10,000 years it will have faded into obscurity. Before it fades, the filaments of Fleming's Triangular Wisp [1] reveal the presence of oxygen and hydrogen ready to seed the next generation of stars.

___As one remnant disperses, so another should be ready to take its place. With an estimated Galactic population of stars that number several hundred billion, there should be one or two cataclysmic explosions every century. There is the remnant from Tycho's supernova that exploded in 1572 and there is Kepler's from 1604 but, since then, no one

has seen another new star in the sky. Just as certainly, however, supernovae must be occurring because the aftermaths are scattered throughout space.

___There is a cloud of gas known as G1.9+0.3, a young supernova remnant that is expanding so fast it must have exploded within the last 140 years. Yet, no records from the nineteenth century speak of such a convulsion of light in the sky. Another supernova remnant, known as Cassiopeia A, must be 330 years old, but there are no sightings of this supernova going off either. What is going on – invisible supernovae? Impossible, they regularly burn with the light of a few hundred billion stars – often outshining all the rest of the stars in their host galaxies put together.

___The answer is covered in dust. The microscopic shards of solid matter that constitute interstellar dust account for about one percent of the mass floating through free space. This is enough to block out most of the stars from our view. And if we can't see the stars, the chances are that we will not see all the supernovae either. So it is the copious dust in the Milky Way that is foxing us here, blotting our view of the drama, even though we have ringside seats.

___The supernovae are happening and leaving their searing signatures in the form of super-heated bubbles of gas. We just have to get better at peering through the dusty shrouds of the Milky Way to spy on them.

LIGHT SECONDS
LIGHT MINUTES
LIGHT YEARS
KILO LIGHT YEARS
MEGA LIGHT YEARS
GIGA LIGHT YEARS

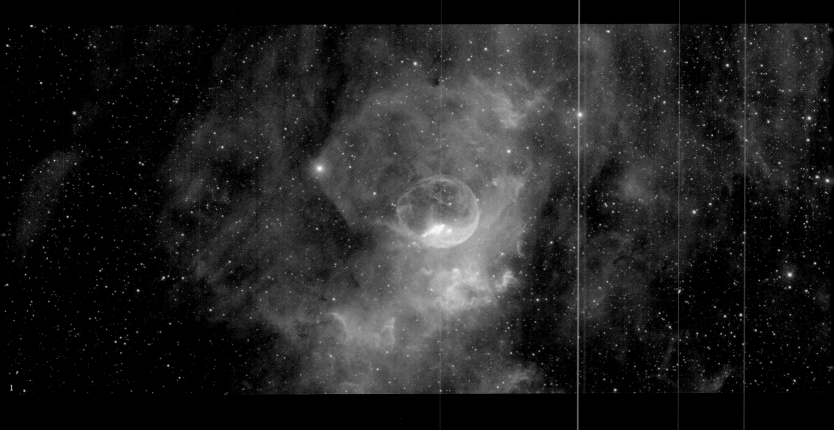

1

Petrifying prospect

Serpentine braids of gas wreath the star at the heart of the the Medusa Nebula. According to mythology, the snake-headed Gorgon was capable of turning flesh into stone. In its own way, this star is also turning things to stone, but one dust grain at a time.

The Medusa Nebula is an old planetary nebula, formed from the dying remnants of a once-proud red giant star. Now billions of years old, back in its heyday the star would have been 200 times larger than the Sun, though it probably contained a similar amount of mass. In such a hugely distended object, the outer layers are so far away from the central core that they are only loosely bound by gravity. The pressure of the dying star's lurching radiation can loft them into space, the first step in the creation of a planetary nebula.

___As these gaseous outflows cool, dust collects like soot in an industrial chimney. The chemicals needed for the dust were created in the star's heart and brought to the surface by mammoth upheavals during which the star exchanged its outer layers for those originally near the nuclear core.

___The dust released by such red giant stars restricts our view of the Milky Way to within a mere 6,000 light years of Earth. Only by looking out of the plane of the Galaxy, or by switching to longer wavelengths of radiation, can we see the rest of the Universe. Without the dust, our view would be unrestricted across the entire Galaxy.

___However, there is an upside to this stellar dust storm. Dust plays an important role in the Galaxy's ecology. It acts as seed for molecules to coalesce around, slowly building the raw ingredients of new stars, planets, moons and, just perhaps, life.

___The more massive a star, the shorter its life span and the earlier it begins to shed its outer layers. In the case of the celestial bubble known as NGC 7635 [1], the giant star at its heart is up to 40 times the Sun's mass, 400,000 times more luminous and just a few tens of millions of years old. Yet it has already begun to shrug off its outer layers.

___In this case, the disgarded material is too hot for dust to form; instead it serves to enrich the interstellar realms with new flavours of gas. These too will find their way into the next generation of stars and planets. And so the cycle begins again...

LIGHT SECONDS
LIGHT MINUTES
LIGHT YEARS
KILO LIGHT YEARS
MEGA LIGHT YEARS
GIGA LIGHT YEARS

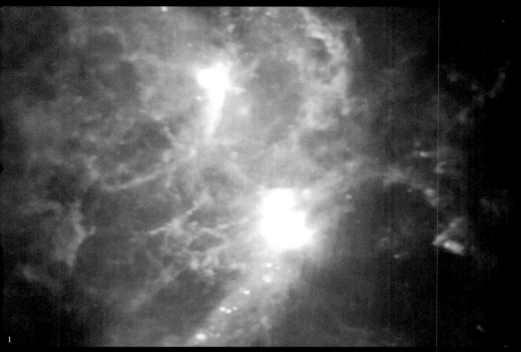

1

2

Star factory

Lying just a celestial stone's throw away from Earth is the Orion Molecular Cloud Complex, a vast, freezing production line that exists with only one purpose: to churn out stars.

The constellation of Orion is one of the largest in the night sky. Its distinctive shape dominates the northern skies in winter. In mythology, Orion is a hunter; in space, he is a giant. His body is 240 light years long and is composed of hundreds of thousands of solar masses of dust and gas [1]. It stretches across the entire constellation [2] and is made of the coldest gas in space, naturally chilled to temperatures as low as –263 °C.

___It is a giant molecular cloud, one of a thousand such conglomerations spread throughout the Milky Way. These clouds are found close to the Galaxy's equator and roughly trace spiral patterns from the galactic centre outwards. They naturally sink towards the equatorial belt of the Galaxy because they are cold, sluggish regions that have little power to resist gravity.

___Such clouds are the sites of star formation and in Orion the process has well and truly started. The entire region is covered with faint traces of glowing hydrogen, a sure sign of active stellar construction. In addition, like icebergs peeping above the polar ocean's surface, brilliant nebulae betray the most vigorous hotbeds of activity.

___Surrounding the Orion cloud complex is an even larger structure known as the Orion-Eridanus bubble. The bubble spans 400 light years of space and is testament to a previous generation of stars that formed from the molecular cloud. Sitting at the epicentre of this bubble is a group of several dozen stars. The most prominent of these mark out Orion's belt and sword.

___Whether it is simply the powerful starlight given out by these stars that has crafted the bubble, or whether it is the last remnants of an old supernova is currently unknown. What is certain is that the eastern extremity of this bubble is marked by a curving arc of glowing hydrogen called Barnard's Loop.

___Whatever created the bubble it is having a profound effect. In contrast to the molecular cloud, the bubble is highly rarefied. What gas there is exists in the form of individual atoms zipping around at relatively high temperatures. In this part of the complex, star formation is impossible.

___But in the denser gas, down in the heart of the molecular cloud, star production is at full throttle. In millions of years' time, all Orion will be alight, glittering like a treasure chest of newborn stellar jewels.

LIGHT SECONDS
LIGHT MINUTES
LIGHT YEARS
KILO LIGHT YEARS
MEGA LIGHT YEARS
GIGA LIGHT YEARS

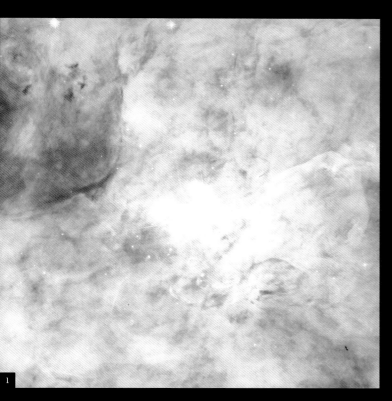

1

2

Orion's monsters

A glowing cave of gas, the Orion Nebula is the lair of the fearsome giant stars that comprise the Trapezium cluster. These four titans swamp space with radiation but may actually be decoys: the real monsters lie hidden behind them.

On their own, the stars in the Trapezium would be terrifying [1]. Even the smallest of the four large stars shines thousands of times more brightly than the Sun. The leader is a star of 40 solar masses, pumping out more energy than 400,000 Suns combined. It is almost solely responsible for carving the opening that is the Orion Nebula.

___The nebula is like a burst blister on the side of the Orion Molecular Cloud facing Earth. As it has ruptured, so it has allowed us to peer into this incandescent hideout and glimpse the giant stars' swarming minions.

___There are thousands of smaller stars, all struggling to survive the ultraviolet onslaught. Some of the smaller stars are surrounded by dusty discs that, left to their own devices,

would have grown into planetary systems. But under the welter of radiation from the Trapezium, the condensing planets are electro-magnetically sandblasted back to their constituent atoms. A bow-shaped shockwave engulfs the star LL Ori as it melts in the face of this unstoppable assault [2]. Chillingly, this sustained violence in nothing compared to that taking place behind the Trapezium.

___Still embedded in the surrounding molecular cloud is a trio of giants, which easily rival the Trapezium stars. Originating from these stars are about 40 iron-tipped cosmic bullets that have been blasted outwards by some sort of savage stellar event. Each bullet is a cloud of iron vapour ten times wider than our Solar System, ploughing through the

surrounding molecular cloud at a speed of 200 km/s and trailing a wake of hydrogen gas. The bullets are hot, blazing at a temperature of 5,000 °C, which is hotter than the surfaces of most stars in the Galaxy. Whatever shot these outward expended tremendous power.

___The event had to be a stellar detonation of some type, and probably in the last few thousand years. The fact that there is iron in the bullet tips betrays that a giant star must be somehow involved because only in such an extreme nuclear furnace can this element be synthesized. But what exactly caused this supreme act of stellar ruination, no one knows for sure.

000.5

LIGHT SECONDS
LIGHT MINUTES
LIGHT YEARS
KILO LIGHT YEARS
MEGA LIGHT YEARS
GIGA LIGHT YEARS

1

Dark knight

It is the equivalent of a stellar shoreline; a cliff-face of
hydrogen gas and dust being pounded by an ocean
of light. As wave upon wave of ultraviolet energy strikes
the interstellar promontory, so it is being eroded away.

The Horsehead itself is a large dusty peninsula, [1] rising out of the expansive gas cloud that covers the lower portion of this image. The equine silhouette is pure chance, blindly sculpted by the forces of nature as the surrounding gases have been eroded away.

___The shadow play would be completely invisible were it not for the bright stars of Sigma Orionis that sit offstage but provide the energy to carve away the gas. The star system is a quintet, five brilliant orbs united by their mutual gravity. Two of them orbit each other every 170 years, with a separation about as wide as our Solar System. They are the hottest stars in the group with surface temperatures of over 30,000 °C.

___Three smaller stars orbit the central pair, and pose a stellar riddle. The furthest of the quintet displays an over-abundance of helium in its makeup. Sigma Orionis E, as it is known, contains seven times the mass of the Sun but once upon a time it was much larger. In its formative days, this celestial glutton sucked in more star-forming material than it could digest, so in a gush of stellar wind the excess material was ejected, driven by the intense radiation generated in the star's core.

___This sudden hiccup reduced its mass but acted predominantly on the lighter hydrogen atoms, flinging them back into space to rejoin the molecular cloud and leaving Sigma Orionis E endowed with more helium than is normal.

___The entire five-star system may also be coming apart at the seams. The gravitational forces acting on each star change constantly as the stellar family swings through a near infinite number of orbital configurations. Almost certainly, this will ultimately result in a falling out, and one or more stars will be ejected from the system to wander space as orphans.

___But for now, the five stars continue to work in uneasy partnership, supplying the power needed to sculpt the Horsehead. As the energized hydrogen rises from the cloud's surface, it is shepherded on its way by the ephemeral magnetic fields that permeate space.

LIGHT SECONDS
LIGHT MINUTES
LIGHT YEARS
KILO LIGHT YEARS
MEGA LIGHT YEARS
GIGA LIGHT YEARS

The hole in space

Once thought to be a dense cloud of obscuring dust, this black patch amid the pearly swathes is now known to be a keyhole, peering into a stellar birth cloud. It is providing a window onto the way young stars burst out of their cradles.

Stars don't so much grow out of their cradles as smash their way to freedom. As the nuclear processes inside them gain a foothold, so the stars become belligerent. They begin to shed particles in great tempests that sweep across space. And sometimes these winds can be confined to relatively narrow jets.

___It is unclear exactly how this happens but, almost certainly, it has something to do both with the planet-forming disc of matter that can surround a stellar newborn, and with the magnetic fields that a nascent star generates. In the former mechanism, the dusty, doughnut-shaped disc acts as a dam, confining the star's radiation to the polar axis. Meanwhile, the magnetic field could also help to focus the

huricane of particles into a jet, because each particle carries an electrical charge, which allows it to be corralled.

___However the jets are formed, they surge into space, spraying particles outward at speeds higher than 100 km/s. They erupt from the top and the bottom of the forming star, boring their way in opposite directions light years into the adjacent clouds of dust and gas. Some parts of the jets can be invisible; at other times they glow brightly. Whenever they hit denser pockets of gas, they create colourful shockwaves that light up their surroundings.

___In the case of the keyhole in NGC 1999, they have carved a recognizable shape out of the cloud's forward face. This act of interstellar

vandalism would have gone unnoticed were it not for the bright star V380 Orionis that sits just outside the cloud. A triple star – three individual stars in close orbits around each other – V380 shines onto the cloud, which reacts like a milky mirror, scattering the light back into space.

___Where the cloud has been blasted away by the jets, there is no dust to perform this reflection and so the hole appears black. But the culprit is not owning up. There is a gang of adolescent stars holed up deep inside this cloud and the jets responsible could be coming from any of them.

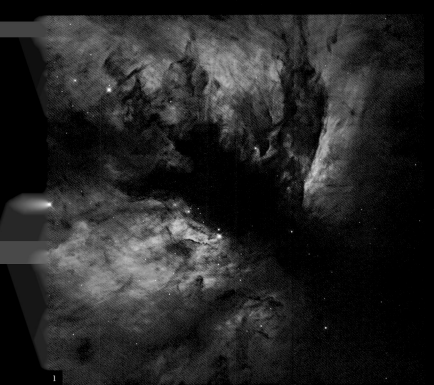

1

2

Hidden fires

They may look like sinister clouds coming to menace these young stars but in reality they are the curtains being pulled back so that the Universe can fully appreciate the newcomers. Already, the stage is radiant with the pure light of stellar youth.

Once again an interstellar cloud is lit up by the stellar debutantes it presents. Ready for the new season, these youngsters are emerging to take their place on the Universal stage.

___M78 occupies a small part of the colossal Orion Molecular Cloud system that stretches for hundreds of light years across space. It is a visible 'iceberg' in the largely unseen cloud and contains around 200 new stars of all sizes. They appear to be forming in families, each a tightly knit cluster that will nevertheless grow further apart as time goes by and the individual stars find their own way through the Galaxy.

___But for now they are united. Some are giants, tens of times more massive than the Sun

and tens of thousands of times brighter, others are destined to be almost identical to our parent star.

___Elsewhere, the cloud is still threaded by rich lanes of dust, the interstellar equivalent of untapped veins of precious ore. They contain the raw material from which yet more stars may form. Dotted about are red beams of gas signifying jets from young stars, fighting their way out of the cloud, queuing for the next season.

___Nearby is the Flame Nebula [1], a star birth conflagration and perhaps a glimpse of what M78 will become once its stars mature a little. The Flame Nebula burns in the brilliant light of Alnitak, the easternmost star in Orion's belt.

A blue supergiant twenty times larger than the Sun, Alnitak holds two other stars captive in orbit around its great bulk.

___Together the three stars muster more than 50 times the mass of the Sun, and pummel the Flame Nebula with a relentless flood of light. The dense core of the nebula is completely hidden to our eyes, but at infrared wavelengths [2] it reveals a smouldering treasure chest of stellar newborns.

___In the nurturing darkness of the cloud, these condensing stars have so far been spared from Alnitak's assault, but their defences won't last. Blue supergiants are the Universe's brightest and hottest stellar spieces and their scouring radiation can't be denied.

LIGHT SECONDS
LIGHT MINUTES
LIGHT YEARS
KILO LIGHT YEARS
MEGA LIGHT YEARS
GIGA LIGHT YEARS

1

The race for life

As soon as the first stars have been born inside an interstellar cloud, an almighty struggle begins. On one side gravity maintains its attempt to pull things together; on the other, radiation pressure tries to blow things apart. At stake are the lives of the as yet unborn stars.

In the confines of a stellar nursery, all is darkness and quiet until the first stars light up. If the newborns are heavyweights, then the effect is dramatic. Their first adult act is to flood their dusty cradles with ultraviolet light blowing away their surroundings of dust and gas.

___But like a giant who doesn't know his own strength, the largest stars do not stop at just blasting away their own surroundings. Their emanations are so powerful that they can reach deep into the rest of the cloud and begin to gnaw away at regions that were nothing to do with them.

___Here, in the Pelican Nebula, is a classic example of this behaviour. The ruddy colours mark a cloud of dust and gas that is well on the path to producing stars. Thousands of them could lie inside this celestial incubator. Yet now their peaceful gestation is threatened – they are in a life or death race against time.

___The leading edge of their dusty incubator is glowing fiercely, being boiled away by the glare from a slightly earlier crop of stellar newborns [1]. Their radiation will carve through the cloud, eroding back into gas any protostars that have yet to start radiating their own energy.

___Towards the top of the cloud some stars do look destined to survive. They cannot be seen directly yet but in the very tip of some tendrils, short jets of gas are appearing – like devils' horns. These are evidence that inside the tip is another young star ready to burst out. They are the lucky ones, but they too will show no mercy to their slower siblings. As soon as they are revealed, their radiation will also contribute to eroding away the rest of the cloud – and any nascent star that gets in the way.

___It is a story that is being repeated throughout the Galaxy.

LIGHT SECONDS
LIGHT MINUTES
LIGHT YEARS
KILO LIGHT YEARS
MEGA LIGHT YEARS
GIGA LIGHT YEARS

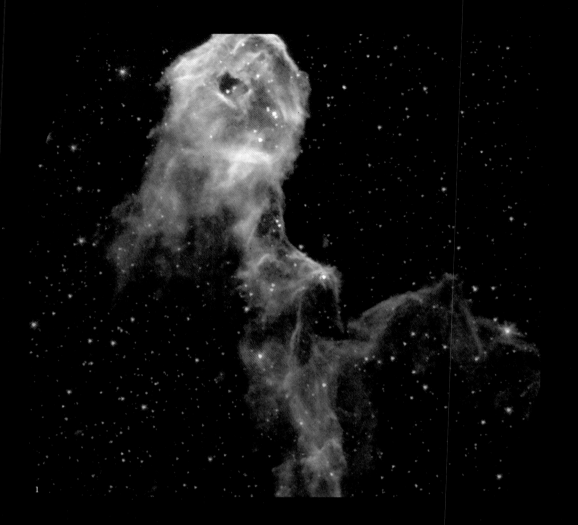

1

Elephant gun

Like a reef in space, the Elephant's Trunk Nebula forms a natural barrier to the sea of starlight around it. But it is fighting a losing battle; not only is it steadily dissolving in the light of nearby stars, but deep within its clouds something unusual is stirring.

Hanging in space, the Elephant's Trunk Nebula is an enormous dusty column that stretches out across 130 light years of space. The sanguine glow of hydrogen gas is all around, testament to the nearby presence of powerful stars.

___Inside its length, new forces are already stirring. It is studded with the dusty fruits of star formation. A pair of slightly older stars has already appeared near the top of the nebula. These are the precocious elder children of the Elephant's Trunk, flexing their luminous muscles and exerting their influence over their surroundings. They have already blown a bubble in the top of the trunk and the compression this is causing is helping to trigger star formation in the rest of the region.

___Hundreds of protostars are forming in this interstellar hatchery. Although impossible to see them at visible wavelengths, some are given away by the infrared light they emit [1], others by a bizarre form of natural laser that so far defies explanation.

___On Earth a laser produces amplified light rays by stimulating their emission from a gas or a crystal. It requires the utmost exactitude in manufacturing because the wavelength of visible light is so small. Microwaves, however, have a much longer wavelength, sitting right at the beginning of the radio frequencies. A laser that produces microwaves instead of light is known as a maser.

___As amazing as it might seem, clouds of molecules around some of the young stars in the Elephant's Trunk appear to be producing maser emission. The molecule responsible is water and, somehow, a large cloud of it can release invisible beams of microwave energy.

___Such natural masers are known elsewhere in the Universe. Saturn's moon Enceladus has produced masers from the clouds of water that it jets into space, as have comets. Some old red giant stars also have tenuous outer envelopes of gas that become natural masers.

___Inside the Elephant's Trunk, although not every new star generates a maser, they do all emit an increasing quantity of radiation as they climb to maturity. As these waves of starlight, infrared, X-rays and microwaves continue to pound the inside of the nebula, so it will be dislodged into space. Eventually this dark dusty reef will be replaced by a shining archipelago of stars.

NGC 2264

EMISSION NEBULA

DIAMETER: 30 LY

LIGHT SECONDS
LIGHT MINUTES
LIGHT YEARS
KILO LIGHT YEARS
MEGA LIGHT YEARS
GIGA LIGHT YEARS

1

Interstellar cloudspotting

Another widespread area of star formation drapes itself across the surface of a giant molecular cloud. As when cloudspotting on Earth, we look for familiar shapes. This one gives the illusion of a fox fur stole, a simple cone and an upside down Christmas tree.

It is tempting to think of star formation as a relatively gentle process in which the dense pockets within giant molecular clouds become unstable. As each pocket passes a certain threshold, so it begins to collapse in on itself. In the process, it will fragment into a number of dense cores, each of which eventually becomes a star. If only it were that simple.

___The fact that stars form in collectives suggests that the process must be more complicated than this orderly ideal. Individual stars are capable of interacting with one another, pinching from each other's food stores, and scrumping extra gas from passing cloudlets. Most of this mischief takes place under the cover of darkness, imposed on the youngsters by the shells of dust that incubate

them, but occasionally we can catch a glimpse.

___The youngest stars in NGC 2264 are not yet visible at optical wavelengths, but can be seen in the infrared. They are arranged in spokes. Each one of these stars is a mere 100,000 years old. If they were humans they would not yet have learnt to crawl, let alone walk. So each is still placed exactly where it formed, following the pattern of dense filaments in the surrounding cloud. As time goes by and these stars do move apart, so the radial pattern will disperse and they will begin to vie for supremacy.

___This cluster inhabits just one part of the surrounding nebula. At 30 light years across, the entire region is so large that different parts of the nebula find themselves at different points

in the evolutionary cycle. A seemingly luxuriant region of hydrogen at the top right is known as the Fox Fur Nebula. Taken together, the entire central region is reminiscent of a Christmas tree, but upside down.

___One of the most developed centres is the Cone Nebula towards the bottom of the region [1]. This is a dusty tower, 2.5 light years long, upon which sits a newly born star. Large by the standards of the Sun, this star is slowly eroding away its seat. The dust is blown downwards, forced away by the pressure of the starlight but the gas is driven off by a different process. Once it absorbs enough energy it lifts itself from the dust column, and begins to fluoresce in the ultraviolet glare. Eventually only the densest parts of this dust column will remain.

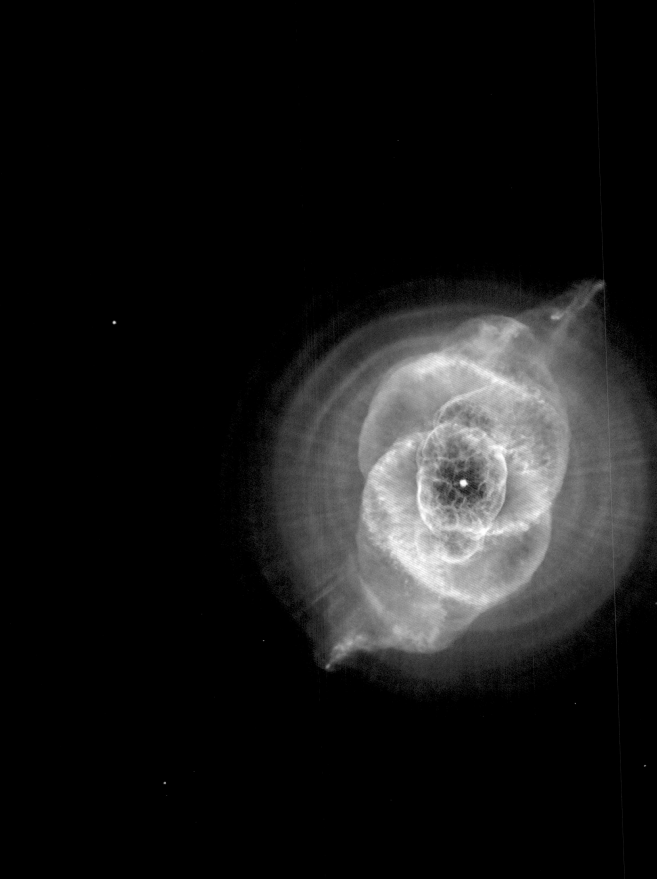

LIGHT SECONDS
LIGHT MINUTES
LIGHT YEARS
KILO LIGHT YEARS
MEGA LIGHT YEARS
GIGA LIGHT YEARS

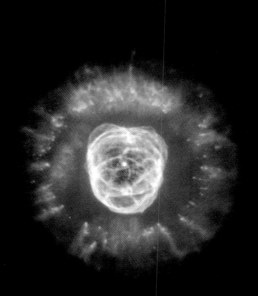
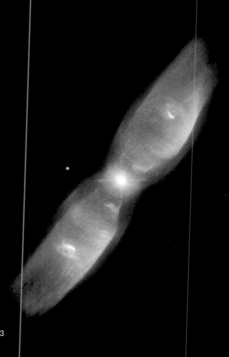

1

2

3

Blaze of glory

The hypnotic spirals of the Cat's Eye Nebula betray a complicated story of protracted stellar death. But as yet, the plot is not completely clear. It seems to involve a sequence of stellar pulsations, tremendous outbursts, and the shadowy influence of a covert companion.

Casting off its outer layers begins the final stellar obsequies. It is thought to be a rather regal process, with the gentle removal of gas and the final revelation of the star's white hot core. Not so in the Cat's Eye Nebula, however.

___The diverse swirls reveal high-speed jets of material cutting through the gossamer sheets, as knots of shocked gas gleam into the darkness. Surrounding the filigree are eleven shells of gas, like a sliced onion, with the Cat's Eye at the centre.

___The onion rings are the oldest components of this complicated structure, having been puffed off by the central star in a series of gentle pulsations. Each one of these slow-motion upheavals lasted 1,500 years, and on every occasion billions of tonnes of gas were lofted into space.

___Initially, the star would have dimmed,

cocooned behind concentric layers of cooling gas and dust. Then, about 1,000 years ago, its behaviour abruptly changed. The pulsations ceased and, inside the cocoon, the Cat's Eye began to form. Instead of a uniform release of matter, things became messy. Jets of gas began to squirt like an out-of-control garden hose, and intense ultraviolet light came hurtling forth from the star's exposed inner layers. The effect on the nebula was overpowering: the gaseous shells were driven into frenzy, lighting up in a glorious blaze of florescence.

___The snowflakes of the stellar realm, no two planetary nebulae are the same [1, 2 & 3]. Their colours are determined by the chemical composition and physical condition of the gases but the mechanism behind their intricate patterns is not always clear.

___The Cat's Eye may owe its form to the action of a companion star, orbiting the dying luminary and disturbing the outpouring gases. But if so, why did it only start stirring things up 1,000 years ago when the star had already been out-gassing? Confounding this idea is that there is no observational evidence to support a companion star. If it is there, it remains hidden.

___Could it therefore be smaller, perhaps a planet? If a gas giant planet were to spiral in towards its central star, it might be able to shape the outflow as it fell.

___Interstellar blooms such as the Cat's Eye were famously misnamed planetary nebulae two centuries ago, and the name has stuck despite their clear relation to stars. Perhaps the Cat's Eye has revealed this label wasn't such a misnomer after all.

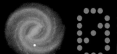

LIGHT SECONDS
LIGHT MINUTES
LIGHT YEARS
KILO LIGHT YEARS
MEGA LIGHT YEARS
GIGA LIGHT YEARS

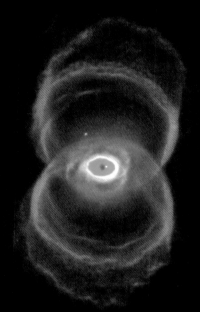

1

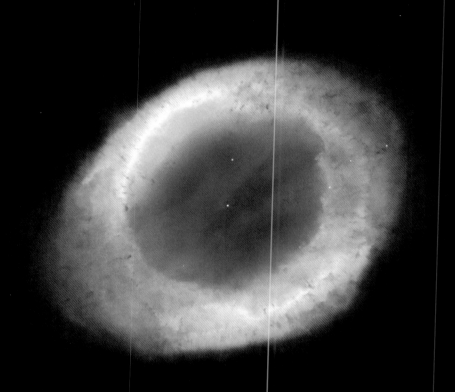

2

Blowing bubbles

So faint it evaded detection for years, this cosmic
'soap' bubble is the picture-perfect end to the life
of a Sun-like star.

Most dying stars like to make a final statement.
They transform themselves from points of
stellar light into giant gaseous sculptures
resembling ants, hour-glasses [1], butterflies,
jelly fish... or anything, so long as it contains
a semblance of symmetry – like a colourful
cosmic inkblot test.

___It is thought these wild variations are
dictated somehow by the amount of matter
lying in orbit around the star and the faltering
way nuclear fusion comes to an end inside the
stellar core. It may also have something to do
with the way the star generates magnetism.

___A star's magnetic field provides highways
and ring roads through its atmosphere for the
gases escaping from its surface. The ring roads
divert the gas back down toward the surface

whereas the highways are the magnetic
fields that flow out into space. Once any
gas is caught in one of these, it is funnelled
off the star. If the Sun is anything to go by,
these magnetic highways are more prevalent
at the rotation poles that at the equator. So
dying stars may already have a propensity
to expel matter off at the poles.

___However, a small number of nebulae
are ring-like. These could be optical illusions
created by looking down the breach of an
hourglass or elliptically shaped nebula.
Such an alignment would be rare but not
impossible. The so-called Ring Nebula, M57,
is the embodiment of such an alignment [2].

___M57 shines in space with a beautiful
concentric ring structure but it is actually a

lozenge-shaped envelope of gas viewed from
one of the pointed ends. Only in a handful of
cases are these ring nebulae genuine bubbles
of gas expanding equally in all directions.

___The Soap Bubble Nebula appears to be
the real deal. This apparently perfect bubble
of gas hangs in front of an emission nebula
where new stars are presently being created.
So, in the midst of all this new stellar life, this
particular star is dying. The bubble has been
expanding into space for thousands of years
and will eventually fade away into nothing.
It has lived its life, probably standing witness
to the Universe for 10 billion years or so.
Now its time has come and with poise and
dignity, it is exiting the stage before the young
celestial turks burst out of their birth clouds.

LIGHT SECONDS
LIGHT MINUTES
LIGHT YEARS
KILO LIGHT YEARS
MEGA LIGHT YEARS
GIGA LIGHT YEARS

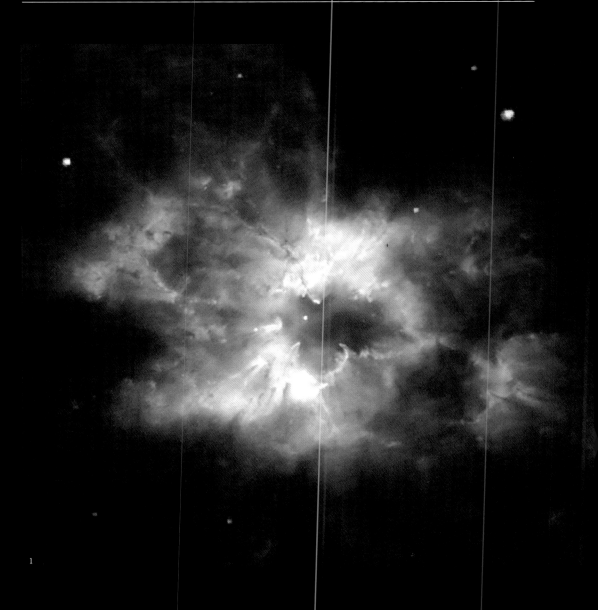

1

Raging butterfly

These dainty butterfly wings are best appreciated from a distance. The gas is tearing through space at more than 270 km/s, having been given a hiding by one of the hottest stars in the galaxy.

Up close, the apparent delicacy of the Butterfly Nebula's wings proves to be an illusion. They are a raging torrent of radiation and atoms, blazing like a moth in a flame. For over 2,000 years, this dying star has been unfurling its wings across space. They are now so large that, were one tip placed by the Sun, the other would reach over halfway to the nearest star.

___The nebula is cinched at the waist, indicating that the star driving this furore must be surrounded by a disc of dust, perhaps even a solar system full of planets. Whatever is there, it is taking the full brunt of this assault, containing the outflow in those directions and giving rise to the butterfly shape.

___The central star is a dense stellar oddment called a white dwarf; although the size of the Earth, it contains the mass of the Sun. It is one of the hottest stars in the galaxy. Measuring a blistering 200,000 °C, it is 35 times hotter than the surface of the Sun.

___Despite this impressive temperature, it is a dull ember compared to what it used to be. Once the forbidding heart of a star, its prodigious nuclear engine, it enjoyed temperatures of 15,000,000 °C.

___It was this fire that the surrounding layers were there to stoke, pressing down on it to keep the nuclear conflagration burning. The outer layers provided a tempering presence on that

searing energy, moulding it into visible light that wouldn't have such a damaging effect on its surroundings. Now those layers have gone, the fires have gone out and the star's slowly cooling heart is laid bare for all to see [1].

___Eventually, the butterfly's wings will fade as the gas drifts off into space and the white dwarf loses its potency. Left on its own, the white dwarf is destined to wander space for the rest of eternity. It will play no further part in the cosmic ecosystem. All the life-giving carbon and the oxygen that could play a role in making habitable planets has been withdrawn, locked firmly by gravity inside the white dwarf.

LIGHT SECONDS
LIGHT MINUTES
LIGHT YEARS
KILO LIGHT YEARS
MEGA LIGHT YEARS
GIGA LIGHT YEARS

1

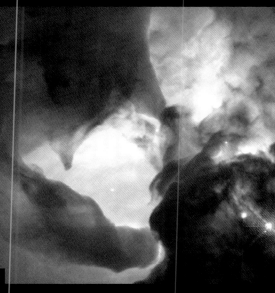

2

Celestial twisters

Not a blue lagoon, but certainly a vast one. On the scale of the Milky Way Galaxy, a lagoon can be a cloud of glowing gas a hundred light years from shore to shore – where the pebbles are whole stars.

In the depths of the Lagoon Nebula lies a cluster of young stars just 2 million years old, numbering about 100 individuals. These stellar pebbles shine brightly enough to keep the whole cloud in a state of blushing brilliance.

___Contrasting with the bright stars, are dark globules. These are the cocoons of the next generation of stars, patiently incubating before they too are born into the cosmos and radiate their contribution of starlight onto the nebula.

___Inside each globule most of the mass will be in the form of gas composed of individual atoms and molecules set spinning in space. They will be heading for a gravitational rendezvous in its centre that will eventually become a star or two. Only one percent of the

matter exists in the form of dust grains, yet each sub-microscopic speck contains several trillions of atoms. Most importantly, these dust grains will go on to form planets, moons and asteroids around these newly forged stars.

___As yet no one knows whether the pattern of planets in our Solar System, with rocky planets innermost and gaseous planets in the outer regions, is unique or the norm. The extrasolar evidence so far suggests that gas giant planets are often found much closer to their central stars.

___At the very heart of the Lagoon is a particularly large conglomeration of dust and gas where the finishing touches are being applied to another cluster of new stars [1].

Of these stars, Herschel 36 is the patriarch. It shines its intense light on an eerie structure known as the Hourglass Nebula [2]. This is made up of a set of twisted funnels of dusty gas that may be swirling, like whirlpools or tornadoes on Earth. But here they are vastly larger: each celestial twister is around half a light year long.

___Herschel 36 pummels the outer surfaces of the funnels in the Hourglass, heating them while their interiors remain cold. When columns of air in Earth's atmosphere are heated from the outside, developing a large temperature difference from the interior, they begin twisting and turn into tornadoes. The same could be happening here.

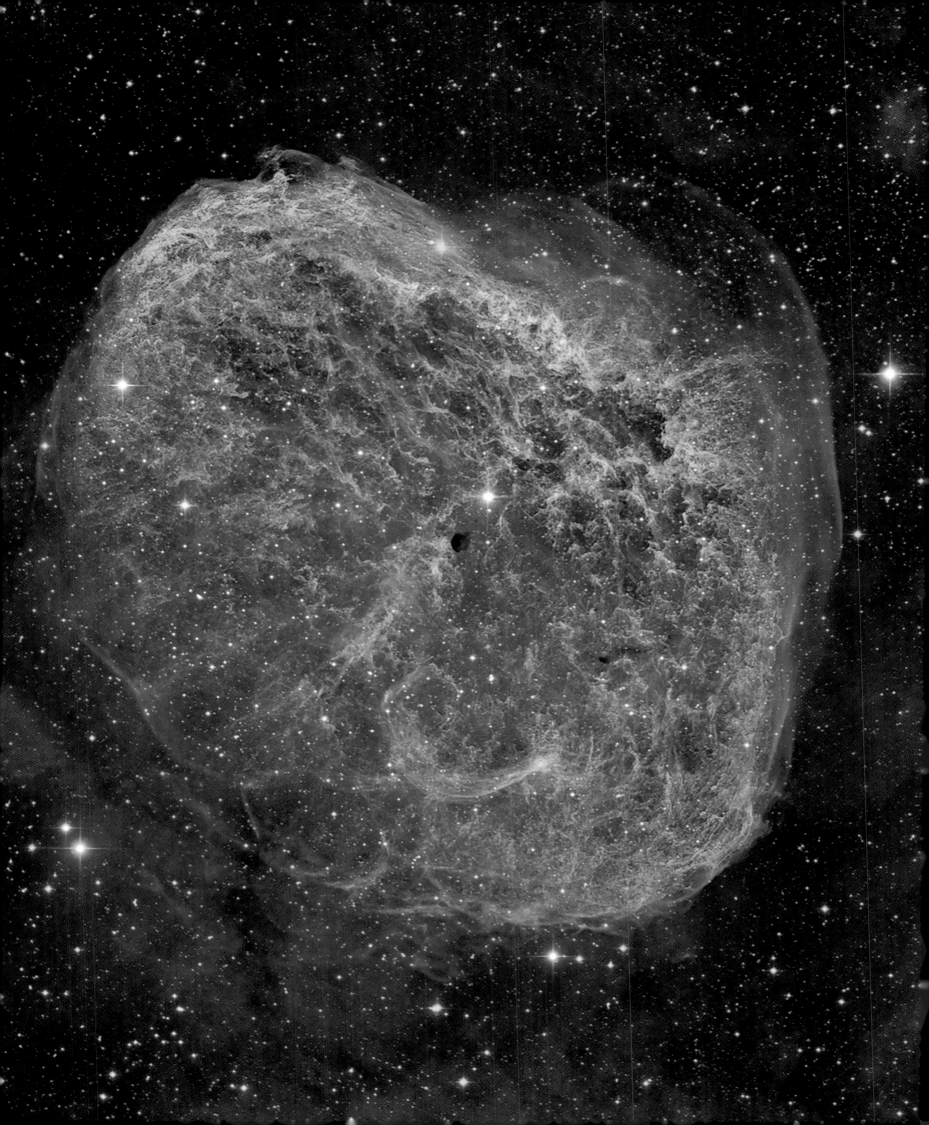

LIGHT SECONDS
LIGHT MINUTES
LIGHT YEARS
KILO LIGHT YEARS
MEGA LIGHT YEARS
GIGA LIGHT YEARS

Wolf at the door

This star is disintegrating before our eyes. Rare and
massive, it is burning too brightly and has created
the Crescent Nebula from its own lifeblood of hydrogen
gas. It can only lead to stellar catastrophe in the form
of a supernova.

Live fast, die young. That has to be the motto
of this star. At the heart of the Crescent Nebula
burns a transitory object called a Wolf-Rayet
star. It contains at least 20 times the mass of
the Sun and glares into space with a surface
temperature not far short of 50,000 °C.

___Unlike most stars, which possess only a
tenuous atmosphere of gases, Wolf-Rayet stars
have a thick atmosphere, sometimes doubling
the extent of the star. This particular example
has gone one step further, actually expelling a
huge quantity of gas. At its current rate of loss,
it is shedding the mass of the Sun every 10,000
years. This is about a billion times faster than
the mass loss from a typical star.

___The process began around 250,000 years
ago, meaning that there is now as much
gas in the nebula as remains in the star:
each containing around 25 times the mass
of the Sun.

___This extraordinary behaviour comes about
because chemical elements such as carbon
and oxygen are formed in the centre of the
star and then gradually pushed outwards
by the irresistible pressure of the escaping
radiation. As these heavier chemical elements
reach the surface layers they mingle with
the transparent hydrogen up there, helping
it to catch the light percolating up from below.
Just like a kite catching the wind and soaring

upwards, so this lifts the star's outer layers.

___First the process creates an atmosphere
and then, if the action is robust enough, it starts
to make the star disintegrate. To have enough
carbon and oxygen to undertake this act of
self-immolation indicates that the nuclear
factory at the star's heart is well into production,
and that the star is nearing the end of its life.

___This star will become a supernova, blowing
itself to smithereens as a result of the nuclear
reactions triggered by the core's collapse.
When this happens, perhaps sometime in the
next few million years, the Crescent Nebula
will be swept away, carelessly erased in the
most violent fate that can befall a star.

LIGHT SECONDS
LIGHT MINUTES
LIGHT YEARS
KILO LIGHT YEARS
MEGA LIGHT YEARS
GIGA LIGHT YEARS

1

Best in show

A shining halo of gas celebrates the birth of a new cluster of stars. The Rosette Nebula is a prominent cloud of star-forming gases, driven into luminescence by the action of its newborn stars, just another battle in the never-ending war between gravity and radiation.

Sitting in a cavity of its own making, the star cluster NGC 2244 floodlights the surrounding gases of its birth nebula. Ten thousand times the mass of the Sun remains in this interstellar swaddling, waiting either to become stars or to be dispersed to obscurity. As ever in the Universe, it is the never-ending fight between gravity and radiation pressure that will determine the outcome.

___Away from the cluster itself, there are patches where gravity appears to be gaining the upper hand. The surrounding Rosette is fringed with towering banks of cloud that glow feverishly in the infrared [1] as new stars make their bid for genesis.

___Hanging above the centre of the main image, at least one of these foetal objects has been revealed prematurely by the retreat of the cloud. It now finds itself in no-man's land,

hopelessly exposed to the onslaught of ultraviolet radiation and having to make its stand early. It is brandishing a single jet of gas as if it were a sword.

___Harsh rays are tearing at its dusty armour, stripping it away and ensuring that whatever destiny once awaited this star, it will now be born greatly diminished in both mass and intensity. If it loses enough mass it could be stillborn, robbed of its ability to generate its own energy and doomed to spend eternity as a brown dwarf.

___It could even be born as a planetary-sized object, and left to make its way around the galaxy with the much larger, bona-fide stars. Such objects, which resemble planets but travel in orbits like stars are called planetars.

___This particular confrontation will be played out time and time again as the nebula evolves.

But the harsh truth is that when individual stars ignite so they turncoat and begin working for the opposition. They contribute their own radiation into the nebula, working against the gravity that has given them life.

___And it is not just radiation, the more massive stars in the nebula produce winds of particles that slam into each other, creating violent shocks that catapult the temperature of the gas to a blistering 6,000,000 °C, helping it escape into space.

___Even if the radiation pressure from the central stars wins this time, and the surrounding gases are flung back into the diffuse interstellar medium, patient gravity will simply begin its work all over again, pulling together the atoms and molecules piece by piece until a new area of star formation takes shape.

006.9 LIGHT SECONDS
LIGHT MINUTES
LIGHT YEARS
KILO LIGHT YEARS
MEGA LIGHT YEARS
GIGA LIGHT YEARS

1

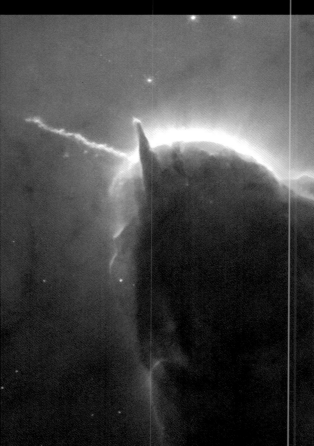

3

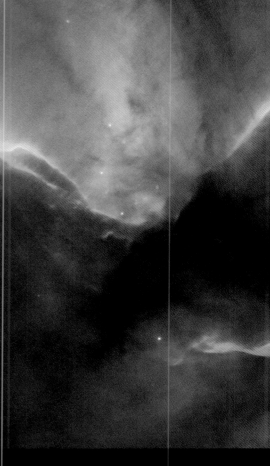

2

Nebulous trinity

Split into three by obscuring dust lanes, the Trifid Nebula is a flashpoint for star formation. Hundreds of newly built stars linger in its interior, creating the differently coloured clouds in this part of space. And there may be more stars on their way.

Smouldering away in the deeper recesses of the Milky Way, the Trifid Nebula combines three different types of nebula into one breathtaking object. There is the pink glow of hydrogen gas that is so characteristic of a stellar nursery where larger stars are being nurtured. Hydrogen is just one of the gases that has been driven into florescence here, sulphur and oxygen have been, too.

___Above this emission nebula is a patch of contrasting blue. This is a reflection nebula created not by gas but by the dust in this part of space. It scatters the blue light from the large stars into all directions through space.

___Dust shows up in the emission nebula as well, but as the dark lanes of obscuring material that cut the nebula into three. Giving the impression of the lead filigree holding a

stained glass window together, these dark channels are likely to be harbouring more individual pockets of gas that are destined to become stars. Only when the rising density, pressure and temperature inside these gaseous blobs passes the critical threshold, will they start generating energy and metamorphose into stars.

___At least three new stars are revealed at the apex of the dust lanes. These are the bright giant stars that are mostly responsible for lighting up the nebulae.

___Infrared views of the emission nebula mimic photographic negatives. At longer wavelengths [1], the darkest regions suddenly show up as bright, because the lower temperature of the dust in these areas stimulates them to release infrared rather than optical light. Shorter

wavelengths [2] have allowed the identification of thirty previously unknown stellar embryos in four knots of dusts, and 120 newborn stars – none of which are yet otherwise visible. The biggest of the stellar embryos are always found in the centre of their respective dusty knot, suggesting that the other stars forming around it feed from its leftovers.

___In the lower part of the emission nebula, a translucent mountain range appears against the background. A close-up of this region [3] reveals spikes of matter reaching upwards. The longest of these measures three-quarters of a light year. The ends of the spikes have been termed EGGs, for evaporating gaseous globules, and they are the dusty incubators of yet more new stars.

LIGHT SECONDS
LIGHT MINUTES
LIGHT YEARS
KILO LIGHT YEARS
MEGA LIGHT YEARS
GIGA LIGHT YEARS

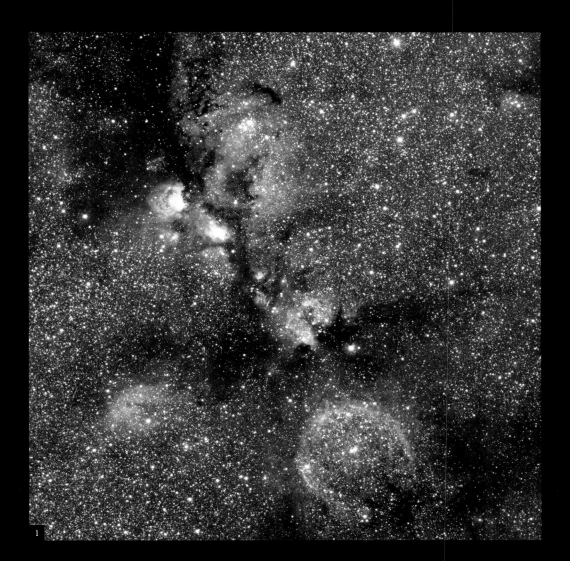

1

Tyger, tyger burning bright

It would have been a large cat indeed that left this paw print. The Cat's Paw Nebula is 60 light years wide and segregated into islands of star formation that give the illusion of the pads on a feline foot. It is the home of tens of thousands of restless stars.

Stars nearly ten times the mass of the Sun have been born in this interstellar cloud during the last few million years. While it is these stellar grandees that snatch the limelight, the region is home to perhaps tens of thousands of smaller stars making it one of the most active nurseries of massive stars in our galaxy.

___The Cat's Paw is buried in the star clouds of the Milky Way, a fact that can be most easily appreciated at infrared wavelengths. Countless stars crowd the view, and rivers of galactic dust seem to flow through this part of space, reaching their confluence at the centre of the Cat's Paw.

___Here the amount of dust is sufficient even to block these wavelengths of infrared light [1], and it is a sure bet that more would-be stars are congregating in this darkness, edging towards their own births.

___The nebula's deep red colour comes not just from the tormented hydrogen in the gas clouds. Lying close to the plane of the Galaxy, the nebula's light must negotiate banks of dust that lie in the 5,500 light years of intervening space between it and Earth. The price of its passage is to lose some of its blue light, hijacked by the dust grains and flung into random directions. Hence, the Cat's Paw's blush becomes deeper.

___One of the most interesting objects in the nebula is the quilted bubble of gases in the bottom right of the image. This is not a signpost of new stellar life, but a warning of impending stellar death. It is the outer layer of a massive star, set free into space by some enormous nuclear upheaval in its central engine. In time, the rest of the star will follow, blasted into space by runaway fusion reactions or the sudden cessation of nuclear activity that triggers the implosion of the star.

___In this avalanche a supernova explosion is generated, and the shockwaves it sends, pummelling into this cloud, will unleash a sudden burst of star formation that completes the process of stellar genesis that gravity had begun.

LIGHT SECONDS
LIGHT MINUTES
LIGHT YEARS
KILO LIGHT YEARS
MEGA LIGHT YEARS
GIGA LIGHT YEARS

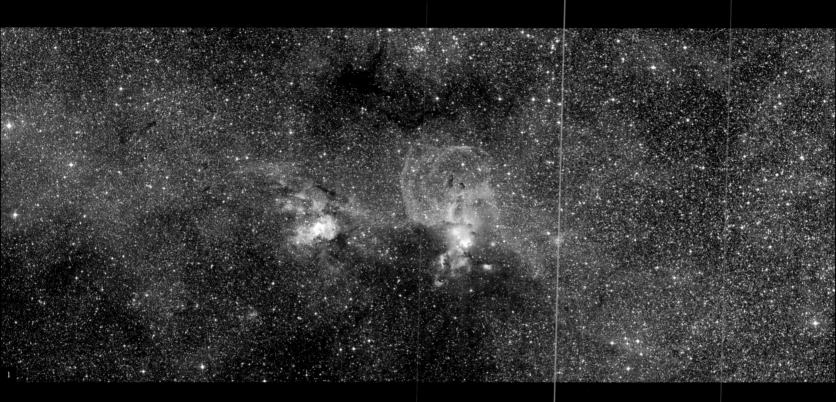

1

Smoky origins of life

Although not obvious from the appearance of these
magnificent looping arches, there is a dreadful form
of dirty pollution suffused in this beautiful cloud.
The irony is that these noxious substances could be
the very stuff that jump-started life on Earth.

Residing in the Sagittarius arm of the Milky
Way [1], NGC 3582 is a jumble of stars, some
of them young, others nearing the ends of their
lives. The giant loops of gas that rise from the
nebula are the result of older stars beginning
to shed their outer layers into space. The stars
responsible will soon be lost to the Universe,
collapsed into dense white dwarfs.

___Meanwhile, there is a new generation
preparing to take their place. Catalogued as
RCW 57, this tight cluster in the centre of the
nebula contains more than 30 massive stars.
Inevitably there will be hundreds of much
smaller stars in here as well, unobservable
in the glare of the bigger ones.

___But it's some of the very smallest objects in
this cloud that make it most interesting. The

objects are molecules, polycyclic aromatic
hydrocarbons to be exact. Such PAHs are
families of molecules, each of which is made
of rings of carbon atoms. They are the most
abundant complex molecules yet discovered
in space. We find them on Earth in the exhausts
given out by cars, the smoke from forest fires
and the charred bits of barbecued meat.

___They can be seen in the tails of comets and
have been found in meteorites. They are thought
to be a key ingredient in the primordial oceans
of Earth. Being composed of carbon atoms,
which make up the backbone in life-giving
molecules of DNA, they may provide one of
the first steps from simply chemistry to life.

___Although not usually soluble in water,
the PAHs can be made so with the help of

ultraviolet light. Light wounds the molecule,
which then bandages itself up with whatever
nearby molecule it can find. Often this will be
made of oxygen and hydrogen and, magically,
the molecule becomes more soluble.

___But not all the parts of the molecule are
comfortable in water. Once submersed, the
PAHs form rings to protect their hydrophobic
parts, like a wagon train making a circle to
protect the interior from attack. As these rings
jostle, the transition to long carbon chains
could be promoted. If so, a step towards DNA
will have been taken.

___While this scenario remains speculative
and untested, should it prove to be true, then
life may be widespread throughout the Galaxy,
because PAHs are everywhere.

LIGHT SECONDS
LIGHT MINUTES
LIGHT YEARS
KILO LIGHT YEARS
MEGA LIGHT YEARS
GIGA LIGHT YEARS

1 .

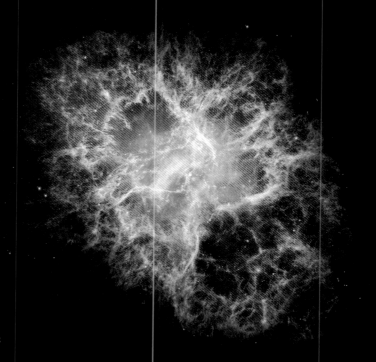

2

Back from the dead?

<u>The striking filaments of the Crab Nebula glow as brightly as they did a thousand years ago, when they were the freshly detonated remains of a giant star. What keeps them powered now? A member of the celestial undead...</u>

This was once a star; all this gas was packed into a dense spherical volume and generating energy. Then in AD 1054 the end came. The core collapsed and the star extinguished itself in a final blaze of glory. Except that not everything was blown to pieces: a stellar cinder of tremendous power remained, and now it energizes the whole remnant, driving it to glow as brightly as it did a millennium ago.

___The early life of this supernova remnant was powered by radioactive decay. The nuclear conflagration that engulfed the star provided the maelstrom in which nature's heaviest elements were forged, including radioactive isotopes.

___As these isotopes such as nickel-56 and cobalt-56 decayed, their energy fed the remnant's appetite and kept it glowing.

The puzzle is that, a thousand years later, the Crab remains as energetic as ever – it is 75,000 times as luminous as the Sun – long after it should have begun to fade. Its secret lies where the star once did, deep inside the Crab, where a new engine is at work.

___It seems barely credible that anything could survive a supernova – several hundred billion stars' worth of energy discharged in one fell swoop. Yet the star's core rode the storm, although not without terrific cost: it lives on as a stellar zombie, or a neutron star.

___Most of the matter from the star's former heart remains – some three times the mass of our Sun – but it is now compressed into a sphere just 20 km across, and it more closely resembles a single, large-scale atomic nucleus than a collection of atoms. It is so dense that a

single teaspoon of neutron star weighs more than 5 billion tonnes and its surface gravity is 200 billion times stronger that Earth's – an object dropped from a height of one metre above a neutron star would hit its surface moving at 7.2 million km/h.

___This particular example is a species of neutron star known as a pulsar, a highly magnetized body spinning in a breathtaking pirouette that it completes 30.2 times a second. As it turns, it acts as a dynamo, accelerating particles to near light speed before spitting them out into the nebula to reinvigorate the remnant's debris clouds. X-ray wavelengths reveal [1] the swirling disc that surrounds the furiously rotating neutron star, while a multi-wavelength [2] image puts it into context with what we can see with our own eyes.

LIGHT SECONDS
LIGHT MINUTES
LIGHT YEARS
KILO LIGHT YEARS
MEGA LIGHT YEARS
GIGA LIGHT YEARS

1

2

Soaring though space

The Eagle Nebula soars through the Milky Way, its gaseous wings outstretched and its colourful plumage on proud display. Its magical eggs will hatch one day not into birds but fully fledged stars.

This particular Eagle is a fearsome beast. Four iconic pillars of dust [1 & 2] nearly 10 light years tall pierce the nebula's clear heart like outstretched talons. All point towards the burning heart of a star cluster, NGC 6611 – the Eagle hatched these stars 1 million years ago.

___Recently, the dark pillars have been found to contain a number of would-be stars. These are the latecomers who have largely missed the party because star formation in the Eagle Nebula is winding down.

___To reinforce this, there are numerous sources of X-rays that dot this nebula. It is most likely that these powerful invisible rays are coming from young stars but they do not appear to be embedded within the dusty pillars. Instead, they are the product of an intermediate round of star formation. When they were just hatching this clutch of stellar eggs would have released so much radiation that the Eagle would likely have spread its wings even further across space.

___From that peak of star formation, 1 million years ago, the trend has been downwards. These days the nebula is on its last legs, with disaster approaching.

___The pillars themselves were carved from a larger, denser portion of the nebula and even now they continue to be visibly eroded. The onslaught is from the ultraviolet light of the nearby star cluster and produces a fringe of yellow light at the top of each pillar. Yet this is nothing compared to the assault racing up from behind.

___The oncoming catastrophe takes the shape of an enormous bubble of super-heated gas. The blast has come from a supernova and it will slam into the pillars in about a thousand years from now. When this barrage hits them, they will topple as they do not contain enough matter to withstand the attack. The pillars will be washed away as if they were sandcastles defending a beach against the incoming tide.

___The Eagle's days are numbered; there is no way for it to fly out of harm's way.

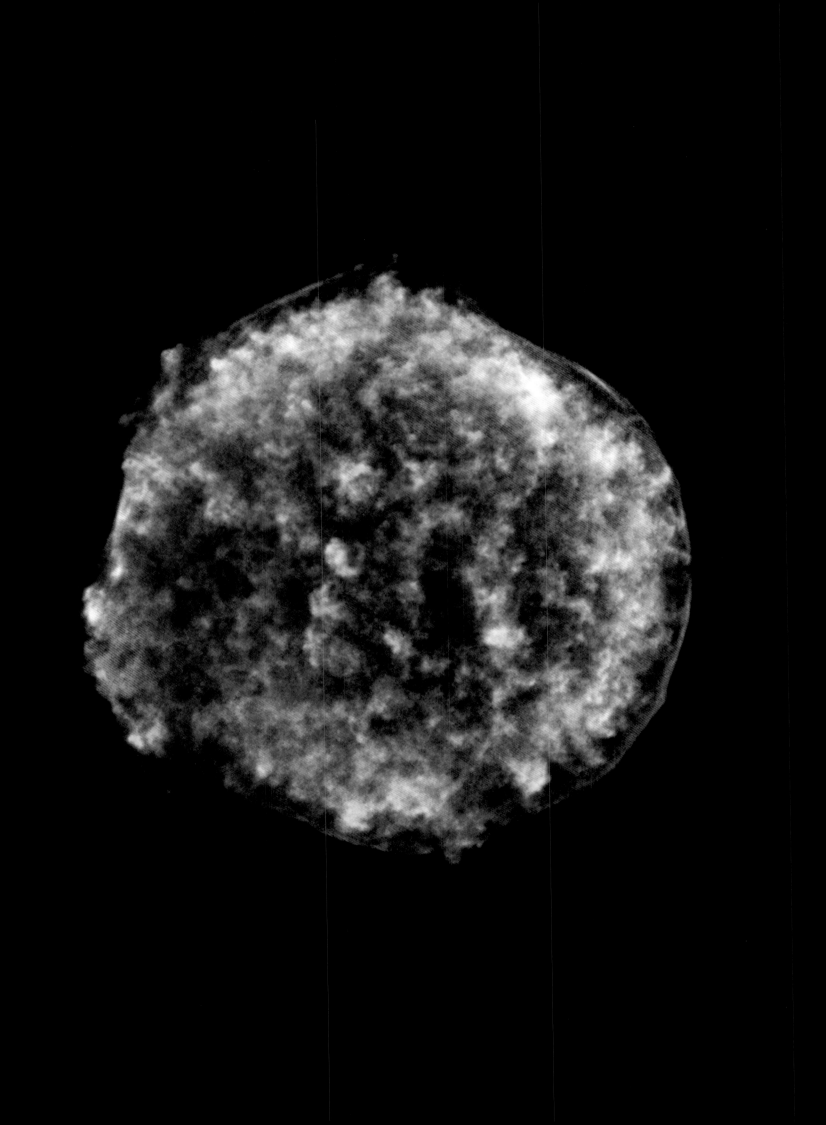

000.6 LIGHT SECONDS
LIGHT MINUTES
LIGHT YEARS
KILO LIGHT YEARS
MEGA LIGHT YEARS
GIGA LIGHT YEARS

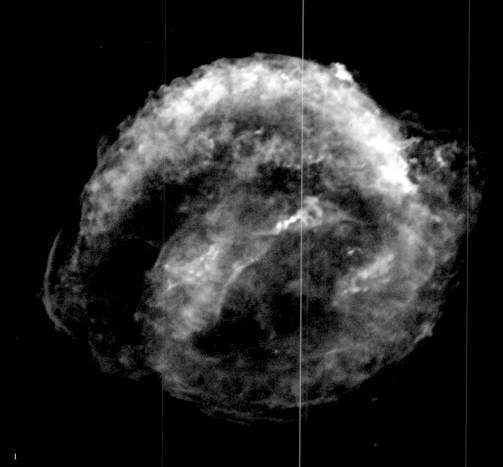

1

The collapse of certainty

This celestial object changed our view of the Universe forever. It was 1572; its unexpected birth – and one man's observation of it – triggered the collapse of 2,000 years of received astronomical wisdom, leading to astronomy as we know it today.

Danish nobleman Tycho Brahe was kidnapped at birth by a jealous uncle, lost the bridge of his nose in a teenage duel, and became the despotic ruler of Hveen Island. He was also the greatest naked-eye astronomer the world has ever known.

___His revelation took place in November 1572, almost four decades before telescopes were invented. Waxed moustache drooping from beneath his disfigured nose, Tycho glanced skyward and saw a new star shining through the chill winter air. Burning more brightly than any other star, not even daylight could drive this stellar herald from the sky. It produced consternation across Europe.

___According to the astrological thinking of the time, an additional celestial influence could only foretell swingeing change and new political landscapes. In England, Elizabeth I summoned her astrologers. Brahe, himself, said it presaged fatal times ahead. Yet it was not kingdoms that fell, but Aristotle's dogmatic view of the Universe.

___According to the ancient Greek, change could only take place below the orbit of the Moon. This view was absorbed into Christian belief as an indication that the Universe was God's perfect creation and therefore incapable of changing, because any alteration would drive it away from perfection. Only on the Earth, then thought to be the centre of the Universe, was corrupting change possible.

___Tycho shattered this belief by measuring the position of the new star night after night, week after week, month after month and finding that it stayed resolutely fixed in the pattern of distant stars, proving that it was at the same distance they were. Any closer to Earth and it would have drifted across the background of fixed stars as the planets do.

___The revelation that the Universe could change emboldened astronomers. Until then everything had seemed so certain. Now they saw that the Universe was in a state of flux. German mathematician Johannes Kepler embodied the new astronomy, questioning 2,000 years of received astronomical wisdom, including the position of the Earth in space. Ironically, Tycho himself never believed that Earth moved.

___In 1604 Kepler spotted his own supernova [1]. Looking in the direction of these stars, we see their superheated remains even today. Although the loss of a star or two is nothing to the Universe, thanks to Tycho's observations and Kepler's mathematics, human perception of the cosmos was changed forever.

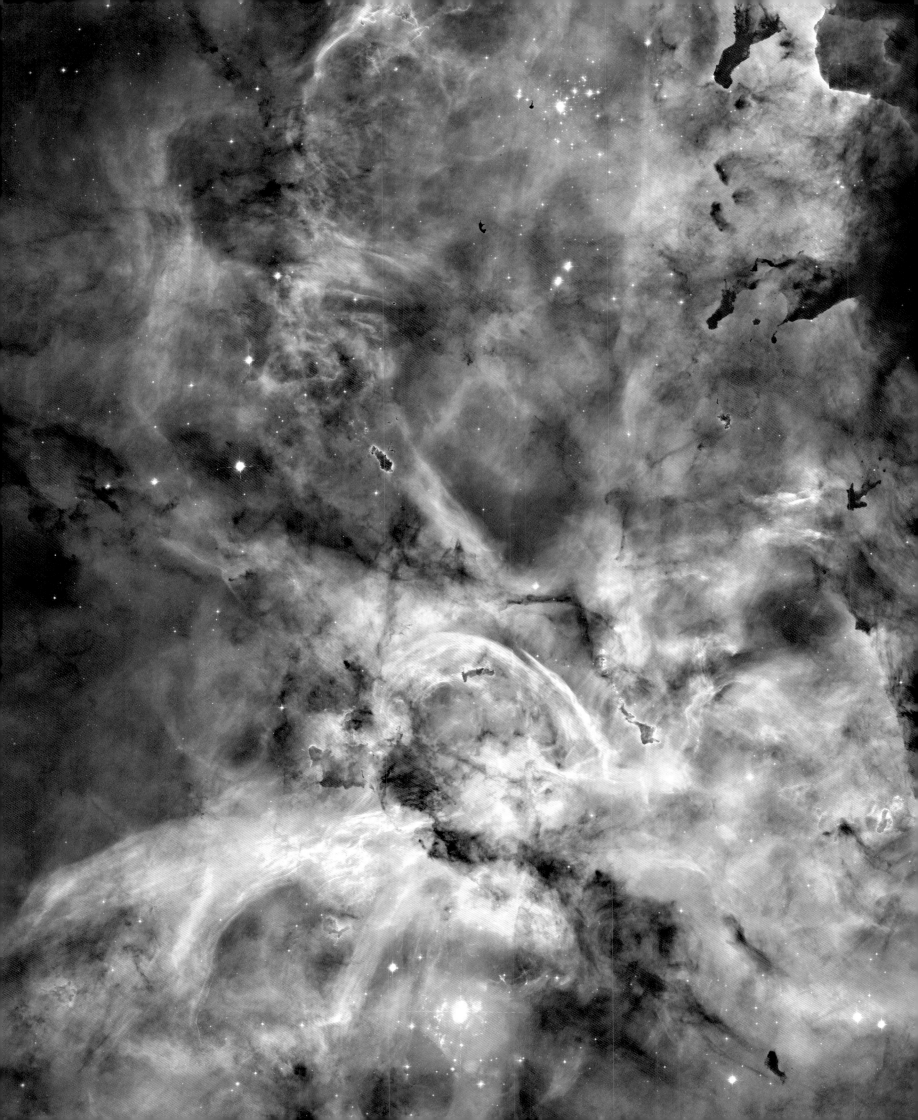

LIGHT SECONDS
LIGHT MINUTES
LIGHT YEARS
KILO LIGHT YEARS
MEGA LIGHT YEARS
GIGA LIGHT YEARS

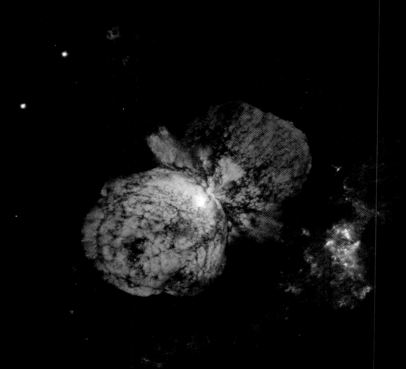

1

2

Hyperstar

Eta Carinae is no ordinary star. Called a blue hypergiant, it is one of the rarest in the Universe. Bulging with between 120–150 times the mass of the Sun, it rages with a luminosity almost 2 million times greater.

Eta Carinae is encased within a dumbbell-shaped nebula [1] that makes up little more than a spot on low centre of the large-scale image opposite. Nevertheless, the star has carved out an expanding bubble and daubed the walls with the opulent colours of energized interstellar gas. The nebula is immense [2] – the inner region alone covers 53 light years – yet it is all that remains of a once even larger giant molecular cloud.

___There are only a few dozen stars like Eta Carinae known to exist in the Galaxy today but 13 billion years ago, they may have been the only kind of stars that could form.

___Back in those ancient days, the chemical composition of the Universe was almost entirely hydrogen and helium. Without any heavier elements, the clouds of gas in space would find it difficult to cool down and collapse into stars, so they just got bigger and bigger. Eventually, they contained so much mass that gravity became overwhelming and forced the giant cloud together, producing extremely massive stars. Some of these stellar mammoths could have swollen to hundreds or even a thousand times the mass of the Sun.

___Almost totally unstable, they would have blown themselves to pieces in just a million years or so, but not before their rapacious nuclear engines had converted about half a percent of the bulk into heavier chemical elements. These were blasted across space in the resulting detonation and created a seasoning of heavier chemicals that stabilized the whole process of star formation.

___They helped the gas clouds radiate energy more easily, making them collapse into the next generation of stars before they reached such gargantuan proportions. So these days, the megastars have largely vanished, replaced by long-lived stars that use their time and energy rather more judiciously than their forebears.

___Nevertheless, Eta Carinae reminds us what these flamboyant individuals must have been like. The cosmos would have been a more dangerous place, but with each one blasting a million times the light of the Sun into space, it would certainly not have been dull.

LIGHT SECONDS
LIGHT MINUTES
LIGHT YEARS
KILO LIGHT YEARS
MEGA LIGHT YEARS
GIGA LIGHT YEARS

1

2

Accident of birth

This moustachioed promontory hides a star approaching adulthood. It will probably be similar to the Sun and, if so, would have a life expectancy of around 9 billion years. But it won't live that long. Through no fault of its own, it is doomed to die in a tiny fraction of that time: less than 10 million years.

This star along with dozens of hidden siblings revealed only in infrared [1] is forming within the last vestiges of the Carina Nebula. The hurricane blast of nearby Eta Carinae's stellar wind and its blistering ultraviolet radiation has compressed the surrounding walls of hydrogen [2] and other gases so much that it has forced a second round of star formation. Within this three-light-year-long mountain of dust lies a young star, almost ready to be born.

___The first sign of its impending arrival is the moustache of light that the promontory is wearing. The two halves are jets created by the star's magnetic field, and they are fuelled by matter from its surroundings that has been busily making planets. They will drill away at this dusty outcrop from within, gradually

whittling it away until the star can shine its light freely across space for the first time.

___On one side the jet has entered a zone of denser gas and this has resulted in a curved bow shock, a kind of sonic boom that rolls through the interstellar gas. On the other side there is no such structure, indicating that this region is largely empty.

___When the jets complete their work, and the star comes into view, it is likely to be a yellow, sun-like star that may shepherd a solar system of planets. There could even be an Earth-like world complete with breathable atmosphere and life.

___But all of it is doomed; not because of any flaw in its make-up but because of the accident of its birth so close to Eta Carinae. When

the nearby giant star rips itself to shreds as a supernova the current stellar wind will appear sweet by comparison.

___Gross energy will tear through space, abrading all the stars and planets that it sweeps across. Even if the atmosphere of the planets is not completely sandblasted away, any protective ozone layer will be disintegrated by the hellish radiation from the supernova.

___Giant supernovae, called gamma ray bursts, may be capable of emitting enough radiation to sterilize a whole galaxy. Thankfully for the rest of the stars and planets in the Milky Way, not even Eta Carinae is big enough to create a gamma ray burst.

LIGHT SECONDS
LIGHT MINUTES
LIGHT YEARS
KILO LIGHT YEARS
MEGA LIGHT YEARS
GIGA LIGHT YEARS

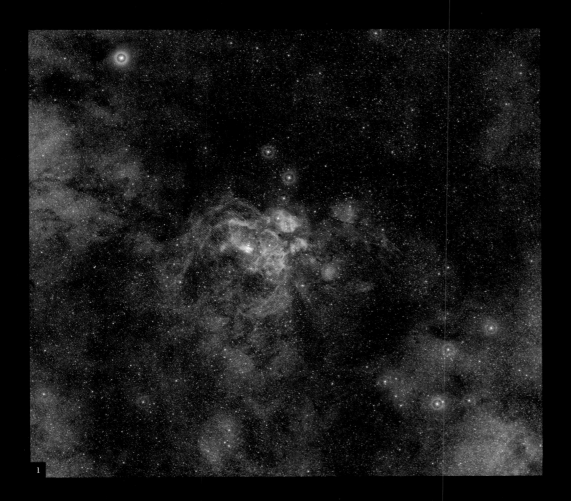

1

Double trouble

A young star cluster hurls its abrasive light into the nebula that gave it life. It has hewn out great pillars of dust that soar upwards, while pushing the rest of the cloud into full retreat. The leader of the attack is the giant star Pismis 24-1, a star whose mass apparently defies reason.

Almost a third of the way towards the Galactic centre, NGC 6357 [1] gave birth to the Pismis 24 star cluster no more than a million or two years ago. The stars immediately turned on their natal cloud, shredding it with radiation. The leader of the attack is Pismis 24-1, the brightest of the stars in the cluster. This titan has all the characteristics of a star containing 200–300 times the mass of the Sun. But if it were truly this big, not only would it be the most massive star in the Galaxy, it would also create a giant scientific headache because such stars are thought to be impossible in the present-day Milky Way Galaxy.

___With the smattering of heavy chemical elements that now exists in the Milky Way, a collapsing gas cloud finds itself less able to resist gravity and so falls together more quickly. As a result it produces smaller stars. Those

stellar behemoths that do manage to emerge lead fitful lives, producing such powerful bursts of energy that they end up coughing and spluttering their outer layers into space. Yet this apparently monstrous star is not surrounded by bubbles of gas and looks entirely stable.

___The mystery is explained because Pismis 24-1 is actually two stars, locked together by gravity, but otherwise separate entities. They are still giants, each containing at least 100 solar masses. Individually, that makes them rare; together the pair could be unique in the Galaxy.

___For every one star created containing 65 solar masses or more, an estimated 18,000 stars similar to the Sun will form. Since giant stars live for only 3 million years or so, while their Sun-like counterparts survive for around 10 billion, there are millions of solar-mass stars for each massive star. And Pismis 24-1 contains two of them.

___In fact, there is another 100-solar mass star elsewhere in this small cluster, making it a true oddity in the Galaxy. Regardless of how three such massive stars were born in such close proximity, the trio are destined to end their lives in spectacular explosions that will destroy the remains of the nebula. As each star goes supernova, so they will leave behind collapsed cores in the form of either neutron stars or black holes.

___The two black holes or neutron stars locked together in Pismis 24-1 could then go on to spiral into one another creating another almighty explosion, greater than their original supernovae.

___Despite the apparently peaceful scene, stellar heavyweights such as Pismis 24-1 are the Galaxy's real troublemakers.

LIGHT SECONDS
LIGHT MINUTES
LIGHT YEARS
KILO LIGHT YEARS
MEGA LIGHT YEARS
GIGA LIGHT YEARS

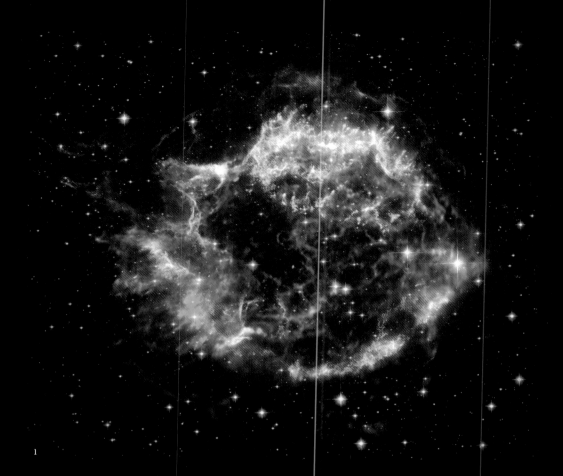

1

Ghost supernova

Although no one saw this star's colossal flare-up, it is more than making up for it today. Visible as a tracery of shockwaves, it screams into the void at radio frequencies. Although more than 300 years old, it is still pelting Earth with smashed atoms.

By all rights, when this star exploded during the mid 17th century, it should have lit up the night sky and probably been visible through daylight, too. Yet there are no records that tell of it gracing the heavens.

___This could be because the star had a false start, coyly surrounding itself with a thick shell of gases after a failed supernova ignition. Later, the star mustered the energy to try again and this time, it succeeded. Its self-destructive ambition tore it to pieces but, to the outside Universe, the intense burst of light was blocked from view by the surrounding shroud of matter.

___Then later still, the blast slammed into the surrounding shell, heating its gases to temperatures of 10,000,000 °C and driving them into a frenzy of emission. Colour coded images taken at a variety of wavelengths [1] reveal the entire blast zone is roiling with clouds of oxygen, sulphur, hydrogen, nitrogen,

neon and aluminium. But this elemental bounty is not the only thing speeding outward from a supernova.

___As the shockwave tumbles outwards, brutally compressing the gas in its path, ambient magnetic fields are squeezed and amplified. Its impact shatters atoms, revealing their electrical charges and making them susceptible to the amplified magnetic fields. As a result, particles stripped by the shockwave can suddenly find themselves accelerated to enormous speeds, transformed into cosmic rays.

___They shoot across the Galaxy, immediately outpacing the shockwave. With no friction in space to slow them down, the cosmic rays speed on, constituting an interstellar radiation field of enormous power.

___Those that happen to be heading in our direction can hit Earth's atmosphere with a

billion times the energy of a particle produced in even the most powerful of man-made particle accelerators. When they strike the molecules in Earth's blanket of gases, they produce a sudden flash of light and burst into a shower of secondary particles, summoned into existence by the sudden release of the cosmic ray's energy.

___As these cascade downwards, they may even trigger discharges of atmospheric electricity that give rise to the forks of lightning seen in thunderstorms.

___High-flying humans are directly affected too. When astronauts close their eyes, they often see faint flashes of light. Each tiny flare is the result of a cosmic ray colliding with a molecule in their eyeball – the pale ghost of a supernova hundreds, or even thousands, of light years away.

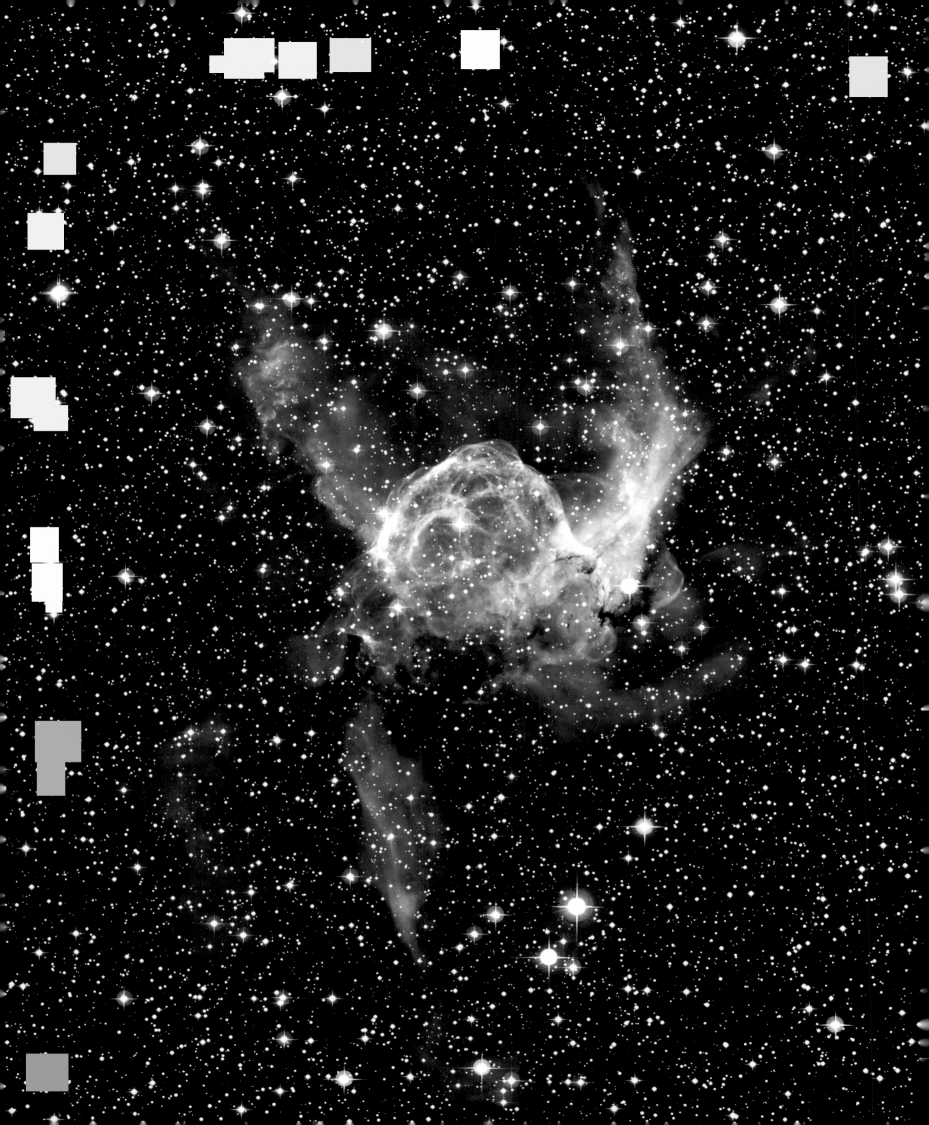

LIGHT SECONDS
LIGHT MINUTES
LIGHT YEARS
KILO LIGHT YEARS
MEGA LIGHT YEARS
GIGA LIGHT YEARS

Final performance

<u>Donning a suitably Wagnerian helmet, this stellar actor is embarking on the role it has always been destined to play. This star will soon become a supernova: a once-in-a-lifetime performance.</u>

It may look as if this blue giant star has already exploded, but in fact this is just the first act in a play with an altogether more violent climax. The star has been preparing for this role since it was born. The moment it garnered more than eight times the mass of the Sun, its fate was sealed. And this one went even further, accumulating more than 20 times the Sun's bulk. and now, it is using this great bulk to light up the heavens.

___Flayed by a stellar wind billions of times of stronger than our Sun's, this star is laying itself bare to its audience of stellar spectators. The first act requires that it casts off the layer of nitrogen and oxygen-rich gases that kept it powered during its youth – this is the material responsible for most of the 30-light-year dome that bubbles and boils around the star here.

___In the next act it will expel layers of carbon-rich gas, remnants of its helium-fusing days. This excruciating striptease is a reminder that age is cruel to massive stars. They are forced to consume heavier and heavier fuels just to keep going. They start on hydrogen, move to helium, then carbon, oxygen and silicon, each transition coming quicker and quicker as they move up the periodic table. The end of the road is iron. No star can fuse iron nuclei. With nothing to burn its nuclear furnaces go out and the star abandons itself to gravity.

___Given free reign, gravity crushes the star's core into the exotic stuff of neutron stars. Such an instant metamorphosis unleashes a prodigious shockwave and a multi-billion degree blaze of radiation that will rip the star open in a matter of hours and flood the heavens with light. This is the big one, the role this stellar heavyweight was always destined to play: that of the leading star in the Galaxy.

___For a few weeks it will shine with the light of hundreds of billions of stars, a final incandescent soliloquy. When the epilogue is over, and its brilliance has faded from the celestial stage, rest assured there will be another star waiting in the wings, preparing for its own once-in-a-lifetime starring performance.

Omega Centauri

NGC 5139

GLOBULAR CLUSTER

DIAMETER: 180 LY

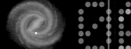

LIGHT SECONDS
LIGHT MINUTES
LIGHT YEARS
KILO LIGHT YEARS
MEGA LIGHT YEARS
GIGA LIGHT YEARS

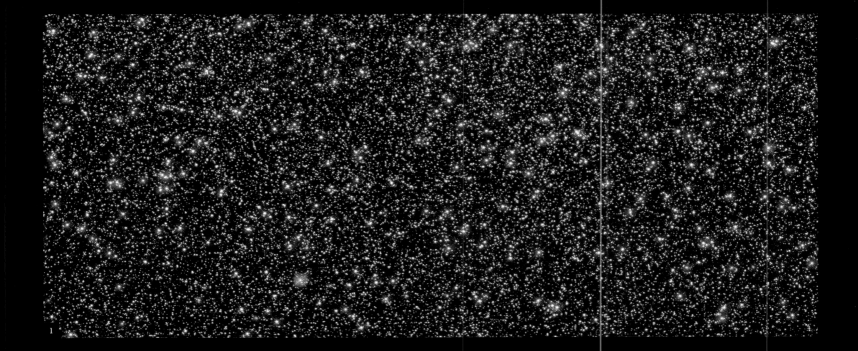

1

Methuselah's metropolis

This gleaming swarm rests in silent witness to the Milky Way. In its core 10 million stars are united by gravity and huddled together into a sphere just 160 light years across. It's a relic from a time gone by and hides a dark secret in its core.

Located beyond the main sweep of stars in our Galaxy, Omega Centauri is the largest of 150 such swarms that circle the Galaxy. Each formed in antiquity, the globular clusters have seen the Milky Way grow and evolve, as they themselves have aged.

___The stars in Omega Centauri are all billions of years old, glowing with the distinctive golden hue of maturity. Some are more advanced, swollen to enormous size and turned red in a final blush of glory before the inevitable collapse into obscurity.

___All traces of star formation are long gone from this cluster: no inky black cocoons to harbour stellar embryos, no rippling nebulae of light to draw attention to the nascent star clusters. Instead, it suffers the inexorable slide into oblivion, the cluster growing ever older, its stellar population diminishing one by one.

But look more closely and there is a paradox.
___Lurking within this astral Methuselah are blue stars – their colour a clear sign of stellar youth [1]. Yet with no star forming regions to have given birth to them, what power lies within to rejuvenate the stars?

___The fountain of stellar youth turns out to be the density of the cluster. This tightly knit community is crowded together, each star roughly 13 times closer to the next than our Sun is to its nearest neighbour. Standing on a planet in this stellar metropolis would be a never forgotten experience, with the night sky full of stars – and as bright as day.

___Jostled together, stellar collisions are commonplace. Each titanic impact results not in the destruction of the stars but in their merger, stoking the now combined nuclear furnace with new fuel and giving the illusion

of stellar youth, as the celestial fire rages.
___But, is Omega Centauri hiding yet another secret? A much larger secret? The stars in its very heart are racing round their orbits, tormented by the gravitational grip of a large black hole, tens of thousands of times the mass of our Sun. This betrays Omega Centauri as a chimera, because true globular clusters don't have black holes, they are not large enough.

___The resolution to the mystery is that Omega Centauri is probably a dwarf galaxy that strayed too close to the Milky Way. Like a bird that has had its flight feathers clipped, so this galaxy has had most of its outer stars ripped away, leaving just the core and a superficial resemblance to a globular cluster. Robbed of its stars and orbital energy, Omega Centauri is now trapped in a gravitational cage of the Milky Way's making.

LIGHT SECONDS
LIGHT MINUTES
LIGHT YEARS
KILO LIGHT YEARS
MEGA LIGHT YEARS
GIGA LIGHT YEARS

Family fortunes

<u>Two whole clusters of stars are popping into view from this molecular cloud, provoking the surrounding hydrogen and oxygen gas into a brilliant display of colour. The newly smelted families of stars are so powerful that they now control the cloud's fate, helping to disperse its remains back into space.</u>

Stars never form in isolation. As huge clouds of dust and gas reach a critical density the process of gravitational collapse is initiated. As the cloud contracts, particular knots collapse faster that their surroundings and these kernels become the hotbeds of star formation. Typically, stars are born in families of a few tens to several thousand individuals.

___About half of these stars will be locked into a gravitational dance with one or more of their neighbours. These binary and multiple stars are destined to spend their entire lives together, endlessly circling each other. In systems of three or more stars, a pair tends to form in the centre and then the other stars revolve around them. Sometimes the dance is more complex: in quadruple star systems, two orbiting couples also pirouette around each other.

___Those siblings not locked into the gravitational dance will slowly drift away into their own separate orbits around the centre of the Galaxy. Eventually it becomes impossible to tell which stars were born together.

___So many stars speckle this image that it is difficult to pick out the two newest born star clusters. One sits directly in the centre, the other resides in a patch of pink gas to its right. Together with the brightest star near the bottom left of the image, they are sculpting the rest of this nebula.

___The dark dust lanes that criss-cross the nebula are places of future star formation but the glowing gas is probably destined to miss out this time. Typically, only around 10 percent of the matter in a cloud of gas is transformed into stars. The rest is set glowing by the newborns and dissipated by their copious radiation. This unwanted gas returns to the diffuse reaches of interstellar space where, in time, it will be press-ganged into a new molecular cloud; ready to take its chances in another round of star formation.

LIGHT SECONDS
LIGHT MINUTES
LIGHT YEARS
KILO LIGHT YEARS
MEGA LIGHT YEARS
GIGA LIGHT YEARS

1

Band of brothers

A collection of stellar jewels peeps out of its hydrogen
birth cloud. Just another in a long line of such young star
clusters? Not so, this one is special; its stars are packed
so tightly that this could be one of the rarest sights in the
whole Universe.

The young stars of NGC 3603 are crammed together, more than 10,000 in a central volume with a diameter of just 3.5 light years. Back at the start of our journey, near the Sun, such a volume of space contains just one star – the Sun – with its nearest neighbour sited 4.3 light years away.

___At this density, the stars of NGC 3603 conjure up so much mutual gravity that it is unlikely that they will ever let go of one another. Most young star clusters float apart, with each individual star eager to make its own way in the Universe. Once free from their siblings, the stars merge into the general stellar population of the Milky Way, eventually making it impossible to recognize other members from the same family.

___This is not the future that awaits NGC 3603; they will always be bound together. And that's a puzzle because the only star clusters that behave in this way are the globular clusters, stellar brotherhoods that orbit the centre of the Milky Way, but in tilted orbits usually far from the plane of the Galaxy.

___So could this star cluster be a newly minted globular cluster? Maybe, and if so it is one of the rarest sights in the Universe because, of the 150 globulars that orbit the Milky Way, all appear uniformly ancient, having formed around 12 billion years ago at the same time as the Milky Way. In short, there are no recent globular clusters around the Milky Way, certainly none with a birthday measured just a few million years ago, as in this case.

___NGC 3603 is small compared to a true globular cluster, nevertheless it represents an exceptional event: a giant gas cloud, supremely dense [1], that collapsed together in a sudden fit of star formation, and has now produced a modern simulacrum of a globular cluster. Only in the case of massive collisions between galaxies can we sometimes see newly formed globulars, recognizable from a great distance because of their bright blue colours. Now, we appear to have one on our cosmic doorstep.

___Whatever triggered this star cluster to form, it is a glimpse of a process mainly long gone from the cosmos. As such, this peculiarly dense star cluster may be showing us what happened before our Galaxy was even born.

LIGHT SECONDS
LIGHT MINUTES
LIGHT YEARS
KILO LIGHT YEARS
MEGA LIGHT YEARS
GIGA LIGHT YEARS

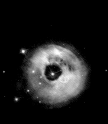
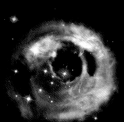
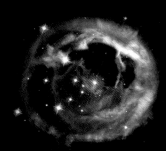

1

Cannibal star

The unexpected bloom of this stellar rose is a celestial mystery staring us in the face. No ordinary stellar explosion, instead of fading away as normal, it became weirder and weirder. Now the conclusion is inescapable, this is a cannibal star – but what did it eat?

V838 Monocerotis, as this star was hurriedly named, came from nowhere. In spite of all the telescopes and the surveys that now scan the heavens, it had evaded detection until its flare-up on 6 January 2002. In March, just as it was fading back into obscurity, it erupted again, then once more in April. From total obscurity it transformed itself into one of the most luminous stars in the whole Galaxy, pumping out a million times the power of the Sun.

___When finally it disappeared from view, it reinvented itself and began emitting most of its energy in the infrared region of the spectrum. If our eyes could have seen in the infrared the star would have pierced the glare of our daylight skies.

___The star swelled up as the mysterious eruption continued until, by October 2002, it was so bloated that if it were to replace the Sun, its outer layers would reach the orbit of Jupiter. Not only that but the light from the eruption began to reflect off giant mantles of gas that had been shrouding the star, giving it the appearance of an enormous celestial rose blooming in space [1].

___Clearly this was no ordinary stellar explosion. Only one explanation fitted such bizarre behaviour: a collision in which the star ate a smaller companion. And a planet wasn't big enough to unleash such havoc; only another star would do.

___In this apocalyptic scenario, the first outburst took place when a large star, perhaps eight times the mass of the Sun, was clipped by a smaller companion, about one-third the Sun's mass. The smaller star survived only to return a month later, resulting in the second outburst. This robbed the smaller star of so much orbital energy that it limped around once more before plunging to its doom. The third encounter ripped it to shreds and surrounded the main star with its debris, creating the cool, bloated object of October 2002.

___How many stars in our Galaxy collide like this? Very few it would seem. Erupting stars that share similarities with this one come along rarely: perhaps one in 1994 and another in the 1670s.

LIGHT SECONDS
LIGHT MINUTES
LIGHT YEARS
KILO LIGHT YEARS
MEGA LIGHT YEARS
GIGA LIGHT YEARS

1

Galactic hubbub

<u>We finally arrive at the hub of the Milky Way, a seething maelstrom of ancient stars surrounded by towering arcs of dust and gas sculpted by stellar winds, magnetic fields, tidal forces and shockwaves.</u>

Forever barred from view at visible wavelengths because of the swathes of dust that lie between us [1], the centre of the Galaxy nevertheless blazes with light in the more exotic parts of the spectrum. It is the kernel around which everything has been built during the last 12 billion years. It is the original seed that condensed out of the primordial ocean of gas that filled the Universe. Like the fledglings of Earth's spring season, it is largely down to luck that it has survived long enough to grow to full adulthood.

___In the beginning there were no large galaxies. Just like all babies, galaxies began small and grew bigger. They did it in one of two ways, either they fed off passing clouds of gas, eating sparingly over the aeons and building new stars at a sustainable rate, or they were

gluttons and cannibalized other galaxies. In the latter case, they wanted it all right there and then. They hid their victim's stars amongst their own and used any spare gas quickly, mixing it with their own and transforming it into a sudden raft of new stars.

___Our Milky Way was more inclined towards the careful line, growing steadily to prominence, and the gravity of this central region was responsible for this circumspect behaviour. In the process, it crafted the spiral pattern of arms that the Sun sits within.

___Now the core forms the gravitational fulcrum of the Milky Way, providing the massive hub around which the curved spokes of the Galaxy rotate. The bestiary of stars that populate the central region swarms across this part of space.

___Within the central three light years of the Galaxy's centre there are thousands of stars, most of them are extremely long-lived, having been formed in ancient times. This is confirmed by the fact that they contain only small amounts of the chemical elements heavier than hydrogen and helium. As these elements are the ones to build up in space with each successive generation of stars, paucity is a clear sign of having been born early in the Galaxy's history.

___But not all the stars found here are ancient. There are more than 100 examples of high-mass stars, all short-lived individuals that must have been created within the last few million years. It is somewhat ironic that the oldest part of the Galaxy contains the largest single collection of young stars.

LIGHT SECONDS
LIGHT MINUTES
LIGHT YEARS
KILO LIGHT YEARS
MEGA LIGHT YEARS
GIGA LIGHT YEARS

1

2

3

Dark heart

The bright white bloom at the centre of this image represents the deadliest radiation field in the Galaxy. And at its very centre, lurks a supermassive black hole, its crushing gravity poised to ambush any celestial object that strays too close.

It is known as Sagittarius A* and, cloaked in a blinding fog of X-rays [1], it has lurked unseen [2] at the centre of our galaxy since the very beginning. It may even be the gravitational seed that pulled together the surrounding swathes of gas that become our Galaxy, but now it is a force of destruction.

___Containing more than 4 million times the Sun's mass, the black hole is crushed into a sphere no bigger than the orbit of Mercury around the Sun. From Earth, it should look no larger than a beach ball on the Moon. Not surprisingly, no one has yet seen it but we know it's there, silently going about its destructive purpose because of the havoc it is wreaking on its surroundings.

___Nothing is immune: stars are being hurled through space by the powerful gravity of the black hole, and any that stray too close are being ripped to shreds and devoured; otherwise parallel filaments of gas are sucked sharply downward towards the bright blob cocooning Sagittarius A* [3].

___Surrounding the black hole is a melting pot of ancient stars, white dwarves, neutron stars, smaller black holes as well as more than 100 of the Galaxy's highest-mass, shortest-lived stars. But how could they get there?

___There is no sign of current star formation. Perhaps they formed out of the debris of other stars pulled to pieces and strewn into a disc surrounding the black hole. No one yet knows. However they got there, they are now in a race against time: will they live out their short lives to explode as supernovae before they are wrenched into their constituent atoms and devoured?

___That's where the X-rays come in. As the stars are pulled apart and the gas races to destruction, it heats up and pours out X-rays. These powerful bursts are the final luminous reminder of the oblivion that lies beyond the black hole's event horizon.

___The event horizon marks the celestial Rubicon. Pass this boundary, and there is no escape. No force in the Universe could propel you back out to safety. Not even light can escape. The only place to go is down towards the singularity, the impossibly compacted region of spacetime that possesses the paradoxical qualities of being infinitely small, yet infinitely dense. Once there, all matter is squeezed out of existence in a process that science cannot yet explain.

M72

NGC 6981

GLOBULAR CLUSTER

DIAMETER: 50 LY

LIGHT SECONDS
LIGHT MINUTES
LIGHT YEARS
KILO LIGHT YEARS
MEGA LIGHT YEARS
GIGA LIGHT YEARS

1

2

3

Stellar survivor

One of the loneliest outposts of the Milky Way, globular cluster M72 is a survivor. Where once there were thousands of similar celestial cities in the sky, now just 150 or so remain. The rest have fallen prey to the Milky Way's unmerciful gravity, been dismembered and scattered to the stellar winds.

In common with other globular clusters – M4 [1], M30 [2], NGC 6397 [3] – M72 follows an inclined orbital path around the central hub of the Galaxy. Usually this keeps it out of harm's way, well separated from the Galaxy's other stars. But every 100 million years or so, M72 must run the galactic gauntlet.

___It plunges through the Milky Way, where it is subjected to stronger gravitational forces than it is used to withstanding. These forces tear at its innards, drawing out vast streams of stars and stringing them across tens of thousands of light years of space. For most of the other globular clusters that once surrounded the Milky Way, this has proved

fatal, eviscerating them to the point of utter destruction as the aeons have passed.

___No one knows how the globular clusters formed. By the ages of the stars they contain, they must have attended the very birth of our Galaxy. In fact, they are older than any surviving structure in our Galaxy. And very few show progressive populations of stars. It seems that the stars in most globular clusters formed at the same time, long ago. Yet although their antiquity is obvious, the other secrets of their formation are under a lock that remains unpicked.

___Globular clusters do, however, prove that the Solar System is not in the centre of the

Galaxy. If we were at the centre of things, the globulars would be distributed randomly around us. As it is, most are located in the southern sky, betraying the centre of the galaxy to be located in that direction.

___Today, just 100,000 stars cling together in M72. It is one of the most distant globular clusters, which has surely helped its survival. As time has marched on, so the stars die off one by one. And they will continue to do so until, where there was once a glittering ball of stars, there will be a black mass of stellar corpses. The price of survival, it seems, is to simply fade away.

INTER
GALACTIC

It is time to leave the glittering stars and their coloured cloaks of gas. As the Galaxy falls away behind us, the magnificent objects that once dominated our view merge into one and we can discern the exquisite finesse of the Galaxy's overall design. Its sweeping spiral arms of blue stars punctuated by the red light of the nebulae, and laced with a tracery of dust.

Turning outwards, we see it is a pattern that is repeated throughout the Universe. The next facsimile galaxy is Andromeda, and a bounty of others grace the night; but to reach them, we need to accelerate again. Andromeda itself lies 2.3 million light years away. Although it is the nearest large galaxy, the first galaxies we encounter on our outward journey are much smaller. They are the Magellanic Clouds, so-called because in the night sky from Earth they appear to be detached fragments of the Milky Way. From our vantage point on the journey we see them as dwarf galaxies a few hundred thousand light years from our Galaxy, close enough for us to see details in their interiors.

___Each Magellanic Cloud serves as a home to a few billion stars, and they are both busily making more. Here we encounter the first surprise in our survey of intergalactic space. Despite their relatively diminutive size, they contain regions of star formation that dwarf anything the Milky Way possesses. If the mighty Tarantula Nebula were to replace the Orion Nebula in our own Galaxy it would dominate the night sky and cast shadows on Earth.

___To truly appreciate the population of intergalactic space we have to reach tens and hundreds of millions of years into the Universe. Here we will find that, as well as the majestic spirals such as the Milky Way and Andromeda, there are barred spirals that support their heavy arms of stars on broad dusty shoulders, and the elliptical galaxies where the stars swarm like bees around a hive. Then there are the irregulars, just fuzzy patches of stars. We will encounter them all, revel in their compelling similarities and wonder at their marked differences. From the scars of dust that score some galaxies, to the deadly wildfire of creation that engulfs others, to the incomprehensible violence of galactic collisions, each galaxy has its own story to tell.

___There is IC 342, turning serenely on its axis, while displaying the grand design of its spiral arms for the Universe to see. The Sombrero Galaxy has had its time of magnificence, and is now losing its spiral arms to contract and fade into a lens-shaped retirement home for old stars. And then there is NGC 1275. There is no growing old gracefully here, it is tearing itself apart from the inside out by blasting bullets of hot gas outwards, drawing colder streams behind them to hang like a freeze-framed firework.

___All the galaxies people could see were once thought to be part of the Milky Way. Their spiral shapes were imagined to be whirlpools of matter settling into a solar system of planets around a central forming star. The image was a seductive one with each galaxy's central bulge of stars resembling an airy star. Then in the early 20th century, the distances of these spiral nebulae were determined and they turned out to be huge.

___They were banished from the Milky Way altogether and shown to be not just far away but vast in size as well. Far from being denizens of our Galaxy, they are whole 'Milky Ways' in their own right; enormous star cities that house hundreds of billions of lustrous stars.

___Galaxies exist across a broad range of size scales. The titans are the elliptical galaxies. In a rich collection of galaxies, one giant elliptical will often be found to have sunk to the dead centre of the cluster, having grown to enormous proportions on a cannibalistic diet. Its vast bulk now forms the fulcrum around which the other galaxies rotate. Spent of any further gas, it has completely lost its ability to breathe life into any new stars. The only way it can replace those that it loses, as they come to an end of their natural lives, is to consume more galaxies. Anything that comes too close will be shown no mercy. They will be dismembered; their lifeblood of stars spilled across space until the giant elliptical mops it all up, using its strong gravity to absorb everything that was once in the other galaxy.

___At the opposite end of the size spectrum, the dwarf galaxies may prove to be some of the most scientifically valuable galaxies existing today. Being so small, they have not produced stars with anything like the profligacy of their much larger brethren. As a result the stellar alchemy that drives the composition of the galaxies to change with each new generation of stars has been arrested. This has preserved the conditions of the early Universe, turning these diminutives into windows onto the distant past.

___The further we journey, the more the arrangement of galaxies becomes apparent. At a scale of hundreds of millions of light years, so the clusters of galaxies come into clear view. Each grouping is the cosmic equivalent of the coliseum, where the galactic gladiators fight to the death.

___Inexorably drawn together into these groups and clusters by the gravity they generate, the galaxies are revealed to be aggressive individuals, always spoiling for a fight. As the galaxies circle, sizing each other up, they rake their gravitational fields across their opponents. Sometimes it is one-on-one, as in the case of M51 and NGC 5196. This David versus Goliath contest sets the smaller NGC 5196 up against a mighty spiral. In contrast to the biblical tale, there is unlikely to be poetic justice here. Unless NGC 5196 can race away, it will be destroyed by M51.

___When two galaxies are evenly matched, as with Antennae Galaxies, there can be no winner. Along the front line where these two spiral galaxies clash, the terrible fires of star formation are ignited. For hundreds of thousands of years, these fires will spread until each cloud of gas is transformed into new stars, as if in a desperate attempt to reinforce each galaxy's army. Finally, drained of energy and reserves, the two warring galaxies will coalesce, reborn as an exhausted, elliptical galaxy.

___At other times, these galactic brawls are pitched battles between numerous galaxies. Stephan's Quintet sees five galaxies all tearing at each other. But not every galactic fight needs to end in the destruction of elegance.

___In a few rare cases, sublime splendour results from these cosmic smash-ups: a ring galaxy, in which the collision creates a ripple of star formation that moves outwards from the bull's eye to the edge. Hoag's Object, 600 million light years away, is one such galaxy, perhaps the best example yet found, with its perfect circular symmetry.

___The galaxies are as individual as human beings. Each possesses its own character and idiosyncrasies, and each has a unique narrative spanning billions of years of cosmic history.

Right: NGC 7217, a tightly bound spiral galaxy in the constellation Pegasus, 41 mega light years distant.

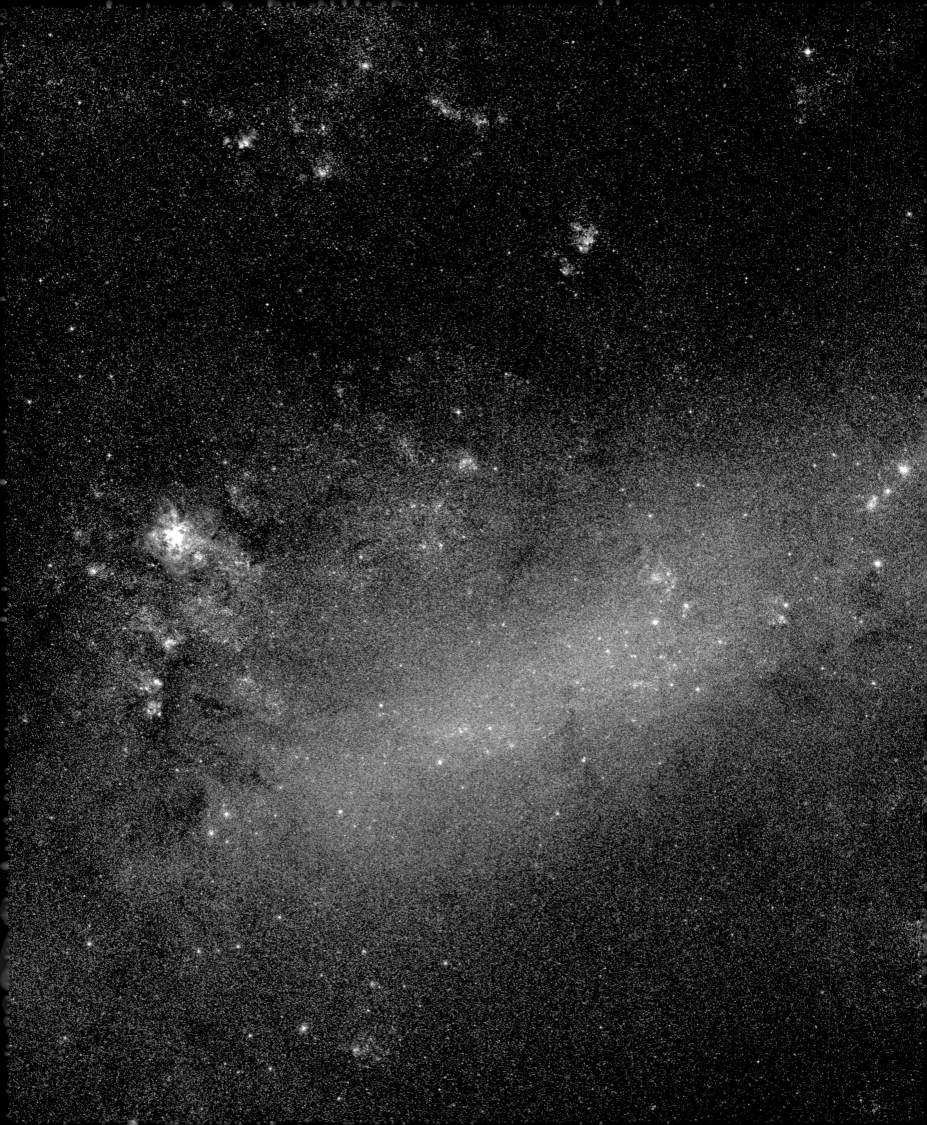

LIGHT SECONDS
LIGHT MINUTES
LIGHT YEARS
KILO LIGHT YEARS
MEGA LIGHT YEARS
GIGA LIGHT YEARS

1

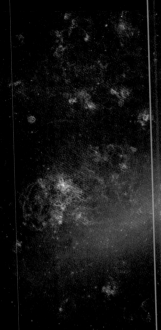

2

Intergalactic visitor

Heralded as one of the Milky Way's finest outposts, the Large Magellanic Cloud is big enough to be thought of as a galaxy in its own right. And the Milky Way may not enslave this satellite galaxy after all; it could be its own master.

Much larger than the globular clusters that surround the Milky Way, and ten times further away, the Large Magellanic Cloud (LMC) displays the trappings and behaviour of a galaxy in its own right. Whereas globular clusters are spent forces and can no longer make stars, the LMC has a full stellar ecosystem at work.

___The entire stellar lifecycle of the LMC is on display here. The smaller stars contribute a suffused glow to a bar across the centre of the galaxy. All told, they number around a few billion. That they are in a bar suggests that this galaxy once had spiral arms of stars, too. They would have curved out from the ends of these bars but are absent today, perhaps ripped away by the gravity of the Milky Way.

___The LMC's heavyweight stars are less ordered, scattered at random around the galaxy. Enshrouded in dust, they show up best at infrared wavelengths, manifesting as glowing knots of red [1]. The green coloured clouds are reservoirs of cooler gas harbouring molecules. These sites are where the next generation of stars will form. Where stellar production is ramping up, bright magenta nebulae gleam with the light of fluorescing hydrogen [2].

___If the globular clusters are the Milky Way's attendants, then the LMC and its smaller cousin the Small Magellanic Cloud (SMC) are honoured guests. However, where they were once thought to be permanent residents, now it seems that they are only paying us a fleeting visit.

___Both galaxies are whipping past at double the speed previously calculated. In the case of the LMC, the speed is nearly 380 km/s. For the SMC progress is a little more sedate: just 300 km/s. At these speeds, the gravity of the Milky Way, huge in reach though it is, would not be able to corral these smaller galaxies into orbit.

___So, instead of satellites, they are merely passers-by, taking in the view before their haste carries them on their intergalactic way. And what a view it is.

___The Milky Way fills a large portion of the sky with its striking spiral shape, arms outlined in silver blue and curled around a core of golden yellow starlight. Glowing red star-forming regions dot those arms and intricate bindings of dust appear to thread everything together.

___With a good star map, it would even be possible to spot the Sun, nestled in the trailing edge of the Orion Spur. Our whole life-giving Sun reduced to a seeming pinprick of light.

060.0

LIGHT SECONDS
LIGHT MINUTES
LIGHT YEARS
KILO LIGHT YEARS
MEGA LIGHT YEARS
GIGA LIGHT YEARS

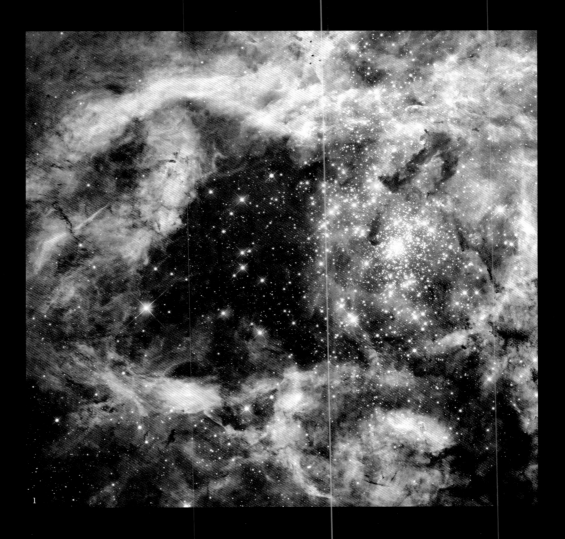

1

Fierce brood

__The giant Tarantula Nebula's gaseous limbs reach
out across 1,000 light years of space, illuminated by
the fiercest centre of star formation in the Local Group
of galaxies.__

We have seen star-forming regions in our own
Galaxy, but nothing like this. The Tarantula
Nebula is 20 times bigger than the Orion Nebula.
If the two were to swap places, the Orion
Nebula would be completely undistinguished,
virtually lost amongst these distant stars.
But the Tarantula would menace the night sky.
It would fill the constellation and cast shadows
across the night-time surface of Earth.
___The Tarantula is so large that no single star
can be responsible for supplying that much
energy to keep it all glowing. Instead, it is
powered by a whole cluster of bright stars [1].
Known as R136, it is a highly compact stellar
bundle. It dates to just a few million years ago
and yet it has already managed to squeeze
stars, to the value of 450,000 solar masses,
into a sphere just 35 light years across.

___Brandishing those statistics, R136 could
be another of the rarest sights in the Universe:
a globular cluster in the process of formation.
Certainly, it is not the first nest of stars that the
Tarantula has built. Another, called Hodge 301,
was born there around 25 million years ago.
That is sufficiently long ago that the more
massive of its stars have already exploded
as supernovae.
___The shock waves from these now dead
stars may have helped R136 to reach its great
proportions by compressing the gas in its
surroundings, thereby forcing more stars to
form while supplying them with plenty of raw
gaseous material. It has led to a dozen stars
with masses more than 40 times that of the Sun;
a couple may be approaching even 100 solar
masses.

___In 1987, a star from the Tarantula Nebula
met its fate. In a sudden nuclear paroxysm,
it was gone: a giant star a dozen times the
mass of the Sun blasted to atoms. Despite
being 160,000 light years away, the light from
the supernova was still powerful enough to
strip a layer of atoms from Earth's atmosphere
when it arrived.
___As the scattered fragments of the former
star reached out into space, travelling much
more slowly than the light from the explosion,
they smashed into a ring of dense gas that
must have been ejected earlier by the star.
As the two debris clouds collided, they lit up
each other in a blaze of X-rays, surrounding
the supernova with a brilliant halo of light. It
will not be the last such event; one by one the
Tarantula's children will meet their own kismet.

200.0
LIGHT SECONDS
LIGHT MINUTES
LIGHT YEARS
KILO LIGHT YEARS
MEGA LIGHT YEARS
GIGA LIGHT YEARS

1

A glimpse of the past

<u>Two and a half thousand pristine new stars burn with
the blue light of stellar youth in this giant interstellar
cloudbank. What kind of giant galaxy houses such a
colossal region of star formation? Not a giant at all,
one of the smallest in the Local Group.</u>

The Small Magellanic Cloud (SMC) [1] contains
only a few hundred million stars. It may
once have had some small measure of spiral
structure but these days it is an irregular fuzzy
ball of stellar light. However, settling down to
a life of quiet mediocrity is not an option. While
most stars in this galactic minnow were created
around 4.5 billion years ago, unknown forces
triggered a new bout of stellar creation some
5 million years ago.

___The emission nebula NGC 346 is the
result of this new episode. Despite its relative
youth it is a celestial time machine, offering a
glimpse into the mighty forces that engulfed
the Universe early in its history. During the
Universe's first billion years, star formation
swept through the cosmos, lighting stellar

fires across the void, populating the Universe
with the first stars.

___NGC 346 has already disgorged one
stellar cargo, with a rippling conglomeration
of massive stars as the vanguard, and it is
preparing its next production run. Embedded
in the dark ribbons of dust that weave through
the blue illumination is a second generation
of new stars in the making. They are busily
pulling together enough mass to take their
place on the nebula's shining stage.

___Because star formation stalled for billions
of years, the SMC has a skewed overall stellar
population. Nevertheless, the trappings of this
latest bout are there for all to see in the shining
nebulae that litter the galaxy.

___Beyond the stars is a rarefied 'atmosphere'

of hydrogen gas. Not only does it surround the
SMC but it reaches to cover the neighbouring
Large Magellanic Cloud, and then extends to
span a much larger volume of space as well.
This common envelope suggests the two
galaxies share a bond; that they are held
together by gravity and travel through space
in company with one another.

___It probably came about when the two
galaxies suffered a near miss some 2.5 billion
years ago. Had they actually collided, the
two would have merged in a lavish display
of star formation that would have smothered
the resulting galaxy in a host of star formation
regions, all resembling the fires of NGC 346.

Andromeda Galaxy

M31

SPIRAL GALAXY

DIAMETER: 141,000 LY

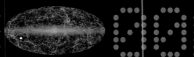

000.0 LIGHT SECONDS
LIGHT MINUTES
LIGHT YEARS
KILO LIGHT YEARS
MEGA LIGHT YEARS
GIGA LIGHT YEARS

2

Stepping stone to the Universe

<u>This beautiful island of stars was the stepping stone to the wider Universe. The furthest object to be visible to the naked eye, it became the subject of serious argument during the early 20th century, as astronomers debated whether it lay inside our Galaxy – or was itself another galaxy in a vastly larger cosmos than had been previously imagined.</u>

The Andromeda Galaxy vies with the Milky Way for domination of the Local Group of galaxies. Locked in combat, the two galactic behemoths are screaming towards each other at 500,000 km/h. In 4 billion years they will collide. In the meantime, Andromeda is harassed by an armada of satellite galaxies that have suceeded in disrupting its spiral structure. In visible light everything appears normal, but infrared wavelengths reveal rings of dust like ripples on a pool [1] and dark arcs devoid of stars within the disc [2]. These are tell-tale signs of a galactic shapeshifter caught between spiral and ring forms.

___The Andromeda Galaxy has always invited speculation about its nature. Dimly visible to the unaided eye as a fuzzy pocket of light, the earliest known recording dates from AD 964 by Persian Astronomer al-Sufi in his *Book of Fixed Stars*, although people must surely have seen it before.

___Viewed through the developing telescopes of the early 20th century, Andromeda intoned a siren's song. To some, its swirling arms convinced them that it was a nearby gaseous whirlpool, perhaps forming a new star. Others wondered whether it could be a whole galaxy, far off in space. But that would mean a revolution in thought, an acknowledgement that the Universe was not just a single collection of stars but broken into

islands and strewn across space as a cosmic archipelago. What was at stake was our understanding of the scale of the Universe.

___Astronomer Edwin Hubble irritated his American colleagues. Originally from Missouri, he studied at University of Chicago and then at Oxford, where the dress sense and pipe smoking that rankled his peers took root. After serving in the US army during the First World War, Hubble turned full time to astronomy.

___He was inspired by observations that showed Andromeda and other spiral nebulae were rotating. His breakthrough came when he identified individual twinkling stars in Andromeda – and not just ordinary stars, but pulsating ones that varied their brightness in regular ways. By comparing them to similar, nearby stars, he showed that Andromeda was a whole galaxy in its own right, containing billions of stars and lying farther away than anyone had previously dared to imagine. This was the true triumph from Hubble's work.

___He showed the world that the Universe extends way beyond the collection of stars that comprises the Milky Way. Our continuation of the work he started has shown that the cosmos is punctuated by billions or even trillions of other galaxies, each containing their own collection of billions of stars. He made the Universe a richer, more detailed place for us all.

1

LIGHT SECONDS
LIGHT MINUTES
LIGHT YEARS
KILO LIGHT YEARS
MEGA LIGHT YEARS
GIGA LIGHT YEARS

1

2

Bejewelled galaxy

The bejewelled arms of the Triangulum Galaxy sparkle into the void. Wrapped around this galaxy's centre, they give the impression of a modest spiral. But looks can be deceiving; Triangulum is bigger than it at first appears.

Not all spiral galaxies are enormous. The Triangulum Galaxy appears to stretch just 50,000 light years across, half the span of our own Galaxy's 100,000 light years. It holds its arms in a wide, relaxed spiral pattern for the Universe to see.

___But don't believe everything your eyes tell you. Switch to infrared and the galaxy reveals its true extent [1]. Tendrils of cold dust reach out, extending the spiral pattern beyond their visible reaches. How these rivers of dark material got there and why they are not forming stars is unknown. What is certain is that they add at least another 10,000 light years onto the diameter of the galaxy.

___Certainly in the visible regions of the galaxy, Triangulum is busily building new stars. The unmistakable red glow of star-forming clouds add sparkle to the galaxy's spiral arms. One particularly impressive construction site is NGC 604 [2]. It draws the eye by dint of its conspicuous size, appearing as a large knot of radiant gas in the outer reaches of one of the galaxy's spiral arms.

___In the centre of this stellar nursery are some 200 hot stars pumping space full of ultraviolet radiation. Now the roles are reversed when compared with our own Galaxy. NGC 604 is 40 times the size of the Milky Way's Orion Nebula, and outshines it by more than 6,000 times.

___As this welter of energy strikes the surrounding gas, it crafts the atoms into a framework of seemingly delicate wisps that drape themselves around the cluster. In reality these gaseous banners stretch for hundreds of light years and have been set into determined retreat by the impact of the starlight.

___There are between 3 and 6 billion solar masses of matter tied up in the stars throughout the Triangulum Galaxy, and a similar amount floating freely as gas and dust. This is roughly a hundred times smaller than the mass of the Milky Way.

___Along with the Tarantula Nebula in the Large Magellanic Cloud, NGC 604 is the other nearest giant star-forming region to Earth. Both of them have been kindled in galaxies much smaller than our own, leaving us to ponder why the Milky Way seems incapable of such a feat. At present, there are no answers.

LIGHT SECONDS
LIGHT MINUTES
LIGHT YEARS
KILO LIGHT YEARS
MEGA LIGHT YEARS
GIGA LIGHT YEARS

Fossil universes

Who would have thought that a class of almost
insignificant galaxies would hold the key to
understanding the earliest stages of the Universe?
Yet this is the promise of the dwarf galaxies
– or fossil universes, as they should be called.

The Sagittarius Dwarf Irregular Galaxy is old school. The stars it contains are keepsakes from a bygone age, more than 10 billion years ago. Back then, galaxies were new and most of the Universe was simply a foamy sea of gas. The foam contained the newly formed stars, cresting on increased densities of gas and loosely aggregating into dwarf galaxies.

___Subsequently, most of those galaxies fell together to form the large galaxies we see today but some remained, isolated and apparently frozen in time. The Sagittarius Dwarf Irregular Galaxy embodies this. It is one of dozens that comprise the most populous members of the Local Group of galaxies. However, in terms of mass and stars, all the dwarf galaxies are completely outweighed by the three main galaxies: our own, M33 and Andromeda.

___SagDIG, as it is known, is a living fossil. Little has changed in this galaxy since the dawn of creation, rather like a sleepy rural hamlet detached from the fashion du jour of the big city. The most obvious sign of this hankering for the past is in the composition of the stars. They share a scarcity of the heavier chemical elements, compared to the modern stars in our Galaxy. Even the central stars in the Milky Way, which are somewhat depleted in the heavier elements, are still more enriched than these stellar anachronisms.

___How can such a primitive object still exist in the modern Universe? Again like a rural hamlet, the pace of life is slower. In SagDIG, this slow motion evolution is because of the comparatively sparse number of stars, just a billion or so. With so few stars there has been little in the way of supernovae to blast heavier

elements back into the gas, stir things up and trigger new stars with more modern compositions.

___Few stars die in SagDIG because few stars formed in the first place. And stellar death of any kind is the essential process by which a galaxy's chemical composition is enhanced with the heavier elements. So although new stars have sluggishly formed, most of the population are between 4–8 billion years old, yet they continue to display the composition that stars would have had 12 or 13 billion years ago.

___When it comes to ingredients for stellar composition, SagDIG continues to use the old recipe, providing a living fossil of the early Universe.

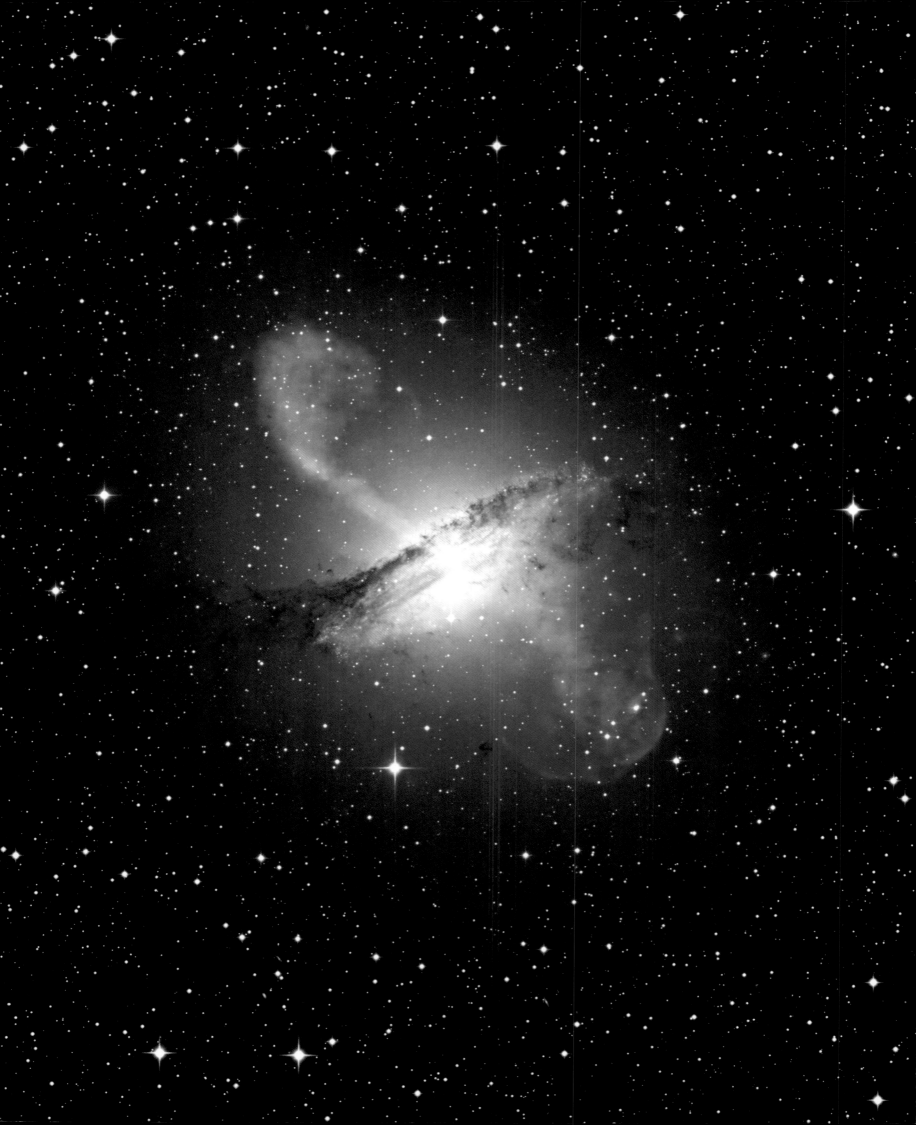

Centaurus A
NGC 5128
ACTIVE GALAXY
DIAMETER: 100,000 LY

LIGHT SECONDS
LIGHT MINUTES
LIGHT YEARS
KILO LIGHT YEARS
MEGA LIGHT YEARS
GIGA LIGHT YEARS

1

2

Galactic glutton

<u>Remarkable jets of particles shoot from the centre of this galaxy. As they interact with the surrounding magnetic fields, so they cry out with radio waves, making them luminous. They are the visible signs of over-indulgence, poorly digested.</u>

Centaurus A almost bit off more than it could chew. One hundred thousand years ago, a smaller companion galaxy drew too close. It was seized and swallowed whole, but it has been giving the greedy galaxy some serious indigestion ever since.

___The remains of the companion can be seen in the obscuring dusty 'tyre-track' that runs across the centre of Centaurus A [1]. But an infrared 'X-ray' [2] provides an even better view of the swallowed galaxy – a bright parallelogram – writhing within its captor. The collision has ignited a maelstrom of star formation, with more than a hundred sites easily visible across the disc. But move away from this disturbed region and there is an air

of false calm. The galaxy's main bulge is composed of old stars, still quietly following their normal orbits.

___The mayhem is repeated in the very heart of the galaxy, for the other winner in this situation lurks there: a billion solar masses compressed into a black hole that is just waiting to devour any stray stars or gas knocked its way. And during the ongoing absorption of the ill-fated companion galaxy, there is plenty for it to feed from.

___As the gas speeds to its deadly rendezvous with the black hole, so it screams out across the Universe, releasing a final cry at radio wavelengths. Somehow, it is also managing to generate sufficient energy to squirt two

enormous jets of electrically charged particles to their salvation, away from the black hole and clean out of the galaxy.

___These jets extend for some 13,000 light years into space and are only slowed because they plough into tenuous gas clouds surrounding the galaxy. A beautiful blue bow shock can be seen surrounding the lower jet, as the faint intergalactic medium is pushed out of the way and set glowing.

___Eventually, when the feeding frenzy is over, Centaurus A will settle down. The black hole and the jets will quieten and the dust lane will disappear, transforming in a plethora of sparkling stars. All will be calm. Order will have been restored.

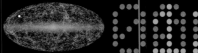

LIGHT SECONDS
LIGHT MINUTES
LIGHT YEARS
KILO LIGHT YEARS
MEGA LIGHT YEARS
GIGA LIGHT YEARS

1

2

3

Might is right

You would be forgiven for thinking that we have turned to look back at the Milky Way. Our own Galaxy certainly shares a similar construction to this one, with its central bulge and winding arms. But no, we are far from home. This is M81 – galactic tyrant.

This beautiful spiral galaxy forms a triumvirate with two other large galaxies. Together, they appear to form a peaceful band of galactic brothers.

___Yet despite its wholesome appearance, there are hints that Bode's Galaxy is a bad apple, and hiding a propensity for violence. There is an ultraviolet surge of new star formation, which is helping to reinforce its spiral arms [1]. The stars are playing the role of the white water on the crests of its density waves. Such events do not just happen by accident; something must be feeding it.

___A central black hole resides at the heart of this galaxy, brooding with a mass of 70 million suns. Although it stands poised, ready to gorge on any star that strays too close, it is quiet for now. So, this is not the reason for the stellar surge.

___More tellingly, the speed of the galaxy's rotation gives away that there are deep reservoirs of matter in the disc and nucleus. Not all of it can have been there from the start or else it would have long since been transformed into stars. So, this spare matter has to be coming from somewhere. Again, this provides an indicator that the galaxy is not the innocent bystander it appears to be.

___The real clue is subtle. In a few places the starry arms break up into mackerel clouds.

And to the left of the nucleus, scars of dust cut across the disc, defying its spiral curve and hinting at a violent past.

___Indeed, not everything is as peaceful as it looks. M81 is ripping two companion galaxies to pieces. Invisible gas is streaming into this galaxy, bolstering its mass, and feeding it with fuel to grow larger and make more stars [2 & 3]. When it comes to satiating its appetite for more gas, this galaxy knows no bounds. But you have to look at its victim, the neighbouring galaxy M82, to truly appreciate the rapacity of its craving.

LIGHT SECONDS
LIGHT MINUTES
LIGHT YEARS
KILO LIGHT YEARS
MEGA LIGHT YEARS
GIGA LIGHT YEARS

1

Into the inferno

Once a spiral galaxy, M82 has been reduced to wreckage. Beginning a few hundred million years ago, a close pass with a neighbouring galaxy stripped it of its finery and transformed it into an inferno of star formation. It has metamorphosed into a galactic throwback.

Star formation in M82 is running hot. In a central region 1,500 light years in diameter, the stellar production line is racing ahead ten times faster than in most galaxies today. Indeed, the Cigar Galaxy is five times brighter than the entire Milky Way, although only a quarter of the size.

___It began during a raid a few hundred million years ago, during which its larger neighbour M81 snatched away vast quantities of gas from M82. This left the remainder of M82 to collapse into itself, kindling a wave of stellar genesis that continues to this day.

___Almost 200 giant star clusters are known to exist in M82, each one holding enough mass to make 20,000 sun-like stars. Much of this mass is locked away temporarily into extremely high-mass stars. These live for

just a few tens of millions of years before blowing themselves to pieces in powerful detonations that contribute even more terrible energy to the centre of the galaxy.

___The result is that the galaxy is now eviscerating itself in fusillade after fusillade of supernovae. This gives rise to the Cigar Galaxy looking like a gigantic galactic explosion, with gaseous debris that has been dragged or blasted from the galaxy now hanging above and below the main disc. This material is now beginning the slow process of raining back down onto the galaxy, helping to trigger a new round of star formation. Higher temperature gas, colour-coded blue [1], leaves the galaxy altogether, destined to be scooped up by M81.

___Such a cacophony of stars and gas could be what most galaxies looked like 10 billion

years ago. Back in those ancient cosmic times, the star formation was uniformly higher in almost every galaxy; the result of smaller galaxies colliding and merging in the bid to grow into the mature galaxies of today. In some cases the stellar output was several hundreds of times the current average.

___As this tremendous starburst engulfed the Universe, so the flood of ultraviolet radiation ripped apart almost every atom, sundering the outer particles, called electrons, from their atomic nuclei. Only one in every thousand atoms escaped.

___This watershed in history is known as the Reionization. It set the stage for the modern cosmos of today, when galaxies came of age and settled into a general state of quiescence, allowing their constituent atoms to combine once more.

LIGHT SECONDS
LIGHT MINUTES
LIGHT YEARS
KILO LIGHT YEARS
MEGA LIGHT YEARS
GIGA LIGHT YEARS

1

2

Firecracker galaxy

<u>Like firecrackers on New Year's Eve, chains of new stars
are bursting into life throughout this galaxy. Baubles of
red gas mark areas of active star formation, indicating
that the stellar production line is in full swing.</u>

NGC 4449 bears a remarkable similarity to
the Milky Way's Large Magellanic Cloud. It is
about the same size as our neighbour, has a
similar number of stars and, most interestingly,
has an elongated shape rather than a
spherical one.

___Such elongated structures are called bars
and are often seen near the centre of much
larger galaxies joining the spiral arms to the
nucleus. In the case of NGC 4449, and indeed
the LMC, the spiral arms are completely missing.

___At invisible radio wavelengths, NGC 4449
no longer seems such a dwarf. The galaxy
sits in the centre of a gigantic bubble of
unilluminated hydrogen, 14 times the
expanse of the visible portion.

___At the core of the galaxy is a tinge of yellow
light, indicating the presence of long-lived
stars. This signals that stars have been forming

here for several billion years, but most of the
visible stars in the rest of the galaxy are vibrant
blue and date to within the last 5 million years.

___Hundreds of thousands of these sparkling
gems now inhabit the galaxy, each one destined
to burn its fuel so quickly that it will exist for
only a hundred million years at the most.
These short-lived stars cluster together into the
equivalent of cities and towns, with the rural
expanses marked out by dark clouds of dust,
held in silhouette against the flaming starlight.

___The huge number of these stars signals an
unusually intense bout of star formation – a
starburst that is continuing to this day. Brilliant
twists of red hydrogen are the heralds of yet
more newly minted stars. If the current rate of
creation continues, the galaxy will transform
all its spare gas into stars within a billion years.

___Such widespread activity is thought to

resemble the primordial galaxies that grew by
merging with one another billions of years ago.
It is highly likely that the same is happening
here, with NGC 4449 sent into frenzy by a
collision with a smaller galaxy.

___Today, no hint of the galactic bullet remains
but its effects are brilliantly visible for all to see.
Whereas starbursts are usually confined to the
central regions of the stricken galaxy, in NGC
4449 they have spilled outwards into streamers
that wind through the whole assemblage.

___Starbursts can rekindle otherwise faded
dwarfs. NGC 1313 [1] is a sickening spiral
galaxy being rejuvenated by a new wave of
starburst activity sweeping round its limbs.
NGC 1569 should be an insignificant island
of stars. Instead, it is being tormented into
blazing activity by a group of 10 surrounding
larger galaxies [2].

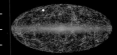

LIGHT SECONDS
LIGHT MINUTES
LIGHT YEARS
KILO LIGHT YEARS
MEGA LIGHT YEARS
GIGA LIGHT YEARS

Grand designs

The spiral pattern of some galaxies is no accident.
They result from waves of denser gas passing round
the galaxy, acting like stellar flypaper and sparking star
formation in their wake. But what triggers these density
waves remains elusive.

Only 10 percent of spiral galaxies display a grand design, making them rare beauties to be cherished. The grand design spirals are those that display prominent arms of blue stars. In many cases, these arms can be traced from the nucleus to the outer edges of the galaxy.

___Seldom do grand designs come much bigger than that at work in the Pinwheel Galaxy. Its sweeping arms curve across 170,000 light years of space. The galaxy rotates, trailing these giant arms and taking about 250 million years to complete one revolution.

___The arms in all spiral galaxies can be more or less tightly wound, suggesting that the pattern is produced by rotation, rather like the way cream swirls in a stirred cup of coffee. But it cannot be this simple. Stars closer to the centre of the galaxy do indeed move faster than those on the outer edges, but this would wind the spirals up within just a few revolutions and there are too many grand design spirals to believe that they have all been observed during this transition phase.

___Instead, the spiral arms are like stellar flypaper, somewhat denser regions of the disc, which attract old stars into them. These stars eventually move back out of the arms but their lingering passage concentrates their starlight, helping the arm to glow.

___Unlike flypaper, the spiral arms also stimulate the growth of new stars. They do this by attracting and compressing clouds of gas that might have not otherwise burst into star formation. As the clouds fall into the spiral arm, they will also tend to collide with one another. Such smash-ups are certain to provoke them into forming stars.

___In this way, the spiral pattern moves around the galaxy at a fixed speed, maintaining its shape by inveigling the help of existing stars.

___But what creates these denser regions in the first place remains unclear. They could be instilled in the galaxy when it first forms as ripples in the primordial gas, or they could be fostered later by the gravitational perturbation of a nearby companion galaxy.

0100.0 LIGHT SECONDS
LIGHT MINUTES
LIGHT YEARS
KILO LIGHT YEARS
MEGA LIGHT YEARS
GIGA LIGHT YEARS

1

Missing limbs

A spiral galaxy but without spiral arms. This is not the only distinction making the Sombrero Galaxy unusual. A large dust lane without star formation, a giant central black hole without activity; it's a galactic enigma.

The Sombrero Galaxy breaks all the rules. The most striking feature of this galaxy is the dust lane that cuts across its equator. Mixed in with this dust are large quantities of cold hydrogen gas, and on the face of it, this should supply plenty of material from which to make stars but there are no clouds of glowing hydrogen to signal any widespread stellar manufacture.

___Its lack of interest or ability in making stars has led to the Sombrero losing its spiral arms – if it ever had any in the first place. The result is a confusing galaxy that displays similarities to both spiral and elliptical galaxies. Like an elliptical, it possesses a large central bulge of stars, but like a spiral it then surrounds this with a disc of older stars, dust and gas [1]. In total, the Sombrero is home to some 800 billion stars, four times the number in the Milky Way, yet it spans only half the size: 50,000 light years.

___The distended central bulge conceals a sleeping giant of a black hole. Judging by the speed at which stars are orbiting the centre of the galaxy, the Sombrero plays host to one of the largest supermassive black holes in the nearby Universe. Clocking up an impressive one billion solar masses, this dark behemoth has certainly been busily devouring other celestial objects. But now, it seems to have lost its appetite.

___There are no jets of gas or cataracts of X-rays shooting from this monster. For now it seems replete, reassuring the stars around it they are safe. Nevertheless, there is a mystery here. A short-wavelength form of radio emission is coming from the centre of the galaxy. Investigation shows it's not coming from the dust, nor the gas, nor the particles caught in the galaxy's magnetic fields. So at present, its origin is completely unexplained.

___Just to complete the picture of this enigmatic galaxy, it is surrounded by a plethora of globular clusters. Estimates place the census at between 1,200 and 2,000, roughly 10 times as many as are gathered around our own Galaxy. No one knows why this should be the case.

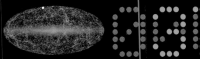

LIGHT SECONDS
LIGHT MINUTES
LIGHT YEARS
KILO LIGHT YEARS
MEGA LIGHT YEARS
GIGA LIGHT YEARS

1

Sinister beauty

Looking for all the world like a whirlpool of stars being
sucked down into the centre of the galaxy, M51 is one
of the grandest of the grand design spiral galaxies.
But beauty is a fragile thing; M51 could so easily have
become an ill-defined mess.

M51 is not the largest of galaxies; it spans just 40,000 light years, about half the size of our Galaxy. Yet its bulk almost equals the Milky Way at some 160 billion solar masses, and it boasts equally mighty coiled arms rendering it one of the most pronounced spiral galaxies in the Universe.

___Two broad arms of brilliant stars wrap themselves around the nucleus, displaying blisteringly hot stars in blue and stellar nurseries in glowing red. One of these stretches onwards, all the way to the faded yellow glow of a dwarf galaxy that sits close by [1]. The smaller galaxy, NGC 5195, has been significantly distorted by the gravitational

might of M51. It may once have been a lenticular shape, but now it is an amorphous clump that defies classification.

___It has made two close passes to M51. The first took place as it approached from behind around 500 million years ago, and the second about 50 million years ago. Now it lies just slightly further away from us than the big spiral.

___Had it smashed into M51, the glorious spiral pattern would have been destroyed, torn apart by the dramatic clash of gravitational forces. The orderly stars would have been thrown from their orbits, creating a random mess that would have settled eventually into an elliptical shape.

___As it was, NGC 5195 missed by just 10,000 light years or so – a hair's breadth in galactic terms. Maybe it was this close shave that bestowed such extreme beauty upon M51. As the weaker gravitational field of the companion swept across the disc of the larger galaxy, so it could have generated or strengthened the ripple of gas that has so clearly defined the spiral arms.

___Now M51 looks as if it is extending an arm to comfort its errant companion. In reality it is probably preparing to drag it the rest of the way to its doom. The bully's crushing strength of gravity has already begun the process of dismembering and devouring the dwarf.

LIGHT SECONDS
LIGHT MINUTES
LIGHT YEARS
KILO LIGHT YEARS
MEGA LIGHT YEARS
GIGA LIGHT YEARS

1

On the edge

Turn this galaxy through 90 degrees, so that it appeared face-on, and it would present a moon-face. Pale and round, it would be almost indistinguishable from an elliptical galaxy. However, viewed from the side, the difference becomes clear: it is rake-thin.

The Spindle Galaxy is only a spindle from this angle. In actuality, it is a flat disc, like NGC 2787 [1], that we happen to be seeing exactly edge-on. It is another example of a spiral galaxy that has lost its spirals.

___It has undoubtedly been a vigorous exponent of star formation in the past because the milky glow of starlight lies all around this galaxy. But over the past few hundreds of millions of years, so the pace has slowed and the spiral shape has disappeared. Now all that remains is a central bulk of stars, an almost featureless disc and a diffuse halo of older stars.

___What this lenticular galaxy lacks in spiral structure, however, it more than makes up for in dust. A dense dust lane runs around its nucleus. It is mostly condensed towards the central regions of the galaxy, petering out in the outer extremities. But this could be enough. Close inspection of this reservoir reveals that all may not be lost for the Spindle Galaxy.

___There are dusty projections that stand proud of the main disc. These elephantine trunks reach outward for hundreds of light years and are more like giant geysers of dust that are being blown upwards to rain down over a large area of the galaxy.

___The only celestial objects that can muster the kind of power necessary to drive such fountains are hot, massive stars that are expelling furiously. Their cascade of light and particles is sufficient to loft huge quantities of dust into these celestial fountains.

___From the number of them, it appears that there could be a widespread renaissance of star formation taking place. Perhaps it is even enough to begin a rippling pattern of density variations around the galaxy to restore it to spiral splendour. Sadly, even if this were to happen, it would be largely lost to our view, as we will continue to look at it side-on.

LIGHT SECONDS
LIGHT MINUTES
LIGHT YEARS
KILO LIGHT YEARS
MEGA LIGHT YEARS
GIGA LIGHT YEARS

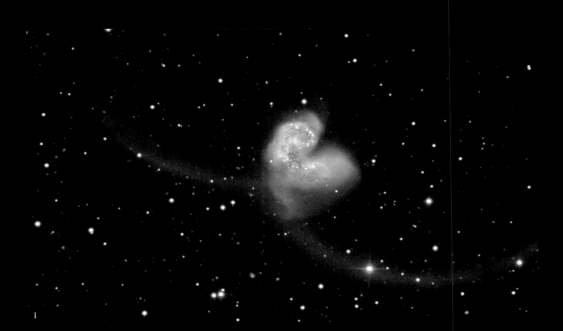

1

Clash of the titans

<u>In galactic terms this is the ultimate heavyweight clash.
Two evenly matched galaxies are going head-to-head.
Yet, in the harsh reality of the Universe, there cannot
be a winner. What started with an undeniable mutual
attraction, now signals the end for both galaxies; and
also a new beginning.</u>

The bout began billions of years ago, when these galaxies felt the first tentative caress of each other's gravity. At that stage they were both preening spirals, basking in the glow of the Universe. Gently at first they began to edge towards one another. With each onward step, so the attraction became stronger until it was impossible to avoid their destiny to be together.

___They began racing onward at an ever-accelerating rate, gripped by an unalloyed gravitational passion to be together. But as they drew nearer so the true nature of the impending encounter became apparent. This was not to be a tender embrace, but a confrontation, a fight to the death.

___When they first touched, just over a billion years ago, the mayhem truly began. They ripped away each other's spiral arms and scattered them to the stellar winds. A firestorm of star formation flared in both galaxies, and the interstellar clouds clashed in mighty collisions.

___Two long tails of stars [1], which give the system its name, mark where these galaxies have cut through space on their way to this deadly embrace. Many other stars in the bulk of the galaxy have yet to be directly affected by the titanic fight going on around them because the space between the stars is so wide. Most stars never actually collide, even during the closest of passes.

___The galaxies have already travelled through each other once, and are now falling back together again for the final round in this match. They are within just 400 million years of becoming one indistinguishable mass of stars. As this conglomeration settles into a new equilibrium, and the spree of star formation subsides, so the two original shapes will entirely disappear, the once spiral grandeur lost for evermore.

___But this is not the very end. In their place will be a mighty elliptical galaxy, presiding over the other galaxies in the locality, youthful beauty replaced by age and the wisdom of having lived through a titanic event.

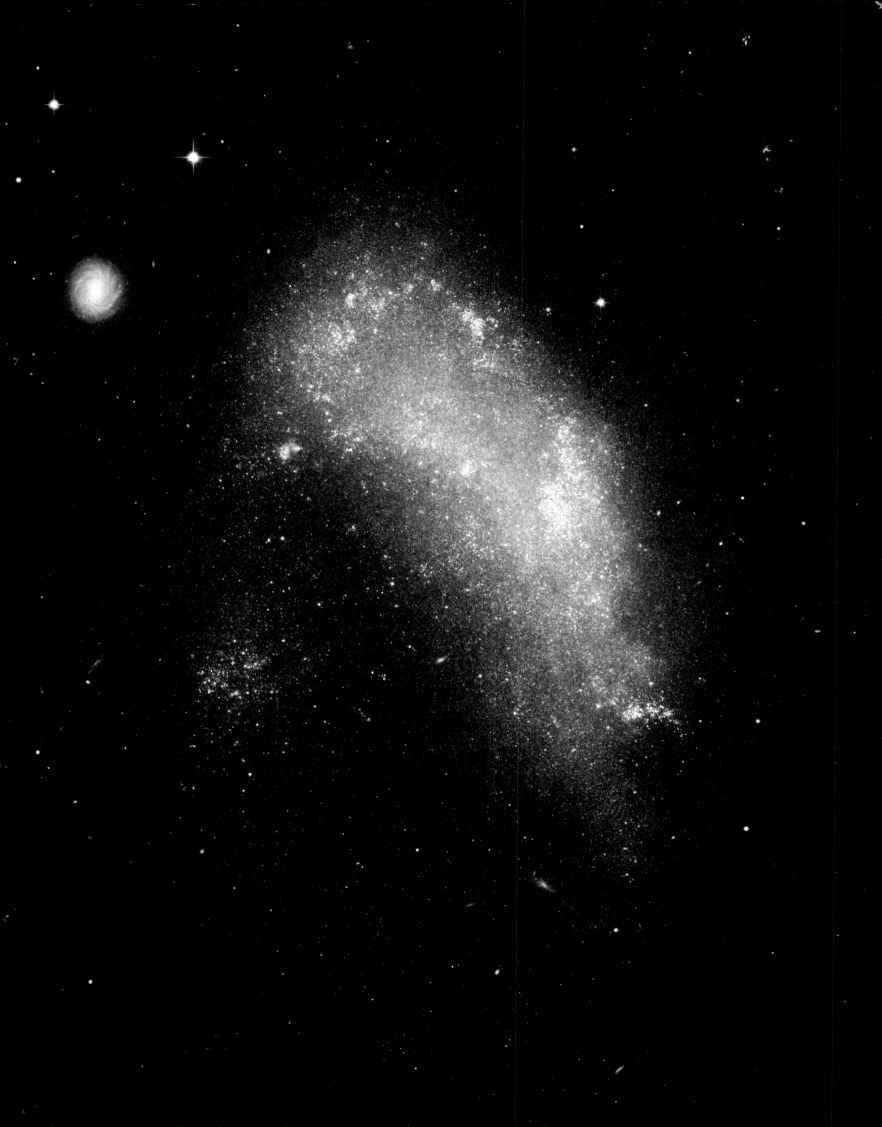

LIGHT SECONDS
LIGHT MINUTES
LIGHT YEARS
KILO LIGHT YEARS
MEGA LIGHT YEARS
GIGA LIGHT YEARS

Surreal stars

It looks like the way Salvador Dali would have painted a galaxy, with one part of it melting away. But this is reality. The brush that fashions NGC 1427A's surreal aspect is a tidal force. On Earth, tides produce the ebb and flow of the ocean; in space they rip galaxies apart.

Doomed is the only word to describe this dwarf galaxy. Its journey through space has taken it too close to a cabal of galaxies called the Fornax Cluster, and their combined gravity has pulled it off course. Now, they are dragging it down into their midst at speeds of more than 600 km/s.

___The galaxy owes its distorted appearance to gravity accelerating its forward edge faster than its rear. This is because gravity weakens progressively with distance and the galaxy, although classified as a dwarf, is still roughly 30,000 light years long. So, the strength of gravity acting on the front is much greater than on the rear, with the result that the galaxy is being stretched.

___This has created a so-called tidal force. They are at work throughout the Universe,

from the oceans of Earth to the moons of Jupiter and beyond; but on intergalactic scales, their power is exaggerated.

___As time goes on, and NGC 1427A dips deeper into the cluster, it will be elongated even more. Eventually it will be pulled into a piece of stellar spaghetti, before losing any final semblance of coherence.

___As it falls, the galaxy is being forced through the cluster's envelope of gas. This creates the intergalactic equivalent of air resistance, and helps to define the 'arrowhead' shape of the galaxy. It also promotes a final round of star formation in NGC 1427A. Short-lived bright blue stars now outline the galaxy, where the intergalactic gas has impacted the margins and compressed the dwarf's own clouds of gas into new stars.

___These stars and the older ones in the centre of the dwarf will eventually be cast off randomly into the cluster. Some will be attracted to the other galaxies and captured by them. Taking their places in the stellar complement, only their eccentric orbits will betray that they were not formed there in the first place.

___Other stars will escape the galaxies' clutches to spend the rest of their lives wandering the cluster in isolation. There must be vast numbers of lonely stars drifting in the orphaned expanses of intergalactic space. However, being such tiny motes against the vastness of the cosmic night, they are rendered almost invisible by sheer distance, and so remain as yet undiscovered.

LIGHT SECONDS
LIGHT MINUTES
LIGHT YEARS
KILO LIGHT YEARS
MEGA LIGHT YEARS
GIGA LIGHT YEARS

1

Spiral evolution

<u>The overwhelming feature of this galaxy is its elongated shape. It has what amounts to a bar of stars running between its nucleus and the beginning of the spiral arms. These elongated galaxies could be the next step in a spiral galaxy's evolution.</u>

The spiral arms themselves are a relatively poor feature of this galaxy, even though they number four in total with two being far more prominent than the others. Overwhelming them all is the large bar that spans more than 60,000 light years and accounts for most of the width of NGC 1672. Rejig the catalogue numbers and you have NGC 6217, another fine specimen of a barred spiral galaxy [1].

___Barred spiral galaxies are more prevalent in the modern Universe. They account for nearly two-thirds of nearby spirals. Tellingly, their numbers have tripled during the last 7 billion years of cosmic history, about half the age of the Universe. This suggests that bars represent the final mature shape of a spiral galaxy.

___The mass of the galaxy helps to determine how quickly a bar can form with the most massive spiral galaxies developing so fast that they manifest bars early. Nowadays, the other spirals are catching up. For example, our Milky Way has a modest bar connecting its nucleus to its spiral arms.

___Bars form in a galaxy when otherwise circular stellar orbits are perturbed and begin to take on elliptical shapes. They start lingering along certain paths and this leads to a bar beginning to build. As the bar forms, so it ensnares more and more stars in it, reinforcing its durability. It also becomes a trap that can funnel dust and gas down into the centre of the galaxy.

___In NGC 1672 this sudden arrival of edible matter has woken up the supermassive black hole in its core. It measures somewhere between 10 million and 100 million solar masses and is presently eating its way through a celestial meal. Being a typically messy eater, it is splashing quantities of hydrogen, helium, nitrogen and oxygen all over the place, which is then lighting up under the glare of the doomed matter nearby.

___Not that the doomed matter is going without a final hoorah. As it is progressively squeezed toward its gravitational Rubicon, so it is giving birth to a teeming mass of new stars. This starburst entirely surrounds the black hole providing its own brilliant radiation.

1

Swimming upstream

NGC 4522 knows what it is like to swim against the current. It is being inexorably pulled down into a morass of giant galaxies. As it is being dragged faster and faster through the surrounding gas, so it is being stripped of its contents.

Spiral swirls of dust and stars lift from this galaxy, apparently forced upwards by the pressure of the surrounding gas through which it is travelling. The galaxy is falling like a stone. Its downward plunge has been clocked at more than 10 million km/h.

___It is just one of the 1,300 members of the Virgo Cluster of galaxies. The great round bulks of the elliptical galaxies are concentrated towards the centre of the cluster, while the flighty spirals are more evenly distributed around the edges, spread throughout a lozenge-shaped region of space that spans millions of light years.

___This is the nearest large grouping of galaxies to the Milky Way, and it dominates the nearby Universe. The Virgo Cluster contains around ten trillion solar masses

of material and is so immense that it is even tugging on our own Local Group of galaxies. So, if we can feel the gravitational attraction towards Virgo, some 60 million light years away, then NGC 4522, situated within it, stands no chance.

___The hapless spiral galaxy is fighting against the pressure of the tenuous mist of gas known as the intergalactic medium. Although this gas is only very sparsely spread through space, it exerts a stinging force when encountered head on at high speed. While it is not enough to lift whole stars out of the galaxy, it is doing a good job of cleaning out the gas.

___As they levitate away from the galaxy, the fleeing gas clouds are being sufficiently compressed to sire new stars, and as these

burst into radiant life they give the illusion that the galaxy is evaporating away.

___While the density of the intergalactic gas is tantamount to nothing, a million billion times more rare than fresh air, it still mounts up when the enormous volumes of space are considered. The pressure from the surrounding gas has actually curved NGC 4402 at the edges; another victim of the Virgo Cluster's titanic pull of gravity [1].

___Fully half of the atoms in the Universe are thought to be located within the intergalactic gas. If the gas stays there, none of it will ever transform into clumps dense enough to form stars and galaxies. Eventually, some may be pulled into nearby galaxies and thus finally take part in the gravitational game of star formation there.

LIGHT SECONDS
LIGHT MINUTES
LIGHT YEARS
KILO LIGHT YEARS
MEGA LIGHT YEARS
GIGA LIGHT YEARS

1

The archetype

So beautiful it's used as a galactic archetype, NGC 1300 is a fine example of a barred spiral galaxy. But that's not all. It is an ordinary spiral galaxy, too. The spiral within a barred spiral can be found embedded in the centre of the galaxy.

At 110,000 light years across, NGC 1300 is large for a spiral galaxy and contains myriad fine details across its arms, bar and nucleus. The entire galaxy is bejewelled with blue and red supergiant stars, clusters of stars, and star-forming regions. Dust lanes braid the arms and the bar, showing marked asymmetries between the opposing sides of the galaxy. The dark dust lanes show up almost like a skeleton, with the starry surrounds providing the celestial equivalent of flesh.

___Star formation is particularly active in the inner regions of the spiral arms, where matter is thought to be queuing up to flow along the bar and into the central bulge of the galaxy.

___And it is in the core of NGC 1300 that there lies a surprise. The central nucleus displays a distinct 'grand design' spiral structure, a small version of the grandest of the spiral galaxies [1]. This miniature replica is about 3,300 light years wide. It could have formed because matter is being funnelled along the bars and into these central regions; certainly on one side of the galaxy, the rate of star formation seems to be much higher than on the other.

___The spiral within a spiral is not the only mystery here. The other is found or, more accurately, not found in the very centre of the galaxy. With all the matter that is supposedly being channelled down that way, one should

expect the supermassive black hole there to be wide awake.

___But the centre of this galaxy is as quiet as the grave: no untoward radio waves or X-rays springing from it. Could this be a galaxy without a central black hole? Maybe, but that would seem to go against everything known about galaxy formation. Yet, if there is a black hole then it is a peculiarly fussy eater, refusing all that is presumably being handed to it.

___Something doesn't add up about NGC 1300. Perhaps it is not quite the archetype it was once thought.

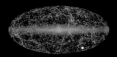

LIGHT SECONDS
LIGHT MINUTES
LIGHT YEARS
KILO LIGHT YEARS
MEGA LIGHT YEARS
GIGA LIGHT YEARS

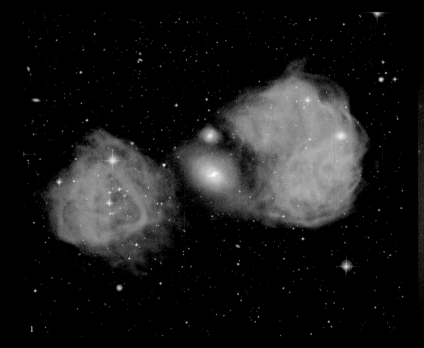

1

2

Dusty chimera

Here's another galactic puzzle: NGC 1316 looks like an elliptical galaxy except that it is riven with dust. Such lanes of raw stellar ingredients are more in keeping with a spiral galaxy. So, just what kind of galaxy is NGC 1316?

Take away the dark markings of dust and NGC 1316 would be an archetypal elliptical galaxy. It is a little on the small side at just 60,000 light years in diameter but, in keeping with the larger ellipticals, it shows no sign of recent star formation and glows with the pale light of older stars.

___However, it does not live in the elliptical galaxy neighbourhood of the Fornax Cluster. Instead of plumping for the centre of town, it chooses a place in the suburbs, where the majority of spiral galaxies can be found.

___Tuning into the celestial radio frequencies shows that, while the galaxy is only modest at visible wavelengths, in reality it is a giant. Two fat lobes of radio emission sit on opposite sides of the galaxy [1]. Individually, each is bigger

than the galaxy itself. In total, from the outer edge of one lobe, across the galaxy to the outer edge of the other, the distance is a million light years.

___The radio lobes themselves must have been excited by incredibly accelerated jets of particles generated in some way near the supermassive black hole at the centre of the galaxy. The particles will have bored their way through the galaxy and out into intergalactic space. Now, however, there is no sign of these jets. The lobes themselves are probably the fading remnants of the previous activity that once lit up this galaxy.

___In the visible outer regions of the galaxies, many structures can be seen: ripples, loops and arcs of stars all point to the idea that two

galaxies are in the final phase of merging here. In the centre of the galaxy is a compact disc of gas that rotates faster than the stars. It is probably what is left of the gas that slid into the central black hole, and created the radio lobes in the process.

___So what is NGC 1316? Is it a stellar shambles that has yet to make up its mind which way it is going? Most likely, it is an elliptical galaxy merging with a spiral galaxy and, like the chimera of lore, it now shows features of both. Galactic chimeras are not uncommon, many galaxies display such mixed features, like the dusty ring wrapped around the otherwise elliptial NGC 7049 [2].

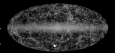

LIGHT SECONDS
LIGHT MINUTES
LIGHT YEARS
KILO LIGHT YEARS
MEGA LIGHT YEARS
GIGA LIGHT YEARS

1

2

3

Tug of war

It's a tug of war between two galaxies. They've been locked into this Herculean struggle for millions of years, and the rope they are using is nothing less than a whole other galaxy.

Not every cluster of galaxies is huge. While it is the giant clusters that most easily grab the attention, there are far greater numbers of smaller galactic groupings. Our own Local Group is one such example with its 30 or so members. But even this looks big compared to the compact groups.

___Each one of these modest galactic gatherings contains from three or four galaxies to just half a dozen or so, but they are every bit as capable of drama as their far-larger cousins. In the case of the Hickson Compact Group (HCG) 90, two of its members are fighting for possession of the third.

___NGC 7173 and NGC 7176 are smoothly contoured elliptical galaxies, existing without much excess gas or dust. Now, they have

developed new appetites for these components and have set about their companion galaxy NGC 7174 to provide them. They have mangled its spiral shape as they continuously plunder its contents, drawing it on a gravitational rack into a long braiding of light and shade.

___These days, the damaged NGC 7174 barely clings to an independent existence, and it will not be long in cosmic terms before it is decimated. The strong tidal forces surging through the galaxy from both of its so-called companions will rip it to pieces. Already significant numbers of its stars have been strewn around the group, forming a diffuse glowing halo.

___So intent on their tug of war are the competing elliptical galaxies that they may

already have crossed the point of no return and are even now heading for their own destruction. Drawn too close together by their greed for NGC 7174, they run the risk of collision. If so, where there was once a group, eventually there will be a single giant galaxy, providing a home for tens to hundreds of times the number of stars in the Milky Way. Such apparently catastrophic collisions are a natural, necessary and not unusual part of galactic life: deep space resounds to the clash of galaxies [1, 2 & 3].

___But it is not always like this. Sometimes, these modest groupings can be elegantly dispersed so that each galaxy has its own space to perform a graceful minuet, rather than HCG 90's feverish tarantella.

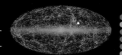

LIGHT SECONDS
LIGHT MINUTES
LIGHT YEARS
KILO LIGHT YEARS
MEGA LIGHT YEARS
GIGA LIGHT YEARS

1

The memory of youth

If our eyes could see in X-rays, this is what galaxies
would look like. Their stars hidden away, all that
remains to be seen are the high-temperature gas
clouds. At the centre of this throng, directing its motion,
lies a supermassive black hole.

One in ten of all galaxies displays some sort
of remarkable activity springing from its core.
It cannot be coming from stars alone because
the quantity and type of light does not match.
Instead, the central engine is a supermassive
black hole containing anything from a few
million to a few billion times the mass of
the Sun.

___The black hole itself cannot release energy.
Once matter crosses the outer boundary known
as the event horizon, it ceases to be able to
communicate in any way with the outside
Universe – this is what makes a black hole
black. But on the way to their doom, the gases
heat up significantly and radiate copious
quantities of farewell energy.

___In the supermassive black holes found in
the young galaxies called quasars, this energy
shines across space as ultraviolet and visible
wavelengths. It is so intense that, despite being
billions of light years away, the quasars were
initially confused with stars. This even gave
rise to their name, which stands for quasi-
stellar object.

___In this particular galaxy, things are a little
more sedate even though the black hole is
still clearly in charge. NGC 4696 [1] is an
elliptical galaxy and the brightest member
of the Centaurus Cluster, a conglomeration of
hundreds of galaxies located about 150 million
light years from Earth.

___The X-rays show up as red and betray vast

mottled clouds of hot gas. The blue lobes on
either side of the galaxy's core are 10,000-light-
year-wide bubbles, hollowed out by particle
jets generated by the strong magnetic fields
that are formed in the vicinity of the black hole.

___The turbulence that this creates within the
galaxy's corpus of gas is enough to prevent
new stars from forming. Any small knots of gas
that do begin to form will soon by swept away
and dispersed back into the galaxy.

___In its youth, this galaxy was almost certainly
a tearaway, blazing across space as a quasar
during those formative years. Even though
it has now settled down, the X-ray glow at
its heart shows that it still remembers what it
was like to be young and powerful.

988.9
LIGHT SECONDS
LIGHT MINUTES
LIGHT YEARS
KILO LIGHT YEARS
MEGA LIGHT YEARS
GIGA LIGHT YEARS

1

Magnetic monster

Like a circular saw slicing through a tree trunk, a spiral galaxy has scythed its way into a larger elliptical. The resulting catastrophe has unleashed a powerful response from the black hole at the heart of the elliptical galaxy.

The dark dust lanes of the attacking galaxy's spiral arms symbolize the teeth of this particular saw blade. It appears to have gone straight for its victim's heart, aiming for the very centre and colliding headlong with the destructive black hole lurking there.

___It has made a particularly foolhardy choice of victim. NGC 1275, also known as Perseus A, is a monumental elliptical galaxy. It sits at the centre of the Perseus Cluster and directs the movement of the other galaxies. Its response to this vicious assault has been immediate and devastating.

___The interplay of titanic forces around Perseus A's central black hole has resulted in the creation of magnetized bubbles of gas, only visible at X-ray energies [1], that have grown to enormous size. Each one now spans

50,000 light years, half the width of our Galaxy.

___Smaller bubbles have risen faster and further, drawing out colder gas behind them to create shining threads that stretch for 20,000 light years into the surrounding intergalactic space. Typically just 200 light years wide, and containing enough gas to make a million stars like the Sun, the threads are so long they must have been forming for 100 million years.

___It is initially baffling that the threads can be this old. The gaseous strands are tens of millions of degrees cooler than the surrounding intergalactic gas and so they should have been buffeted and blown about, losing their carefully delineated shapes long ago. If the winds in the 70,000,000 °C intergalactic medium failed to disrupt them, then the gravity of the parent galaxy should have ripped them apart. But no,

something is magically holding them in place.

___In fact, it is not magic but magnetism. Magnetic fields must be corralling these threads, binding them together and strengthening them against the destructive forces that would otherwise seek to bring them down. The more fragile-looking the filament, the stronger the magnetic bracing required to keep it stable.

___The pulled threads of NGC 1275 are a striking example of intergalactic magnetic fields and highlight another way, other than gravity, that the supermassive black holes in giant galaxies reach out and attempt to control their wider environments.

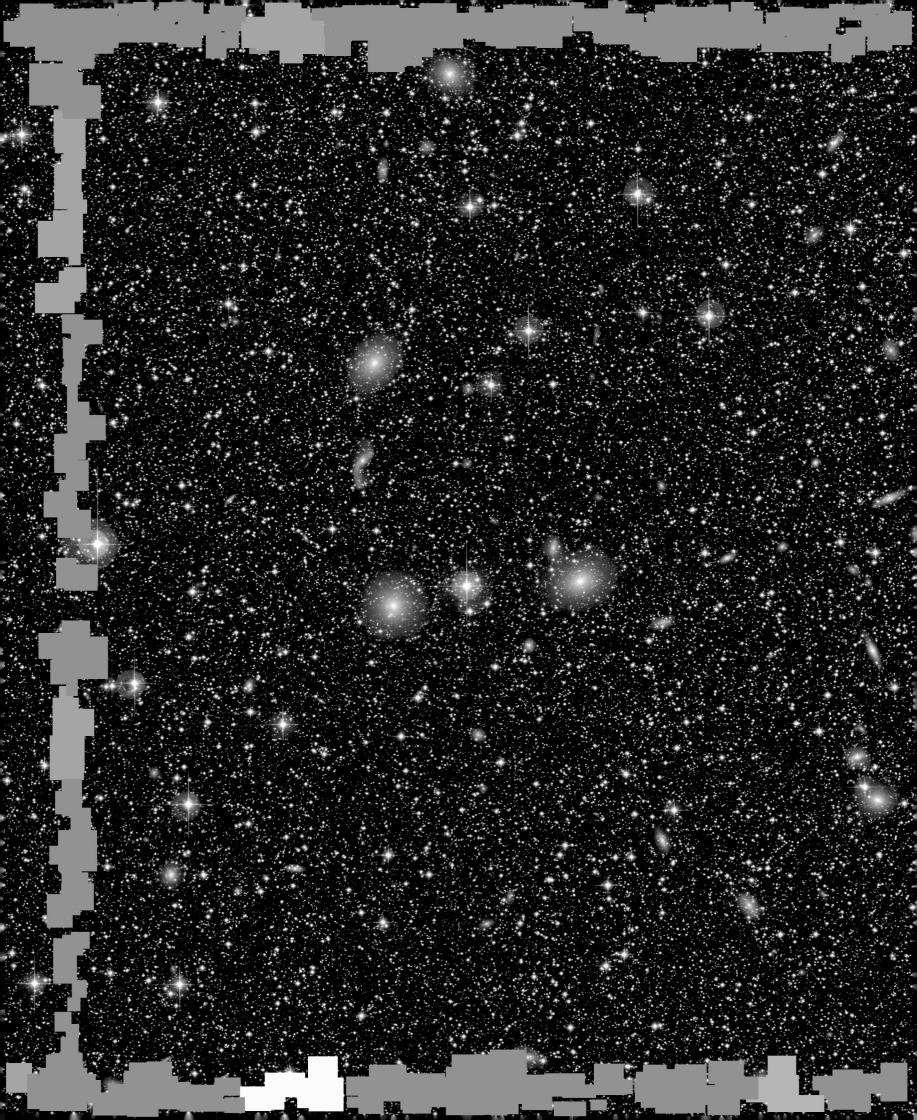

LIGHT SECONDS
LIGHT MINUTES
LIGHT YEARS
KILO LIGHT YEARS
MEGA LIGHT YEARS
GIGA LIGHT YEARS

Towards the Great Attractor

Galaxies glow green in this colour-coded image of the Norma Cluster. Thousands of galaxies are estimated to live here. Moreover, this is no ordinary galaxy cluster; it sits in a gravitational anomaly known as the Great Attractor.

Many galaxies are part of larger groupings. If the group contains more than 100 individual galaxies it is known as a cluster, and the Norma Cluster is one of the largest in the local Universe. It is estimated to contain the equivalent of several thousand galaxies the size of the Milky Way.

___It sits in a region that was dubbed the Great Attractor because, when the movement of all the galaxies in the nearby Universe is taken into account, they are clearly streaming towards the Norma Cluster at speeds of hundreds or even thousands of kilometres per second. Millions of galaxies are involved in this headlong rush through space, firey trails of hot gas streaming behind them [1].

___The cluster, while massive, does not seem to contain anything like the necessary abundance of galaxies to perform this feat of attraction and so, for a while, it was thought that this region of space must contain an egregious quantity of extra matter, and most of it probably in a form unknown on Earth. Such 'dark matter' would outweigh the normal matter by ten to one.

___Calculations showed that it must be spread over an area 400 million light years across. However, fate has rendered the region largely invisible as it sits hidden behind the bulk of the Milky Way in the Zone of Avoidance, locked away from further investigation. To underline this cosmic censorship, the stars of the Milky Way in this direction appear as dense as snowflakes in a blizzard, as if occupied in the attempt to conceal the distant galaxies from view.

___Recently, however, the Great Attractor has been shown to be an imposter. While there is a clear enhancement of matter in this region of space, it is not as large as first thought. We were being fooled by an even larger collection of galaxies lurking behind the Norma Cluster.

___Called the Shapley Supercluster this gargantuan grouping is responsible for dragging the Milky Way and all the other galaxies in the nearby groups and clusters. Approximately 650 million light years away, the supercluster is a cluster of galaxy clusters, containing 20 times the number of galaxies as there are in our immediate galactic neighbourhood. It is the largest concentration of galaxies in the nearby Universe and it is making sure we don't ignore it.

The Mice

NGC 4676A, 4676B

COLLIDING GALAXIES

DIAMETER: 300,000 LY

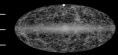

LIGHT SECONDS
LIGHT MINUTES
LIGHT YEARS
KILO LIGHT YEARS
MEGA LIGHT YEARS
GIGA LIGHT YEARS

1

2

3

The tale of two galaxies

These colliding galaxies are known as the Mice because of the starry tails that stretch out behind them, but if you were to speed up time they would remind you more of a massing flock of starlings swooping and merging as the fancy took them.

In reality, the drama of these merging galaxies will play out in apparent slow motion over the course of billions of years. But if the cosmic film could be speeded up, then their behaviour would seem very different. Its the old story: galaxy meets galaxy against the cold backdrop of space, they feel an immediate attraction, but then it all starts to go horribly wrong. Snapshots of three other merging galaxies stand in to provide the opening frames of the story, showing this first encounter [1, 2 & 3].

___Then, as the Mice circle each other, so the tails lose their blue sheen as the massive stars die. They tarnish to the dull yellow of longer-lived stars, before experiencing a final flush as those stars swell into red giants and die.

___The galaxies draw ever closer and their stars surge this way and that like flocks of birds until eventually the two galaxies plunge together forming a single system of stars. The newly formed gestalt galaxy wobbles like a jelly, as the stars jostle for position, acclimatizing to the suddenly cramped environment in which they find themselves.

___But the real drama is just starting. Across the galaxy, the individual clouds of dust and gas are ploughing into one another, triggering giant compression waves as they slam together. As they merge, growing darker and more menacing with each passing moment, eventually something has to give. When the celestial thunderhead finally bursts, jagged forks of star formation leap across the clouds. Initially red with the hue of fluorescent hydrogen, they turn almost immediately to blue as the searing brilliance of the most massive stars reveals itself. Then abruptly the fireworks really start.

___Star after star bursts vividly and then disappears from view. These are supernovae. They blast bubbles in the galaxy, transforming the dense environs into Swiss cheese. Dust and gas are launched away into space, only to form fountains of matter as the galaxy jealously grabs them back, pulling them down into the fold once more.

___Eventually, when all the spare dust and gas have been used up and the maelstrom has died down, the surviving stars are left to huddle together. Comforted by the warm glow of their fellows, they apparently settle to their new way of life as an elliptical galaxy. But the newly enlarged galaxy is constantly alert. Its bolstered gravitational field is ready to grasp and consume any tasty galactic morsel that strays too close.

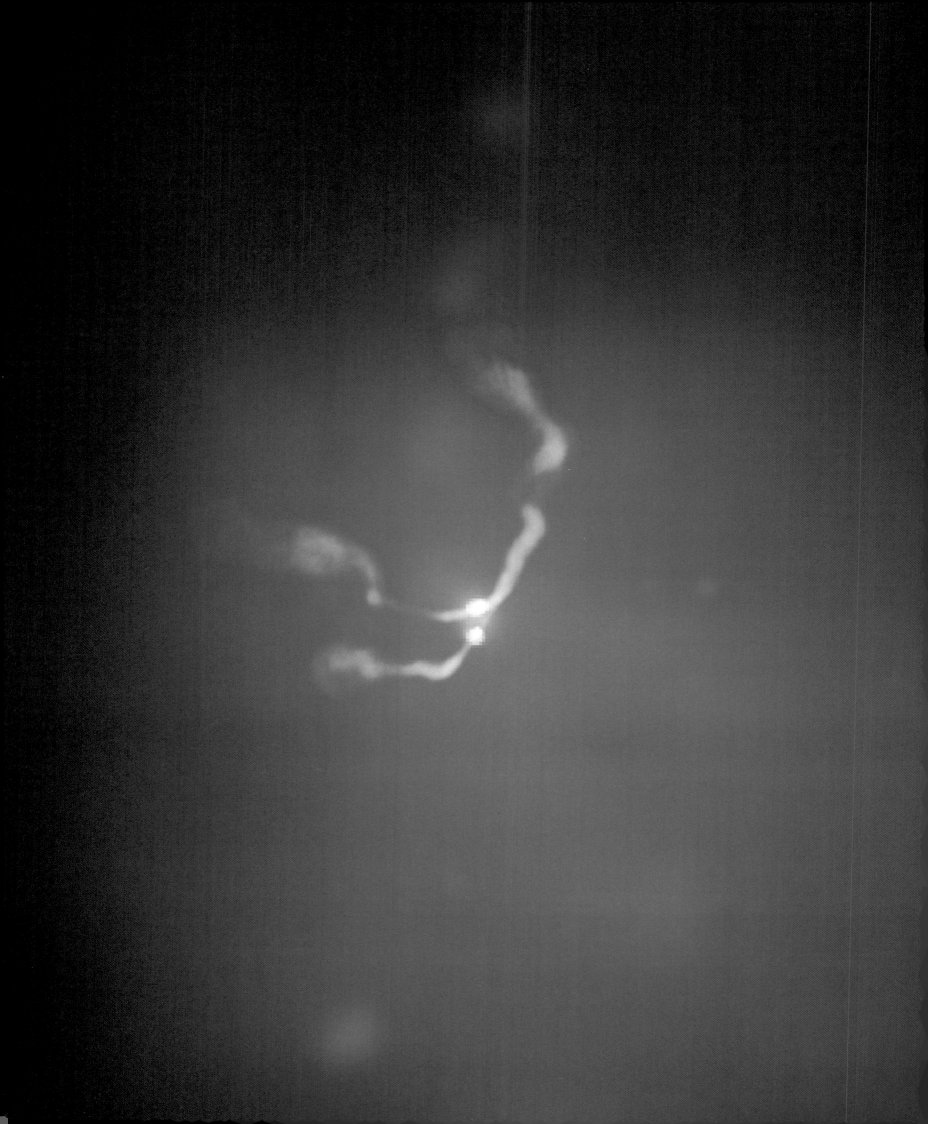

3C 75
_____
COLLIDING GALAXIES
DIAMETER: 100,000 LY

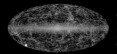

LIGHT SECONDS
LIGHT MINUTES
LIGHT YEARS
KILO LIGHT YEARS
MEGA LIGHT YEARS
GIGA LIGHT YEARS

1

2

Black hole collision

This cosmic X-ray of a colliding galaxy pair sees right through the stars and into the guts of the system. It shows a brace of supermassive black holes heading for a deadly heart to heart – a collision that will unleash a blast of energy more powerful than the light of every single star in the Universe combined.

Trailing devil horns of gas, these two gigantic black holes are heading for Armageddon. Once upon a time, each was the heart of a separate galaxy. Now the galaxies are merging to form a larger collection of stars, and the black holes are circling each other like predators, sizing each other up before a duel.

___As they complete each revolution of the other, so they inch closer. They are spiralling together, separated now by just 25,000 light years and plunging headlong through their ever-decreasing orbits at 1,200 km/s. This is just the first of three phases.

___The second phase happens quickly and is known as the plunge. This is the moment when the black holes touch. Exactly what happens next is unknown for sure because black holes continue to defy our understanding, but most likely there will be an extraordinary release

of energy – bad news for the merging galaxy in which they live.

___The calculated quantities of energy that will be liberated in the plunge defy imagination. Such an event is second only to the Big Bang itself in terms of the energy that is released. In the case of the Big Bang, the Universe was created and all of cosmic history was set in motion. For a black hole merger, the burst could spell death and destruction for hundreds of thousands of star systems. The radiation will vaporize nearby stars and planets, rip atmospheres off otherwise habitable worlds, and blast away clouds of star-forming material. Not only this, it will set the very fabric of space quivering in this third and final phase, known as the ringdown.

___Space itself acts like netting, supporting

the Universe's various celestial heavyweights. Catastrophic meetings of extreme mass, such as black-hole mergers, set off disturbances in this netting that ripple through space at the speed of light. They distort the shape of everything they pass through: stars, planets, moons – nothing escapes their temporary warping ability.

___But the size of the distortion is so small, being just a fraction of the width of a hydrogen atom's nucleus, that so far such ripples have completely evaded detection.

___3C 75 is not the only object doomed to suffer this fate. NGC 6240 also harbours two supermassive black holes spiralling towards each other [1]. Already their interaction has lit X-ray fires that threaten to engulf the galaxy [2].

196
197

LIGHT SECONDS
LIGHT MINUTES
LIGHT YEARS
KILO LIGHT YEARS
MEGA LIGHT YEARS
GIGA LIGHT YEARS

1

When galaxies go to war

This is intergalactic war. No ray guns or rockets but whole galaxies tearing each other limb from limb. The galaxies in Stephan's Quintet are all engaged in the deadliest of battles. But one combatant is a sham, a bystander, tricking us into believing that it is involved.

The first compact galactic group to be identified, Stephan's Quintet is a battleground. The conflict consists of full-sized galaxies waging war against each other for gravitational control of the environment.

___Starbursts blaze in all the galaxies like cities set aflame, and rashes of star formation scream out across the combatants' weary bodies. A magnificent arc of starburst activity curves around two of the galaxies, NGC 7318A and B. It appears to be a shield of light, protecting the individuals behind it. Instead, it is a monstrous shockwave created as NGC 7318B charges into the attack at millions of kilometres per hour, heading for the centre of the fray. It shines particularly brightly at X-ray wavelengths [1].

___NGC 7318A and B are both under attack from the larger barred spiral galaxy NGC 7319, but they are inflicting telling damage on their assailant. NGC 7319 trails a wounded arm of star formation, dislocated from its bulk by the gravitational force of the two smaller galaxies. Or maybe it has been inflicted by a sneak attack from behind by the spiral galaxy NGC 7320C, just out of shot at the top of this image. NGC 7320C shares a similar distance from Earth to the rest of the galaxies and, although it appears to be separate from them, the tidal arm does curve in its direction.

___At the bottom of the image, the compact elliptical galaxy NGC 7317 is biding its time, choosing its moment carefully, as if waiting for

its hot-headed neighbours to weaken themselves sufficiently before sweeping in for the kill.

___The flanks of the beleaguered pair NGC 7318A and B also seem to be coming under attack from the bright spiral galaxy to the left. This is NGC 7320, the brightest galaxy in the grouping. When the group was first discovered it was thought to be a full member. However, subsequent investigations have shown that it is sited far away from the others, separated by around 160 million light years.

___Even though NGC 7320 is not part of the group, that is cold comfort to the other members, engaged in this most bitter of intergalactic conflicts.

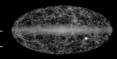

LIGHT SECONDS
LIGHT MINUTES
LIGHT YEARS
KILO LIGHT YEARS
MEGA LIGHT YEARS
GIGA LIGHT YEARS

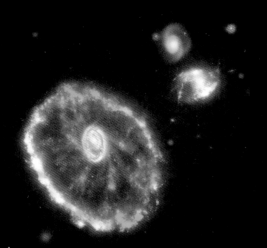

1

Brief encounter

This galaxy wears a spectacular ring encrusted with stellar diamonds. Most galaxies that collide with their neighbours end up as addled ellipticals but once in a blue moon, something magnificent happens and the galaxy ends up more beautiful than ever.

Ring galaxies are forged when an intruder plunges through the disc of a spiral galaxy like a bullet piercing a paper target. The aggressor has to be another galaxy that packs about the same mass as its victim so it can punch cleanly through. Such an impact sets off a ripple of star formation around ground zero that forms a ring as it spreads out across the target's disc.

___In the majority of galaxy collisions, both parties are equally to blame, enticing the other closer and closer in a swirling orbital dance. Ring galaxies are an exception. They are the product of truly accidental collisions, two galaxies on entirely independent paths that just happen to be in the wrong place at the wrong time.

___The nucleus of the target galaxy is not disrupted because it is tightly bound by gravity and the spaces between the stars are large enough for the galaxies to slide through one another with few actual stellar collisions. If it were not for their mutual gravity, the galaxies would then continue on their journeys into the eternal night, like passing ships.

___As it is, the collision sets in motion a giant shockwave that rolls outwards, compressing the gas and kindling a ring of star formation. In AM 0644-74, the ring looks elliptical. This is probably because the ring is tilted from our line of sight. Not so easy to explain is the fact that the yellow nucleus is also offset. This could

mean that the galaxy is denser on one side than the other, so the shockwave is finding it harder to propagate in that direction.

___The Cartwheel Galaxy [1] is an example of an older ring galaxy. About 200 million years ago it was a spiral galaxy, perhaps similar to our own, but then disaster struck as a smaller, compact galaxy ripped through it. Now, with the shockwave reaching the outer rim of the galaxy, the spiral arms have a chance to reform, looking like the spokes in a wheel. In another 100 million years, the Cartwheel will have completely forgotten the attack, the ring will have faded and it will once again regain its spiral composure.

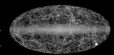

LIGHT SECONDS
LIGHT MINUTES
LIGHT YEARS
KILO LIGHT YEARS
MEGA LIGHT YEARS
GIGA LIGHT YEARS

1

The time of giants

This is the shape and size of things to come. Across the
Universe, where currently there are whole groups of
galaxies, eventually only gargantuan ellipticals will
remain. The subtle dwarfs and the splendid spirals that
once ruled space will all have merged together, giving
rise to giant unstructured galaxies.

Although referred to as a fossil group, NGC
1132 really demonstrates a taste of things
to come. It was once a collection of dozens
of galaxies, all bound in gravitational
brotherhood. But as time has passed, so the
brothers lost energy and inched towards
the centre of the group, making things more
crowded and pushing up the chances of
collision. One-by-one, the galaxies slammed
into one another. In the resulting havoc,
stars were flung from their established orbits
and the bulk of the galaxies merged together
into a single indistinguishable clump of stars.

___The survivors of those numerous collisions
are the thousands of orphaned globular

clusters that now swarm around this galaxy,
each parent digested somewhere inside
NGC 1132's lustrous bulk. The globulars
themselves look like stars in this image but,
by pinpointing them, subtle differences such
as the age of their stars and their compositions,
can reveal how many galaxies went into the
making of this giant.

___Switch to X-ray wavelengths [1] and NGC
1132 becomes larger still, sitting in an ocean of
hot gas ten times larger than the collection of
stars. This gas has been heated by the violence
of the collisions and spread throughout space
as a tenuous mist, far too insubstantial to clump
together to form new stars. As future aeons

pass it will gradually cool and sink back
down towards the giant elliptical.

___Our own Galaxy seems destined to become
a giant elliptical. The process may already
have begun, because the Milky Way and the
Andromeda Galaxy are heading towards each
other. The two spirals are closing at a speed
of 120 km/s but, given that there are 2.5 million
light years separating the two, any collision
is still more than 3.5 billion years in the
future. By this time, the Earth will already be
uninhabitable because of the Sun's evolution
to higher temperatures.

NGC 4921 _____
SPIRAL GALAXY _____
DIAMETER: 180,000 LY _____

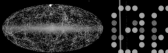

LIGHT SECONDS
LIGHT MINUTES
LIGHT YEARS
KILO LIGHT YEARS
MEGA LIGHT YEARS
GIGA LIGHT YEARS

1

Fountain of youth

<u>Anaemic is the only word that can describe this galaxy.
Its pallid arms are revealed in infrared as glowing milky
white, and star formation has all but stopped. With no new
stars to replenish its bulk, this galaxy could even be dying.</u>

NGC 4921 is undoubtedly a faded beauty. Its remaining structure, while delicate, is a mere palimpsest of what it must have been. In its prime, this galaxy would have drawn attention to its graceful arms by draping them in azure-blue stars, bold indicators of youth and beauty. Now, the only signs of stellar vigour are to be found in a dusty necklace surrounding the nucleus. Here, massive stars are visible, radiating their characteristic blue light.

___The rest of the galaxy is simply fading away as the stars die out. In another billion years or so, the arms will probably have withdrawn completely into the shadows. At that point, NGC 4921 will have to be reclassified as a lenticular galaxy. All that will remain is the central stock of stars in the elongated nucleus.

___As if that were not bad enough, the galaxy is bleeding hydrogen into space, losing the very gas that could make new stars. But there may just be a fountain of youth from which to revive this galaxy.

___It exists in a rich assemblage of other galaxies called the Coma Cluster [1]. The galaxies float like islands in a vast ocean of gas and are composed almost exclusively of large ellipticals and lenticulars.

___In dense clusters such as Coma, spiral galaxies tend to be endangered species. The crowded environment promotes interactions and mergers that erode the delicate patterns and transform the spirals into messy elliptical galaxies. As a result there are fewer spirals in this 1,000-strong grouping than in other quieter

corners of the Universe. Of those that do live here NGC 4921, despite its palid appearance, remains the brightest.

___But encounters need not always be destructive. As the myriad galaxies weave their orbits, they often draw close without actually colliding. Proximity allows the galactic neighbours to gravitationally reach out and touch each other. Such interactions can reignite quiescent galaxies, breathing new fire into them by prompting the remaining gas clouds to collapse in frenzies of star formation.

___If this were to happen to NGC 4921 it would experience a brief renaissance, a final lease of life before the inevitability of age caught up with it once and for all.

LIGHT SECONDS
LIGHT MINUTES
LIGHT YEARS
KILO LIGHT YEARS
MEGA LIGHT YEARS
GIGA LIGHT YEARS

1

Another brick in the wall

Unlike the larger, richer clusters, which tend to destroy their spiral galaxies in collisions, Hercules is more sedate and the pace of life is slower. But, this doesn't mean that the Hercules Cluster is some galactic backwater, it is actually part of the largest structure we have yet come across.

A hundred galaxies gather together in loose association in the Hercules Cluster. Most of them are spirals, affording us a look at what many clusters used to be like before infighting produced populations of mostly elliptical galaxies.

___Within the extended family of this cluster, there are a number of smaller units. Arp 272 is a beautiful pair of galaxies [1]. Look closely and they appear to be cradling a third, smaller galaxy in their arms. Yet these galaxies are anything but loving parents; the same old fights are kicking off, driven by the same gravitational jealousies and greed.

___These two galaxies are in a neck-and-neck race to consume the smaller galaxy. Not even that will satiate their appetites, once they have despatched their hapless victim, they will turn on each other, each galaxy attempting to

cannibalize the other. The only winners in this dog-eat-dog situation will be the three giant black holes, one from each galaxy. They will gorge themselves on as much of the stellar carrion as they can before merging into a single supermassive black hole. When that has happened, the galaxy will take its place with the other ellipticals in the cluster.

___There is a marked difference in the colours of the different galaxy types. Blue marks out the recently formed, short-lived stars in the spirals while gold denotes the older, long-lived stars, which dominate elliptical galaxies. Yet, 400 million light years from Earth, individual galaxies are becoming less important, relegated to the status of building blocks for the clusters of galaxies that dominate the Universe on this scale.

___The Hercules Cluster itself is the densest

collection of galaxies within a larger gravitationally bound structure called the Hercules Supercluster. Whereas the clusters and the superclusters are cloud-like, their three dimensions being roughly equal, there is a marked change of shape in the larger groupings. There are no cloud-like mega-clusters. Instead there are long wall-like filaments and sheets of galaxies, and the Hercules Cluster is just another brick in the Great Wall.

___Stretching for a length of at least 500 million light years and a height of 300 million light years, this extraordinary structure of galaxies is just 15 million light years deep. And the length of the Great Wall is a conservative estimate, because it disappears behind the Milky Way's Zone of Avoidance and is lost from view.

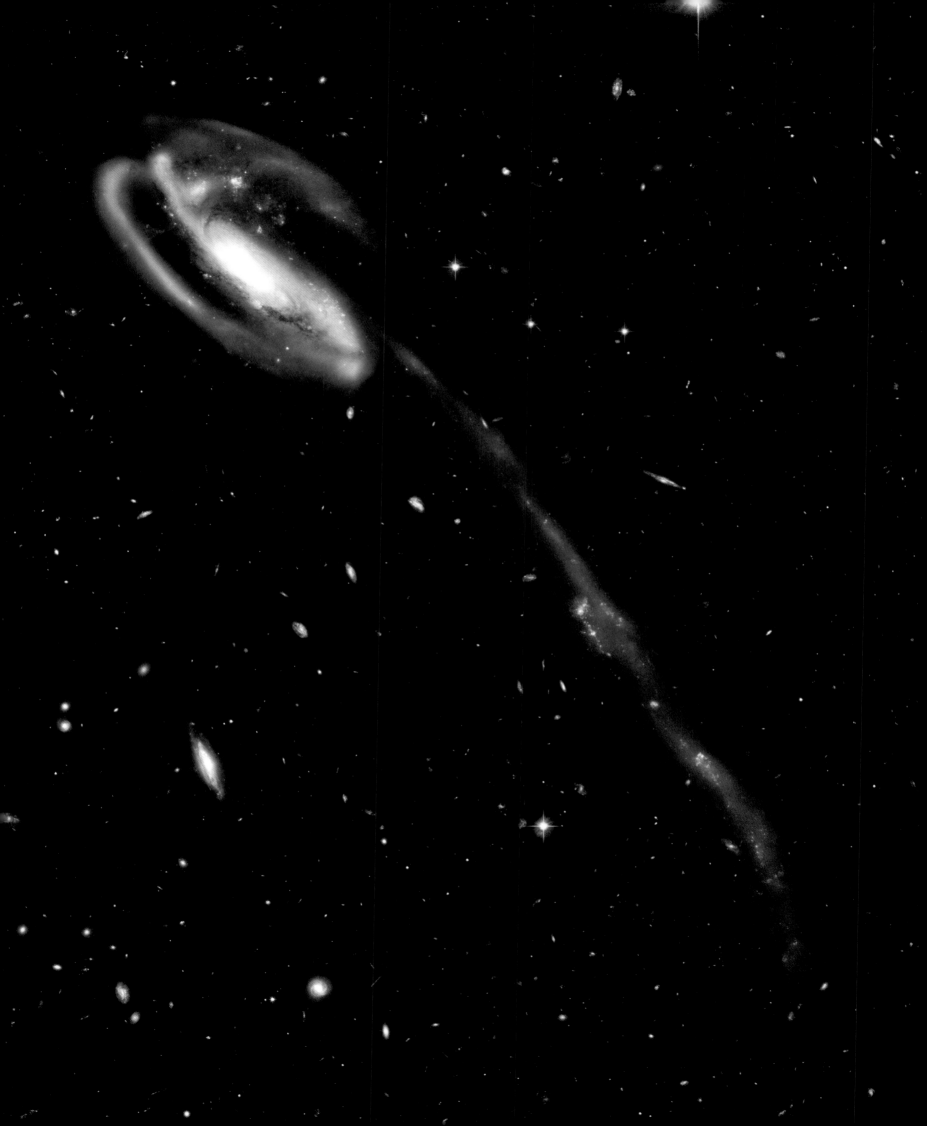

LIGHT SECONDS
LIGHT MINUTES
LIGHT YEARS
KILO LIGHT YEARS
MEGA LIGHT YEARS
GIGA LIGHT YEARS

1

2

Knight in shining armour

<u>This galactic knight is ready for the joust. Its lance of stars is poised, 280,000 light years long. But there is something missing from this contest. While the galaxy has obviously been damaged from a previous round, at first sight there is no sign of its opponent.</u>

Tadpole-like tidal tails are not uncommon [1&2], but there is something unusual about this particular one. Wherever they appear, they are a sure sign of a grand gravitational conflict between two galaxies. But in this image only one somewhat battered barred spiral is obvious. Six thousand other galaxies share the image but not one of them can be the missing combatant because they are all much further away. They are there simply to provide a tapestry backdrop.

___The mystery of the missing galaxy deepens. For a while it was thought that perhaps an entirely invisible galaxy was crossing swords with the Tadpole, and we were seeing just the visible portion of this galaxy's struggle with the dark side.

___A plethora of star clusters have been kindled by the galaxy collision. These are not just visible along the tidal tail but around the spiral arms too. Each one of these stellar associations can contain around a million stars, each one 10 times hotter than the Sun and a million times brighter.

___But wait, there is something bigger buried in there too – much bigger – near the nucleus of the Tadpole. Just to its top left is a knot of stars much too large to be a star cluster. It is the core of the interloping galaxy. It must be a dense galaxy, punching well above its weight to take on the whole Tadpole. It has passed by once, drawing out the tidal tail and is currently 300,000 light years behind the Tadpole.

___No one knows whether the small galaxy has finished harassing the larger one or whether it has more mischief in mind. Assuming that it now decides against a second pass, then the Tadpole Galaxy, just like its terrestrial namesake, will eventually lose its tail as the bright stars fade away. But a legacy will remain; a couple of dwarf galaxies are forming within the tail. They will linger in train with the main galaxy, or may even begin orbiting around it.

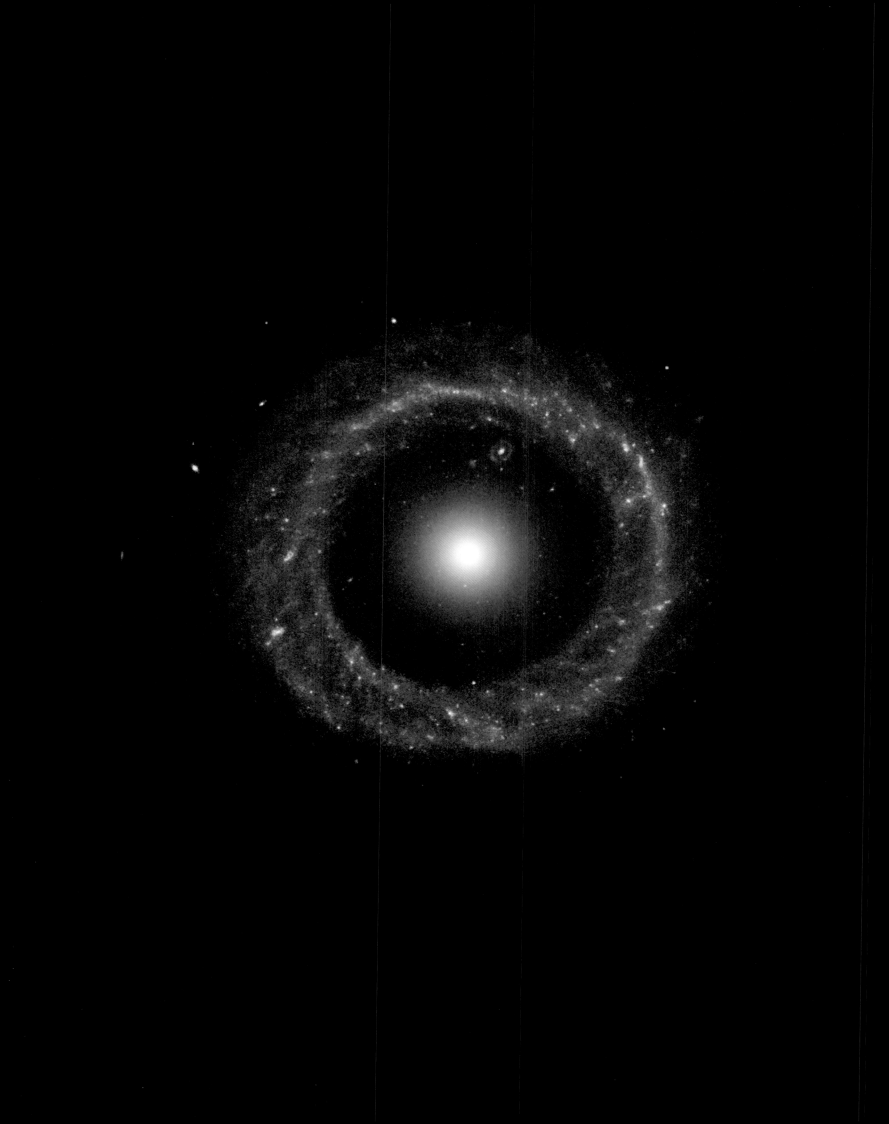

Hoag's Object

PGC 54559

RING GALAXY

DIAMETER: 100,000 LY

LIGHT SECONDS
LIGHT MINUTES
LIGHT YEARS
KILO LIGHT YEARS
MEGA LIGHT YEARS
GIGA LIGHT YEARS

Direct hit

Hoag's Object took it on the chin. Another galaxy
smacked it fairly and squarely, passed straight through
and continued on its way. In response, a shockwave
developed around Hoag's old nucleus, creating this
shimmering halo of new stars.

Such intergalactic bull's eyes are rare events,
afflicting far less than one percent of the
galaxies in the Universe. Even when such a
ring galaxy forms, it is usually distorted in
some way. Hoag's Object is remarkable for its
delectable symmetry: a spherical nucleus in
the dead centre of the perfectly circular ring
of stars.

___As rare as ring galaxies are, by the luckiest
of cosmic coincidences another one appears in
the background, reddened by its distance and
shrunken by perspective. Nevertheless, it is
another almost perfect ring galaxy.

___Most ring galaxies are thought to form
as one galaxy passes through another. Such
an encounter is dramatically captured in
Arp 148 [1]. Like a bullet through a bubble, the

target galaxy gives the illusion of having been
shattered by the impact. Both galaxies have
been distorted by the collision but, in this case,
only one will emerge as a ring galaxy.

___An incredible double pair of ring galaxies
form the Arp 147 system [3]. Although they
lack the perfect symmetry of Hoag's Object,
they are a vanishingly rare sight. The starry
blue ring, some 30,000 light years in diameter,
was most probably created when the galaxy
on the left dived through an existing spiral
galaxy. The orange knot at the lower left of the
blue ring is the vestige of the target galaxy's
original nucleus. But most fittingly, in a rare
case of poetic justice, the left-hand intruder has
also been transformed by the encounter into
a ring galaxy.

___There is a subset of galaxies that are
more puzzling. They are called the polar
ring galaxies [2] and, as the name suggests,
their adornments are not equatorial but
perpendicular. They are still formed when
two galaxies approach each other too closely
but, instead of one galaxy slamming through
the other, the larger one drapes the smaller
around itself like a scarf on a winter's day.
Or it draws out a seam of gas, transforming
it into a starry necklace.

___Some polar rings are to be found around
elliptical galaxies. However, most of them
surround lenticular galaxies, indicating that
the central galaxy paid for its adornment by
losing its spiral arms,

INTER
TEMPORAL

We finally reach the largest scales of the Universe. Just as planets gave way to stars, which gave way to galaxies as our vista expanded, now the galaxies give way to the clusters. On distances of over a billion light years, we see a significant fraction of the cosmos, and the large-scale structure is revealed: a cosmic web of galaxy clusters that string themselves across the entire Universe.

Each cluster contains from a few hundred to a few thousand galaxies. These collections can be elongated or spherical in shape, and can contain predominantly spirals or be overwhelmingly composed of elliptical galaxies. There are numerous smaller groups, each of a few dozen galaxies or so, but on these cosmic scales they are too small to concern us.

___It is the distribution of the clusters that catches the eye on these scales. They are but individual enhancements in the much larger grouping, superclusters that twist through space. They are strung into filaments that weave around large empty bubbles of cosmic wasteland, the voids.

___Also at this scale, gravity begins to lose its overwhelming influence. So far in our journey, all the celestial objects we have encountered have been bound together by this universal force. Now, the distances are vast enough that gravity is so weakened that other factors come into play. One of the most obvious is the expansion of the Universe.

___In the big bang, our Universe's most extraordinary moment of creation, all matter and energy were created and hurled outwards at tremendous force. It set the Universe into a state of expansion that continues to this very day. Early in Universal history, all matter followed this expansion, carried along like so much flotsam on the cosmic ocean. But as gravity went to work, so pockets of gas drew themselves together, becoming islands in which gravity was the master.

___Today these islands are the clusters of galaxies, in which the cosmic drama plays out on the individual stages of galaxies, stars and planets, and the clusters are bound to others creating the archipelagos of the superclusters.

___Mysteries abound at these scales, not only are we pushing the limits of our ability to see, we are also encountering the current boundaries of human knowledge. There are strong hints that other forces are at work on these scales, forces that build up and only become apparent over cosmic distances. For example, the movement of galaxies within individual clusters is much faster than we expect. Something must be pulling them harder than our understanding of gravity allows. Could this mean that we simply do not understand how gravity works on these distances? Or does it mean that there is more

matter hidden in the galaxies themselves? If it is extra matter, it must be invisible and totally different to normal atoms or our understanding of the way the chemical elements have built up in the Universe will be invalidated. To differentiate the hypothetical stuff from atoms, it is called dark matter.

___Just as galaxies occasionally collide, so whole galaxy clusters can smash into one another. Such impacts give us clues that can either be interpreted in favour of dark matter or in favour of a modified theory of gravity. As yet, there is no way to tell, although the weight of modern opinion rests on the side of dark matter.

___As the space between superclusters continues to expand, driving them ever further away from one another, so the fate of the Universe rests in the strength of gravity versus this expansion. Gravity is subtle, and has time on its side. It will tenaciously attempt to still the cosmic expansion, clawing back the superclusters little by little. If there is sufficient matter – atomic or dark – to generate enough gravity, then the expansion will be reversed and everything will eventually fall back together, creating an inescapable Armageddon called the big crunch. If there is not enough mass, then the Universe will continue to expand forever, eventually driving the superclusters so far away from one another that they become lost to each other's sight.

___In the fight over the fate of the Universe another dark force has come to light. Although its nature is dimly perceived at present, it appears that a weak form of antigravity may permeate the universe. This unanticipated force of nature has been termed 'dark energy' to emphasize its unknown nature. If it exists, it is not predicted by any current theory. It might not be a force; it could be a form of energy in space, or an unanticipated aspect of gravity.

___Or it could simply be an illusion brought about because we happen to live in a lower density region of the cosmos. With less gravity being generated around, so the expansion of space can move faster.

___Distances and motions are not the only confounding issues in the intertemporal zone. As the name suggests, our perception and treatment of time needs to be taken into account. At the simplest level, this means that light has taken billions of years to cross these distances

and that in that time, not only have the celestial objects changed but the expansion of space has driven them ever further away. So what we perceive to have been located at 13 billion light years distance, will in reality be much further away, out to some 45 billion light years or so.

___As if that was not brain-bending enough, the rate at which time passes changes from place to place as well. This is because time is affected by gravity, which behaves like molasses, retarding every natural process and effectively slowing down time.

___If we were to measure the age of the cosmos in a region of space with a greater density of galaxies and other matter, we would register a younger Universal age because the gravity in that region has forced the clock to run more slowly. If so, it means our perception of the age of the Universe may not tally with other age estimates elsewhere. In this case, the Universe would not just be a cosmic landscape but a cosmic timescape as well.

___At the furthest limits of our view is the cosmic microwave background radiation. This universal barrier prevents us looking any further through time or space; it walls off the big band from our direct view. The cosmic microwave background shows us what the Universe looked like just 380,000 years after the big bang, when all space was filled with just a diffuse ocean of gas. A few slight crests and troughs were the only variation that existed and they became the large-scale structure of galaxies that we see today.

___But what of the big bang? What was it? What set it into motion? In other words, why did our Universe begin? No one knows. Ideas abound; from believing that it is just a statistical quantum fluke, to the idea that it is the aftermath of two whole universes colliding. But as yet, we have no real evidence for either. Only when our ideas of space and time, matter and energy, force and motion are more developed will we stand any chance of moving towards a wider understanding.

___And it is this journey that makes the Universe such a rewarding thing to study. The more we look, the more we find, the more knowledge we possess, the richer the ever wider Universe becomes.

Right: a computer simulation reveals a web of dark matter filaments flecked with bright galaxies

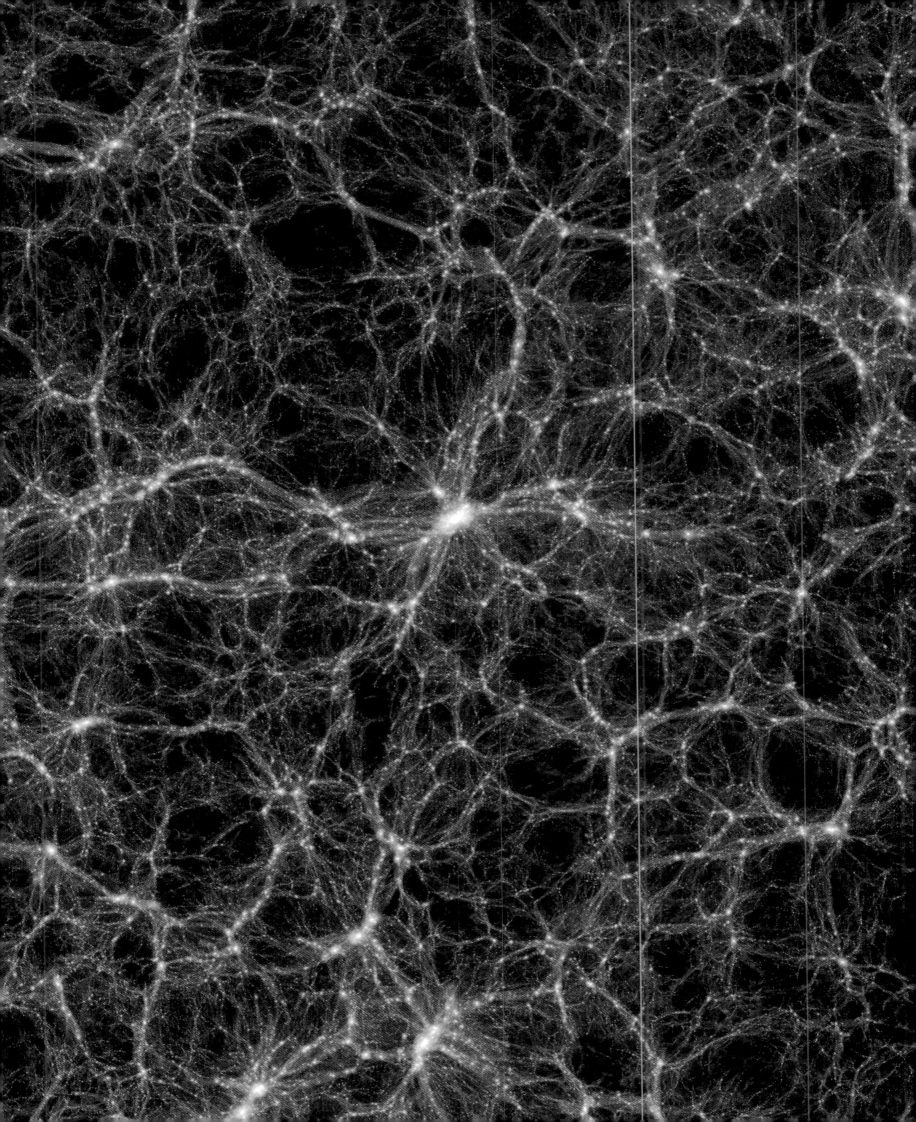

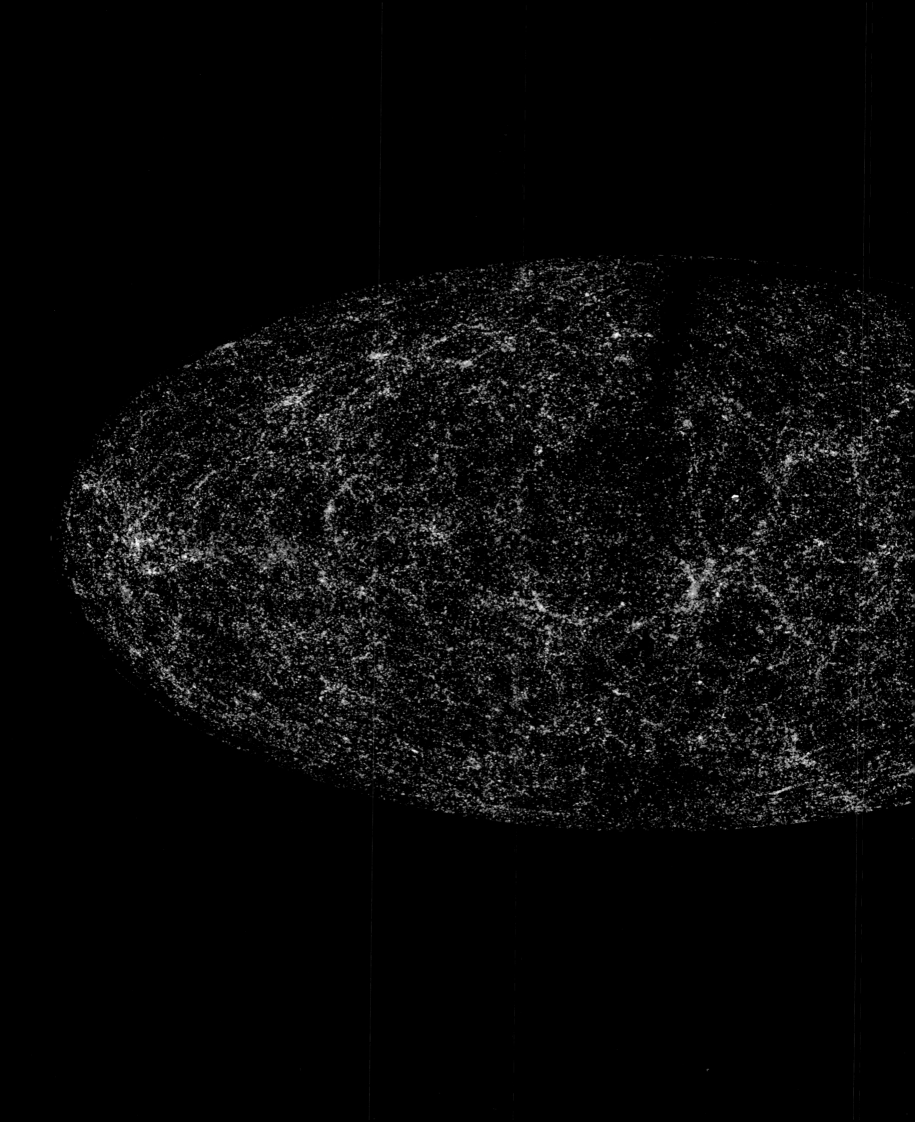

LIGHT SECONDS
LIGHT MINUTES
LIGHT YEARS
KILO LIGHT YEARS
MEGA LIGHT YEARS
GIGA LIGHT YEAR

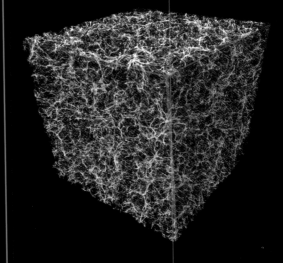

1

The cosmic web

Hundreds of billions of galaxies populate the Universe.
They form a cosmic web that stretches all the way
across it. Everywhere we look, the galaxies are
gathered into filaments and walls that surround vast
empty spaces. This is the cosmic architecture but how
it was constructed is still not well understood.

Bright alignments of galaxies are the dominant
feature on scales of a few hundred million
light years and greater. These filaments thread
themselves around giant inky voids, revealing
a cosmic web, the framework from which the
galaxies, their clusters and their superclusters
are suspended.

___In this infrared map, 1.5 million galaxies
have been sifted and placed in their correct
position to show the web. The nearest galaxies
are displayed as blue, with green, yellow
and red signifying increasing distance. The
superclusters are revealed as knots of colour.
As many as half the atoms in the Universe
exist in the form of a hot gas that permeates
the filaments rather than sitting in the actual
galaxies.

___The voids reveal themselves as emptier
regions. They are bubbles of low-density that
can reach from tens to hundreds of millions
of light years across space. Isolated galaxies
can be found in the voids, but no clusters
or superclusters. At the grandest scales, the
Universe resembles a vast coral sponge,
as this three-dimensional computer simulated
chunk of spacetime shows [1].

___Such an obvious pattern cannot have
developed by pure chance. Somewhere back
in cosmic history, there must have been forces
at work to produce today's cosmic web. Gravity
was clearly an architect but there must be
other forces at work to drape the galaxies that
gravity created into the filaments.

___The expansion of the Universe plays an
important role. Instilled into the Universe by the
fury of its creation, space is in a constant state
of expansion. Without gravity, the matter in
the Universe would have been spread into an
ever-thinner soup of particles, spread more or
less evenly throughout space. Only in those
areas that happened to be sufficiently dense,
did gravity gain the upper hand and force the
formation of galaxies and clusters.

___Helping to resist gravity, the expansion
may be aided by a mysterious form of energy,
or even a previously unanticipated force
of nature. Whichever it is, it appears to be
accelerating the expansion of space, stretching
the cosmic web even more. The enigmatic
assistant has been dubbed dark energy,
though what it truly is – if it even exists at all –
remains unknown.

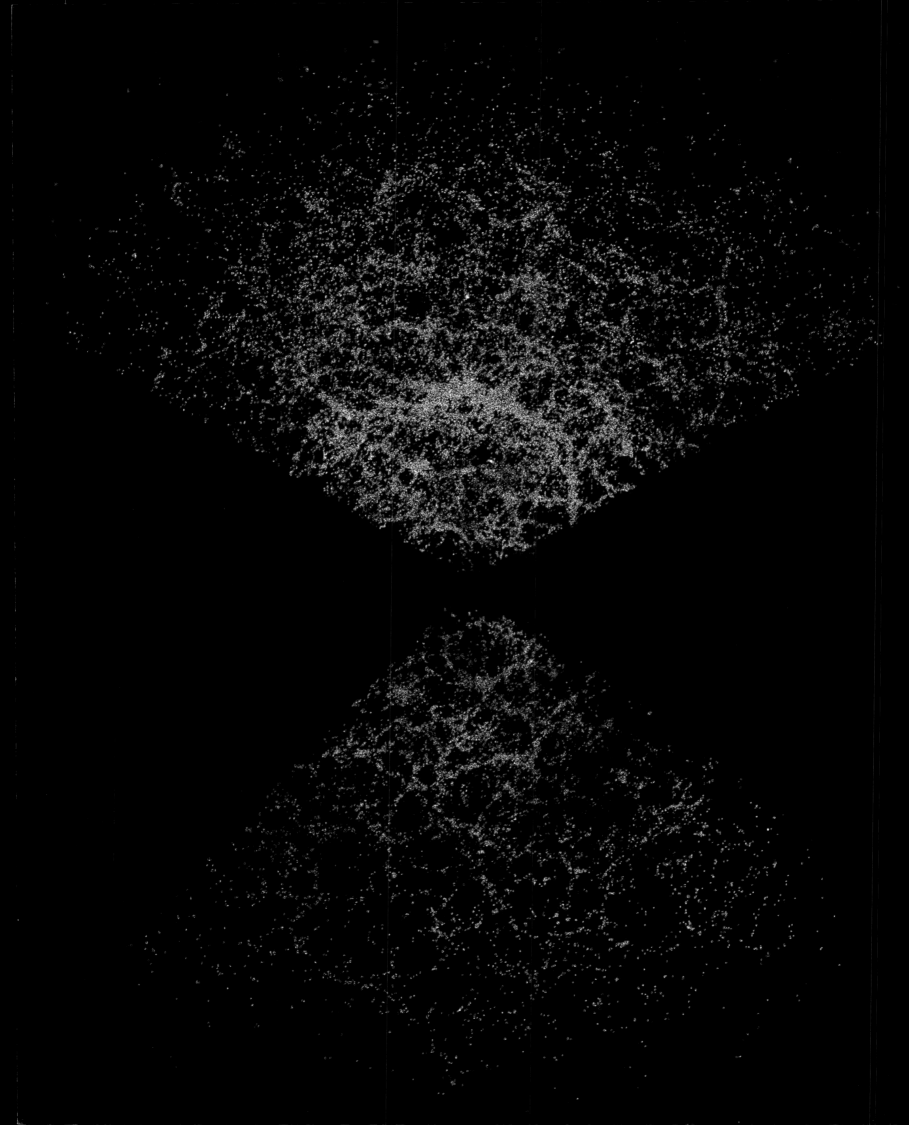

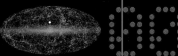

LIGHT SECONDS
LIGHT MINUTES
LIGHT YEARS
KILO LIGHT YEARS
MEGA LIGHT YEARS
GIGA LIGHT YEAR

The end of greatness

The Sloan Great Wall of galaxies measures approximately 1.37 billion light years across, at least twice the size of the previously encountered Great Wall. Situated a billion light years from Earth, and visible in this map as a bright arc across the top cone, Sloan is the largest known structure in the Universe. But is it really a structure?

The great walls are gargantuan sheets of galaxies, hundreds of millions of light years or more in length and width. Yet they are only tens of millions of light years deep. Five have been positively identified, with a handful of others under investigation. Our own Galaxy could be part of a great wall that stretches through the Local Supercluster and off in the direction of the southern constellation Centaurus. Verifying this association is difficult, however, because it passes through the Zone of Avoidance, behind the Milky Way.

___The Sloan Great Wall is so large that the gravity from one side has reduced to virtually nothing by the time it reaches the other. This means it cannot be a gravitationally bound object. Instead, it may be just a chance alignment of galaxy superclusters, a lingering memory of where they happened to form.

___It signals the end of greatness, a strange term perhaps to apply when we arrive at the very grandest scales of the Universe. But by greatness we mean the ability of gravity to bind objects together. At this scale or larger, the lumpiness created by gravity gives way to a more or less smooth distribution of matter. Each volume of space larger than 300 million light years contains roughly the same amount of mass as any other volume of a similar size.

___This is crucial to our understanding of the Universe as a whole because our current level of mathematical ability only allows us to calculate the behaviour of the cosmos if the distribution of matter is roughly uniform. Fluctuations will be present because of the random way the structures collapsed in the first place. Hence there will be chance alignments like the Sloan Great Wall and the mighty Eridanus Supervoid, which some estimates suggest stretches for almost a billion light years across space.

___Such deviations from uniformity are known as the cosmic variance and they will impact upon our understanding, making the Universe behave somewhat differently from the idealized calculations. But, by and large, the mass of the Universe on these scales can be thought of as homogeneously distributed.

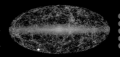

LIGHT SECONDS
LIGHT MINUTES
LIGHT YEARS
KILO LIGHT YEARS
MEGA LIGHT YEARS
GIGA LIGHT YEARS

A secret matter

Thousands of galaxies from across space and time
dot this image. Only a few stars from our own Galaxy
show up; everything else represents individual
collections of billions of stars, shrunken to almost
point-like stellar proportions by their extreme distance.

The yellow galaxies in the lower left section of the image form the galactic metropolis called Abell 315. They are the galactic equivalent of bees around a hive, each travelling on a curving path but never straying too far away – and that's a riddle looking for a solution.

___The paths these galaxies take should be dictated by the combined mass of their companions, which creates a cluster-wide gravitational field. The problem is that they are all moving too fast to be corralled by the gravity of their companions, even though each galaxy contains the mass of a few hundred billion stars. Taken at face value, this would mean this cluster is in the process of disintegration with each of the galaxies now intent on forging its own path through space. But such behaviour is repeated in every single

other galaxy cluster strewn throughout the entire universe.

___They can't all be flying apart otherwise there would not be any left in the Universe today. So what does this mean? Either our understanding of gravity breaks down on the largest scales and the force pulls a little harder in those realms, or there are vast reserves of matter hiding in every galaxy and galaxy cluster.

___If it is matter rather than the behaviour of gravity, then it cannot be formed from ordinary atoms or there would be many more galaxies – and the ones that we do have would be much bigger. Instead, it is possible that this invisible matter could be made up of undiscovered particles that played crucial roles during the origin of the Universe and the establishment of

its physical laws but are now relics, sitting in space like ash at the bottom of a fire. As such particles would not emit or absorb light (otherwise we would have seen them), their sole way of communicating with the rest of the Universe would be through the gravity they generate. As a result, they are collectively referred to as dark matter.

___If this picture is true then each galaxy is the equivalent of an iceberg – a brightly visible tip atop a great bulk of hidden matter.

___If, however, a misunderstanding of large-scale gravity is responsible for the gulf between a galaxy's mass and its gravitational influence, then we are going to need a contemporary Newton or Einstein to move our knowledge onwards.

LIGHT SECONDS
LIGHT MINUTES
LIGHT YEARS
KILO LIGHT YEARS
MEGA LIGHT YEARS
GIGA LIGHT YEARS

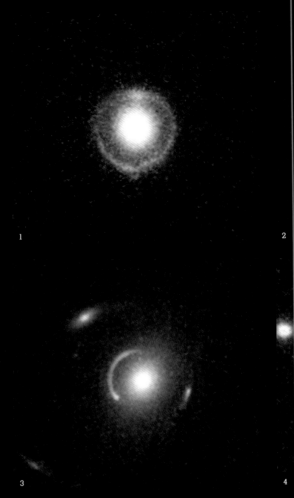

1

2

3

4

Space warp

The combined mass of this cluster of galaxies is so great that it visibly warps space around it. Light can no longer travel in straight lines through these buckled realms and so becomes distorted and even duplicated – but this offers an enormous bonus.

The thin blue cobwebs surrounding Abell 1689 are the malformed images of exceptionally distant galaxies, brought into view only because the gravity of this galaxy cluster acts like a gigantic natural zoom lens and amplifies the light.

___Just as diverging light rays are bent to a focus by a normal lens, be it a glass lens in a telescope or an organic one in an eye, so space can perform a similar feat. It takes the combined mass of trillions of stars, all held in a giant cluster of galaxies, to distort space so much that it takes on the shape of a lens two million light years wide.

___The more massive the cluster, the better it acts as a gravitational lens. Even then, it is a

slightly peculiar one. Unlike a normal lens, it does not bring light to a sharp point but instead tries to spread it into a halo. If the alignment is perfect between the observer, the lens and the target object, then the image produced is a circle, known as an Einstein ring [1]. When the alignment is not ideal, arcs are created [2, 3 & 4].

___Abell 1689 lens sits 2.2 billion light years away and shows us hundreds of galaxies much further away, spread into the concentric threads of a cosmic spider's web. Some of these distorted galaxies date from the beginning of galaxy formation, a billion or so years after the big bang.

___The distribution of the cobwebs, especially where they deviate from a symmetrical pattern,

allows the gravitational field of the lensing cluster to be mapped out. Such efforts corroborate the realization that our understanding of gravity is flawed. Calculating the amount of mass needed to generate the lensing seen leaves the cluster wanting. There are simply not enough galaxies in there to do the job. So again, either there is an enormous stock of dark matter in there, outweighing the normal matter ten to one, or our understanding of the way gravity is generated on the large scale is flawed.

___Regardless of how they manage the task, gravitational lenses provide a way of seeing further into the cosmos than would otherwise be currently feasible.

LIGHT SECONDS
LIGHT MINUTES
LIGHT YEARS
KILO LIGHT YEARS
MEGA LIGHT YEARS
GIGA LIGHT YEARS

Taking a bullet

As if galaxy collisions weren't big enough, the Bullet Cluster is the head-on smash between a pair of whole galaxy clusters. Thousands of billions of solar masses of gas have been ripped out of each cluster, and the elusive dark matter may have been revealed.

Like two charging armies, a pair of galaxy clusters has ripped right through each other and both clusters are currently speeding out of the other side. The collision took place 150 million years ago and, whereas all the galaxies have survived, the surrounding oceans of hot gases have been dragged out of each cluster. Coloured in red, the gas blisters at 70–100 million °C. The smaller cluster has had its gas forged into a bullet shape as it powered through the large one.

___The blue areas are colour codings that show where the majority of each cluster's mass should be, according to the way they behave as gravitational lenses. Both regions still clearly surround the two galaxy clusters involved in the collision indicating that most of the mass contained in each remains intact.

___The amount of lensing also allows the mass within each cluster to be calculated and it is much more than can be contained within just the visible parts of the galaxies. So could this be another piece of evidence for dark matter? Maybe, maybe not.

___The collision speed has been estimated at 10 million km/h and this is faster than expected for two clusters of this type. It is as if something is pulling them a little harder than anticipated from our understanding of gravity.

___Another galaxy cluster collision that displays a similar pattern to the Bullet Cluster is MACS J0025.4-1222 [1]. The hot gas has been stripped from the galaxy clusters in a textbook example of how you would expect dark matter to behave in a cosmic collision. But not every galaxy collision is so simple.

___Abell 520 is a chaotic mess [2] with hot gas and supposed dark matter intermixed to such an extent that the only way to explain it is by postulating that a new force of nature must exist to pull on the dark matter. Alternatively, perhaps gravity behaves differently from the way we expect on the largest of the cosmic scales and maybe dark matter does not exist at all.

___Yet another, MACSJ0717.5+3745, is a multiple pile-up of four galaxy clusters [3]. Here too is a confusing picture, with two of the galaxy clusters having been separated from their supposed dark matter.

___Like the expressionist paintings they resemble, these images capture the grandeur of cluster collisions, yet only hint at the physical reality that underpins them.

CL 0024+17
GALAXY CLUSTER
DIAMETER: 2,600,000 LY

LIGHT SECONDS
LIGHT MINUTES
LIGHT YEARS
KILO LIGHT YEARS
MEGA LIGHT YEARS
GIGA LIGHT YEARS

1

Ring of truth?

The Universe just got weirder, a lot weirder. The blue shading surrounding this cluster of galaxies shows where space is warped the most. But it should be in the centre of the cluster, not spread around the outer edges.

In the battle to uncover the invisible behaviour of dark matter, the warping of space is now a front-line weapon. A menagerie of distant galaxies exists in every direction one looks [1] and can be analyzed for subtle contortions that betray the curvature of space.

___Each crooked galactic visage is the result of a weak version of gravitational lensing. Analyzed across a whole cluster they map out hills and valleys in the fabric of space. This can then be colour coded and overlain on images of the same region to see whether the topography corresponds to luminous groupings of matter.

___A found galaxy cluster Cl 0024+17 it does not. The dark matter thought responsible for the majority of its mass does not appear to be concentrated in the centre of the cluster.

Rather, it is spread around its outskirts in a ring that measures 2.6 million light years across. Such an arrangement runs against the grain of traditional theory and begs an explanation.

___One possible solution is that this cluster of galaxies collided with another between one and two billion years ago. The smash took place directly in our line of sight so that one cluster is now directly behind the other and difficult to see. Somehow, this collision set the dark matter rippling outwards to become the ring-like structure now revealed by the weak lensing. But if so, it would seem to pull in the opposite direction to some of the other galaxy cluster collisions that suggest that dark matter particles pass straight through each other undisturbed.

___So, how should the blue areas be interpreted if dark matter does not exist? They could show where the curvature of space is greater than expected from the mass contained in that volume. And if that were to be the case, our fundamental understanding of gravity on the large scale would have been wrong.

___For the moment, although the weight of opinion swings towards the dark matter explanation for all gravitational anomalies in the Universe, it is by no means proven. Ambiguous findings, such as in Cl 0024+17, do not help and while they remain inexplicable, the mystery continues.

LIGHT SECONDS
LIGHT MINUTES
LIGHT YEARS
KILO LIGHT YEARS
MEGA LIGHT YEARS
GIGA LIGHT YEARS

A vision of infinity

This is what infinity looks like. Vast stretches of the darkest
night punctuated by the occasional island of light. These
particular islands are the first galaxies, the first motes of
hope in a previously black existence, the first inklings of
the grandeur that was to burst across the cosmos.

This is the end of the dark ages. Before this
moment, the giant oceans of gas created in the
big bang had yet to fall together to become
the first stars and galaxies. But here we see the
moment when star formation truly ignited
across the Universe and galaxies were born.
___They are unmasked from the blackness in
the deepest image of the Universe ever taken.
No existing ground-based telescope can see
these galactic youngsters; only the Hubble
Space Telescope so far has the power – and
then only by staring myopically at the same
patch of sky for eleven and a half days.
___Light from the very faintest of these objects
trickled in at just one photon per minute,
compared with the usual rate of millions
per minute from nearer galaxies. Having
completed its 13-billion-year-long journey,
each photon was recorded and amassed until

the galaxies responsible for these dim celestial
fires materialized.
___Many of these galaxies appear as they
did just 800 million years after the Big Bang,
or around 13 billion years ago; some may be
as they appeared just 400 million years after
the big bang. They are youthful, perhaps
even foetal galaxies, just emerging from
their first growing pains to begin to resemble
the fully fledged adults they will become.
Yet astronomers search in vain for familiar
galactic shapes. There are no grand spirals
or giant ellipticals. These shapes will come
later, over the course of billions of years, as
these galactic infants collide and merge.
___There are 10,000 galaxies in this image
alone, each one home to billions of stars.
For all it can tell astronomers about our cosmic
origins, it is still the poorest scrap of information

about the Universe at large. This is because
the whole panorama only covers one fiftieth
of the area of the full moon in the night sky.
To observe the whole sky at this level of
precision would take almost a million years
of uninterrupted observing time with the
Hubble Space Telescope.
___Stepping back from the Hubble Space
Telescope's unprecedented level of detail,
a widefield view of deepest space from
the Herschel Space Observatory is just as
astounding [1]. It reveals a pointillist blizzard
of 10–12 billion-year-old galaxies, reminiscent
of densest starfields of the Milky Way. In actual
fact, there are many more galaxies in the
Universe than there are stars in the Milky Way.
Clearly we are a long way from mapping the
entire Universe, and there are secrets enough
in eternity to keep us busy for aeons.

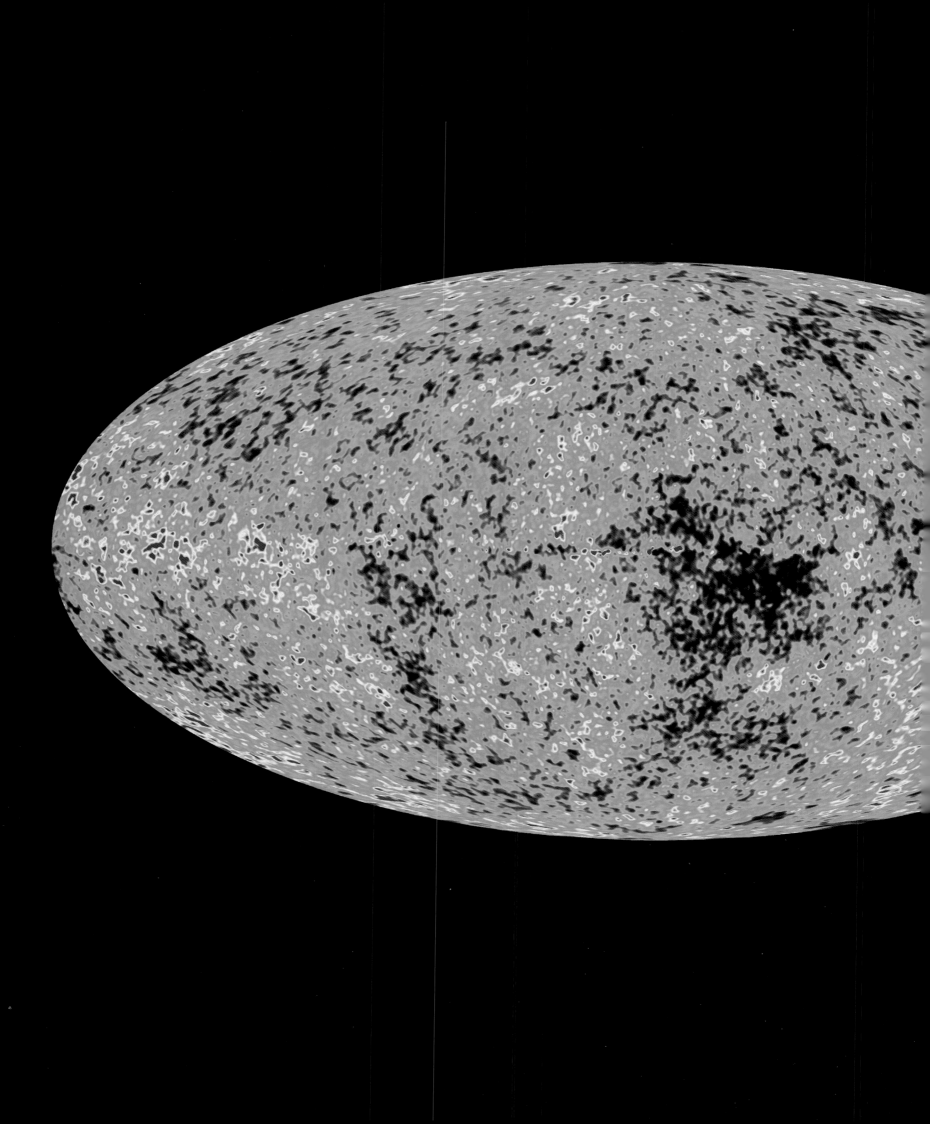

LIGHT SECONDS
LIGHT MINUTES
LIGHT YEARS
KILO LIGHT YEARS
MEGA LIGHT YEAR
GIGA LIGHT YE.

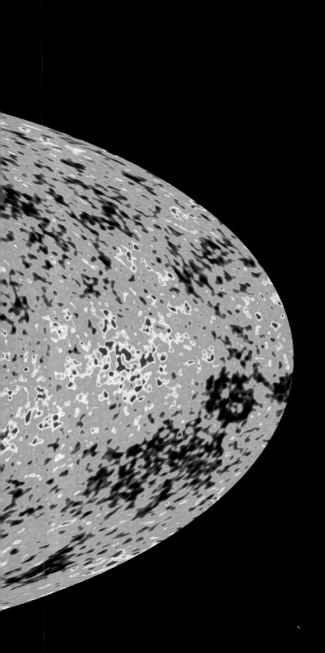

The cosmic blueprint

This is what the Universe looks like to microwave eyes. Gone are the planets, the stars and the galaxies. In their place is an all-pervading glow of microwaves that shows up as a faint hiss on Earthly radios. But make no mistake, this static is significant: it is the echo of the Big Bang and the blueprint for the Universe.

This is what the Universe looked like just 380,000 years after the Big Bang. Before any celestial objects were born there were only atoms and light. The light was a flood of X-rays that, enfeebled with age and distance, now appears as this wall of microwave radiation.

___We can see no further than this, it is an impenetrable barrier that blocks our view of the creation of the Universe. The energy locked in this all-pervading radiation was produced when more than a billion times the amount of matter in the entire Universe today annihilated itself against an equal quantity of antimatter just a fraction of a second after the Big Bang.

___This galactic cataclysm produced a tiny residue of matter that has been sufficient to build every planet, every star and every galaxy in the Universe around us. But for the first few hundreds of thousands of years, the clouds of gas and energy fought for supremacy. Then, as atoms formed, so the radiation broke free and

___Now it is everywhere, having been travelling for about 13.7 billion years. In all that time, roughly the age of the Universe, space has expanded greatly, stretching the radiation and transforming it from X-rays to microwaves. In the far future, it will be stretched even further into radio waves.

___The blotches on this all-sky view represen small differences in gas density at the momer of the radiation's escape. The cooler, denser regions went on to become the filaments, the great walls and the superclusters of galaxies

___The expansion has also driven this barrie ever further from the Milky Way. Now it sits at a distance of 46.5 billion light years. For all practical purposes, it marks the edge of our observable universe and the end of our journey. As befits the weirdness of intertemporal space, we have come the furtherest possible distance in order to see the very nearest possible image, so

GL⬤SSARY

ABSOLUTE ZERO
The lowest theoretical temperature possible. Is equivalent to –273 °C, and known as zero on the Kelvin scale. There is no upper limit on temperature.

ABSORPTION NEBULA
A sufficiently dense cloud of interstellar dust and gas which can block the light from more distant celestial objects.

ACCRETION DISC
A disc of dust and gas formed as material spirals down into the gravitational field of a body, such as a forming star or a black hole.

ACTIVE GALACTIC NUCLEUS (AGN)
The core of an active galaxy. The energy generated inside an AGN can outshine all the other stars in that galaxy. There is now persuasive evidence that an AGN is powered by the heating of an accretion disc as it spirals into a supermassive black hole. Although most galaxies are thought to contain a supermassive black hole, only one in ten display activity.

ACTIVE GALAXY
A galaxy that emits more energy from its centre than can be accounted for by its normal components: stars, dust and gas. It is thought that a central supermassive black hole is feeding, creating an AGN.

ASTEROID, NEAR-EARTH ASTEROID
A small rocky body orbiting the Sun, each one up to 1,000 km in diameter. Most are found in the Asteroid Belt between Mars and Jupiter but some have more elliptical orbits and swing past the inner planets. Eros is a good example of such a near-Earth asteroid.

ASTRONOMICAL ICES
Water, ammonia and methane. When found beyond the Asteroid Belt, they are so far from the heat of the Sun that they are usually in solid form.

ATMOSPHERE
A shell of gas around a planet or moon. Atmospheres exist in a variety of combinations and densities.

AURORA
Incoming solar particles can excite the atoms in a planet's atmosphere, usually near the poles of a planet with a magnetic field, to produce vivid colours.

BARRED SPIRAL GALAXY
A form of spiral galaxy in which the arms do not connect directly to the central bulge. Instead, they peel off from a central bar of stars running across the bulge.

BIG BANG
The event that marks the origin of the Universe 13.7 billion years ago. At this time, the Universe exploded into existence and has been expanding ever since.

BILLION
10^9 or 1,000,000,000 (a thousand million).

BLACK HOLE
A dense celestial object with a gravitational field so strong that within a certain radius, known as the event horizon, nothing can escape. Even light is trapped inside. At the end of its life, a particularly massive star collapses under its own weight to form a black hole. A supermassive black hole can form in the centre of a galaxy, either from collapsing gas clouds or from black hole mergers.

BLUE SUPERGIANT STAR
The most massive stars, often containing between 30 and 150 solar masses of material. With a surface temperature greater than 30,000 °C, their light appears bluish-white.

BOK GLOBULE
A dark, dense cloud of dust and gas in which star formation is taking place.

BROWN DWARF
A failed star, containing less than eight percent of the Sun's mass. Unable to sustain the nuclear fusion of hydrogen atoms, brown dwarfs probably look like somewhat larger versions of the planet Jupiter.

CALDERA
A volcanic crater, found in the top of a volcano.

CELSIUS

CEPHEID VARIABLE
A type of variable star that undergoes cyclic changes in its brightness, closely related to its average luminosity. By measuring the periods of variation in Cepheids in distant galaxies, astronomers can estimate their average luminosities and then calculate their distances.

COMET, LONG-PERIOD, SHORT-PERIOD
Leftovers from the formation of the Solar System, comets are kilometres-wide chunks of dust and ice. Those that orbit the Sun in less than 200 years are termed short-period comets; long-period comets can take millions of years to return. They are the icy, outer Solar System equivalent of the asteroids.

CORE
The densest centre of a moon, planet or star.

COSMIC MICROWAVE BACKGROUND RADIATION (CMBR)
A faint glow of microwave radiation across the entire sky. It is believed to be the afterglow of the big bang itself, now cooled to –270 °C or just 2.7 °C above absolute zero by the expansion of the Universe.

CRATER
The usually circular scar left by an impact on the surface of rocky body.

CRUST
The uppermost solid layer on a rocky body.

CRYOVOLCANISM
Volcanic activity involving astronomical ices rather than molten rock.

DEEP FIELD
An extremely long exposure to reveal faint galaxies, usually located billions of light years away in space.

DUST
Tiny particles of chiefly silicates and carbon occupying deep space alongside gas. Dust clouds absorb visible light but infrared wavelengths can pass through them.

DWARF GALAXY
A small, faint galaxy, either irregular or elliptical in structure.

DWARF PLANET
A small round object orbiting the Sun. The definition of small means that it is incapable of controlling its wider environment through gravity.

ELECTROMAGNETIC RADIATION
A form of energy that propagates across the Universe as a combination of electrical and magnetic waves. The most familiar form is visible light, whose colours correspond to different wavelengths and energies. The full electromagnetic spectrum runs from extremely energetic gamma rays, via X-rays, ultraviolet, visible and infrared light, and microwaves to low-energy radio waves. Electromagnetic radiation can also be described as a stream of particles known as photons.

ELLIPTICAL GALAXY
A galaxy that appears spherical or American football shaped, with no specific internal structure. Its constituent stars are all in randomly inclined orbits.

EMISSION NEBULA
A cloud of gas that shines with its own light, usually by absorbing ultraviolet radiation from blue supergiant stars and re-emitting it at visible wavelengths. Planetary nebulae, supernova remnants, and many star-forming clouds are all emission nebulae.

GALACTIC HALO
A spherical region around a spiral galaxy that contains dim stars and globular clusters. It is also thought to contain dark matter. The radius of the halo surrounding the Milky Way extends some 50,000 light years from the galactic centre.

GALAXY
A gravitationally bound system of dust, gas and stars. Galaxies range in size from a few hundred, to hundreds of thousands of light years across, and are classified according to their appearance. The most common types are spiral, barred spiral, elliptical, lenticular and irregular.

GALAXY CLUSTER
A collection of hundreds or thousands of galaxies bound together by gravity.

GALAXY SUPERCLUSTER
A grouping of perhaps a dozen or more neighbouring galaxy clusters.

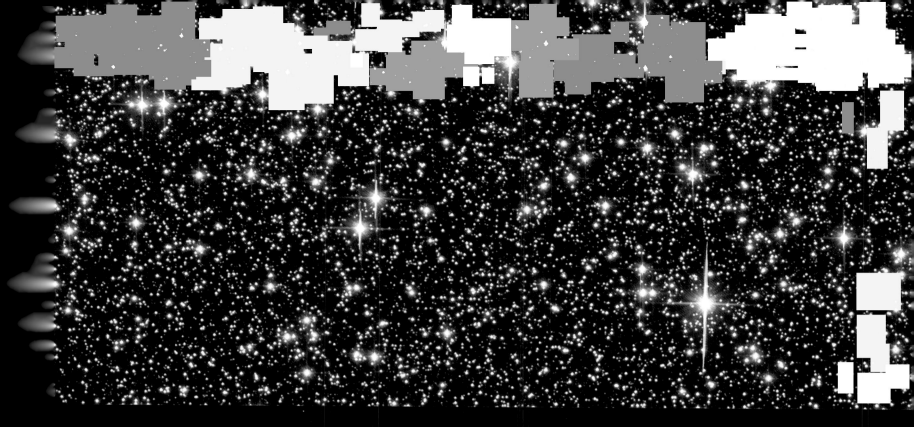

GAMMA RAY
The most energetic form of electromagnetic radiation.

GAMMA RAY BURST
A brief but immensely powerful burst (measured in minutes at most) of gamma rays from space. Usually seen to emanate from the distant realms of the Universe, they are believed to be triggered by the detonation of the first stars to form in the Universe, or the collisions between neutron stars or between black holes.

GAS GIANT PLANET
Vast planets, such as Jupiter or Saturn, with extraordinarily thick atmospheres.

GENERAL RELATIVITY
Albert Einstein's theory that explains gravity as a distortion or warping of space and time.

GLOBULAR CLUSTER
A distinct, densely packed ball of mostly old stars in orbit around a central galaxy. These are some of the oldest objects found in the Universe.

GRAVITY
A mutual attraction between masses, proportional to the masses and the distance between them, manifesting itself as a force.

HICKSON COMPACT GROUP
A collection of a handful of galaxies that is unusually compact. Often, the galaxies in a compact group will be close enough to interact

ICE GIANTS
Gas giant planets with a high proportion of astronomical ices in their make-up. Uranus and Neptune are ice giants.

INDEX CATALOGUE (IC)
A two-part supplement, published in 1895 and 1908, adding 5,386 astronomical objects to the New General Catalogue (NGC).

INFLATION
An event just after the big bang in which, for a fraction of a second, the entire Universe was driven to expand much faster than normal.

INFRARED RADIATION
A section of the electromagnetic spectrum invisible to human eyes but sensed as heat or thermal radiation.

INTERSTELLAR MEDIUM
The rarefied material scattered through the space between the stars, typically consisting of 90 percent hydrogen, 9 percent helium and 1 percent dust.

IONIZATION
The process that produces ions – atoms that are electrically charged by the capture or loss of electrons. Atoms can be stripped of their electrons by high-energy radiation (from stars, for example). Material that has been completely ionized is known as plasma.

IRREGULAR GALAXY
Any galaxy that lacks the necessary structures to be classified as an elliptical, spiral or

LANDER
A man-made vehicle designed to safely land on the surface of a celestial body and take scientific measurements.

LENTICULAR GALAXY
A galaxy that resembles a spiral galaxy, with a central nucleus and a disc, but without spiral arms.

LIGHT
The electromagnetic radiation detectable to the human eye. However, the term is loosely applied to other forms of electromagnetic radiation, especially in the ultraviolet and infrared.

LIGHT SECOND
The distance covered by light in a vacuum during one second: 299,791 km.

LIGHT MINUTE
The distance covered by light in a vacuum during one minute: 17.9 million km.

LIGHT HOUR
The distance covered by light in a vacuum during one hour: 1 billion km.

LIGHT YEAR
The distance covered by light in a vacuum during one year: 9.5 trillion km.

LOCAL GROUP
A collection of approximately 30 galaxies spread over 10 million light years, dominated by our own Milky Way and the Andromeda

LOOK-BACK TIME
The time difference associated with looking at a distant object, due to the finite speed of light. Look-back time is just an interesting curiosity within our cosmic neighbourhood, but on the largest scales, when it amounts to billions of years, it reveals the Universe in a significantly earlier stage of its development.

MAGELLANIC CLOUDS
Two nearby irregular galaxies that could be in orbit around the Milky Way, or simply passing through space close to us.

MAGMA
Hot material shot up from under the crust of a body during a volcanic eruption.

MAGNETIC FIELD
The region of influence of the magnetic force of a body.

MANTLE
An intermediate shell of material covering the core but beneath the crust of a rocky body.

MASS
In astronomy there is a careful distinction between mass, the amount of matter in a body, and weight, defined as the force acting on a body in a gravitational field.

MESSIER CATALOGUE (M)
A list of about 100 nebulous-looking astronomical objects compiled by French astronomer Charles Messier between 1758 and 1781. Most were later identified as galaxies or gaseous nebulae; a few as star clusters.

METEORITE
A piece of rock ejected by one planetary body that lands on another.

METEOR SHOWER
The lights in the sky created by the Earth's atmosphere travelling through debris left by a comet, as the particles burn up.

MILKY WAY
Our Galaxy: the name is derived from our perception of it as a misty band of stars that divides the night sky. The Milky Way is, in fact, a large barred spiral galaxy spanning 100,000 light years and containing around 200 billion stars. Our Solar System lies about two-thirds of the way towards the edge of its disc, in a truncated spiral arm.

MILLION
10^6 or 1,000,000 (a thousand thousand).

MOLECULAR CLOUD
An accumulation of dust and gas, significantly denser than the interstellar medium, which spans hundreds of light years and is the site of star formation.

MOON, SHEPHERD MOON
A moon is a natural satellite of a planet. There are more than 140 in the Solar System of which the Moon orbits Earth. Shepherd moons affect rings around a planet.

NEUTRON STAR
An extremely dense stellar remnant produced during a supernova explosion when huge gravitational forces compress electrons and protons together to produce neutrons.

NEW GENERAL CATALOGUE (NGC)
A compilation of 7,800 astronomical objects published in 1888 by JLE Dreyer and based on earlier observations made by William and John Herschel.

NUCLEAR FUSION
The process that powers stars. Two or more atomic nuclei are forced together, forming a single larger nucleus and releasing energy. Most stars spend the majority of their lives converting hydrogen into helium; more massive, hotter stars can fuse heavier elements.

OBSERVABLE UNIVERSE
That part of the Universe that we are able to study, limited by look-back time to a sphere of space apparently 13.7 billion light years in radius, but really much larger (45 billion light years), centred on our own location. At the edge of the observable Universe in every direction, we are looking back to within 400,000 years after the Big Bang itself.

OORT CLOUD
The swarm of comets surrounding the Solar System at a distance of half to one light year from the Sun.

OPEN STAR CLUSTER
A group of young stellar siblings, born from the same molecular cloud but only loosely bound together by gravity. Such clusters are usually dominated by short-lived brilliant blue stars, but are fated to disperse over a period of several hundred million years.

ORBIT, ORBITAL PERIOD

The trajectory of one celestial body around another. The time it takes one body to travel all the way around another body is called the orbital period.

PHOTON

A particle of light; the quantum (smallest possible) unit of the electromagnetic force.

PLANET

A large body in orbit around a star that can control its wider orbital environment with gravity. Pluto has recently been re-classified as a dwarf planet because it shares a similar orbit with a group of smaller, icy asteroids known as Plutinos.

PLANETARY NEBULA

A shell of debris flung out by a red giant star as it becomes unstable, which fades over 100,000 years as the remaining white dwarf star cools. Misnamed because of their appearance through early telescopes.

PULSAR

A rotating neutron star that emits a sweeping beam of high-energy radiation from its magnetic poles.

QUASAR

The very bright, very distant core of an extremely powerful active galaxy. The name is derived from 'quasi-stellar radio source' – so-called because this class of object was first identified through its radio emissions.

RADIATION PRESSURE

The pressure exerted on an object by a stream of photons; it sculpts gas clouds in space.

RADIO GALAXY

A type of active galaxy, usually elliptical, that emits large quantities of radio radiation. Often this is in the form of jets from the centre of the galaxy that create vast clouds of radio emission on either side of the galaxy, hundreds of thousands of light years across.

RED DWARF

A small and relatively cool star with a diameter and mass of less than one-third that of the Sun. Red dwarfs comprise the vast majority of stars.

RED GIANT

An ageing star that has exhausted all the hydrogen in its core and is supported by a thin spherical shell of hydrogen fusion around the core or, later, the fusion of heavier elements within the core. This change of processes boosts the star's brightness, but also causes it to balloon in size, allowing its surface to cool and turn red.

REFLECTION NEBULAE

A cloud of dust and gas in space, where the dust scatters the light from nearby stars.

ROCKY WORLDS

Planets formed predominantly from rock, sometimes with an atmosphere around them.

ROTATION PERIOD

The time it takes a body to spin once on its axis.

SAGITTARIUS A*

The supermassive black hole at the centre of the Milky Way; it is a source of intense radio and X-rays.

SEYFERT GALAXY

A spiral galaxy with an unusually bright core. The activity around a central supermassive black hole is the cause of the bright core. Seyfert galaxies are a type of active galaxy.

SOLAR MASS

A comparative unit used to express the mass of other stars in relationship to our Sun. One solar mass is equal to 2×10^{30}kg.

SOLAR SYSTEM

The Sun and its family of planets, moons and smaller bodies. Many stars could have associated solar systems.

SPIRAL GALAXY

A galaxy with a spherical central bulge of older stars; surrounded by a flattened disc containing a spiral pattern of young, hot stars. The Milky Way is a spiral galaxy.

STAR

A massive ball of hydrogen and helium bound together by gravity and shining for most of its life with the light of nuclear fusion. Stars of many different sizes are born in nebulae and open clusters, and spend most of their lives, sometimes in pairs, fusing hydrogen into helium before evolving into red giants. Depending on their mass stars die as planetary nebulae or supernovae. The stellar remnants

STAR CLUSTER

A loose formation of stars born at the same time from the same cloud.

STAR FORMATION

The process by which stars gravitationally condense from molecular clouds.

STARBURST GALAXY

A galaxy (often irregular in structure) experiencing an intense burst of star formation. Most starbursts are triggered by interaction – or even collision – with other galaxies.

STELLAR WIND

A stream of particles radiated away from a star.

SUN

The star at the centre of our Solar System.

SUPERGIANT

An extremely massive star that has exhausted the supply of hydrogen in its core, increased in luminosity as it enters a phase equivalent to a red giant, and ballooned in size. While the expansion of Sun-like stars means their surfaces cool down to become red or orange, some supergiants produce so much energy that their surface remains hot, and they can have almost any colour.

SUPERMASSIVE BLACK HOLE

A black hole with a mass of millions or billions of solar masses. Most, if not all, galaxies are thought to harbour a supermassive black hole at their core.

SUPERNOVA

The explosive demise of a star. Supernovae come in two types: Type I and Type II. A Type I supernova involves the collapse of an existing white dwarf into a neutron star; a Type II supernova is the explosion that marks the demise of a star of eight solar masses or more. Depending on the mass of the star, either a neutron star or a black hole is left at the centre of the conflagration.

SUPERNOVA REMNANT

An expanding shell of dust and gas – the debris of a supernova explosion, mixed together with swept-up interstellar matter.

TRILLION

10^{12} or 1,000,000,000,000 (a million million).

ULTRAVIOLET RADIATION

Electromagnetic radiation with a shorter wavelength than violet light.

UNIVERSE

The entirety of space, time and everything that it contains. See also observable Universe.

WAVELENGTHS

Electromagnetic radiation is emitted at many different wavelengths, collectively known as the electromagnetic spectrum. Radio wavelengths are the longest. Infrared is invisible to human eyes but sensed as heat. Visible wavelengths are detected by the human eye as light. Ultraviolet radiation has a shorter wavelength than violet in the visible spectrum. X-rays are higher-energy than ultraviolet radiation but less energetic than gamma rays, which are the shortest wavelengths of all.

WHITE DWARF

The dense, cooling ember of a star that has exhausted its nuclear fuel and collapsed under the force of its own gravity. All but the most massive stars will end their days as white dwarfs.

WOLF–RAYET STAR

A particularly massive, short-lived star, usually containing more than 25 solar masses of material. Wolf–Rayets have powerful stellar winds that strip away the outer layers of their own atmospheres, leaving their interiors exposed.

X-RAYS

High-energy electromagnetic radiation. Less energetic than gamma rays, but more so than ultraviolet radiation.

INDEX

Abell 315 221
Abell 520 225, *225*
Abell 1689 223
absolute zero 10, 232
absorption nebula 69, *69*, 83, *83*, 91, *91*, 93, *93*, 232
accretion disc 232
active galactic nucleus (AGN) 232
active galaxies 191, *191*, 232
AMO644-741 ring galaxy 201, *201*
Andromeda Galaxy 10, 12, 144, 153, *153*, 157
Antares 63
Antennae Galaxy 144, 175, *175*
Apollo Moon landings 21, *21*, 71
Apophis 33
Aristotle 117
Arp 147 system 211, *211*
Arp 148 galaxy 211, *211*
Arp 272 galaxies 207, *207*
asteroids 8, 12, 16, 21, 31, 33, 37, 45, 232
    near-Earth asteroid 232
astronomical ices 232
atmosphere 232
    Earth 49, 71, 101, 125
    Jupiter 16, *37*
    Mars 23, 29, *29*
    Venus 23
atoms: stripped of electrons 27
aurora 16, 232

background radiation 10, 214, 231, 233
Barnard's Loop 79
barred spiral galaxies 144, 179, *179*, 183, *183*, 232
Big Bang 9, 10, 197, 214, 223, 229, 231, 232
billion 232
black holes 12, 13, 60, 123, 139, *139*, 159, 169, 179, 183, 185, 189, 191, 197, 207, 232
    supermassive 237
blue stars 129, *129*, 144, 167, 177
blue supergiant stars 60, 183, 232
Bode's Galaxy (M81) 161, *161*, 163
Bok globule 232
bow shock 121, 159
brown dwarves 105, 232
Bullet Cluster 225
Butterfly Nebula 99, *99*

C10024+17 galaxy cluster 227, *227*
caldera 232
Caloris Basin, Mercury 25
carbonaceous chondrites 31
Carina Nebula 60, 119, *119*
Cartwheel Galaxy 199, *199*, 201, *201*
Cassini Division 43
Cassiopeia A supernova remnant 75, 125, *125*
Cat's Eye Nebula 95, *95*
Cat's Paw Nebula 109, *109*
celsius 232
Centaurus A 12, 159, *159*
Centaurus Cluster 189
cepheid variable 233
Ceres 16, 57
chaos regions 41
Charon 16
Cigar Galaxy (M82) 161, 163, *163*
colliding galaxies 175, *175*, 195, *195*, 197, *197*

Coma Cluster 205, *205*
Comet Holmes 35
Comet Tempel 1 35, *35*
comets 16, 35, 37, 60, 111, 233
Compact Galactic Group 199
Cone Nebula 93, *93*
Copernicus, Nicolaus 12
core 8, 25, 27, 37, 123, 127, 137, 179, 209, 233
Corona Australis Complex III *71*
cosmic acceleration 13
cosmic microwave background radiation 214, 231, 233
cosmic rays 125
Crab Nebula 113, *113*
crater 233
Crescent Nebula 103
crust 233
cryo-volcanism 47, 233
Cygnus Loop 75, *75*

Dactyl 33, *33*
dark energy 13, 214, 217
dark matter 60, 193, 214, 221, 223, 225, 227
Death Star (in *Star Wars*) 45
deep field 233
Deep Impact probe 35
Deimos (moon of Mars) 31, *31*
dinosaurs 33, 43
DNA 41, 67, 111
dust 233
dwarf galaxies 171, *171*, 209, 233
dwarf irregular galaxies 157, *157*, 165, *165*, 177, *177*
dwarf planets 16, 55, 57, 233

E ring 47, *47*
Eagle Nebula 60, 115, *115*
Earth
    age of 19
    atmosphere 49, 71, 101, 125
    as centre of Universe 12
    core 25
    gravity 47
    in inner solar system 16
    life on 8, 19, 21, 41, 53
    movement of continents 19, 21
    oceans 39, 47, 111, 177
    orbit around the Sun 12
    surface water 16
EGGs (evaporating gaseous globules) 107
Einstein, Albert 12
Einstein ring 223, *223*
electromagnetic radiation 9, 233
electromagnetic spectrum 9
electrons 27, 163
Elephant's Trunk Nebula 91, *91*
Elizabeth I, Queen 117
elliptical galaxies 9, 169, 175, 185, *185*, 187, 189, *189*, 191, 195, 203, *203*, 205, 207, 211, 214, 233
emission nebulae 81, *81*, 89, *89*, 101, *101*, 103, *103*, 105, *105*, 107, *107*, 109, *109*, 111, *111*, 123, *123*, 131, *131*, 149, *149*, 151, *151*, 233
Enceladus (moon of Saturn) 8, 47, *47*, 91
Ericke Division 43
Eridanus Supervoid 217
Eris 57
Eros (asteroid) 33
Eta Carinae 119, 121

Europa (moon of Jupiter) 8, 41, *41*, 47
European Space Agency 10
Everest, Mount 39
exoplanets 16

Fleming's Triangular Wisp 75, *75*
Fornax Cluster 177, 185
Fox Fur Nebula 93

G1.9+0.3 gas cloud 75
galactic halo 233
galaxies: definition 233
    see also ring galaxies; spiral galaxies
galaxy clusters 9, 13, 193, *193*, 207, *207*, 214, 221, 223, 225, *225*, 227, *227*, 217, 233
galaxy filaments 217, 219
galaxy superclusters 9, 13, 217, 219, 233
gamma ray burst 121, 234
gamma rays 9, 27, 234
gas giant planets 16, 234
Gaspra 33, *33*
general relativity 12, 234
globular clusters 60, 63, 129, *129*, 133, 141, *141*, 147, 149, *149*, 169, 203, 234
Gould's Belt 60
gravitational fields 12, 31, 51, 144, 195, 223
gravitational lenses 223, 225, 227
gravity
    definition 234
    Earth 47
    Jupiter 16, 37, 39
    Mars 31
    Moon 21, 31
    Saturn 47
Great Attractor 193
Great Wall, the 207

halos 60
Haumea 57
Helix Nebula 67, *67*
Herbig-Haro Objects 65
Hercules Cluster 207
Hercules Supercluster 207
Herschel, William 67
Herschel 36 star 101
Herschel Crater, Mimas 45
Herschel Space Observatory 229, *229*
Hickson Compact Group (HCG) 90 187, *187*, 234
Hoag's Object 144, 211
Hodge 301 149
Horsehead Nebula (Barnard 33) 83, *83*
Hourglass Nebula 101, *101*
Hubble, Edwin 153
Hubble Space Telescope 9, 229
Hubble Ultra Deep Field 229
Hyperion (moon of Saturn) 16, 51, *51*, 53

Iapetus (moon of Saturn) 53, *53*, 60
IC 4592 *71*
ice giants 234
Ida 33, *33*
Index Catalogue (IC) 234
inflation 234
infrared 9, 63, *63*, 67, 91, 105, *105*, 107, 147, 153, *155*, 159, *159*, 217, 234
interstellar medium 234
intertemporal zone 9, 231

Io (moon of Jupiter) 8, 16, 39, *39*, 41
ionization 234
iron 73, 127
irregular galaxies 234

Jupiter
    atmosphere 16, *37*
    and comets 35
    gravity 16, 37, 39
    Great Red Spot 37, *37*, 55
    mass 37
    moons 8, 177
    in outer solar system 16
    shrinkage 37
    storm system 37, *37*

Kepler, Johannes 12, 117
Kepler's supernova 75, 117, *117*
keyholes 33, 85

Lagoon Nebula (M8) 60, 101, *101*
lander 234
Large Magellanic Cloud (LMC) 147,, *147*, 155, 165
lasers 91
lava 19, 21, 39, *39*
lenticular galaxies 169, *169*, 173, *173*, 205, 211, 234
life 121
    on Earth 8, 19, 21, 41, 53
    on Europa 41
    on Mars 23
    on Venus 23
light 9, 12, 234
    bent light rays 223
    speed of 9-10, 27
light hour 234
light minute 234
light second 234
light year 234
LL Ori 81, *81*
Local Group 12, 151, 153, 181, 187, 234
Local Supercluster 217
look-back time 10, 12, 235

M4 63
M33 157
M51 144
M72 141, *141*
M78 87, *87*
M82 161
Maat Mons 23, *23*
McNeil's Nebula 87
MACS J0025.4-1222 225, *225*
MACSJ0717.5+3745 225, *225*
Magellanic Clouds 10, 144, 235
magma 235
magnetic fields 8, 83, 85, 97, 121, 125, 137, 159, 169, 191, 235
magnetism 19
Makemake 57
mantle 235
Mars
    atmosphere 23, 29, *29*
    gravity 31
    in inner solar system 16
    potential life on 23
    volcanoes 29
    winds of 8
masers 91
mass: definition 235
Mathilde 33, *33*
Medusa Nebula (Abell 21) 77
Mercury

core 25
   fault lines 25
   in inner solar system 16
   orbit of 16, 139
   rocks on 8
   temperature 25
Messier Catalogue (M) 235
meteor shower 235
meteorites 8, 31, 35, 45, 111, 235
Mice, The (colliding galaxies) 195, *195*
microwaves 9, 10, 91, 231
Milky Way 8, 9, 10, 12, 60, 63, 75, 77,
   79, 107, 115, 121, 123, 129, 133, 141,
   144, 147, 153, 155, 157, 171, 179, 187,
   193, 203, 229, 231, 235
   core 137, *137*
Milky Way III 111
million 235
Mimas (moon of Saturn) 16, 43, *43*,
   45, *45*
molecular clouds 60, 79, *79*, 93, 119,
   131, 235
Moon 16, 21, 235
   Apollo landings 21, *21*, 71
   gravity 21, 31
   tidal forces 39
mountains 8, 16, 19, 39, 53, *53*, 60, 107

NASA 35
nebulae *see* absorption nebulae;
   emission nebulae; individual
   names of nebulae; reflection
   nebulae
Neptune
   gravity 57
   Great Dark Spot 55, *55*
   in outer solar system 16
   slow orbit round the Sun 57
   storms and clouds of 55
   and Uranus 55
neutron stars 73, 113, 123, 127, 235
New General Catalogue (NGC) 235
NGC 346 151, *151*
NGC 604 155, *155*
NGC 1132 203, *203*
NGC 1300 183, *183*
NGC 1313 165, *165*
NGC 1316 185, *185*
NGC 1427A 177, *177*
NGC 1555 65
NGC 1569 165
NGC 1672 179, *179*
NGC 1999 85
NGC 2244 105
NGC 2264 93
NGC 2787 *173*
NGC 3582 111, *111*
NGC 3603 133, *133*
NGC 4402 181, *181*
NGC 4449 165, *165*
NGC 4522 181
NGC 4696 189, *189*
NGC 4921 205, *205*
NGC 5195 171
NGC 5196 144
NGC 6217 179
NGC 6240 197, *197*
NGC 6357 123, *123*
NGC 6611 115
NGC 7049 185, *185*
NGC 7173 187
NGC 7174 187
NGC 7176 187
NGC 7317 199

NGC 7318A 199
NGC 7318B 199
NGC 7318C 199
NGC 7320 199
NGC 7320C 189, 199
NGC 7635 77, *77*
Norma Cluster 193, *193*
Nu Scorpii *71*
nuclear fusion 65, 235
nuclei, merger of 27

observable universe 235
Omega Centauri globular cluster
   129, *129*
Oort cloud 235
open star cluster 235
orbit 236
Orion Molecular Cloud Complex 79,
   79, 81, 87
Orion Nebula 10, 60, 71, 81, *81*, 144,
   147, 149, 155
Orion-Eridanus bubble 79
ozone layer 121

PAHs (polycyclic aromatic
   hydrocarbons) 111
Pan (moon of Saturn) 43
particle accelerators 125
paterae 39
Pelican Nebula 89, *89*
Perseus A 191, *191*
Perseus Cluster 191
Phobos (moon of Mars) 31, *31*, 33
Phoebe (moon of Saturn) 53
photons 9, 229, 236
Pinwheel Galaxy 167, *167*
Pismis 24-1 star cluster 123
Planck (spacecraft) 10
planetars 105
planetary nebulae 67, *67*, 77, *77*, 95,
   95, 97, *97*, 99, *99*, 236
planets: definition 236
plunge, the 197
plutinos 16
Pluto 16, 55, 57
polar ring galaxies 211, *211*
pulsars 113, 236

quasars 189, 236

R136 globular cluster 149, *149*
radiation 9, 91, 103, 105, 125, 127, 131,
   179, 197, 231, 236
radiation pressure 236
radio galaxy 236
radio waves 9, 43
radioactive decay 113
radioactive isotopes 113
rainbow 9
RCW57 star cluster 111
red dwarf stars 37, 60, 236
red giant stars 49, 67, 77, 91, 195, 236
red supergiant stars 183
reflection nebulae 65, *65*, 71, *71*, 85,
   87, *87*, 107, 236
Reionization 163
Rho Ophiuchi nebula 63
Rigel 71
ring galaxies 201, *201*, 211, *211*
Ring Nebula 97, *97*
ringdown, the 197
rocky planets 8, 16, 19, 101, 236
Rosette Nebula 105, *105*
rotation period 236

Sagittarius A* 139, *139*, 236
Sagittarius Dwarf Irregular Galaxy
   (SagDIG) 157, *157*
satellites 9
   geostationary 33
Saturn
   clouds 8, 43
   gravity 47
   moons 43
   opalescent complexion 43, *43*
   in outer solar system 16
   rings 8, 43, *43*
   storms 43
Scorpius 60
Seyfert galaxy 236
Shapley Supercluster 193
shepherd moon 235
Sigma Orionis 83
Sigma Orionis E 83
Skull & Crossbones Nebula 131
Sloan Great Wall 217
Small Magellanic Cloud (SMC) 147,
   151, *151*
Snake Nebula (Barnard 72) 69, *69*
Soap Bubble Nebula 97
solar mass 8, 236
Solar System 12, 16, 236
solar wind 236
Sombrero Galaxy 169, *169*
South Boösaule Montes, Io 39
Southern Cross 60
spacetime 217, *217*
Spindle Galaxy 173, *173*
spiral galaxies 8, 144, 153, *153*, 155,
   155, 161, *161*, 165, 167, *167*, 169, 171,
   171, 181, *181*, 201
star clusters 63, 105, 111, 115, 123, 131,
   133, *133*, 163, 209, 237
star formation 8, 13, 237
Star Wars (films) 45
starburst galaxies 163, *163*, 237
stars
   birth of 65, *65*
   definition 236
   movement of 12
   stellar death 95, 97, *97*, 99, 157
   stellar explosions 10
   stellar winds 83, 121, 127, 137, 175,
   237
Stephan's Quintet 144, 199, *199*
al-Sufi: *Book of Fixed Stars* 153
Sun 147, 237
   and comets 33
   core 27
   density 27
   energy 16, 27
   gravity 27
   heart of the solar system 27
   mass 16, 37, 63, 73, 83, 99, 103, 113,
   123, 135, 139, 149
   a middle-aged star 8, 27
   orbit around the centre of the
   Milky Way 12
   as a red giant 49
   seen as centre of Universe 12
   temperature 27, 99, 203
   ultraviolet light 23, 39
sunspots 27, *27*
supergiant 237
supernova remnants 73, *73*, 75, *75*,
   113, *113*, 125, *125*, 237
supernovae 10, 60, 75, 103, 113, 115,
   121, 123, 149, 195, 237

T Tauri 63, 65
Tadpole Galaxy 209, *209*
Tarantula Nebula 144, 149, *149*, 155
telescopes 9, 12, 229
thermal vents 41
Thor's Helmet 127
3C 75 colliding galaxy 197, *197*
tidal forces 39, 41, 177, 187
Titan (moon of Saturn) 16, 49, *49*, 51,
   60
Trapezium cluster 81, *81*
Triangulum Galaxy 155, *155*
Trifid Nebula 107, *107*
trillion 237
Triton (moon of Neptune) 57, *57*
tsunamis 33, 73
2 MASS Survey *217*
Tycho Brahe 117
Tycho Supernova Remnant 75, 117,
   117

ultraviolet radiation: defined 237
Universe
   age of 9
   creation of 197, 214
   definition 237
   expansion 217
   mass 217
   size 12
Uranus 55, *55*, 67
   falls on its side 55
   and Neptune 55
   in outer solar system 16

V380 Orionis 85
V838 Monocerotis 135, *135*
Vela supernova 10, 73, *73*
Venus *23*
   atmosphere 23
   clouds 23
   in inner solar system 16
   potential life on 23
   volcanoes 23, *23*
Virgo Cluster of galaxies 12, 181
volcanoes 19, 29, 39

War & Peace Nebula 123, *123*
wavelengths: definition 237
Whirlpool Galaxy 171, *171*
white dwarf stars 99, 111, 139, 237
Witch Head Nebula 71, *71*
WMAP survey 231, *231*
Wolf-Rayet star 103, 237

X-rays 9, 12, 60, 113, 115, 139, *139*, 149,
   169, 189, *191*, 197, *197*, 199, *199*, *203*,
   231, 237

Zone of Avoidance 193, 207, 217

[redacted]REDITS

p2: NASA; p11: [1] ESA/LFI & HFI Consortia; p13: [1] Atlas Image courtesy of 2MASS/UMass/IPAC-Caltech/NASA/NSF/G. Kopan, R. Hurt, [2] ESA & SPIRE Consortium & HerMES consortia; p14: NASA/JPL/Space Science Institute; p17: NASA; p18: NASA; p19: [1] NASA/Science Faction, [2] Image Analysis Laboratory/NASA Johnson Space Center; p20: Image Analysis Laboratory/NASA Johnson Space Center; p21: [1] Mike Constantine/NASA; p22: NASA/JPL/Mosaic by Mattias Malmer; p23: [1] NASA/JPL-Caltech, [2] NASA/JPL-Caltech; p24: NASA/Johns Hopkins University Applied Physics Laboratory/Carnegie Institution of Washington; p25: [1] NASA/Johns Hopkins University Applied Physics Laboratory/Carnegie Institution of Washington, [2] NASA/Johns Hopkins University Applied Physics Laboratory/Arizona State University/Carnegie Institution of Washington, [3] NASA/Johns Hopkins University Applied Physics Laboratory/Smithsonian Institution/Carnegie Institution of Washington; p26: Göran Scharmer, Kai Langhans, Mats Löfdahl, ISP, SST, Royal Swedish Academy of Sciences; p27: [1] NSO/AURA/NSF; p28: NASA/JPL/University of Arizona; p29: [1] NASA/JPL/University of Arizona, [2] NASA/JPL/University of Arizona, [3] NASA/JPL/University of Arizona; p30: NASA/JPL-Caltech/University of Arizona; p31: [1] NASA/JPL-Caltech/University of Arizona, [2] NASA/JPL-Caltech/University of Arizona; p32: NASA/JPL-Caltech; p33: [1] NASA/JPL-Caltech, [2] NASA/JPL-Caltech, [3] NASA/JPL-Caltech; p34: Canada-France-Hawaii Telescope/Coelum/J.-C. Cuillandre & [illegible]Anselmi; p35: [1] NASA/JPL/UMD, [2] NASA/JP[illegible]altech/UMD; p36: NASA/JPL/Space Science Institute; p3[illegible]] NASA/JPL-Caltech, [2] NASA/JPL/Space Science Institute; p38: NASA/JPL/University of Arizona; p39: [1] NASA/JPL-Caltech; p40: NASA/JPL/University of Arizona; p41: [1] NASA/JPL/University of Arizona/University of Colorado, [2] NASA/JPL-Caltech; p42: NASA/JPL/Space Science Institute; p43: [1] NASA/JPL/Space Science Institute, [2] NASA/JPL/Space Science Institute, [3] NASA/JPL/Space Science Institute; p44: NASA/JPL/Space Science Institute; p45: [1] NASA/JPL/Space Science Institute; p46: NASA/JPL/Space Science Institute; p47: [1] NASA/JPL/Space Science Institute/Universities Space Research Association/Lunar & Planetary Institute, [2] NASA/JPL/Space Science Institute, [3] NASA/JPL/Space Science Institute; p48: NASA/JPL/Space Science Institute; p49: [1] NASA/JPL/Space Science Institute, [2] NASA/JPL/Space Science Institute, [3] NASA/JPL/Space Science Institute; p50: NASA/JPL/Space Science Institute; p51: [1] NASA/JPL/Space Science Institute; p52: NASA/JPL/Space Science Institute; p53: [1] NASA/JPL/Space Science Institute, [2] NASA/JPL/Space Science Institute, [3] NASA/JPL/Space Science Institute; p54: Voyager 2, NASA; p55: [1] NASA/JPL-Caltech, [2] NASA/JPL-Caltech; p56: NASA/JPL-Caltech; p57: [1] NASA/JPL-Caltech, [2] NASA/JPL; p58: ESO/J. Emerson/VISTA. Acknowledgment: Cambridge Astronomical Survey Unit; p61: NASA, ESA and AURA/Caltech; p62: Robert Gendler, Jim Misti, Steve Mazlin; p63: [1] ESO/S. Guisard, [2] NASA/JPL-Caltech/Harvard-Smithsonian CfA; p64: T.A. Rector/University of Alaska Anchorage, H. Schweiker/WIYN and NOAO/AURA/NSF; p65: [1] J. Morse/STScI, and NASA, [2] NASA/ESA and The Hubble Heritage Team (AURA/STScI), [3] NASA and The Hubble Heritage Team (AURA/STScI); p66: NASA, NOAO, ESA, the Hubble Helix Nebula Team, M. Meixner (STScI), and T.A. Rector (NRAO); p67: [1] J. L. Hora (Harvard Smithsonian Center for Astrophysics); W. B. Latter (NASA/Herschel Science Center); M. Marengo (Harvard Smithsonian Center for Astrophysics); G.G. Fazio (Harvard Smithsonian Center for Astrophysics); H.A. Smith (Harvard Smithsonian Center for Astrophysics), [2] NASA/JPL-Caltech/J. Hora (Harvard-Smithsonian CfA); p68: Robert Gendler, Jim Misti; p69: [1] Canada-France-Hawaii Telescope/Coelum/J.-C. Cuillandre & G. Anselmi, [2] NASA, ESA, and The Hubble Heritage Team (STScI/AURA), Acknowledgment: P. McCullough (STScI); p70: Image Data: Digitized Sky Survey; Color Composite: Noel Carboni; p71: [1] Robert Gendler, Martin Pugh, [2] Robert Gendler, Jim Misti, Steve Mazlin; p72: Anglo-Australian Observatory/David Malin Images; p73: [1] NASA/SAO/CXC, [2] NASA and The Hubble Heritage Team (STScI/AURA), Acknowledgment: W. Blair (JHU) and D. Malin (David Malin Images); p74: NASA, ESA, the Hubble Heritage (STScI/AURA)-ESA/Hubble Collaboration, and the Digitized Sky Survey 2. Acknowledgment: J. Hester (Arizona State University) and Davide De Martin (ESA/Hubble); p75: [1] T.A. Rector/University of Alaska Anchorage, H. Schweiker/WIYN and NOAO/AURA/NSF; p76: H. Schweiker/NOAO/AURA/NSF and T. A. Rector/University of Alaska Anchorage and NOAO/AURA/NSF; p77: [1] T.A. Rector/University of Alaska Anchorage, H. Schweiker/WIYN and NOAO/AURA/NSF; p78: Robert Gendler; p79: [1] Infrared Processing and Analysis Center, Caltech/JPL, [2] Infrared Processing and Analysis Center, Caltech/JPL; p80: NASA,ESA, M. Robberto (Space Telescope Science Institute/ESA) and the Hubble Space Telescope Orion Treasury Project Team; p81: [1] NASA,ESA, M. Robberto (Space Telescope Science Institute/ESA) and the Hubble Space Telescope Orion Treasury Project Team, [2] NASA,ESA, M. Robberto (Space Telescope Science Institute/ESA) and the Hubble Space Telescope Orion Treasury Project Team; p82: T.A.Rector (NOAO/AURA/NSF) and Hubble Heritage Team (STScI/AURA/NASA); p83: [1] ESO; p84: NASA and The Hubble Heritage Team (STScI); p86: T. A. Rector/University of Alaska Anchorage, H. Schweiker/WIYN and NOAO/AURA/NSF; p87: ESO/IDA/Danish 1.5 m/R. Gendler, J.-E. Ovaldsen, C. Thöne and C. Féron, ESO/J. Emerson/VISTA. Acknowledgment: Cambridge Astronomical Survey Unit; p88: University of Colorado, University of Hawaii and NOAO/AURA/NSF; p89: [1] Digital Sky Survey, Acknowledgment: Charles Shahar; p90: T.A. Rector (University of Alaska Anchorage) and WIYN/NOAO/AURA/NSF; p91: [1] NASA/JPL-Caltech /W. Reach (Caltech); p92: ESO; p93: [1] NASA, H. Ford (JHU), G. Illingworth (UCSC/LO), M.Clampin (STScI), G. Hartig (STScI), the ACS Science Team, and ESA; p94: NASA, ESA, HEIC, and The Hubble Heritage Team (STScI/AURA); p95: [1] ESA/Hubble and NASA, [2] NASA, Andrew Fruchter and the ERO Team [Sylvia Baggett (STScI), Richard Hook (ST-ECF), Zoltan Levay (STScI)];[3] Bruce Balick (University of Washington), Vincent Icke (Leiden University, The Netherlands), Garrelt Mellema (Stockholm University), and NASA; p96: T.A. Rector/University of Alaska Anchorage, H. Schweiker/WIYN and NOAO/AURA/NSF; p97: [1] Raghvendra Sahai and John Trauger (JPL), the WFPC2 science team, and NASA, [2] Hubble Heritage Team (AURA/STScI/NASA); p98: NASA, ESA, and the Hubble SM4 ERO Team; p99: [1] NASA and The Hubble Heritage Team (AURA/STScI); p100: ESO/S. Guisard (www.eso.org/~sguisard); p101: [1] ESO/IDA/Danish 1.5 m/R. Gendler, U.G. Jørgensen, K. Harpsøe, [2] A. Caulet (ST-ECF, ESA) and NASA; p102: Daniel López, IAC; p104: T. A. Rector/University of Alaska Anchorage, WIYN and NOAO/AURA/NSF; p105: [1] ESA/PACS & SPIRE Consortium, Frédérique Motte, Laboratoire AIM Paris-Saclay, CEA/IRFU - CNRS/INSU - Uni. Paris Diderot, HOBYS Key Programme Consortia; p106: ESO; p107: [1] NASA/JPL-Caltech/J. Rho (SSC/Caltech), [2] NASA/JPL-Caltech/J. Rho (SSC/Caltech), [3] NASA and Jeff Hester (Arizona State University); p108: T.A. Rector/University of Alaska Anchorage, T. Abbott and NOAO/AURA/NSF; p109: [1] ESO/J. Emerson/VISTA, Acknowledgment: Cambridge Astronomical Survey Unit; p110: T.A. Rector/University of Alaska Anchorage, T. Abbott and NOAO/AURA/NSF; p111: [1] NASA, ESA, and the Digitized Sky Survey 2. Acknowledgment: Davide De Martin (ESA/Hubble); p112: NASA, ESA, J. Hester and A. Loll (Arizona State University); p113: [1] NASA/CXC/ASU/J. Hester et al. And NASA/HST/ASU/J. Hester et al., [2] X-ray: NASA/CXC/J.Hester (ASU); Optical: NASA/ESA/J.Hester & A.Loll (ASU); Infrared: NASA/JPL-Caltech/R.Gehrz (Univ. Minn.); p114: T.A. Rector and B.A. Wolpa (NRAO/AUI/NSF); p115: [1] NASA, ESA, and The Hubble Heritage Team (STScI/AURA), [2] NASA, Jeff Hester and Paul Scowen Arizona State University; p116: NASA/CXC/Rutgers/J. Warren & J.Hughes et al; p117: [1] NASA, CXC and S. Holt (F.W. Olin College of Engineering); p118: NASA, ESA, N. Smith (University of California, Berkeley), and The Hubble Heritage Team (STScI/AURA); p119: [1] Jon Morse (University of Colorado), and NASA/ESA, [2] NOAO/AURA/NSF; p120: NASA, ESA, and M. Livio and the Hubble 20th Anniversary Team (STScI); p121: [1] NASA, ESA, and M. Livio and the Hubble 20th Anniversary Team (STScI), [2] NASA/JPL-Caltech/N. Smith (Univ. of Colorado at Boulder); p122: NASA, ESA and Jesús Maíz Apellániz (Instituto de astrofísica de Andalucía, Spain). Acknowledgment: Davide De Martin (ESA/Hubble); p123: [1] Davide De Martin (ESA/Hubble), the ESA/ESO/NASA Photoshop FITS Liberator & Digitized Sky Survey 2; p124: NASA, ESA, and the Hubble Heritage (STScI/AURA)-ESA/Hubble Collaboration, Acknowledgment: R. Fesen (Dartmouth College) and J. Long (ESA/Hubble); p125: [1] NASA/JPL-Caltech/O. Krause (Steward Observatory); p126: Canada-France-Hawaii Telescope/Coelum/J.-C. Cuillandre & G. Anselmi; p128: NASA, ESA, and the Hubble Heritage Team (STScI/AURA), Acknowledgment: A. Cool (San Francisco State University) and J. Anderson (STScI); p129: [1] NASA, ESA, and the Hubble SM4 ERO Team; p130: ESO; p132: NASA, ESA, and the Hubble Heritage (STScI/AURA)-ESA/Hubble Collaboration, Acknowledgment: J. Maíz Apellániz (Institute of Astrophysics of Andalucía, Spain); p133: [1] NASA/JPL-Caltech/UCLA; p134: NASA, ESA, and H. Bond (STScI); p135: [1] NASA and The Hubble Heritage Team (AURA/STScI); p136: NASA, ESA, SSC, CXC and STScI; p137: [1] ESO, Digitized Sky Survey 2 & S. Guisard (www.eso.org/~sguisard); p138: NASA, ESA, SSC, CXC and STScI; p139: [1] NASA/CXC/MIT/F.K. Baganoff et al., [2] ESO/S. Gillessen et al., [3] NRAO/VLA F.Zadeh et al; p140: ESA/Hubble & NASA; p141: [1] NOAO/AURA/NSF, [2] NASA/ESA, [3] NASA, ESA and H. Richer (University of British Columbia); p142: NASA, ESA, and the Hubble Heritage (STScI/AURA)-ESA/Hubble Collaboration; p145: NASA/ESA; p146: ESO; p147: [1] NASA/JPL-Caltech/M. Meixner (STScI) & the SAGE Legacy Team, [2] C. Smith, S. Points, the MCELS Team and NOAO/AURA/NSF; p148: ESO; p149: [1] NASA, ESA, and F. Paresce (INAF-IASF, Bologna, Italy), R. O'Connell (University of Virginia, Charlottesville), and the Wide Field Camera 3 Science Oversight Committee; p150: NASA, ESA and A. Nota (STScI/ESA); p151: [1] ESA/Hubble and Digitized Sky Survey 2. Acknowledgments: Davide De Martin (http://www.skyfactory.org); p152: Robert Gendler; p153: [1] NASA/JPL-Caltech/P. Barmby (Harvard-Smithsonian CfA), [2] NASA/JPL-Caltech/P. Barmby (Harvard-Smithsonian CfA); p154: T.A. Rector (NRAO/AUI/NSF and NOAO/AURA/NSF); p155: [1] NASA/JPL-Caltech, [2] NASA and The Hubble Heritage Team (AURA/STScI); p156: NASA, ESA, and The Hubble Heritage Team (STScI/AURA), Acknowledgment: Y. Momany (University of Padua); p158: X-ray: NASA/CXC/CfA/R.Kraft et al; Submillimeter: MPIfR/ESO/APEX/A.Weiss et al; Optical: ESO/WFI; p159: [1] NASA/JPL-Caltech/J. Keene (SSC/Caltech), [2] E.J. Schreier (STScI) and NASA; p160: NASA, ESA, and The Hubble Heritage Team (STScI/AURA) Acknowledgment: A. Zezas and J. Huchra (Harvard-Smithsonian Center for Astrophysics); p161: [1] X-ray: NASA/CXC/Wisconsin/D.Pooley & CfA/A.Zezas; Optical: NASA/ESA/CfA/A.Zezas; UV: NASA/JPL-Caltech/CfA/J. Huchra et al; IR: NASA/JPL-Caltech/CfA, [2] ESA/Hubble and Digitized Sky Survey 2. Acknowledgments: Davide De Martin (ESA/Hubble), [3] Chynoweth et al., NRAO/AUI/NSF, ESA/Hubble & Digitized Sky Survey 2. Acknowledgments: Davide De Martin (ESA/Hubble); p162: NASA, ESA, and The Hubble Heritage Team (STScI/AURA), J. Gallagher (University of Wisconsin), M. Mountain (STScI), and P. Puxley (National Science Foundation); p163: [1] NASA, ESA, CXC, and JPL-Caltech; p164: NASA, ESA, A. Aloisi (ESA/STScI) and The Hubble Heritage (STScI/AURA)-ESA/Hubble Collaboration; p165: [1] ESO, [2] NASA, ESA, the Hubble Heritage Team (STScI/AURA), and A. Aloisi (STScI/ESA); p166: NASA, ESA, K. Kuntz (JHU), F. Bresolin (University of Hawaii), J. Trauger (Jet Propulsion Lab), J. Mould (NOAO), Y.-H. Chu (University of Illinois, Urbana), and STScI; p168: NASA and The Hubble Heritage Team (STScI/AURA); p169: [1] NASA/JPL-Caltech and The Hubble Heritage Team (STScI/AURA); p170: NASA, ESA, S. Beckwith (STScI), and The Hubble Heritage Team (STScI/AURA); p171: [1] NASA, ESA, S. Beckwith (STScI), and The Hubble Heritage Team (STScI/AURA); p172: NASA, ESA, and The Hubble Heritage Team STScI/AURA); p174: NASA, ESA, and the Hubble Heritage Team (STScI/AURA)-ESA/Hubble Collaboration, Acknowledgment: B. Whitmore (Space Telescope Science Institute); p175: [1] NOAO/AURA/NSF, B. Twardy, B. Twardy, and A. Block (NOAO); p176: NASA, ESA, and The Hubble Heritage Team (STScI/AURA), Acknowledgment: M. Gregg (Univ. Calif.-Davis and Inst. for Geophysics and Planetary Physics, Lawrence Livermore Natl. Lab.); p177: [1] NASA/ESA and The Hubble Heritage Team; p178: NASA, ESA, and the Hubble Heritage Team (STScI/AURA)-ESA/Hubble Collaboration; p179: [1] NASA, ESA, and the Hubble SM4 ERO Team; p180: NASA & ESA; p181: [1] NASA & ESA; p182: NASA, ESA, and The Hubble Heritage Team (STScI/AURA), Acknowledgment: P. Knezek (WIYN); p183: [1] NASA, ESA, and The Hubble Heritage Team (STScI/AURA), Acknowledgment: P. Knezek (WIYN); p184: NASA, ESA, and The Hubble Heritage Team (STScI/AURA), Acknowledgment: P. Goudfrooij (STScI); p185: [1] NRAO/AUI and J. M. Uson, [2] NASA, ESA and W. Harris (McMaster University, Ontario, Canada); p186: NASA, ESA, and R. Sharples (University of Durham); p187: [1] NASA, ESA, the Hubble Heritage Team (STScI/AURA)-ESA/Hubble Collaboration and A. Evans (University of Virginia, Charlottesville/NRAO/Stony Brook University), [2] NASA, ESA, the Hubble Heritage Team (STScI/AURA)-ESA/Hubble Collaboration and A. Evans (University of Virginia, Charlottesville/NRAO/Stony Brook University), [3] NASA, ESA, the Hubble Heritage Team (STScI/AURA)-ESA/Hubble Collaboration and A. Evans (University of Virginia, Charlottesville/NRAO/Stony Brook University); p188: X-ray: NASA/CXC/KIPAC/S.Allen et al; Radio: NRAO/VLA/G. Taylor; Infrared: NASA/ESA/McMaster Univ./W.Harris; p189: [1] NASA & ESA; p190: NASA, ESA and Andy Fabian (University of Cambridge, UK); p191: [1] X-ray: NASA/CXC/IoA/A.Fabian et al; Radio: NRAO/VLA/G. Taylor; Optical: NASA/ESA/Hubble Heritage (STScI/AURA) & Univ. of Cambridge/IoA/A. Fabian; p192: European Southern Observatory; p193: [1] X-ray: NASA/CXC/UVa/M. Sun, et al; H-alpha/Optical: SOAR (UVa/NOAO/UNC/CNPq-Brazil)/M. Sun et al; p194: NASA, H. Ford (JHU), G. Illingworth (UCSC/LO), M.Clampin (STScI), G. Hartig (STScI), the ACS Science Team, and ESA; p195: [1] NASA, ESA, the Hubble Heritage Team (STScI/AURA)-ESA/Hubble Collaboration and A. Evans (University of Virginia, Charlottesville/NRAO/Stony Brook University), [2] NASA, ESA, the Hubble Heritage Team (STScI/AURA)-ESA/Hubble Collaboration and A. Evans (University of Virginia, Charlottesville/NRAO/Stony Brook University), [3] NASA, ESA, the Hubble Heritage Team (STScI/AURA)-ESA/Hubble Collaboration and A. Evans (University of Virginia, Charlottesville/NRAO/Stony Brook University); p196: X-ray: NASA/CXC/AIfA/D.Hudson & T.Reiprich et al; Radio: NRAO/VLA/NRL; p197: [1] X-ray (NASA/CXC/MIT/C.Canizares, M.Nowak); Optical (NASA/STScI), [2] X-ray (NASA/CXC/MIT/C.Canizares, M.Nowak); Optical (NASA/STScI); p198: NASA, ESA, and the Hubble SM4 ERO Team; p199: [1] X-ray (NASA/CXC/CfA/E.O'Sullivan); Optical (Canada-France-Hawaii-Telescope/Coelum; p200: NASA, ESA, and The Hubble Heritage Team (AURA/STScI); p201: [1] Kirk Borne (STScI), and NASA; p202: NASA, ESA and the Hubble Heritage (STScI/AURA)-ESA/Hubble Collaboration. Acknowledgment: M. West (ESO, Chile); p203: [1] NASA, ESA, M. West (ESO, Chile), and CXC/Penn State University/G. Garmire, et al; p204: NASA, ESA, K. Cook (Lawrence Livermore National Laboratory, USA); p205: [1] NASA, ESA, and the Hubble Heritage Team (STScI/AURA) Acknowledgment: D. Carter (Liverpool John Moores University) and the Coma HST ACS Treasury Team; p206: Canada-France-Hawaii Telescope/Coelum/J.-C. Cuillandre & G. Anselmi; p207: [1] NASA, ESA, the Hubble Heritage Team (STScI/AURA)-ESA/Hubble Collaboration and K. Noll (STScI); p208: NASA, H. Ford (JHU), G. Illingworth (UCSC/LO), M.Clampin (STScI), G. Hartig (STScI), the ACS Science Team, and ESA; p209: [1] NASA, ESA, the Hubble Heritage Team (STScI/AURA)-ESA/Hubble Collaboration and A. Evans (University of Virginia, Charlottesville/NRAO/Stony Brook University), [2] NASA, ESA, the Hubble Heritage Team (STScI/AURA)-ESA/Hubble Collaboration and A. Evans (University of Virginia, Charlottesville/NRAO/Stony Brook University); p210: NASA and The Hubble Heritage Team (STScI/AURA); p211: [1] NASA, ESA, the Hubble Heritage Team (STScI/AURA)-ESA/Hubble Collaboration and A. Evans (University of Virginia, Charlottesville/NRAO/Stony Brook University), K. Noll (STScI), and J. Westphal (Caltech), [2] The Hubble Heritage Team (AURA/STScI/NASA), [3] NASA, ESA, and M. Livio (STScI); p212: MacFarland, Colberg, White (Munchen), Jenkins, Pearce, Frenk (Durham), Evrard (Michigan), Couchman (London, CA) Thomas (Sussex), Efstathiou (Cambridge), Peacock (Edinburgh)/National Science Foundation/NASA; p215: Volker Springel, Max-Planck-Institute for Astrophysics; p216: 2MASS/T. H. Jarrett, J. Carpenter, & R. Hurt; p217: [1] NASA, ESA, and E. Hallman (University of Colorado, Boulder); p218: Acknowledgment: Richard Gott et al; p220: ESO/J. Dietrich; p222: NASA, N. Benitez (JHU), T. Broadhurst (Racah Institute of Physics/The Hebrew University), H. Ford (JHU), M. Clampin (STScI), G. Hartig (STScI), G. Illingworth (UCO/Lick Observatory), the ACS Science Team and ESA; p223: [1] NASA, ESA, A. Bolton (Harvard-Smithsonian CfA) and the SLACS Team, [2] NASA, ESA, A. Bolton (Harvard-Smithsonian CfA) and the SLACS Team, [3] NASA, ESA, A. Bolton (Harvard-Smithsonian CfA) and the SLACS Team, [4] NASA, ESA, A. Bolton (Harvard-Smithsonian CfA) and the SLACS Team; p224: X-ray: NASA/CXC/CfA/M.Markevitch et al; Optical: NASA/STScI; Magellan/U.Arizona/D.Clowe et al; Lensing Map: NASA/STScI; ESO WFI; Magellan/U.Arizona/D.Clowe et al; p225: [1] X-ray(NASA/CXC/Stanford/S.Allen); Optical/Lensing(NASA/STScI/UC Santa Barbara/M.Bradac), [2] X-ray: NASA/CXC/UVic./A.Mahdavi et al. Optical/Lensing: CFHT/UVic./A.Mahdavi et al., [3] X-ray (NASA/CXC/IfA/C. Ma et al.); Optical (NASA/STScI/IfA/C. Ma et al.); p226: NASA, ESA, M.J. Jee and H. Ford (Johns Hopkins University); p227: [1] NASA, ESA, M.J. Jee and H. Ford (Johns Hopkins University); p228: NASA, ESA, S. Beckwith (STScI) and the HUDF Team; p229: [1] ESA & SPIRE Consortium & HerMES consortia; p230: NASA/WMAP Science Team; p232: NASA/JPL-Caltech/S. Stolovy (SSC/Caltech); p234: NASA, ESA, and K. Sahu (STScI); p236: NASA, ESA, and M. Livio and the Hubble 20th Anniversary Team (STScI).

For Elizabeth Grace, who sees castles among the stars – SC

And for Faye Zephyrine, who sees bananas – NC

First published in hardback in Great Britain in 2010 by Atlantic Books and Callisto, imprints of Atlantic Books Ltd.

Copyright © Stuart Clark, Nicolas Cheetham 2010

The moral right of Stuart Clark & Nicolas Cheetham to be identified as the authors of this work has been asserted in accordance with the Copyright, Designs and Patents Act of 1988.

All rights reserved. No part of this publication may be reproduced, stored in a retrieval system, or transmitted in any form or by any means, electronic, mechanical, photocopying, recording, or otherwise, without the prior permission of both the copyright owner and the above publisher of this book.

The picture credits constitute an extension of this copyright page.

Every effort has been made to trace or contact all copyright holders. The publishers will be pleased to make good any omissions or rectify any mistakes brought to their attention at the earliest opportunity.

A CIP catalogue record for this book is available from the British Library.

Callisto ISBN: 978 0 85740 021 5
Atlantic Export ISBN: 978 1 84887 946 1

Designed by Grade Design Consultants, www.gradedesign.com
Printed in China

10 9 8 7 6 5 4 3 2 1

Callisto and Atlantic Books
Imprints of Atlantic Books Ltd
Ormond House
26–27 Boswell Street
London
WC1N 3JZ

www.atlantic-books.co.uk

240